7/97

44. 50

HISTORICAL DICTIONARIES OF RELIGIONS,
PHILOSOPHIES, AND MOVEMENTS
Edited by Jon Woronoff

Historical Dictionary of the Olympic Movement

by
Ian Buchanan
Bill Mallon

Historical Dictionaries of Religions,
Philosophies, and Movements,
No. 7

The Scarecrow Press, Inc.
Lanham, Md., and London

SCARECROW PRESS, INC.

Published in the United States of America
by Scarecrow Press, Inc.
4720 Boston Way
Lanham, Maryland 20706

4 Pleydell Gardens, Folkestone
Kent CT20 2DN, England

British Cataloguing-in-Publication Information Available

Library of Congress Cataloging-in-Publication Data

Buchanan, Ian
Historical dictionary of the Olympic movement / by Ian Buchanan and
Bill Mallon.
p.   cm. — (Historical dictionaries of religions, philosophies and
movements ; no. 7)
Includes bibliographical references.
1. Olympics—History—Dictionaries. 2. Olympics—Records.
I. Mallon, Bill. II. Title. III. Series.
GV721.5.B83   1995   796.48—dc20   95-22858   CIP

ISBN 0-8108-3062-0 (cloth ; alk. paper)

CONTENTS

FOREWORD

It is an encouraging beginning to the second century of the modern Olympic Movement that two eminent Olympic scholars have taken on the formidable task of attempting the first comprehensive effort to compile in dictionary format a workable summary of important data of use to both casual and academic readers. It is the mark of a great idea that when it becomes a reality, it appears so obvious that everyone wonders why they did not think of it in the first place. This is a perfect example. Of course, the idea is one thing. Having the energy and resolve to undertake the enormous amount of work to produce the concrete expression of it is quite another. We can only admire and applaud the authors and their colleagues for their remarkable achievement and hope that they have paced themselves so that they are already working on the next edition.

There is a rapidly growing body of material and information concerning the Olympic Games and the Olympic Movement. Much of it, however, is not easily accessible without a specific knowledge of where to look or even where to start to look. This work will be of valuable assistance to anyone who wishes to pursue casual or in-depth inquiry.

The Olympic Movement is little understood by the public at large, which tends to be aware of the celebration of the Olympic Games, formerly every four years and, since 1994, every two years with a rotation between the "Summer" and "Winter" Games. While undoubtedly the engine that drives the Olympic Movement, the Games are really only the culmination of the efforts of a vast series of interdependent national and international organizations that operate around the clock every day of the year.

The Olympic Movement is unique in many respects. It is truly and unrepentantly international in scope and character. Its purpose is to unite the youth of the world in peaceful congress through sport, free of discrimination of every sort. It channels an important part of the energies of the youth of the world - numbering in the billions - into sport. It is available to everyone, regardless of ability; one can practice Olympism within the limits of physical ability and self-discipline, whatever they may be, and in all aspects of life.

In addition to the greatest resource on this planet - its youth - the Olympic Movement has as its very foundation the efforts of volunteers, which provides a stability that is lacking in virtually every other field of endeavor. It is the voluntary and selfless dedication of hundreds of millions of teachers, coaches, organizers, and officials that makes sport possible. The consensual goodwill that leads to sport and organized sport has made it possible for sport to become international and to survive the strains of an evolution in society over the past century that has been unparalleled in any other period of our history. It is no accident that the Olympic Movement has survived and flourished when so many other international organizations have foundered and sunk without trace.

This work does not purport to be a complete history of the Olympic Movement. That would be well beyond the scope of any single publication. It does, however, contain a wealth of information that would otherwise be almost impossible to find. The reader can discover, for example, all the cities that bid to host the Games on each occasion and how their candidacies fared before the International Olympic Committee. Each edition of the Games is reviewed briefly, to give a "flavor" of the occasion and to recall the background and some of the great Olympians who made them special. The arrangement of the material has been simplified to make the dictionary easy to use and readable at whatever level the user desires.

How often have we wanted to find the name of a final torch bearer or to know who may have been guilty of doping, but had no idea where to look? Which public figures opened the Games on a particular occasion? What festivals were the precursors of the modern Olympic Games? When did the Soviet Union first enter the Games? What happened when the Soviet Union disintegrated? When was South Africa expelled from the Olympic Movement? When was it readmitted? What is the real name of IOC President Lord Killanin? Who are the competitors who have won the most Olympic medals and in what sports did they compete? How many athletes competed in each Olympic Games? How many of these were women? The answers to these questions and thousands more are now available in a single volume.

The authors have collected references to works that deal in more depth with many aspects of the Olympic Movement, whether of specific Games or more general topics that will lead the way into detailed research for those with narrower targets of study. Just as an ordinary dictionary does not teach anyone how to write, but is a reference tool to keep one on the right track, so, too, this *Historical Dictionary of the Olympic Movement* is a guide to more thorough knowledge of the field. More importantly, with the sources available to the authors, it should serve as a most useful cross-reference to facts and dates that appear in other sources, such as the media, where reliability may have been compromised by the need to get information disseminated quickly at the time an event or as the story unfolds.

The beauty of this dictionary is that it can be expanded and updated over time. Any reference tool that has this capacity can become powerful indeed and benefit from the continued scholarship not only of the authors, but also of Olympic afficionados throughout the world who can add to the information in this first edition and suggest other entries that will enhance the wealth of information already within its covers. This work will undoubtedly become a stimulus and challenge to all Olympic scholars and to those who can add to Olympic lore.

Olympic education, in its broadest sense, is a calling that is actively encouraged by the International Olympic Committee. This work fills an important gap in the material available to the general public and to the academic community. On behalf of the International Olympic Committee, I commend the authors for their important contribution to this field.

Richard W. D. Pound, Q.C.
International Olympic Committee
Member, Executive Board

Montreal, Quebec, Canada
March 1995

EDITOR'S FOREWORD

Of the many movements included in this series, there is nothing quite like the Olympic Movement in scope. The original Olympic Games were held nearly three millennia ago and the next Olympics are never more than two years away. The flame from the old to the new Games was carried by dedicated individuals, Pierre de Coubertin and other pioneers, and is now borne by tens of thousands of organizers, athletes, trainers, sponsors and fans, and observed by a public that numbers in the hundreds of millions. Whereas only Greeks participated in the original Olympic Games, participation has now spread around the world, including persons of every race, religion, and nationality. Despite a need for organization and the creation of institutions, this remains a people's movement more than any other.

Given the vast scope of the Olympic Movement, this book had to cover an unusually broad range of persons, places, and events as well as an extended time horizon. It has done so extremely well with a helpful chronology and concise recapitulation of the modern Olympic Games and with entries on Olympic bodies, significant pioneers, organizers and athletes, the various sporting events and associations, and a multitude of countries. The appendices provide handy information on leading figures in the movement and the outstanding athletes. An extensive bibliography suggests further reading.

This *Historical Dictionary of the Olympic Movement* was written by an exceptional team of authors, Ian Buchanan and Bill Mallon. Both have an abiding interest in sports and have actively supported the Olympic Movement. Among other things, they helped found the International Society of Olympic Historians (ISOH), of which Ian Buchanan is the President and Bill Mallon the Secretary-General. They have already written a number of significant works on the Olympic Games and again combine their knowledge and insight in a book that is not only informative but readable and will be an excellent guide for countless readers who wish to know more.

Jon Woronoff
Series Editor

AUTHORS' PREFACE

The Olympic Games are one of humanity's longest surviving institutions; their origins date to at least 776 B.C., and probably to as early as 1100 B.C. in Ancient Greece. Though the Games were abandoned by decree of the Roman Emperor Theodosius in 393 A.D., they were revived in 1896 by the efforts of a remarkable Frenchman, the Baron Pierre de Coubertin. Since 1896, the Olympic Games have become one of the most watched and publicized spectacles in the world. It has been noted that they now constitute the largest peacetime gathering of humanity in the history of the world. One former U.S. Olympic competitor, Elliott Denman (a walker), reflected on the Olympic Games: "[The Olympics] bring the world together. They are a remarkable cause for the good of mankind. In a planet beset with divisiveness, the Games continue to promote both the magnificent diversity of mankind, and the commonality of all" (Program at 60th Anniversary of Shore Athletic Club, *Asbury Park Press*, 30 October 1994).

Although the world watches the Olympic Games every four years and wonders at the feats of the athletes, the Olympic Movement and its philosophy of Olympism go on daily and are the cornerstones of the work of the International Olympic Committee (IOC). The Olympic Movement does not receive the publicity received by the Games themselves, but it has the ability to serve and has served as a major force for international goodwill. U.S. Vice-President Al Gore recently pointed out, correctly, that "the IOC is the oldest multinational, non-governmental continuous organization in the world" (*Olympic Review*, *XXV(1)*: 43, February–March 1995).

When we first began this work, we thought it might be a rehashing of work we had done together on earlier projects. Quickly, we realized it was not, and that the need for a complete dictionary of the Olympic Movement was a real one. Though we have both studied the Olympic Games and Olympic Movement extensively, we do not think a comparable work exists that allows the student of the Olympics to find background references on all aspects of the Olympic Games and Olympic Movement in one source.

We would like to thank Jon Woronoff, the series editor of Scarecrow's Historical Dictionaries of Religions, Philosophies, and Movements. We have been helped in our research particularly by Karel Wendl of the IOC, who first suggested our names to Jon Woronoff. We would also like to thank Wolf Lyberg (SWE), Joachim K. Rühl (GER), Ture Widlund (SWE), and David Young (USA). Lyberg, Rühl, Wendl, Widlund, and Young are all members relatively new organization devoted to studying the Olympic Games and Olympic Movement. We also extend special thanks to IOC and ISOH member Dick Pound (CAN), who wrote the foreword but also carefully edited many sections of the book.

In addition to the above, many members of ISOH have been instrumental with their help, either with direct answers to our questions or by earlier research that we have used for our sources. We would particularly like to thank the following: Tony Bijkerk (BEL), Juan Fauria Garcia (ESP), Arild Gjerde (NOR), Stan Greenberg (GBR), Rupert Kaiser (GER), Erich Kamper (AUT), Ove Karlsson (SWE), Karl Lennartz (GER), Jos Luypaers (BEL), Lia Manoliu (ROM), Giuseppe Odello (ITA), Jaroslav Pruner (CZE), Donald Sayenga (USA), Daniel Schamps (FRA), Markku Siukonen (FIN), Athanasios Tarassouleas (GRE), and Benjamin Wright (USA).

Naturally, we extend special thanks to the two indispensable people in our lives who often wonder about those crazy husbands sitting behind their computers – Jeanne Buchanan and Karen Mallon.

Ian Buchanan
Burgh Next Aylsham, Norwich, England

Bill Mallon
Durham, North Carolina, USA

July 1995

ABBREVIATIONS AND ACRONYMS USED

Three-Letter Sport Abbreviations

ARC	Archery
ASK	Alpine Skiing
ATH	Athletics (Track & Field)
BAS	Basketball
BDM	Badminton
BIA	Biathlon
BOB	Bobsledding
BOX	Boxing
BSB	Baseball
CAN	Canoe & Kayaking
CUR	Curling
CYC	Cycling
DIV	Diving
EQU	Equestrian Events
FEN	Fencing
FKL	Freestyle Skiing
FSK	Figure Skating
FTB	Football, Association (Soccer)
GYM	Gymnastics
HAN	Team Handball
HOK	Hockey (Field)
ICH	Ice Hockey
JUD	Judo
LAX	Lacrosse
LUG	Luge
MOP	Modern Pentathlon
MTB	Motorboating
NSK	Nordic Skiing
POL	Polo
ROW	Rowing & Sculling
RUG	Rugby Football
SHO	Shooting
SKE	Skeleton
SSK	Speed Skating (Long-track)
STK	Short-track Speed Skating
SWI	Swimming
TEN	Tennis (Lawn Tennis)
TOW	Tug-of-War
TTN	Table Tennis
VOL	Volleyball
WAP	Water Polo
WLT	Weightlifting
WRE	Wrestling
YAC	Yachting

Three–Letter National Abbreviations

AFG	Afghanistan
AHO	Netherlands Antilles
ALB	Albania
ALG	Algeria
AND	Andorra
ANG	Angola
ANL	Antilles (West Indies)
ANT	Antigua and Barbuda
ARG	Argentina
ARM	Armenia
ARU	Aruba
ASA	American Samoa
AUS	Australia
AUT	Austria
AZE	Azerbaijan
BAH	The Bahamas
BAN	Bangladesh
BAR	Barbados
BDI	Burundi
BEL	Belgium
BEN	Benin
BER	Bermuda
BHU	Bhutan
BIH	Bosnia–Herzegovina
BIR	Burma
BIZ	Belize
BLR	Belarus
BOH	Bohemia
BOL	Bolivia
BOT	Botswana
BRA	Brazil
BRN	Bahrain
BRU	Brunei
BUL	Bulgaria
BUR	Burkina Faso
CAF	Central Africa
CAM	Kampuchea
CAN	Canada
CAY	Cayman Islands
CEY	Ceylon
CGO	Congo
CHA	Chad
CHI	Chile
CHN	China

Three-Letter National Abbreviations (continued)

CHN	China
CIS	Commonwealth of Independent States (aka EUN)
CIV	Ivory Coast
CMR	Cameroon
COK	Cook Islands
COL	Colombia
COM	Comoros Islands
CPV	Cape Verde
CRC	Costa Rica
CRO	Croatia
CUB	Cuba
CYP	Cyprus
CZE	Czech Republic
DEN	Denmark
DJI	Djibouti
DMA	Dominica
DOM	Dominican Republic
ECU	Ecuador
EGY	Egypt
ESA	El Salvador
ESP	Spain
EST	Estonia
ETH	Ethiopia
EUN	Unified Team (aka CIS)
FIJ	Fiji
FIN	Finland
FRA	France
FRG	Federal Republic of Germany
GAB	Gabon
GAM	The Gambia
GBR	Great Britain
GDR	German Democratic Republic
GEO	Georgia
GEQ	Equatorial Guinea
GER	Germany
GHA	Ghana
GNB	Guinea-Bissau
GRE	Greece
GRN	Grenada
GUA	Guatemala
GUI	Guinea
GUM	Guam
GUY	Guyana
HAI	Haiti
HKG	Hong Kong

Three-Letter National Abbreviations (continued)

HUN	Hungary
INA	Indonesia
IND	India
IOP	Independent Olympic Participant
IRI	Iran
IRL	Ireland
IRQ	Iraq
ISL	Iceland
ISR	Israel
ISV	U. S. Virgin Islands
ITA	Italy
IVB	British Virgin Islands
JAM	Jamaica
JOR	Jordan
JPN	Japan
KAZ	Kazakhstan
KEN	Kenya
KGZ	Kyrgyzstan
KOR	Korea (South)
KSA	Saudi Arabia
KUW	Kuwait
LAO	Laos
LAT	Latvia
LBA	Libya
LBR	Liberia
LCA	Saint Lucia
LES	Lesotho
LIB	Lebanon
LIE	Liechtenstein
LTU	Lithuania
LUX	Luxembourg
MAD	Madagascar
MAR	Morocco
MAS	Malaysia
MAW	Malawi
MDV	Maldives
MEX	Mexico
MGL	Mongolia
MKD	Macedonia
MLD	Moldova
MLI	Mali
MLT	Malta
MON	Monaco
MOZ	Mozambique
MRI	Mauritius

Three-Letter National Abbreviations (continued)

MTN	Mauritania
MYA	Myanmar
NAM	Namibia
NCA	Nicaragua
NED	The Netherlands
NEP	Nepal
NGR	Nigeria
NIG	Niger
NOR	Norway
NRU	Nauru
NZL	New Zealand
OMA	Oman
PAK	Pakistan
PAN	Panama
PAR	Paraguay
PER	Peru
PHI	The Philippines
PLE	Palestine
PNG	Papua–New Guinea
POL	Poland
POR	Portugal
PRK	Democratic People's Republic of Korea (North)
PUR	Puerto Rico
QAT	Qatar
RHO	Rhodesia
ROM	Romania
RUS	Russia
RWA	Rwanda
SAF	South Africa
SAM	Western Samoa
SCO	Scotland
SEN	Senegal
SEY	Seychelles
SIN	Singapore
SKN	St. Kitts and Nevis
SLE	Sierra Leone
SLO	Slovenia
SMR	San Marino
SMY	Smyrna
SOL	Solomon Islands
SOM	Somalia
SRI	Sri Lanka
STP	São Tomé and Príncipe
SUD	The Sudan
SUI	Switzerland

Three-Letter National Abbreviations (continued)

SUR	Suriname
SVK	Slovakia
SWE	Sweden
SWZ	Swaziland
SYR	Syria
TAN	Tanzania
TCH	Czechoslovakia
TGA	Tonga
THA	Thailand
TJK	Tadzhikistan
TKM	Turkmenistan
TOG	Togo
TPE	Chinese Taipei
TRI	Trinidad and Tobago
TSL	Thessalonika
TUN	Tunisia
TUR	Turkey
UAE	United Arab Emirates
UGA	Uganda
UKR	The Ukraine
URS	Soviet Union
URU	Uruguay
USA	United States
UZB	Uzbekistan
VAN	Vanuatu
VEN	Venezuela
VIE	Vietnam
VIN	St. Vincent and the Grenadines
VOL	Upper Volta
YAR	Yemen Arab Republic (North)
YEM	Yemen
YMD	Yemen Democratic Republic (South)
YUG	Yugoslavia
ZAI	Zaire
ZAM	Zambia
ZIM	Zimbabwe

Other Abbreviations Used

ACNO	Association des Comités Nationaux Olympiques
ACNOA	Association des Comités Nationaux Olympiques d'Afrique
ACNOE	Association des Comités Nationaux Olympiques d'Europe
AGFIS	Association Générale des Fédérations Internationales de Sports

Other Abbreviations Used (continued)

AIBA	Association Internationale de Boxe Amateur
AIWF	Association of the International Winter Sports Federations
ARISF	Association of the IOC Recognized International Sports Federations
ASOIF	Association of Summer Olympic International Federations
COJO	Comité d'Organisateur des Jeux Olympiques
EOC	European Olympic Committees
FEI	Fédération Equestre Internationale
FIBA	Fédération Internationale de Basketball
FIBT	Fédération Internationale de Bobsleigh et de Tobogganing
FIC	Fédération Internationale de Canoë
FIE	Fédération Internationale d'Éscrime
FIFA	Fédération Internationale de Football Association
FIG	Fédération Internationale de Gymastique
FIH	Fédération Internationale de Hockey
FIL	Fédération Internationale de Luge de Course
FILA	Fédération Internationale de Luttes Associées
FINA	Fédération Internationale de Natation Amateur
FIS	Fédération Internationale de Ski
FISA	Fédération Internationale des Sociétés d'Aviron
FITA	Fédération Internationale de Tir à l'Arc
FIVB	Fédération Internationale de Volleyball
GAISF	General Association of International Sports Federations
IAAF	International Amateur Athletic Federation
IBA	International Baseball Federation
IBF	International Badminton Federation
IF(s)	International Federation(s)
IHF	Fédération International de Handball
IIHF	International Ice Hockey Federation
IJF	International Judo Federation
IOA	International Olympic Academy
IOC	International Olympic Committee
IPC	Institut Pierre de Coubertin
IPC	International Paralympic Committee
ISF	Fédération Internationale de Softball
ISOH	International Society of Olympic Historians
ISU	International Skating Union
ITF	International Tennis Federation
ITTF	International Table Tennis Federation
IWF	International Weightlifting Federation
IYRU	International Yacht Racing Union
NOC(s)	National Olympic Committee(s)
OCA	Olympic Council of Asia
OCOG	Organizing Committee of the Olympic Games
ODECABE	Organización Deportiva Centroamericana y del Caribe

Other Abbreviations Used (continued)

ODEPA	Organización Deportiva Panamericana
ONOC	Oceania National Olympic Committees
PASO	Pan American Sports Organization
q.v.	*quod vide*, literally "which see," meaning "See also"
qq.v.	*quae vide*, literally "which see," meaning "See also (several)"; plural of *q.v.*
TOP	The Olympic Programme
UCI	Union Cycliste Internationale
UIPMB	Union Internationale de Pentathlon Moderne et Biathlon
UIT	Union Internationale de Tir
WCF	World Curling Federation

CHRONOLOGY OF THE OLYMPIC MOVEMENT

776 B.C. First recorded Ancient Olympiad celebrated in Olympia on the Peloponnesus Peninsula in Ancient Greece. The Olympic Games initially consist of a single race of about 190 meters in length, termed a *stadion* race. The first winner is Coroebus, a cook from the city–state of Elis.

582 B.C. The first Pythian Games are held at Delphi in Ancient Greece.

582 (?581) B.C. The first Isthmian Games are held at the Isthmus of Corinth in Ancient Greece.

573 B.C. The first Nemean Games are held at Nemea in Ancient Greece.

393 A.D. The Ancient Olympic Games end after 12 centuries when they are prohibited by the imperial decree of Roman Emperor Theodosius I.

1612 – 1642 Robert Dover's Games, an early attempt at revival often called the Cotswold Olimpick Games, are held annually in the Cotswolds (England) on Thursday and Friday of Whitsun Week. They stop shortly after Dover's death in 1641 but are revived during the reign of King Charles II in the 1660s.

22 Oct 1850 The Much Wenlock Olympian Games, the brainchild of British sports enthusiast Dr. William Penny Brookes (1809–1895), are held for the first time in Much Wenlock, England, a small town in rural Shropshire. The Much Wenlock "Olympics" are a major influence on Pierre de Coubertin, who visits them in 1889.

15 Nov 1859 The 1st Zappas Olympic Games, an early attempt at revival of the Olympics, are held

	in Athens. The Games were initiated and financed by a wealthy grain dealer, Evangelis Zappas (1800–1865).
1 Jan 1863	Pierre Frédy, the Baron de Coubertin, is born in Paris, France, to Charles Louis Frédy, the Baron de Coubertin, and the former Agathe Marie Marcelle Gabrielle de Grisenoy de Mirville.
15 Nov 1870	The 2nd Zappas Olympic Games are held in Athens. They are considered the most successful of the Zappas Olympics.
18 May 1875	The 3rd Zappas Olympic Games are held in Athens.
18 May 1889	The 4th Zappas Olympic Games are held in Athens.
1891	The 1st Panhellenic Gymnastic Society Games, modeled after the Zappas Olympics, are held in Athens.
25 Nov 1892	Meeting of sports dignitaries at the Sorbonne celebrating the fifth anniversary of the Union des Sociétés Françaises de Sports Athlétiques (USFSA), at which Coubertin first broached the idea of the revival of the Olympic Games. His speech ended with the now famous summons, "Let us export rowers, runners, and fencers; there is the free trade of the future, and on the day when it is introduced within the walls of old Europe the cause of peace will have received a new and mighty stay. This is enough to encourage your servant to dream now about the second part of his program; he hopes that you will help him as you have helped him hitherto, and that with you he will be able to continue and complete, on a basis suited to the conditions of modern life, this grandiose and salutary task, the restoration of the Olympic Games."

1893	The 2nd Panhellenic Gymnastic Society Games, modeled after the Zappas Olympics, are held in Athens.
16 – 24 Jun 1894	The Paris International Athletic Congress is organized by Coubertin at the Palais de la Sorbonne in Paris. Although titularly to be a congress with amateurism as its main theme, the program lists ten points to be discussed, the last three of which concern the reestablishment of the Olympic Games. This is later regarded as the First Olympic Congress.
23 Jun 1894	The International Olympic Committee is formed at the end of the Sorbonne Congress and consists mostly of sports dignitaries who had attended the Congress.
23 Jun 1894	Demetrios Vikelas of Greece elected as the first President of the International Olympic Committee at the end of the First Session of the IOC.
6 – 15 Apr 1896	Athens, Greece – Celebration of the Games of the Ist Olympiad of the modern era.
10 Apr 1896	Baron Pierre de Coubertin of France elected as the second President of the International Olympic Committee at the Second Session of the IOC.
23 – 31 Jul 1897	Le Havre, France – Second Olympic Congress celebrated at the Town Hall of Le Havre with "Sports Hygiene and Pedagogy" as the theme.
20 May – 28 Oct 1900	Paris, France – Celebration of the Games of the IInd Olympiad.
1 Jul – 23 Nov 1904	St. Louis, Missouri, USA – Celebration of the Games of the IIIrd Olympiad.
9 – 14 Jun 1905	Brussels, Belgium – Third Olympic Congress celebrated at the Palais des Académies with "Sport and Physical Education" as the theme.

22 Apr – 2 May 1906	Athens, Greece – Intercalated Olympic Games are held in Athens during the interim between the celebrations of the Olympiad.
23 – 25 May 1906	Paris, France – Fourth Olympic Congress celebrated at the Comédie Française et Touring Club with "Art, Literature, and Sport" as the theme.
27 Apr – 31 Oct 1908	London, England – Celebration of the Games of the IVth Olympiad.
5 May – 27 Jul 1912	Stockholm, Sweden – Celebration of the Games of the Vth Olympiad.
7 – 11 May 1913	Lausanne, Switzerland – 5th Olympic Congress celebrated at the Palais de l'Université with "Sports Psychology and Physiology" as the theme.
15 – 23 Jun 1914	Paris, France – 6th Olympic Congress celebrated at the Palais de la Sorbonne with "Olympic Regulations" as the theme.
Dec 1915 – Feb 1917	Baron Godefroy de Blonay of Switzerland is appointed interim IOC President by Coubertin, who enlists to help the French war effort. Coubertin felt the IOC should not be headed by a soldier.
Summer 1916	The Games of the VIth Olympiad, scheduled to be held in Berlin, Germany, are cancelled due to World War I.
Feb 1917	Baron Pierre de Coubertin resumes his post as President of the International Olympic Committee.
23 Apr – 12 Sep 1920	Antwerp, Belgium – Celebration of the Games of the VIIth Olympiad.
2 – 7 Jun 1921	Lausanne, Switzerland – 7th Olympic Congress celebrated at the Casino de Montbenon with "Olympic Regulations" as the theme.

25 Jan – 4 Feb 1924

Chamonix, France – Celebration of the "Semaine internationale des sports d'hiver," which was later designated retroactively as the 1st Olympic Winter Games.

4 May – 27 Jul 1924

Paris, France – Celebration of the Games of the VIIIth Olympiad.

28 May 1925

Count Henri de Baillet–Latour of Belgium elected as the third President of the International Olympic Committee at the 24th Session of the IOC in Prague.

29 May – 4 Jun 1925

Prague, Czechoslovakia – 8th Olympic Congress celebrated at the Prague Town Hall with "Sports Pedagogy and Olympic Regulations" as the theme. The Congress is notable for Coubertin's retirement as IOC President.

11 – 19 Feb 1928

St. Moritz, Switzerland – Celebration of the 2nd Olympic Winter Games.

17 May – 12 Aug 1928

Amsterdam, The Netherlands – Celebration of the Games of the IXth Olympiad.

25 – 30 May 1930

Berlin, Germany – 9th Olympic Congress celebrated at the Aula of the Friedrich Wilhelm University with "Olympic Regulations" as the theme.

4 – 15 Feb 1932

Lake Placid, New York, USA – Celebration of the 3rd Olympic Winter Games.

30 Jul – 14 Aug 1932

Los Angeles, California, USA – Celebration of the Games of the Xth Olympiad.

15 Sep 1935

At a rally in Nuremburg, Hitler announces the enactment of the Nuremburg Laws, stripping Jews of their German citizenship and their rights under German law. This gives new impetus to consideration to boycott the 1936 Olympics, both to be based in Germany.

6 - 16 Feb 1936   Garmisch-Partenkirchen, Germany –
                   Celebration of the 4th Olympic Winter
                   Games.

7 Mar 1936   Hitler orders three battalions of the German
                   army into the Rhineland, violating the
                   Treaty of Versailles. In response, France
                   considers the possibility of a boycott of the
                   1936 Olympics.

1 - 16 Aug 1936   Berlin, Germany – Celebration of the
                   Games of the XIth Olympiad. Despite calls
                   for a boycott from multiple nations, almost
                   all IOC member nations participate at
                   Berlin.

2 Sep 1937   Pierre de Coubertin dies while walking
                   through Lagrange Park in Geneva,
                   Switzerland.

26 Mar 1938   At a ceremony in Ancient Olympia, the
                   heart of Pierre de Coubertin, which had
                   been removed from his body shortly after
                   his death, is placed for perpetuity in a
                   marble stele on the Kronos hill, near the
                   Ancient Olympic stadium.

Winter 1940   The 5th Olympic Winter Games are
                   cancelled due to World War II. The Games
                   were originally awarded to Sapporo, Japan,
                   which withdrew on 16 July 1938. They
                   were reassigned to St. Moritz, Switzerland,
                   which withdrew as host on 9 June 1939.
                   The Games were then reassigned to
                   Garmisch-Partenkirchen, Germany.

Summer 1940   The Games of the XIIth Olympiad,
                   originally scheduled to be held in Tokyo,
                   Japan, and later (after the withdrawal of
                   Tokyo on 16 July 1938) awarded to
                   Helsinki, Finland (awarded 3 September
                   1938), are cancelled due to World War II.

6 Jan 1942   Count Baillet-Latour dies. The IOC
                   presidency will remain vacant during the
                   remainder of World War II, although

Sweden's Sigfrid Edström assumes the position of interim President.

Winter 1944 The 5th Olympic Winter Games, tentatively scheduled for Cortina d'Ampezzo, Italy, are cancelled due to World War II.

Summer 1944 The Games of the XIIIth Olympiad, originally scheduled to be held in London, England, are cancelled due to World War II.

4 Sep 1946 J[ohannes] Sigfrid Edström of Sweden elected as the fourth President of the International Olympic Committee at the 40th Session of the IOC in Lausanne.

30 Jan – 8 Feb 1948 St. Moritz, Switzerland – Celebration of the 5th Olympic Winter Games.

29 Jul – 14 Aug 1948 London, England – Celebration of the Games of the XIVth Olympiad.

14 – 25 Feb 1952 Oslo, Norway – Celebration of the 6th Olympic Winter Games.

16 Jul 1952 Avery Brundage of the United States elected as the fifth President of the International Olympic Committee at the 48th Session of the IOC in Helsinki.

19 Jul – 3 Aug 1952 Helsinki, Finland – Celebration of the Games of the XVth Olympiad.

26 Jan – 5 Feb 1956 Cortina d'Ampezzo, Italy – Celebration of the 7th Olympic Winter Games.

10 – 17 Jun 1956 Stockholm, Sweden – Celebration of the Equestrian Games of the XVIth Olympiad. The Equestrian Games were made necessary because of Australia's highly restrictive animal quarantine restrictions.

29 Oct 1956 Israel invades the Sinai peninsula, a part of Egypt. Egypt, Lebanon, and Iraq withdraw from the Melbourne Olympics in protest.

4 Nov 1956	Soviet troops enter Budapest, Hungary in an effort to stop rising political insurgency. This eventually leads to boycotts of the Melbourne Olympics by Spain, Switzerland, and the Netherlands, protesting the Soviet action.
22 Nov – 8 Dec 1956	Melbourne, Victoria, Australia – Celebration of the Games of the XVIth Olympiad. In an attempt to solve the problem of the two Germanys, a unified German team representing both East (GDR) and West (FRG) Germany competes at the IOC's behest.
18 – 28 Feb 1960	Squaw Valley, California, USA – Celebration of the 8th Olympic Winter Games.
25 Aug – 11 Sep 1960	Rome, Italy – Celebration of the Games of the XVIIth Olympiad.
Nov 1963	GANEFO – the Games of the New Emerging Forces – are held in Jakarta, Indonesia. GANEFO refuses to admit athletes from Israel or Taiwan, and the international federations for track & field athletics, swimming, and shooting ban all athletes who competed at GANEFO from competing at Tokyo in 1964. The IOC did not support this as a blanket ban on all athletes competing at GANEFO.
29 Jan – 9 Feb 1964	Innsbruck, Austria – Celebration of the 9th Olympic Winter Games.
10 – 24 Oct 1964	Tokyo, Japan – Celebration of the Games of the XVIIIth Olympiad.
6 – 18 Feb 1968	Grenoble, France – Celebration of the 10th Olympic Winter Games.
2 Oct 1968	Student protests against the Mexico City Olympics come to a head in the capital city. On this day, student protesters hold a rally in the Plaza of Three Cultures, and government troops open fire, killing almost

	300, with thousands injured and imprisoned.
12 – 27 Oct 1968	Mexico City, Mexico – Celebration of the Games of the XIXth Olympiad.
3 – 13 Feb 1972	Sapporo, Japan – Celebration of the 11th Olympic Winter Games.
21 Aug 1972	Sir Michael Morris, The Lord Killanin of Dublin and Spittal (Ireland) elected as the sixth President of the International Olympic Committee at the 73rd Session of the IOC in Munich.
26 Aug – 11 Sep 1972	Munich, Federal Republic of Germany – Celebration of the Games of the XXth Olympiad.
5 Sep 1972	Terrorists representing the Black September group forever change the Olympic Games when they take hostage and then savagely murder 11 members of the Israeli Olympic team. The deaths occur at Fürstenfeldbruck airport on the outskirts of Munich.
30 Sep – 4 Oct 1973	Varna, Bulgaria – 10th Olympic Congress, the first in 43 years, celebrated at the Sports Palace with "Sport for a World of Peace – The Olympic Movement and Its Future" as the theme.
4 – 15 Feb 1976	Innsbruck, Austria – Celebration of the 12th Olympic Winter Games.
17 Jul – 1 Aug 1976	Montreal, Quebec, Canada – Celebration of the Games of the XXIst Olympiad.
25 – 26 Nov 1979	The two–China question is finally resolved. On 25 November 1979, mainland China, the People's Republic of China is recognized officially by the IOC. The next day, the Chinese Taipei Olympic Committee is given official IOC recognition under that name, agreeing to compete using only that name, and not as the Republic of China. This clears the way

for both Chinese Olympic Committees to compete together at the Olympic Games.

25–27 Dec 1979

The Soviet Union invades Afghanistan, precipitating an eventual boycott of the Moscow Olympics.

4 Jan 1980

In retaliation for the Soviet invasion of Afghanistan, U.S. President Jimmy Carter announces, for the first time, the possibility of a U.S. boycott of the 1980 Moscow Olympics.

13 – 24 Feb 1980

Lake Placid, New York, USA – Celebration of the 13th Olympic Winter Games.

16 Jul 1980

Juan Antonio Samaranch [Torellos] elected as the seventh President of the International Olympic Committee at the 83rd Session of the IOC in Moscow.

19 Jul – 3 Aug 1980

Moscow, USSR – Celebration of the Games of the XXIInd Olympiad. Approximately 60 countries boycott the Olympics in protest of the Soviet Union's invasion of Afghanistan.

23 – 28 Sep 1981

Baden–Baden, Federal Republic of Germany – 11th Olympic Congress celebrated at Baden–Baden's Kurhaus with "United By and For Sport" as the theme, with three sub-themes: 1) The Future of the Olympic Games; 2) International Cooperation; and 3) The Future Olympic Movement.

8 – 19 Feb 1984

Sarajevo, Yugoslavia – Celebration of the 14th Olympic Winter Games.

8 May 1984

The Soviet Union announces it will not attend the Los Angeles Olympic Games, citing concerns over the safety of its athletes in Los Angeles, and because of "anti-Communist activities" in the United States.

28 Jul – 12 Aug 1984	Los Angeles, California, USA – Celebration of the Games of the XXIIIrd Olympiad. Fourteen invited countries join the Soviet-inspired boycott. Of the Soviet-bloc nations, only Romania defies the boycott and competes.
13 – 28 Feb 1988	Calgary, Alberta, Canada – Celebration of the 15th Olympic Winter Games.
17 Sep – 5 Oct 1988	Seoul, Republic of Korea – Celebration of the Games of the XXIVth Olympiad.
8 – 23 Feb 1992	Albertville, France – Celebration of the 16th Olympic Winter Games.
25 Jul – 9 Aug 1992	Barcelona, Spain – Celebration of the Games of the XXVth Olympiad. For the first Olympics since 1960, no politically inspired boycott or other serious political problems mar the Games.
12 – 27 Feb 1994	Lillehammer, Norway – Celebration of the 17th Olympic Winter Games.
23 Jun 1994	The 100th Anniversary of the founding of the Modern Olympic Games is celebrated with a ceremony at the Sorbonne, where Coubertin held the First Olympic Congress which re-established the Modern Olympic Games.
29 Aug – 3 Sep 1994	Paris, France – 12th Olympic Congress celebrated with four main themes: 1) The Olympic Movement's Contribution to Modern Society, 2) The Contemporary Athlete, 3) Sport in Its Social Context, and 4) Sport and the Media. The 12th Olympic Congress is held in celebration of the 100th Anniversary of the Olympic Movement.
19 Jul – 4 Aug 1996	Atlanta, Georgia, USA – scheduled celebration of the Games of the XXVIth Olympiad, the Centennial Olympic Games.
7 – 22 Feb 1998	Nagano, Japan – scheduled celebration of the 18th Olympic Winter Games.

16 Sep – 1 Oct 2000   Sydney, New South Wales, Australia – scheduled celebration of the Games of the XXVIIth Olympiad.

Feb 2002   Salt Lake City, Utah, USA – scheduled celebration of the 19th Olympic Winter Games.

THE OLYMPIC GAMES AND OLYMPIC WINTER GAMES

The Games of the Ist Olympiad (1896)   The Games of the Ist Olympiad were held in Athens, Greece from 6 to 15 April 1896. (At the time, Greece recognized the Julian Calendar, not the Gregorian Calendar used by much of the world then and now used universally. In Greek terms, the Games were held from 25 March to 3 April 1896.) London was initially to have been the site but the Sorbonne Congress of 1894 elected Athens as the host city by acclamation. The only other city seriously considered was Paris.

Fourteen nations competed at Athens, with approximately 200–230 athletes – it cannot be determined with certainty. No women competed. The first Olympic champion of the modern era was James Connolly of the United States who won the hop, step and jump in track & field athletics (now called the triple jump). Greece won the most medals with 50, while the United States won the most gold medals with 11, including most of the track & field athletics events. The highlight of the Games was the marathon victory of Spiridon Loues of Greece. When he neared the stadium, messengers came into the ancient stadium and cried out, "Hellas! Hellas! (A Greek! A Greek!)," sending the crowd into a frenzy. The Olympic pride based on millennia of Olympic tradition was then realized by the home crowd, which had been rather disappointed by the results of the Greek athletes. Loues won the race and became a hero, offered gifts and riches by many different Greek merchants. But he asked only for a cart to help him carry and sell his water and he returned to being a shepherd in his small town of Amarousi.

Many people wanted the Games to remain permanently in Athens, and in 1896 the American athletes wrote a letter to *The New York Times* asking that this be done. But Coubertin insisted that the Games be spread to various countries to emphasize the international flavor of the Olympic Games.

The Games of the IInd Olympiad (1900)   The Games of the IInd Olympiad were held in Paris, France from 20 May through 28 October 1900. They were a disaster. If one had to nominate the "worst modern Olympics" ever, 1900 and 1904 would surely lead the voting.

In 1900, Paris hosted a great World's Fair, the Exposition Universelle Internationale de 1900 à Paris. Coubertin made plans to hold the Olympics as part of the fair and planned to organize the events. But the organizers of the Fair relegated Coubertin to a relatively minor administrative position and took over the organization of the sporting events connected with the Fair. Most of the events we today consider "Olympic" were not even labeled as such in 1900, often being called the "Championnats d'Exposition," or "Championnats Internationaux." Years later, many athletes did not know they had competed in the Olympic Games, believing that their sport had been only a part of the World's Fair. Only the athletics (track & field) events were really publicized in the media as being part of the Olympics.

The Games were stretched out over five months (May–October) and formal opening and closing ceremonies were not held. It is difficult to know, because of the confusion over titles, and the many, many events held at the Fair, what events should actually be considered "Olympic" and which should not. The IOC had no real control of this and thus one sees various listings. Many unusual sports and events were contested such as motorboating, balloon racing, underwater swimming, and an obstacle swimming race. Thus, the number of nations and athletes competing is completely conjectural.

Women made their Olympic debut, with the first known competitors being two croquet players listed only as Mme. Brohy and Mlle. Ohnier (on 28 June). Charlotte Cooper (GBR) won the first championships by a woman, in tennis singles and mixed doubles. Margaret Abbott (USA) won the "Olympic" golf championship in early October. Neither of those two sports was labeled as Olympic by the organizers. Years later, Abbott's relatives did not know for certain that the title she won that day had been for the Olympic championship. In many sports, medals were not awarded. Most of the listed prizes were cups and other similar trophies. In several sports, notably fencing and shooting, professional events were held and yet were considered later by the IOC to be of "Olympic" stature.

The Games of the IIIrd Olympiad (1904)   The Games of the IIIrd Olympiad were held in St. Louis, Missouri, USA, from 1 July through 23 November 1904. After the debacle of 1900, Coubertin was hoping for better from the United States in 1904, but did not see his hopes realized. The Games were awarded to Chicago. However, St. Louis was to host a major world's fair in 1904, the Louisiana Purchase Exposition, and the St. Louis organizers wanted the Olympics as part of the fair. They threatened to hold competing Olympics if Chicago did not allow them to have the Games. Chicago eventually acquiesced.

The Games were very similar to 1900 – they lasted almost five months, many of the events were not labeled as Olympic but only as championships of the Fair, it is difficult to know which sports and events were definitely on the Olympic program, a number of unusual sports and events saw their way to the program, and the Games were mostly an afterthought to the Fair. Again, the number of competing nations and athletes cannot be determined with any accuracy. Coubertin vowed after 1904 that he would never again hold the Olympics as a sideshow to a fair. Notably, he did not even attend the Olympics in 1904, sending two IOC delegates from Hungary and Germany in his place. He was appalled when he heard of the happenings in St. Louis, but never more so than when he heard about the "Anthropological Days." The Fair organizers included several days of "Olympic" competitions among several so-called primitive tribes which were being exhibited at the Exposition. Among these were Pygmies, Patagonians, Filipinos, Native American Indian tribes, Japanese Ainus, and certain Asian tribes. Events included throwing bolos, mud fighting, and climbing a greased pole.

Again, only the athletics (track & field) received any great publicity as being an Olympic sport. These events were virtually an American club championship, and, in fact, a trophy was donated by Albert Spalding for the American club scoring the most points in the event.Though surpassed by athletes in other sports, the American foursome of Archie Hahn, Harry Hillman, James Lightbody, and Ray Ewry won three gold medals each in track & field and received the bulk of the media attention. In other sports, American dominance was almost as complete, owing to the fact that only a few other countries attended the Games, and very few foreign athletes competed.

Two black Zulu tribesmen who were part of the Boer War exhibition at the fair, Lentauw and Yamasini, also competed in the marathon. Ironically, they are considered to be the first Olympic competitors from South Africa.

The Intercalated Olympic Games of 1906   The Olympic Games of 1906 were held in Athens, Greece from 22 April through 2 May 1906. Twenty nations attended with 826 athletes competing (820 men and 6 women). (Fifteen Danish women also gave a gymnastics exhibition in 1906.)

Today, the IOC and some historians do not consider the 1906 Intercalated Olympics to be "true" Olympic Games. By doing so, they neglect the Games that may have helped save the Olympic Movement. After the debacles of 1900 and 1904, the Olympics were in desperate straits. The Greeks had wanted to host more Olympics and they proposed holding "interim" Olympics, every four years in the even year between the Olympics. The first of these was scheduled in 1906. The Greeks later scheduled interim Olympics for 1910 and 1914 but political and economic events in Greece prevented those from being held.

The Games of 1906 were not of the caliber of many Olympics of later years, but they were the best Olympics to that date.

Again, many of the facilities were not of the highest quality. However, as in 1896, the Greeks approached their responsibility with enthusiasm and the most international field to date competed in these Olympics. A true opening ceremony was conducted for the first time, with the athletes marching with their teams following a flag bearer from their own country.

The newspapers considered these Games to be the Olympics and labeled them as such. Coubertin, at first opposed to the idea, subsequently embraced them as Olympics when he saw that the Greeks were organizing the best "Olympics" of the modern era. The IOC made no official determination of the status of these events at first, but later declared them not to be official. The Olympics of 1906 deserve that title much more so than do the farces that were 1900 and 1904. They resurrected the flagging Olympic movement.

The Games of the IVth Olympiad (1908)   The Games of the IVth Olympiad were held in London, England from 27 April to 31 October 1908. Twenty–two nations attended with 2,035 athletes competing (1,999 men and 36 women). The Games were originally awarded to Rome, Italy, which was chosen over Berlin, Germany at the 6th IOC Session in London on 22 June 1904. But in 1906, Mt. Vesuvius erupted near Naples, and the Italian government felt it needed the money to rebuild the area around the volcano and asked that the 1908 Rome Olympics be relocated. London gladly accepted.

These Olympics were by far the best organized to date. They also had the most international flavor of any Olympics yet held. By now the Olympics were becoming "known" to the world and athletes everywhere wanted to compete, and managed to find ways to do so. Still, the Games, though superbly run, are best known for multiple political arguments and other bickering that occurred.

The problems began at the Opening Ceremony. The Swedish and United States flags did not fly over the stadium, as the organizers stated they could not find them. This so infuriated the Swedes that when a dispute arose over wrestling rules later in the Games, they threatened to withdraw from the competition. The Finns marched in the ceremony without a flag. Finland was a territory of Russia in 1908, but Russia allowed them to compete separately, provided they did so under the Russian flag. The Finns, in protest, marched under no flag. The United States later protested the officiating in multiple track & field athletics events.

The most memorable event of the 1908 Olympics was the marathon. The race was to start at Windsor Castle so that Queen Alexandra's grandchildren could watch the beginning. The distance from there to the finish line at the Shepherd's Bush stadium was 26 miles, 385 yards. This was the first time this distance was chosen for a marathon and it later became the standard.

The leader for most of the second half of the race was Dorando Pietri, a candymaker from Capri, Italy. But when Pietri entered the Stadium, he was totally exhausted. Like a drunken sailor, he staggered and fell several times before the finish line. He also turned in the wrong direction twice during the last lap. Officials, urged on by sympathetic fans, helped him to his feet and directed him to the finish line. He finished the race first and was declared the winner. A few hundred meters behind him finished Johnny Hayes of the United States. An immediate protest was lodged and Pietri was disqualified, with Hayes winning the gold medal.

The Games of the Vth Olympiad (1912)   The Games of the Vth Olympiad were held in Stockholm, Sweden, from 5 May through 27 July 1912. After the problems of 1908, the pseudo–Olympics of 1900 and 1904, and the meager international participation of 1896, Stockholm, Sweden should be credited with the first truly modern Games of Olympic proportions. No other city was seriously considered as host for 1912 and Stockholm was elected by acclamation at the 10th IOC Session in Berlin on 28 May 1909. Twenty-eight nations attended, with 2,547 athletes competing (2,490 men and 57 women).

The Games were marvelously organized. The only significant political problems concerned the entries of Finland and Bohemia. Both nations wished to compete as independent nations, but in 1912, Finland was a part of Russia, and Bohemia was a part of the Austro–Hungarian Empire. As in 1908, both were allowed to compete but were not allowed to use their own flags.

But probably more than any other, the 1912 Olympics belonged to one person, Jim Thorpe. Jim Thorpe was a Sac and Fox Indian from Oklahoma who had attended the Carlisle Indian School. In 1912, Thorpe decided to compete in the two new Olympic events testing the all–around abilities of the track & field athletes – the decathlon of ten events, and pentathlon of five events. He won by enormous margins. When awarded his prizes by King Gustav V, the King supposedly said, "Sir, you are the greatest athlete in the world." Thorpe's reply was supposedly, "Thanks, King." But, in 1913, it was discovered that Thorpe had played minor league professional baseball in 1909 and 1910, and he was stripped of his medals. Seventy years later, in 1982, the IOC finally relented and restored the medals to Thorpe's family – he had died in 1953.

Hannes Kolehmainen of Finland, the first of the great Flying Finn distance runners, also made his debut at the 1912 Olympics. He won four medals: three gold in the 5,000 meters, 10,000 meters, and individual cross–country, and a silver in the team cross–country. When Kolehmainen won, the Russian flag was raised because of Finland's subjugation to the Russians at that time. "I would almost rather not have won, than see that flag up there," he said. (Lord Killanin and John Rodda, *The Olympic Games 1984*, p. 77. Salem, New Hampshire: Michael Joseph, 1983.)

The 1912 Olympics were also noteworthy for the first swimming events for women. Previously, women had competed at the Olympics to any degree only in tennis, with minor appearances in archery, golf, yachting, and croquet in 1900, 1904, and 1908. There were only two swim events for women, a 100 meter freestyle and a freestyle relay, as well as a high diving event, but they were important as they were the first truly "athletic" events in which women were allowed to compete at the Olympics. The list of events in which women compete would increase with each Olympiad.

The Games of the VIth Olympiad (1916)   The Games of the VIth Olympiad were originally awarded to Berlin, Germany, which was chosen at the 14th IOC Session in Stockholm on 4 July 1912 over Budapest, Hungary. Other cities which expressed interest to host the 1916 Olympics were Alexandria, Egypt; Amsterdam, The Netherlands; Brussels, Belgium; and Cleveland, Ohio, USA. Because of World War I, the Games were not celebrated.

The Games of the VIIth Olympiad (1920)   The Games of the VIIth Olympiad were held in Antwerp, Belgium from 23 April through 12 September 1920. Other cities which had expressed interest to host the 1920 Olympic Games were Amsterdam, The Netherlands; Atlanta, Georgia, USA; Budapest, Hungary; Cleveland, Ohio, USA; Havana, Cuba; and Philadelphia, Pennsylvania, USA. The offer from Lyon was seriously considered during World War I when Belgium was being ravaged by the effects of the War, but Antwerp was officially chosen at the 17th IOC Session in Lausanne on 5 April 1919. However, eventually 29 nations attended the Games in Antwerp, with 2,670 athletes competing (2,593 men and 77 women).

The War was only over a year when the 1920 Olympics were finally awarded to war-ravaged Belgium. Coubertin decided that, though the War would be over less than two years, the VIIth Olympiad should be celebrated as scheduled. Although the Games were decidedly austere, the Belgian people and organizing committee did an amazing job in preparing for the Games on such short notice.

The opening ceremonies were notable for the first use of the Olympic flag at the Olympics, the first time the Olympic oath was taken by a competitor (Victor Boin), and the first release of homing pigeons as a symbol of peace. Of the 29 countries competing, missing were Germany, Austria, Hungary, and Bulgaria, as the IOC barred them because of their aggressiveness in World War I.

The Olympics were most notable for the debut of Paavo Nurmi of Finland, probably the greatest distance runner ever. Nurmi competed in four events, losing only in the 5,000 meters. His countryman, Hannes Kolehmainen, returned eight years after his Stockholm victories in the 5,000 and 10,000 meters, and won the marathon. The shooting program contained 20 events, including 10 team events, allowing Willis Lee and Lloyd Spooner of the United States to win seven medals, and Carl Osburn (USA) to win six. Nedo Nadi (ITA) was much decorated as he won five gold medals in fencing.

The Antwerp Olympics helped the world recover from the Great War. Coubertin summarized them in the Antwerp Town Hall when he addressed the IOC in the presence of King Albert of Belgium:

> This is what the seventh Olympiad has brought us: general comprehension; the certainty of being henceforward understood by all . . . These festivals . . . are above all festivals of human unity. In an incomparable synthesis the effort of muscles and of mind, mutual help and competition, lofty patriotism and intelligent cosmopolitanism, the personal interest in the champion and the abnegation of the team–member, are bound in a sheaf for a common task.

The 1st Olympic Winter Games (1924)   The 1st Olympic Winter Games were held in Chamonix, France from 25 January through 4 February 1924. Sixteen nations attended with 258 athletes competing (245 men and 13 women).

In June 1922, the French Olympic Committee held a congress in which representatives of skiing, skating, and ice hockey were present. They arranged to hold an International Winter Sports Week in Chamonix in early 1924. The contests were not originally called the Olympic Games, but the opening speech, while not using the word Olympic in their title, did state that they were under the "high patronage of the International Olympic Committee." Their original official title was the "Semaine internationale des sports d'hiver." On 27 May 1925, the IOC amended its charter to begin a cycle of Olympic Winter Games. The Chamonix events were never officially mentioned as the 1st Olympic Winter Games in this proclamation. It is felt, however, that this was an error of the secretary taking the minutes as the IOC has long since recognized the 1924 Chamonix events as the 1st Olympic Winter Games.

The politics of declaring these as Olympic Games may have been more interesting than the Games themselves. The 1924 Winter Olympics saw Clas Thunberg and Thorleig Haug crowned as multiple champions in skating and skiing, respectively. Gillis Grafström repeated his title in men's figure skating which he had won at the

Summer Games in Antwerp in 1920.   In women's figure skating, Herma Planck–Szabó of Austria won the title but the eighth, and last, place finisher would later become the greatest women's figure skater ever, Sonja Henie.

The Games of the VIIIth Olympiad (1924)   The Games of the VIIIth Olympiad were held in Paris, France from 4 May through 27 July 1924.   Other cities considered as hosts were Amsterdam, The Netherlands; Barcelona, Spain; Los Angeles, California, USA; Prague, Czechoslovakia; and Rome, Italy.   Forty–four nations attended the 1924 Olympics, with 3,092 athletes competing (2,956 men and 136 women).   After the difficulties of the 1900 Olympics in Paris, Coubertin fervently desired to see his home city host another Olympics.   Paris was elected to host the 1924 Olympics at the 19th IOC Session in Lausanne on 2 June 1921 and nicely redeemed itself.

In swimming, Johnny Weissmuller (USA) made his first Olympic appearance and showed why he would someday become known as the world's greatest swimmer.   He would compete in the 1928 Olympics as well, and then turned to Hollywood where he became famous as Tarzan, portraying that character in 19 movies.

The Games themselves were the personal playground of Paavo Nurmi, who took up where he left off in 1920.   Nurmi won five gold medals and could have won more had the schedule allowed him time to compete in more events.

The 1924 Olympics are today most famous as the Olympics of Harold Abrahams and Eric Liddell, the Olympics of *Chariots of Fire*.   In 1981, the movie *Chariots of Fire* was made celebrating the lives of Harold Abrahams and Eric Liddell and their route to the 1924 Olympics.   The movie won the Academy Award for Best Picture of the Year.   It was an excellent movie, but much of the story was apocryphal, with ample use of poetic license.

Besides its heralded stars, the 1924 Olympics unveiled several other notable firsts.   The Olympic motto – "Citius, Altius, Fortius" – was used for the first time.   And at the closing ceremony the practice of raising three flags – one for the IOC, one for the host nation and one for the succeeding host nation – was instituted for the first time.

The 2nd Olympic Winter Games (1928)   The 2nd Olympic Winter Games were held in St. Moritz, Switzerland from 11 to 19 February 1928.   Other cities considered by the IOC as possible hosts were Davos, Switzerland and Engelberg, Switzerland, but St. Moritz was awarded the Games at the 27th IOC Session in Lausanne on 10 April 1929.   Twenty–five nations attended with 464 athletes competing (438 men and 26 women).

The 1928 Olympic Winter Games were highly successful but the organizers had to contend with poor weather. The föhn, a strong wind coming down the leeward side of a mountain and carrying warm weather with it, postponed several events and forced the cancellation of one. On the morning of the 50 kilometer cross-country skiing, the temperature was about 0° C. (32° F.) but during the competition, the föhn came in and temperatures rose to 25° C. (77° F.) by mid-day, playing havoc with the snow and waxing conditions.

Later that night, the warm weather brought rain which poured down and ruined the ski courses. Fortunately snow and frost over the next few days rescued them. But the föhn affected several other events as well. In the 10,000 meter speed skating, the United States' Irving Jaffee had the best time after the first few runs as the föhn was bringing in warm weather and melting the rink. The event was halted because of the conditions and it was never restarted. Jaffee is listed by some American sources, incorrectly, as having won the event, but it actually was never contested to a conclusion. The five-man bob race also suffered the wrath of the föhn, when the bob course was thawed and the four-run contest was shortened to only two runs.

The individual stars of the Games were Clas Thunberg, who won two more golds in speed skating; Johan Grøttumsbråten, who won two Nordic skiing golds; Gillis Grafström, who won his third consecutive figure skating title; and Sonja Henie, who won her first of three Olympic figure skating championships. But perhaps the real star of the 1928 Winter Olympics was the Canadian ice hockey leviathan which, in the absence of American participation, was unchallenged in winning the title with a goal margin of 38–0.

The Games of the IXth Olympiad (1928)   The Games of the IXth Olympiad were held in Amsterdam, The Netherlands from 17 May through 12 August 1928. The only other city seriously considered as a host was Los Angeles, California, USA. Amsterdam was chosen as host of the 1928 Olympics at the 19th IOC Session in Lausanne on 2 June 1921. Forty-six nations attended with 3,014 athletes competing (2,724 men and 290 women).

The 1928 Olympic Games were remarkable for the return of Germany to the Olympic Games for the first time since 1912, after it had not been invited in 1920 or 1924. In addition, an Olympic flame burned at the Olympic stadium for the first time ever. It burned atop the marathon tower, although it was not lit at the end of a torch relay.

The 1928 Olympics were an unusual event in that no single athlete dominated. Paavo Nurmi was back and he won three more medals, but only one of them was gold. Johnny Weissmuller was back and again won two gold medals. But the biggest story of the 1928 Olympics was probably the emergence of women.

The Ancient Olympic Games did not allow women as competitors, or even as spectators. If they were found to be watching they were supposedly put to death. Baron de Coubertin did not want women in the Olympics and he explicitly said so several times in his writings. In the modern Olympics, probably because of Coubertin's opposition, women were admitted slowly and only grudgingly.

Women had competed at the Olympics since 1900 but in small numbers and never in track & field athletics. Track & field athletics has always been the showcase sport of the Olympics. Women were not allowed to compete in this sport until the 1928 Olympics. Track & field is controlled by the IAAF (International Amateur Athletic Federation) and it did not support the admission of women's track & field to the Olympics. So the women formed a separate organization, the FSFI (Fédération Sportive Féminine Internationale). The FSFI held its own events, the Women's "Olympics" in 1922 in Paris, and the 1926 "2nd International Ladies' Games" in Göteborg, Sweden.

It was only after these games proved the success of women's athletics that the IAAF acquiesced and allowed the sport into the Olympics. However, in 1928, only five events were held for women. The 1928 Olympic track & field events were so few and in such varied disciplines that no single woman could dominate. They were marred when several women finalists were on the verge of collapse after the 800 meters, a not uncommon sight among men either. The IOC reacted by barring the women from running distances over 200 meters, and this was not changed until 1960.

The 1928 Olympics were one of the last truly peaceful and fully attended Olympics. The depression had not yet occurred, which would mar the 1932 Olympics. Hitler was still in prison and the post–World War II boycotts had not yet occurred. They were missing the single standout athlete and one other thing. Because of illness, Coubertin missed his first Olympics since 1906. He did not get to see women compete in track & field.

The 3rd Olympic Winter Games (1932)   The 3rd Olympic Winter Games were held in Lake Placid, New York, USA from 4 to 15 February 1932. Seventeen nations attended with 252 athletes competing (231 men and 21 women). Multiple other U.S. cities submitted candidatures to the IOC as well as Montreal, Quebec, Canada, but Lake Placid was chosen to host at the 27th IOC Session in Lausanne on 10 April 1929.

The biggest news of these Games was the controversy over the manner in which the speed skating events were contested. For the first time in Olympic history, the European method of skating time trials in pairs was not used. (It became a separate facet of the sport again in 1992 at Albertville.) Instead the American method of pack racing was used to determine the Olympic champions. The Europeans, unaccustomed to the style, fared badly, and the great Clas Thunberg, still a viable competitor at age 39, refused to compete in protest of the change. Norway's Ivar Ballangrud did compete, but managed only a silver medal in the unfamiliar style.

The pack style did make heroes of two U.S. skaters. Hometown boy Jack Shea came home from Dartmouth and won the 500 and 1,500 meter races. He also delivered the oath of the athletes and, in 1980, would be a member of the organizing committee when the Winter Olympics returned to Lake Placid. Irving Jaffee won the other two events, the 5,000 and 10,000 meters. A few years later, during the depths of the depression, he pawned the gold medals and never saw them again.

In figure skating, Gillis Grafström competed again but was finally defeated as Austrian Karl Schäfer won the title with Grafström second. Sonja Henie repeated in the women's competition. In bobsledding, U.S. teammates Billy Fiske and Clifford Grey repeated as gold medalists from 1928.

The Games of the Xth Olympiad (1932)   The Games of the Xth Olympiad were held in Los Angeles, California, USA from 30 July through 14 August 1932. It was the only city which applied to host the Olympics, as the world was in the midst of a terrible economic depression. Los Angeles was awarded the Games by acclamation at the 21st IOC Session on 8 April 1923. Only 37 nations attended, the first time the number of competing nations had not increased at an Olympics. There were 1,408 athletes who competed (1,281 men and 127 women). The depression and the travel distance from Europe kept the international turnout low. Less then half as many athletes competed as in 1928 as many nations sent only small squads.

The 1932 Olympics also saw the unveiling of a woman to rival the male feats of Jim Thorpe. Mildred Ella "Babe" Didrikson was an 18-year-old Texas tomboy in 1932. She was from Dallas and was heralded even before the Olympics. Restrictions on women's participation prevented Babe from showing her true colors. She was allowed to enter only three events, though no such restriction existed for men. She won the javelin throw, and won the high hurdles (in a virtual dead-heat with Evelyne Hall [USA]). She was second in the high jump although she tied for first with Jean Shiley, but lost in a jump-off. Had she been able to compete in more events, it is likely that Babe could have won several more medals. After the Olympics, Babe Didrikson took up golf and became the greatest women's player in that sport.

Paavo Nurmi also attempted to compete at the 1932 Olympics but did not. Shortly before the Games the IOC declared him a professional for having received money for a tour of Germany.

He planned to run the marathon in 1932 and it is almost certain that he would have won that race, had he been allowed to compete. The United States dominated what was close to a domestic Olympics, winning 41 gold medals and 103 medals in all. This was more than the winning totals of the next four best nations combined.

The 4th Olympic Winter Games (1936)   The 4th Olympic Winter Games were held in Garmisch–Partenkirchen, Germany from 6 to 16 February 1936. Garmisch–Partenkirchen was chosen by the IOC at its 31st Session in Vienna on 8 June 1933. Other candidate cities were Montreal, Quebec, Canada and St. Moritz, Switzerland. Twenty–eight nations attended with 668 athletes competing (588 men and 80 women).

The 1936 Olympic Winter Games were held under the Nazi regime of Adolf Hitler. When IOC president, Henri Baillet-Latour, was traveling to Garmisch to see the Games, he was astonished to see roadsigns en route declaring "Dogs and Jews not allowed." Baillet-Latour demanded an audience with Der Führer and demanded that the signs be taken down. Hitler replied that he thought it usual, when a guest entered a person's home, that the guest followed the wishes of the host. Baillet-Latour responded that when the flag of Olympia flew over the area, he became the host and Hitler was only the invited guest. Hitler acquiesced and had the signs removed.

The Games were opened in a blinding snowstorm. They ended with the ski jump being watched by a record attendance of 150,000 people. In between, Ivar Ballangrud won three more gold medals in speed skating. Sonja Henie won her third consecutive gold medal in figure skating but the victory was a bit controversial. Henie had become a favorite of Der Führer, and it was thought that he wished her to win. She was not undeserving, but Britain's Cecilia Colledge was much improved and some thought that her second place finish was less than it could have been.

The biggest upset of the 1936 Olympic Winter Games occurred in ice hockey when the British team defeated the Canadians. The victory was aided by the scheming of J. F. "Bunny" Ahearne, general secretary of the British Ice Hockey Federation. Ahearne had a "mole" working in the Canadian Amateur Hockey Association and by 1934 had a complete list of all Canadian registered players who had been born in the British Isles. He contacted many of them and the team that won in Garmisch was led by eight ersatz Brits, several of whom had been imported from Canada. The Canadians howled in protest but to no avail.

The Games of the XIth Olympiad (1936)   The Games of the XIth Olympiad were held in Berlin, Germany from 1 through 16 August

1936. At least 11 other cities were considered by the IOC as possible hosts but Berlin was chosen in the final vote over Barcelona, Spain by 43-16 at the 29th IOC Session in Barcelona on 26 April 1931. Forty-nine nations attended, with 4,066 athletes competing (3,738 men and 328 women).

Because of Nazi policies against Jews and their aggressive national tendencies, there were many protests against the Olympics being held in Berlin in 1936. The Americans came the closest to boycotting in protest although the British and French both considered the option. At the IOC Session in Vienna on 7 June 1933, the membership discussed the discrepancy between Nazi doctrine and Olympic Principles, with two American members questioning the German members about their country's policies. At the 33rd IOC Session in Athens on 15 May 1934, Lord Aberdare, a British member, then expressed concerns about reports from Germany. He pointedly asked the German IOC members if their government's pledges were trustworthy. In September 1934, future IOC President Avery Brundage traveled to Germany to inspect the country and its policies. He later recommended that the Games go on in Germany, but calls for a boycott continued, although they were never realized.

And the Games were magnificently staged, as Hitler spared no expense and used them as a propaganda tool to demonstrate the beauty and efficiency of the Third Reich. He had Leni Riefenstahl, a renowned German filmmaker, produce a wondrous movie, *Olympia*, to ensure that the propaganda would not end at the closing ceremonies.

No other Olympics belonged to a single non-competitor as much as the 1936 Olympics with Adolf Hitler. But these Olympics were actually dominated by Jesse Owens. He showed up Hitler's Aryan supremacy theories and dominated the Berlin Games. Owens, a black American, won four gold medals in track & field athletics, winning the 100 meters, the 200 meters, the long (broad) jump, and the 4x100 meter relay. He was the most heralded and most popular athlete of the 1936 Olympics.

The greatest innovation of the 1936 Olympics was conceived by Dr. Carl Diem, head of the organizing committee. He proposed that a torch relay be instituted to carry a flame from Ancient Olympia to the Berlin Stadium and then to light the Olympic flame at the stadium. On 20 July 1936, 15 Greek maidens clad in short, belted smocks representing the robes of priestesses, gathered on the plain at Ancient Olympia and the flame was lit there by the rays of the Greek sun off a reflector. The high priestess presented the flame to Kyril Kondylis, the first Greek runner, to begin a torch relay. After several thousand miles, the flame arrived in Berlin where it was lit in the stadium by Fritz Schilgen.

The 1940 Olympic Winter Games   The 5th Olympic Winter Games, scheduled for 1940, were originally awarded to Sapporo, Japan at the 36th IOC Session in Warsaw on 9 June 1937. Sapporo withdrew on 16 July 1938, and the Games were awarded to St. Moritz at the IOC Executive Board meeting in Brussels on 3 September 1938. St. Moritz withdrew on 9 June 1939 at the 38th IOC Session in London and the 1940 Olympic Winter Games were then awarded to Garmisch-Partenkirchen, which eventually also withdrew. The Games were not held because of World War II.

The Games of the XIIth Olympiad (1940)   The Games of the XIIth Olympiad were to have been held in 1940, but did not take place because of the onset of World War II. At the 35th IOC Session in Berlin on 31 July 1936, the Games were originally awarded to Tokyo, Japan, in a vote of 36-27 over Helsinki, Finland. Other cities which had expressed interest in hosting the 1940 Olympics were Alexandria, Egypt; Buenos Aires, Argentina; Dublin, Ireland; Athens, Greece; Rio de Janeiro, Brazil; Barcelona, Spain; Budapest, Hungary; and either Toronto or Montreal, Canada. On 16 July 1938, Tokyo withdrew as host. On 3 September 1938, at the IOC Executive Board meeting in Brussels, the Games were awarded to Helsinki. The Games were canceled late in 1939.

The 1944 Olympic Winter Games   After the 1940 Olympic Winter Games were not held, the 5th Olympic Winter Games were scheduled for 1944 and were awarded to Cortina d'Ampezzo, Italy (16 votes in round two), which was chosen over Montreal, Quebec, Canada (12 votes in round two); and Oslo, Norway (2 votes in round two) at the 38th IOC Session in London on 9 June 1939. The Games were not celebrated because of World War II.

The Games of the XIIIth Olympiad (1944)   The Games of the XIIIth Olympiad were to have been held in 1944, but did not take place because of World War II. The Games had been awarded to London, England, which won the IOC nomination with 20 votes over Rome, Italy (11 votes); Detroit, Michigan, USA (2 votes); and Lausanne, Switzerland (1 vote) at the 38th IOC Session in London on 9 June 1939.

The 5th Olympic Winter Games (1948)   The 5th Olympic Winter Games were held in St. Moritz, Switzerland from 30 January through 8 February. Twenty-eight nations attended with 669 athletes competing (592 men and 77 women). The only candidate which opposed St. Moritz for 1948 was Lake Placid, New York. St. Moritz was chosen by the IOC Executive Board which met in Lausanne on 4 September 1946 and made its decision.

St. Moritz hurriedly put together excellent arrangements for the Games which were again disturbed, though less severely, by the föhn. Ice hockey matches (held outdoors) and the 10,000 meters speed skating had to be delayed but no events were canceled this time.

Alpine skiing made its true Olympic debut. A few combined events had been held in 1936 but this time there were three events for both men and women. Two athletes won a second "St. Moritz" Olympic medal, as "Bibi" Torriani played on the Swiss ice hockey team to match his bronze from 1928; and John Heaton (USA) also repeated his silver medal from the skeleton race in 1928. The skeleton race, a form of tobogganing unique to the St. Moritz resort, was held at the Olympics for only the second, and probably the last, time.

The Games of the XIVth Olympiad (1948)   The Games of the XIVth Olympiad were held in London, England from 29 July through 14 August 1948. For the only time in Olympic history, the Games were awarded to London by a postal vote after the IOC recommended the site to its members. The vote was confirmed by the IOC membership at its 39th Session in Lausanne on 4 September 1946. Other candidate cities were Baltimore, Maryland, USA; Lausanne, Switzerland; Los Angeles, California, USA; Minneapolis, Minnesota, USA; Philadelphia, Pennsylvania, USA. Fifty-nine nations attended with 4,099 athletes competing (3,714 men and 385 women).

As in 1920, the IOC decided that it was necessary to resurrect the Olympic Movement at the earliest scheduled time. Thus, although England had been ravaged by Hitler's air raids, the Games of the XIVth Olympiad were awarded to London in 1948. In spite of years of difficulties caused by rationing of food, clothes and other essential materials, the English organizing committee did an outstanding job.

No great innovations accompanied the Games themselves, as most of the protocols of the opening, closing and victory ceremonies were by now established. However, these Games were significant as they were televised for the first time, although only to small local audiences. Television sets were still quite rare.

One country which was missed was the Soviet Union. The USSR had competed in 1946 at the European Championships in track & field athletics and it was thought that perhaps it would return to the Olympics in 1948. This was not to be and the reasons for its failure to compete have never been revealed.

As a very popular sport in England, track & field was truly the focus of these Olympics, as it is so often. Three athletes stood out in the athletics stadium. "Fanny" Blankers-Koen (NED), a 30-year-old mother of three children in 1948, won the 100 meters, 200 meters, 80 meter high hurdles, and helped win gold in the 4x100 meter relay. Bob Mathias (USA), a 17-year-old schoolboy, won the decathlon despite a torrential downpour throughout much of the two-day event. In the next few years he would prove it not to be a fluke. He would win again in 1952 at Helsinki and was never defeated in his decathlon career. Finally, Emil Zátopek (TCH) won the 10,000 meters and finished second in the 5,000. It was only a prelude to his heroics of 1952.

The 6th Olympic Winter Games (1952)   The 6th Olympic Winter Games were held in Oslo, Norway from 14 to 25 February 1952. Thirty nations attended with 694 athletes competing (585 men and 109 women). At the 40th IOC Session in Stockholm on 21 June 1947, Oslo was chosen by the IOC with 18 votes over Cortina d'Ampezzo, Italy (9 votes) and Lake Placid, New York, USA (1 vote).

The Olympic Winter Games were finally held in a Nordic country and an Olympic flame was first lit at the Olympic Winter Games. Unlike the summer flame, however, this flame was originally lit from the hearth of the house in Morgedal, Norway, where Sondre Norheim, the outstanding pioneer of modern skiing, was born. At the end of a ski relay, the flame was lit in the Bislett Stadium by Eigil Nansen, grandson of the explorer Fridtjof Nansen.

Norway's athletes dominated the events, especially so Hjalmar Andersen who won three gold medals in speed skating. In Alpine Skiing, the handsome Stein Eriksen of Norway seemed the embodiment of a modern ski hero. He won the giant slalom and was second in the slalom. Dick Button of the United States won his second consecutive men's figure skating championship. In women's skiing, Andrea Mead-Lawrence (USA) won two events by upsetting the European women.

In bobsledding, Germany won both the two-man and four-man events. Its "athletes" in this event were so large that their momentum helped them win by increasing their speed. This caused the International Bobsleigh Federation to change its rules to place a weight limit on bobsled teams.

The Games of the XVth Olympiad (1952)   The Games of the XVth Olympiad were held in Helsinki, Finland from 19 July through 3 August 1952. At the 40th IOC Session in Stockholm on 21 June 1947, Helsinki won the vote in the second round over Los Angeles, California, USA; Minneapolis, Minnesota, USA; Amsterdam, The Netherlands; Detroit, Michigan, USA; Chicago, Illinois, USA; and

Philadelphia, Pennsylvania, USA. Sixty-nine nations attended with 4,925 athletes competing (4,407 men and 518 women).

In 1952, the biggest news from Helsinki was that the Soviets were there. After the Bolshevik Revolution of 1917, the USSR had not competed in the Olympics until the Helsinki Games. The world braced for the athletic battles between the Soviet Union and the United States – in effect, a cold-war Olympics. The Soviets were accorded one rather unusual allowance. They were set up in a separate Olympic Village and housed only with athletes from the Eastern Bloc countries of Hungary, Poland, Bulgaria, Romania, and Czechoslovakia.

It is always an exciting moment when the Olympic torch enters the stadium. In 1952, the excitement was palpable when the Finnish crowd realized that the torch bearer was the Finnish hero of heroes, Paavo Nurmi. Although now a 55-year-old, Nurmi carried the torch on high and still had the very familiar stride. Not only the crowd, but even the athletes were excited. They broke ranks to run to the side of the track to get closer to the distance running legend. Some Finnish football players then brought the torch from the track to the top of the tower, handing it to Hannes Kolehmainen, second only to Nurmi in the Finnish pantheon of sporting heroes. The 62-year-old Kolehmainen then lit the Olympic flame at the top of the tower.

Given that the Games were opened by two of the greatest distance runners ever, it was fitting that the 1952 Olympics were dominated by a distance runner who even surpassed a few of their feats. Emil Zátopek, the Czech who had won the 10,000 meters in 1948, was by now the greatest distance runner in the world. He entered the 5,000 and 10,000 meters and won both of them rather easily. He then entered the marathon, a race he had never before run. Still, the extra distance did not deter Zátopek. He was running with the favored Jim Peters of Great Britain for the first half of the race when he turned to Peters and asked him if the pace wasn't a bit slow. With no reply, Zátopek took off and was never seen again by Peters. Zátopek won the race by over 2½ minutes, while Peters failed to finish.

The Americans and the Soviets met several times in these Olympics, most notably in the boxing ring. In 1952, the Americans had the best of it, though the Soviets would improve in the coming years. The press made a big thing out of the medal counts, which were led early by the Soviet Union, although the United States eventually won the most medals and gold medals. This too would change in later Olympics.

The 7th Olympic Winter Games (1956)   The 7th Olympic Winter Games were held in Cortina d'Ampezzo, Italy from 26 January through 5 February 1956. Thirty-two nations attended with 820 athletes competing (688 men and 132 women). Cortina d'Ampezzo was chosen at the 43rd IOC Session in Rome on 28 April 1949 with 31 votes over Montreal, Quebec, Canada (7 votes); Colorado Springs, Colorado, USA (2 votes); and Lake Placid, New York, USA (1 vote).

The Cortina Olympics began ominously when the torch bearer at the opening ceremonies, speed skater Guido Caroli, tripped over a microphone wire and fell. However, he was not harmed and the torch did not go out. After that initial difficulty, the Games were a wonder.

The big news was the entrance of the Soviets into the Winter Olympics. The Soviet Union immediately excelled at speed skating and, in an upset, began its domination of ice hockey when its team defeated the Canadians.

The hero of the Cortina Olympics was movie idol-handsome Toni Sailer of Austria, "The Blitz from Kitz" (Kitzbühel). Sailer won all three Alpine Skiing events by large margins of victory each time. In ski jumping, the Finns introduced a new aerodynamic style when they placed their arms against their sides rather than forward in front of their heads. With the new method Antti Hyvärinen and Aulis Kallakorpi took first and second, respectively. The figure skating competitions saw two very close contests as Americans swept the men's medals, with Hayes Alan Jenkins winning. Among the women, Tenley Albright barely defeated Carol Heiss. Heiss and Jenkins would later marry.

The 1956 Equestrian Olympic Games   After the IOC awarded the Games of the XIVth Olympiad to Melbourne, Australia, they learned that Australian quarantine laws would not allow the importation of horses for the equestrian events without an extended quarantine period. This precluded Melbourne from being able to host the equestrian events at the 1956 Olympic Games. It was decided, actually in violation of the Olympic Charter, to contest separate Equestrian Olympic Games in Stockholm, Sweden, from 10 to 17 June 1956. At the 49th IOC Session in Athens on 13 May 1954, Stockholm was chosen with 25 votes over Paris, France (10 votes); Rio de Janeiro, Brazil (8 votes); Berlin, Germany (2 votes); and Los Angeles, California, USA (2 votes).

The Equestrian Games of 1956 were held without major incidents and were contested by 29 nations and 158 athletes (145 men and 13 women). The opening ceremony was quite unusual as all competitors came in on their mounts, including the flag bearers. The Olympic flame was brought into the stadium on horseback by Hans Wikne who lit the main torch. Karin Lindberg and Henry Eriksson held torches which were lit. They ran towards the stadium tower with the torches and lit flames there. Sweden's Henri Saint Cyr recited the oath of the athletes while on his horse, and later won two gold medals, in individual and team dressage. This was matched by Germany's Hans Günter Winkler, who won gold medals in the individual and team show jumping events. The only controversy of the 1956 Equestrian Games came in the three-day event when one horse broke his leg and had to be destroyed. The SPCA (Society for the Protection of Cruelty to Animals) was very upset and a lengthy debate followed.

The Games of the XVIth Olympiad (1956)   The Games of the XVIth Olympiad were held in Melbourne, Victoria, Australia from 22 November through 8 December 1956. At the 43rd IOC Session in Rome on 28 April 1949, Melbourne was awarded the Olympics by a single vote in the fourth round over Buenos Aires, Argentina. Other candidate cities were (with round of elimination from voting): Los Angeles, California, USA (third round); Detroit, Michigan, USA (3rd round); Mexico City, Mexico (second round); Chicago, Illinois, USA (first round); Minneapolis, Minnesota, USA (first round); and Philadelphia, Pennsylvania, USA (first round). Sixty-seven nations eventually competed in Melbourne, with 3,184 athletes competing (2,813 men and 371 women).

This was the first time the Games were held in the southern hemisphere and necessitated the Games being held very late in the year to take advantage of the early part of the Australian summer. Because of Australian quarantine laws, it was decided, in violation of the Olympic Charter, to contest separate Olympic Equestrian Games in Stockholm, Sweden from 10-17 June 1956. (See The 1956 Equestrian Olympic Games)

But between June and the Melbourne Olympics, the world was thrown into turmoil. On 29 October, Israel invaded Egypt's Sinai peninsula. Then on 4 November 1956, 200,000 Soviet troops entered Budapest, Hungary, to quell political uprisings in that country. Egypt, Lebanon and Iraq withdrew in protest at Israel's action. The Netherlands, Spain, and, somewhat surprisingly, Switzerland withdrew in protest at the Soviet action. Switzerland kept alive its record of competing in every modern Olympics only because it had already been represented by athletes in Stockholm. These protests constituted the first true boycott in modern Olympic history, though the scene would be repeated many times in the coming decades.

With that background, water polo had the unusual distinction of being perhaps the most awaited event of the Olympics. In a final round match, the Soviet Union met the Hungarians, usually a water polo power. The athletes from both countries wasted no time in breaking all known rules and niceties of water polo. The water was literally blood red in several areas during the match and several players had to be helped out of the water because of bleeding. Hungary achieved some measure of revenge for the invasion of the country when it won, 4–0.

The Games were less well attended than those of other years because of the travel distance to Australia. Still, all the major sporting countries were represented. In a precursor of problems to come, the People's Republic of China (Beijing, then Peking) withdrew because the Republic of China (Taiwan) was allowed to compete. The question of the two countries' representation would not be resolved for 28 years.

The 8th Olympic Winter Games (1960)   The 8th Olympic Winter Games were held in Squaw Valley, California, USA from 18 to 28 February 1960. Thirty nations attended with 665 athletes competing (522 men and 143 women). At the 50th IOC Session in Paris on 14 June 1955, Squaw Valley won a close contest by two votes over Innsbruck, Austria (32–30 in the second round). Garmisch–Partenkirchen, Germany, and St. Moritz, Switzerland were also candidate cities, but were eliminated in the first round of voting.

When the 1960 Olympic Winter Games were awarded to Squaw Valley, all that existed there was a hotel. The ski village was the dream of Alexander Cushing and he succeeded in convincing the IOC to hold the Olympics there. After the award the Europeans verbally attacked the site for various reasons. The ski courses were not up to FIS calibre in the Alpine competitions, while in the Nordic races, the altitude (2,000 meters [6,650 feet]) was felt to be too stressful for the competitors. The Squaw Valley organizers polled the Winter Olympic nations and found that only nine would send a bobsled team so they elected not to build a run and not to contest the sport. In all, despite the initial misgivings about the site, the Games were well run with few problems. And U.S. television was present showing the events to the American people for the first time.

Biathlon was introduced as a sport for the first time. Women's speed skating also made its Olympic debut and saw the arrival of Lidiya Skoblikova (URS) who won two gold medals. In figure skating, Hayes Alan Jenkins' brother, David Jenkins, won the men's titles, while David Jenkins' future sister–in–law, Carol Heiss, avenged her 1956 defeat to easily win the women's title. In the Nordic combined event, Georg Thoma (FRG) became the first non–Scandinavian to win a Nordic event. In ice hockey, the United States pulled a major upset when it defeated the Soviet Union in the semi–final match. The U.S. went on to defeat Czechoslovakia in the finals and win the gold medal. Not as well publicized as the miracle of 1980, the U.S. victory in 1960 was equally astonishing.

The Games of the XVIIth Olympiad (1960) The Games of the XVIIth Olympiad were held in Rome, Italy from 25 August through 11 September 1960. At the 50th IOC Session in Paris on 16 June 1955, Rome was awarded the Games in the third round over Lausanne, Switzerland by a vote of 35–24. The other candidate cities (with round of elimination from voting) were Detroit, Michigan, USA (second round); Budapest, Hungary (second round); Brussels, Belgium (first round); Mexico City, Mexico (first round); and Tokyo, Japan (first round). Eighty-three nations attended the Games, with 5,346 athletes competing (4,736 men and 610 women).

Rome had been awarded the 1908 Olympics but eventually turned them down after Mt. Vesuvius erupted. Fifty-two years later the Olympics would return to the eternal city. Never before, and possibly never again, were the ancient and modern civilizations so intertwined at an Olympics. The 1960 Olympics were a wonder. With the boycotts, massacres and political problems that were to come, many Olympic afficionados would later yearn for the glory that was Ancient Greece and the grandeur that was Modern Rome.

Many of the events took place in settings thousands of years old. Wrestling was held in the Basilica of Maxentius, where similar competitions had taken place two millennia previously. Gymnastics events were contested in the Terme di Caracalla. The marathon began in front of the ancient Roman capitol, on Capitoline Hill, and finished along the Appian Way neath the Arch of Constantine. For modern facilities the Italians provided Stadio Olimpico, a beautiful track & field complex, the Sports Palace for boxing, and the Velodrome for cycling.

A number of heroes emerged from the Games. In women's athletics, the Italians and the world thrilled to the feats of Wilma Rudolph, an American sprinter from Tennessee. Long-legged and attractive, she was dubbed by the European press as "La Gazelle Noire" – the black gazelle. She won the women's 100 meters, 200 meters and anchored the sprint relay.

In basketball and boxing, two of the greatest practitioners ever of those sports were on display. In basketball, the U.S. men's team won very easily as the team was led by Oscar Robertson, Jerry West, Jerry Lucas, Walt Bellamy, and Terry Dischinger. Certainly the greatest amateur team ever, it rivals many of the great NBA teams. In boxing, the light–heavyweight gold medal was won by Cassius Marcellus Clay, who as Muhammad Ali would thrill the world for the next two decades as "The Greatest."

The 1960 Olympics were the first Summer Olympics televised in the United States, although all events were shown on tape delay after the film was flown from Rome to New York. And also for the first time since the 1912 marathon, the Olympics saw the death of a competitor. In the cycling road race, Knut Enemark Jensen (DEN) collapsed and later died. He was found to have taken amphetamines and his death was partially responsible for the institution of drug testing in the mid-1960's.

The 9th Olympic Winter Games (1964)   The 9th Olympic Winter Games were held in Innsbruck, Austria from 29 January through 9 February 1964. Thirty-six nations attended with 1,091 athletes competing (891 men and 200 women). At the 55th IOC Session in Munich, Germany on 26 May 1959, Innsbruck (49 votes) was chosen over Calgary, Alberta, Canada (9 votes); and Lahti, Finland (0 votes).

Innsbruck was an almost unanimous choice to host the 1964 Olympic Winter Games. And few better choices have ever been made by the IOC. Innsbruck became the first city, winter or summer, to spread the Olympic events around geographically a bit with some events being held 30 km. (20 miles) from Innsbruck center. Because of this and the central location of the city, well over a million spectators saw these Olympics. In addition, television now transmitted them to over a billion viewers. Computers were also present for the first time at an Olympics, as the electronic age came to Olympia.

With all this, there were a few problems. The organizing committee forgot to order snow for the events. In the last few days, the Austrian army hauled 20,000 cubic meters of snow to the ski courses so they would be well packed. In practice before the Games, two athletes were killed – Ross Milne, an Australian skier, and Kazimierz Skrzypecki, a Polish-born British luger.

Soviet women were the biggest winners at Innsbruck. Lidiya Skoblikova produced one of the great performances of the Olympic Winter Games when she won all four women's speed skating gold medals in four days. In women's cross-country skiing, Klavdiya Boyarskikh won gold medals in all three women's events. The Soviets also ensured there would be no repeat of 1960 and won the ice hockey title easily. But in bobsledding, both events produced big upsets. The two-man title was won by Britain's Tony Nash and Robin Dixon, while the four-man champion sled from Canada was driven by Vic Emery. Neither country had a bobsled run in 1964.

The Games of the XVIIIth Olympiad (1964)   The Games of the XVIIIth Olympiad were held in Tokyo, Japan from 10 through 24 October 1964. At the 55th IOC Session in Munich, Germany on 26 May 1959, Tokyo (34 votes) won the final vote in the first round over Detroit, Michigan, USA (10 votes); Vienna, Austria (9 votes); and Brussels, Belgium (5 votes). Ninety-three nations attended with 5,140 athletes competing (4,457 men and 683 women).

For the first time, the Olympic Games were celebrated in an Asian country. The Japanese were eager to prove that they had recovered from the horrors of World War II and, to emphasize the point, they chose as the final torch bearer Yoshinori Sakai, who had been born in Hiroshima on the day the atom bomb immolated that city.

Before the Games began there was a minor controversy when Indonesia and North Korea withdrew because several of their athletes were declared ineligible. The affected athletes had competed in the Games of the New Emerging Forces (GANEFO) in Jakarta, Indonesia in November 1963. Indonesia did not allow Taiwan or Israel to compete at those Games, so the international federations for athletics, swimming, and shooting banned any athlete from the Tokyo Olympics who had competed at GANEFO. Because this affected several of their athletes, Indonesia and North Korea withdrew from Tokyo in protest. The only significant athlete missing was Dan Sin-Kim of North Korea, unofficial women's world record holder in the 800 meters.

In athletics, Billy Mills of the United States pulled off one of the biggest upsets in Olympic history when he won the 10,000 meter run. The most decorated hero of the Games was swimmer Don Schollander who won four gold medals in men's swimming. Schollander could have won a fifth gold medal but he was left off the medley relay team by U.S. coaches, although he was America's fastest freestyler.

The Japanese were gracious hosts but they were helped in their own efforts by two new Olympic sports: judo and volleyball. In volleyball the Japanese women, coached by the martinet-like Hirofumi Daimatsu, were easily victorious. In judo, the Japanese won three of the four gold medals. But the one they lost, in the open class to Holland's Anton Geesink, was a crushing blow to the hosts.

The Games were beautifully run and the minor boycott had minimal effect. The 1964 Olympics were the last Olympics to be held for 28 years without major political overtones and boycotts.

The 10th Olympic Winter Games (1968)   The 10th Olympic Winter Games were held in Grenoble, France from 6 to 18 February 1968. Thirty-seven nations attended with 1,158 athletes competing (947 men and 211 women). At the 62nd IOC Session in Innsbruck on 28 May 1964, Grenoble was chosen on the third ballot over a large field of candidate cities which included Calgary, Alberta, Canada (third round); Lahti, Finland (second round); Sapporo, Japan (first round); Oslo, Norway (first round); and Lake Placid, New York, USA (first round).

The controversy so often associated with the Olympic Games began to reach Winter Olympia in 1968 at Grenoble. Though the Games went fairly well, there were many problems. It began before the Olympics when the IOC decided it wished to curb advertising on skis and clothing by the Alpine skiers. They threatened to expel certain skiers, while the skiers threatened to withdraw en masse in revolt. A compromise was reached eventually in which the skiers agreed to remove all equipment with advertising prior to being photographed or interviewed. The Games' hero of heroes was Jean-Claude Killy who had grown up and learned to ski in the neighboring mountains. He was favored, and expected by France to duplicate Toni Sailer's 1956 feat and win all three Alpine Skiing gold medals. He succeeded but not without a major controversy in the slalom. The race was held in fog and both Karl Schranz (AUT) and Håkon Mjøn (NOR) posted faster times. But both were disqualified for missing gates. Schranz appealed, stating that he had been interfered with and replays showed he had. He was allowed a restart and again posted a winning time. But he was then disqualified when further investigation revealed that the interference on the first run occurred after Schranz had missed his gates. And Killy had his third gold medal and France had its hero.

In the bobsled events, held on l'Alpe d'Huez, site of so much heroism and suffering during the Tour de France, Eugenio Monti of Italy finally succeeded in winning an Olympic gold medal. In fact he won two. In pairs figure skating, the lyrical, almost poetic team of Lyudmila Belousova and Oleg Protopopov won their second consecutive championship.

The Games of the XIXth Olympiad (1968)   The Games of the XIXth Olympiad were held from 12 through 27 October 1968 in Mexico City, Mexico. At the 60th IOC Session in Baden-Baden, Germany on 18 October 1963, Mexico City had been awarded the Games on the first ballot in 1963 with 30 votes over Detroit, Michigan, USA (14 votes); Lyon, France (12 votes); and Buenos Aires, Argentina (2 votes). One hundred twelve nations attended with 5,530 athletes competing (4,749 men and 781 women).

In 1963, the IOC awarded the Olympics to Mexico despite some warnings about the effects of competing at the altitude (2,134 meters) of Mexico City. The warnings would prove prophetic, both for good and bad, but also prominent at Mexico City was the first large-scale incursion of politics into the Olympic scene since 1936.

Political problems first manifested themselves as protests by Mexican students before the Games. The students were upset that so much money was spent on the Olympics in the face of such widespread poverty in their own country. As the protest movement gathered momentum leading up to the Games, the Mexican army took charge on the night of 2 October. As 10,000 people demonstrated in the Square of the Three Cultures in Mexico City, the army surrounded the crowd and opened fire. More than 250 people were killed and over a thousand were injured.

In the United States, Harry Edwards, a professor at San Jose State University, urged blacks to boycott the Olympics to protest the rampant racism of American society. The boycott never materialized. However, his efforts came to fruition in the victory ceremony of the 200 meters. The race was won by Tommie Smith (USA) with the bronze medal going to John Carlos (USA). On the victory platform, as "The Star–Spangled Banner" played in the background, almost unheard, the two black Americans stood barefooted, heads bowed, and raised a singled black–gloved fist in their own form of protest. The IOC banned the two from future Olympic participation and ordered them to leave the Olympic village immediately.

On a positive political note, the Federal Republic of Germany (West Germany) and the German Democratic Republic (East Germany) entered separate national teams for the first time, although they competed wearing the same emblems and flag, and using a joint anthem for medal ceremonies.

The altitude severely affected many track & field events. Bob Beamon used the lesser gravity to set a stunning world record in the long jump of 8.90 meters (29'2½"). In the 100, 200, 400, 400 meter hurdles, 4x100 relay, 4x400 relay, and the triple jump, all sprint events not requiring much oxygen, and aided by the lessened pull of gravity, new world records were set by the men. Many of these records would not be broken for years. But the distance running events saw very slow times, as the runners gasped for the oxygen that was not there.

The 11th Olympic Winter Games (1972)   The 11th Olympic Winter Games were held in Sapporo, Japan from 3 to 13 February 1972. Thirty–five nations attended with 1,006 athletes competing (800 men and 206 women). At the 64th IOC Session in Rome on 26 April 1966, Sapporo was chosen on the first ballot (32 votes) over Banff, Alberta, Canada (16 votes); Lahti, Finland (7 votes); and Salt Lake City, Utah, USA (7 votes).

The controversy that had started in Grenoble four years earlier continued and erupted at the beginning of the Games. Avery Brundage insisted on ending commercialization by skiers and singled out Austrian star, Karl Schranz, who was expelled from the Games.

Another controversy occurred when Canada refused to send its ice hockey team, protesting professionalism by the Soviets. The USSR won that gold medal quite easily, though it is unlikely the Canadians would have made a difference, as by 1972, the Soviets were showing that they could now play well against the NHL (National Hockey League).

Ard Schenk (NED) was the best publicized athlete at these Olympics as he won three championships in speed skating. His triple was matched in women's cross-country skiing by Galina Kulakova

(URS), though a bit more surreptitiously to the world's media. The Japanese, not usually a winter sports power, were exultant when three of their ski jumpers, led by Yukio Kasaya, swept the medals in the 70 meter ski jumping.

The Games of the XXth Olympiad (1972)   The Games of the XXth Olympiad were held in Munich, Germany (Federal Republic/West) from 26 August through 11 September 1972. At the 64th IOC Session in Rome in 1966, Munich had been awarded the Games on the second ballot (31 votes) over Montreal, Quebec, Canada (15 votes); Madrid, Spain (13 votes); and Detroit, Michigan, USA (eliminated after round one). One hundred twenty-one nations attended with 7,123 athletes competing (6,065 men and 1,058 women).

The Munich Olympics began as The Games of Joy, in which the West German government attempted to atone for the militaristic Nazi image so associated with the 1936 Berlin Games. They ended as The Games of Terror and Tragedy.

The first 11 days of the 1972 Olympics were perhaps the most beautiful celebrations of Olympia ever seen. But on the morning of 5 September, the Games were interrupted when eight Arab terrorists, representing the militant Black September group, entered the Olympic Village and took hostage 11 members of the Israeli Olympic team. While the world watched on television and waited, the terrorists occupied the building of 31 Connollystraße, and demanded freedom for several Arabs held in Israeli prisons. The Israeli government refused this as a day of tense negotiations ensued.

Late in the evening of 5 September, the terrorists took their hostages to Fürstenfeldbruck, an Army air base near Munich. There, in a few quick minutes of fighting as the Germans tried to save them, all the Israelis were murdered by a bomb the terrorists had set in the helicopter which was to take them to freedom. Several of the terrorists were killed, but most escaped. A few were later captured but none ever came to trial.

The murdered Israeli athletes and coaches were David Marc Berger, Zeev Friedman, Yossef Gutfreund, Eliezer Halfin, Yossef Romano, Amitzur Shapira, Kehat Shorr, Mark Slavin, Andrei Spitzer, Yacov Springer, and Moshe Weinberg.

There were some marvelous athletic performances at the 1972 Olympics, notably Mark Spitz winning seven gold medals, and setting seven world records, but they seemed of little consequence. The Games were halted for one day as a memorial service was held for the Israelis. When they resumed the Olympic Games would never again be the same.

The 12th Olympic Winter Games (1976)   The 12th Olympic Winter Games were held in Innsbruck, Austria from 4 to 15 February 1976.   Thirty-seven nations attended with 1,123 athletes competing (892 men and 231 women).   Innsbruck was not originally even a candidate city for the 1976 Olympic Winter Games.   At the 69th IOC Session in Amsterdam on 13 May 1970, the original choice of the IOC was Denver, Colorado, USA which won out on the third ballot (39 votes) over Sion, Switzerland (30 votes in round three); Tampere, Finland (second round); and Vancouver, British Columbia, Canada (first round).   In November 1972, the citizens of Colorado, in a referendum, indicated that they did not wish the Olympics to be held in Denver, fearing a negative impact on the environment.   Denver officially withdrew as host on 12 November 1972.   Innsbruck, which had held the Games so successfully in 1964, was able to step in on short notice, after being selected over hastily arranged bids from Lake Placid (USA), Chamonix (FRA), and Tampere (FIN).   And once again Innsbruck demonstrated how well an Olympic Winter Games could be staged.

The competitions were well-contested though no single athlete could be said to dominate, as in years past.   Rosi Mittermaier (FRG) was perhaps the best publicized.   She won the downhill and slalom early in the Games and had a chance to equal the feats of Toni Sailer and Jean-Claude Killy by winning the giant slalom.   Older than many of the competitors, close to retirement, and born nearby, just across the German border at Reit im Winkl, she was a heavy sentimental favorite.   But it was not to be.   Canada's Kathy Kreiner defeated Mittermaier by 12/100th's of a second in the giant slalom. In men's skiing Austria's Franz Klammer electrified fans and the television audience with a spectacular run, in which he skied to the edge and was on the verge of falling several times, to win the downhill gold medal over Switzerland's Bernhard Russi.

In figure skating, Irina Rodnina (URS) again won a pairs gold medal, but with a different partner than in 1972.   In men's figure skating Britain's John Curry and Canada's Toller Cranston introduced a more balletic style than in years past.   Among the women, Dorothy Hamill of the United States became a media favorite with her ability and style, her wholesome looks, and pixie-like hairdo.

The Games of the XXIst Olympiad (1976)   The Games of the XXIst Olympiad were held in Montreal, Quebec, Canada from 17 July through 1 August 1976.   At the 69th IOC Session on 13 May 1970, Montreal had been awarded the Games in the second round of balloting (41 votes) by the IOC over Moscow, USSR (28 votes) and Los Angeles, California, USA (eliminated after round one). Ninety-two nations eventually competed in the Montreal Games, with 6,026 athletes competing (4,779 men and 1,247 women).

The city of Montreal spent extravagantly to host the Games, leaving the citizens of Canada and Quebec with a tax debt they would be repaying for years, and the Games were dubbed the billion-dollar circus by the Canadian press. In 1994, the debt still remaining to the Quebec citizenry was estimated at $304 million (US). Much of the debt, however, was incurred to finance structures which would have been necessary to build eventually.

Shortly before the 1976 Olympics were to start they were marred by a boycott of 22 African countries, Guyana, and Chinese Taipei (then Taiwan). The African/Guyanan boycott was in protest of a recent tour of South Africa by the New Zealand national rugby team. As South Africa was ostracized from international sporting competition, the African nations demanded that New Zealand not be allowed to compete at Montreal. But the IOC had little control over this problem, as rugby had no current affiliation with the Olympic Movement. New Zealand competed and most of Africa did not.

The Taiwan boycott occurred when Canada at first considered refusing to allow the team to enter the country, as the Canadian government did not recognize the island nation. This was in direct violation of their agreement as host country to admit all eligible nations in honoring the Olympic Charter. The Canadians acquiesced and allowed the Taiwanese to compete, but refused to allow them to do so under the title of the Republic of China, the official national name. Several other countries protested and threatened withdrawal, notably the United States, if the Taiwan athletes were not allowed to compete. However, these protests were short-lived and the IOC finally gave in to the Canadian government. Taiwan withdrew and did not compete.

Twenty-six nations eventually boycotted the Montreal Olympics. Twenty-two of these did not compete at all and are as follows: Algeria, Central Africa, Chad, People's Republic of Congo, Ethiopia, The Gambia, Ghana, Guyana, Iraq, Kenya, Libya, Malawi, Mali, Niger, Nigeria, Sudan, Swaziland, Tanzania, Togo, Uganda, Upper Volta, and Zambia. In addition, Egypt, Cameroon, Morocco, and Tunisia also boycotted, although they are listed as competing nations, because some of their athletes competed on the first two days of the Olympics before they officially withdrew.

After all this the Olympics began. Despite the absence of some top African track athletes, they were well run and the boycotts had minimal effect on competition. The fans thrilled to the exploits of Romania's Nadia Comăneci in gymnastics as she dominated the competition, scoring the first perfect 10s ever awarded at the Olympics. The major effect on track & field athletics was in the 1,500 meters, in which John Walker (ironically of New Zealand) and Filbert Bayi (Tanzania) were to compete. They were the two best milers in the world by far, but Walker had only himself to beat, and he managed a comfortable gold medal victory. The most spectacular athlete on the track was probably Cuba's Alberto Juantorena, who won the 400 and 800 meter runs.

The 13th Olympic Winter Games (1980)   The 13th Olympic Winter Games were held in Lake Placid, New York, USA from 13 to 24 February 1980. Thirty-seven nations attended with 1,072 athletes competing (839 men and 233 women). Lake Placid was unopposed in its bid and was chosen by the IOC at its 75th Session in Vienna on 23 October 1974.

Lake Placid, like St. Moritz and Innsbruck before it, was given a second chance to host the Olympic Winter Games. In the era of spiraling costs, Lake Placid promised a simpler Olympics. But the complexity of television and millions of spectators almost proved too much for the small upstate New York village. Transportation and communication was difficult and the IOC vowed never to return the Games to such a small venue.

As if these were not enough problems, shortly before the Olympics, the Soviet Union invaded Afghanistan. President Jimmy Carter promptly called for a U.S.-led boycott of the Moscow Olympics. And he used Secretary of State Cyrus Vance to lecture the IOC at its session in Lake Placid days before the Games started.

But Lake Placid had two great redeeming features – Eric Heiden and the U.S. ice hockey team. In speed skating, Heiden was the greatest skater in the world and pre-Games predictions had him winning five gold medals, though few believed he would actually win all five. But he did. He ended his Olympic dominance with a gold medal in the 10,000 meters. Racing in the second pair with Viktor Lyoskin (URS), Heiden set a world record by six seconds and earned his fifth gold medal.

In ice hockey, the Soviet Union was by now conceded the gold medal at all Olympics. A week before the Olympics, the USA and the USSR played an exhibition game in Madison Square Garden and the Soviets won, 10–3. But the U.S. team had more fortitude than anyone suspected and were led by a coach, Herb Brooks, who brought more out of them than they knew they had. The Americans could not, and would not, be intimidated.

In the semi-finals they faced the Soviets. The score was tied in the third period when captain Mike Eruzione scored to put the U.S. ahead, 4–3. As time ran out with that same score, Al Michaels, ABC television announcer, echoed everybody's thoughts when he asked, "Do you believe in miracles?" Two nights later, the Americans came from behind to defeat Finland and win the gold medal.

The Games of the XXIInd Olympiad (1980)   The Games of the XXIInd Olympiad were held in Moscow, Russian Republic, USSR from 19 July through 3 August 1980. At the 75th IOC Session in Athens on 18 May 1978, Moscow was awarded the Games by a vote of 39–20 over Los Angeles, the only other city which bid for the Olympics. Eighty countries eventually competed in Moscow, with 5,217 athletes competing (4,092 men and 1,125 women).

In late December 1979, Soviet tanks invaded Afghanistan. After the Soviet invasion of Afghanistan, United States' President Jimmy Carter called for a boycott of the Moscow Olympics if the Soviets did not withdraw before 20 February 1980. They did not. Carter pressed his efforts, attempting to enlist other countries to join his boycott. But American allies Britain, Finland, France, Ireland, Italy, New Zealand, Spain, and Sweden all competed at Moscow. Carter made his announcement public to the IOC via Secretary of State Cyrus Vance, who rather rudely addressed the IOC at the Lake Placid Games in February.

Approximately 63 countries eventually boycotted the Moscow Olympics (see below). Notable among these were the United States, Canada, West Germany, Japan, China, Kenya, and Norway (a full list follows at the end of this section). Several countries who did not boycott protested at the Olympic ceremonies. Ten countries elected not to march at the opening ceremonies, while six other nations marched behind flags of their national Olympic committees, or the Olympic flag, rather than their national flags. Several countries chose not to have their national anthems played at victory ceremonies, substituting instead the Olympic hymn. Finally, at the closing ceremony President Carter refused to allow the American flag to be raised as the host country of the next Olympics. The flag of Los Angeles was raised instead.

The Games suffered in level of competition but they were marvelously run, although spectators spoke often of the military atmosphere as Soviet soldiers were on every street corner with automatic weapons. The most awaited races matched two British athletes in the 800 and 1,500 meters in the track and the boycott had no effect on them. Sebastian Coe was favored in the 800 and Steve Ovett in the 1,500. They each won a gold medal, but in the "other man's" event. The most bemedaled athlete in Moscow was Soviet gymnast Aleksandr Dityatin, who won medals in all eight gymnastics events, three of them gold.

It is almost impossible to be certain how many nations boycotted or chose not to attend the 1980 Olympic Games in response to the Soviet invasion of Afghanistan. The United States' Government dogmatically stated numerous times that 65 nations joined the U.S.-led boycott but that number is almost certainly wrong and too high. Because of political repercussions, many nations simply stated that they could not attend because of financial or other reasons, when in likelihood they were joining the boycott. On the other hand, among the non-participating nations, it is likely that a few were not boycotting, but did not compete for other reasons. No definitive further conclusions can be drawn concerning the number of boycotting nations.

For the record, the following 63 nations did not compete in Moscow but were IOC members, and eligible to compete in the Olympics, as of 27 May 1980, the date due for acceptance of invitations to the 1980 Olympic Games: Albania, Antigua, Argentina, Bahamas, Bahrain, Bangladesh, Barbados, Belize, Bermuda, Bolivia, Canada, Cayman Islands, Central Africa, Chad, Chile, China, Egypt, El Salvador, Federal Republic of Germany, Fiji, Gabon, The Gambia, Ghana, Haiti, Honduras, Hong Kong, Indonesia, Israel, Ivory Coast, Japan, Kenya, Korea, Liberia, Liechtenstein, Malawi, Malaysia, Mauritania, Mauritius, Monaco, Morocco, Netherlands Antilles, Niger, Norway, Pakistan, Panama, Papua-New Guinea, Paraguay, Philippines, Saudi Arabia, Singapore, Somalia, Sudan, Suriname, Swaziland, Thailand, Togo, Tunisia, Turkey, United States, U.S. Virgin Islands, Upper Volta, Uruguay, and Zaire.

As stated, the deadline for responding to the Moscow invitation to compete at the Olympic Games was 27 May 1980. The above nations can be separated into three categories based on this deadline - 1) declined the invitation, 2) did not respond to the invitation, and 3) accepted the invitation but eventually did not compete.

Twenty-eight nations declined the invitation to compete, as follows: Albania, Argentina, Bahrain, Bermuda, Canada, Cayman Islands, China, Federal Republic of Germany, The Gambia, Honduras, Hong Kong, Indonesia, Israel, Kenya, Liechtenstein, Malawi, Malaysia, Mauritania, Pakistan, Paraguay, The Philippines, Saudi Arabia, Singapore, Thailand, Tunisia, Turkey, United States, and Uruguay.

Twenty-nine nations did not respond to the invitation to compete by 27 May 1980, as follows: Antigua, Bahamas, Bangladesh, Barbados, Belize, Bolivia, Central Africa, Chad, Chile, Egypt, El Salvador, Fiji, Ghana, Haiti, Ivory Coast, Japan, Korea, Liberia, Monaco, Morocco, Netherlands Antilles, Norway, Papua-New Guinea, Somalia, Sudan, Swaziland, Togo, U.S. Virgin Islands, and Zaire.

Six nations accepted the invitation to compete, but eventually chose not to, as follows: Gabon, Mauritius, Niger, Panama, Suriname, and Upper Volta. The reasons for these nations' eventually choosing not to participate are not clear.

There were two further categories of IOC-"member" nations in 1980. Both Chinese Taipei and Iran had been member nations of the IOC but at the time of the Moscow invitation they were in suspension and were not eligible to compete at the 1980 Olympic Games.

Finally, three nations were accepted into IOC membership at the IOC Executive Board Meeting in Lausanne on 9–10 June 1980, after the due date for acceptances to the Moscow invitation. These were Mozambique, Qatar, and the United Arab Emirates. These nations were, therefore, not technically eligible to compete at Moscow. However, Mozambique did compete, although Qatar and the United Arab Emirates did not. It is likely that, because of the boycott, late invitations were extended to these three nations to fill out the list of competing nations in Moscow, and that Mozambique chose to, and was able to field a team in time.

The 14th Olympic Winter Games (1984)   The 14th Olympic Winter Games were held in Sarajevo, Bosnia–Herzegovina Province, Yugoslavia from 8 to 19 February 1984. Forty-nine nations attended with 1,274 athletes competing (1,000 men and 274 women). At the 80th IOC Session in Athens on 18 May 1978, Sarajevo was chosen in the second round of balloting (39 votes) over Sapporo, Japan (36 votes); and Göteburg, Sweden (eliminated after round one).

After the controversy, problems, and excitement that were Lake Placid, Sarajevo's Winter Olympics were much quieter, in marked contrast to the Yugoslavian civil war that would come to Sarajevo within the next decade. The only difficulties were early weather problems. An initial concern about lack of snow was alleviated when a blizzard hit shortly after the opening ceremonies, forcing the men's downhill to be postponed twice.

In Nordic Skiing, Marja–Liisa Hämäläinen (FIN) won three cross-country skiing gold medals. But Nordic Skiing rarely captures the press notices of figure skating, Alpine Skiing or ice hockey, and Hämäläinen's feat was noted with little fanfare outside Finland.

In ice hockey, the Soviets restored the status quo when they easily won the gold medal. The Canadians, having returned to Olympic ice hockey in 1980, were thought to have a chance as some professionals could now be used. But the USSR played seven games, won seven games, and won the gold medal.

In ice dancing, the British couple, Jayne Torvill and Christopher Dean, was heavily favored based on past performances. Their final program was quite controversial, however, as it probably violated ice dancing protocol by being based on a single piece of music, Ravel's "Bolero." Their performance to "Bolero" was mesmerizing, building to an almost orgiastic finish which brought the crowd to a frenzy. The judges awarded the British pair the highest scores ever seen in figure skating, with 12 perfect 6.0s out of 18 marks.

In singles figure skating, Scott Hamilton (USA) and Katarina Witt (GDR) won gold medals. Hamilton was expected to win as he had been nonpareil since the 1980 Olympics. Witt was not as well-known and was not favored, but her stunning beauty helped to make her a crowd favorite.

The Games of the XXIIIrd Olympiad (1984)   The Games of the XXIIIrd Olympiad were held in Los Angeles, California, USA from 28 July through 12 August 1984. Los Angeles was awarded the Olympics by acclamation at the 80th IOC Session in Athens on 18 May 1978. No other candidate cities bid for these Olympics. One hundred forty nations attended the Los Angeles Olympics with 6,797 athletes competing (5,230 men and 1,567 women).

In May 1984, the Soviet Union announced that it would not attend the Olympics in Los Angeles, citing concerns over the safety of its athletes because of the "anti-Soviet and anti-Communist activities" in the Los Angeles area. Most people considered the boycott one of retribution for the United States' refusal to compete in Moscow. Most of the Eastern European countries joined in the Soviet-bloc boycott, notably East Germany (GDR), and it was joined by Cuba. Although only 14 invited countries did not compete in Los Angeles, the absence of the USSR, Cuba, and the GDR made many of the events mere shadows of what was anticipated.

Still, more countries and athletes competed at Los Angeles than in any previous Olympics. However, what the 1984 boycott lacked in numbers relative to the 1980 boycott, it made up for in its impact on the competition. Boxing, weightlifting, wrestling, gymnastics, and, to a certain extent, track & field would have been dominated by the boycotting nations. The nations which did not compete were: Afghanistan, Bulgaria, Cuba, Czechoslovakia, Ethiopia, German Democratic Republic, Hungary, Laos, Mongolia, North Korea, Poland, South Yemen, Vietnam, and the U.S.S.R. Bravely, Romania defied the boycott and competed at the Olympics, receiving an ovation at the opening ceremonies second only to that of the host country.

China also returned to the Olympic Games at Los Angeles in 1984, after an absence of 32 years (China had competed at the Olympic Games of 1932, 1936, 1948 and 1952). It had competed at the 1980 Olympic Winter Games in Lake Placid, but China's appearance at the opening ceremonies was greeted warmly by the American crowd, especially in light of the Soviet boycott. Yugoslavia, not Soviet dominated, was the only other country from Eastern Europe to compete.

After all that, the Olympics were very well run, although the Europeans had numerous complaints, mostly about customary American methods of doing business. American television concentrated on U.S. athletes, which infuriated the Europeans. For the first time ever, the Games were managed in an entrepreneurial fashion. Organizing committee President Peter Ueberroth insisted that the Olympics be designed to break even or even provide a profit. Again, the Europeans, used to the simon-pure idealistic image of the Olympics for the Olympics' sake, rebelled against this philosophy. But Ueberroth was determined that the Games would be financially independent and he succeeded admirably in that regard. Ueberroth's marketing methods, though decried by the Europeans, have since been copied by all organizing committees and even the IOC itself.

As to the sports themselves, the competition was good, though diluted in many ways because of the boycott. Carl Lewis emerged as the American men's star, equaling Jesse Owens' 1936 feat of winning four gold medals in track & field. But Lewis did not have Owens' appeal to the American public and his image, almost obsequiously nurtured by his manager, failed to live up to his deeds on the track.

Failing Lewis, the American public reached instead to Mary Lou Retton, an American gymnast who won the all-around individual gold for the first time in history. To win she needed a perfect 10 on her last event, the horse vault. Given two vaults, she achieved the 10, not once, but twice.

After the difficulties of Munich and Montreal, Los Angeles had been the only bidder for the Games of 1984. But Los Angeles, despite its problems, revitalized the Olympic Movement to some degree. Having shown that the Olympics did not need to be a "loss-leader" and could, in fact, produce an operating profit, many cities now were interested in hosting the Olympics. Shortly after the 1984 Olympics, six cities would submit official bids to host the 1992 Games.

The 15th Olympic Winter Games (1988)   The 15th Olympic Winter Games were held in Calgary, Alberta, Canada from 13 to 28 February 1988. Fifty-seven nations attended with 1,423 athletes competing (1,110 men and 313 women). At the 84th IOC Session in Baden-Baden, Germany on 30 September 1981, Calgary was chosen on the second round (48 votes) over Falun, Sweden (31 votes); and Cortina d'Ampezzo, Italy (eliminated after round one).

In ice hockey, the Soviets again were dominant. Speed skating's hero was the unlikely Yvonne van Gennip of The Netherlands. All attention was focused on the GDR's quartet of Karin Kania, Andrea Ehrig, Christa Rothenburger, and Gabi Zange, and the United States' Bonnie Blair. They skated well, with Blair winning the 500 and Rothenburger the 1,000, and between them, those five won 12 of the available 15 medals. But the other three were won by van Gennip who won the 1,500, 3,000, and 5,000 meters, defeating the favored Ehrig and Zange in the long-distance races.

One of the media heroes was Italian Alpine skier Alberto Tomba, who won two gold medals, and delighted the press with his nightly antics. He attempted to date the GDR's Katarina Witt, who won her second consecutive figure skating gold medal, but he got nowhere, which further delighted the media.

In men's speed skating, the real hero was probably a man who never finished a race. Dan Jansen was a favorite in the 500 meters, and in the 1,000, he was thought to have a chance to win. But the morning of the first race, the 500, he found out that his sister, who had been ill with leukemia, had died. He elected to skate that night, but fell on the first turn. A few days later, he hoped to redeem himself in the 1,000 meters and through 600 meters, he had the fastest pace. But he fell again. The world watched and suffered with him but Dan Jansen offered no excuses. He was gracious and magnanimous throughout. Years of effort were lost, certainly by the emotions of the moment, but he responded with the grace so often requested of our Olympians, and yet so rarely offered.

The Games of the XXIVth Olympiad (1988)   The Games of the XXIVth Olympiad were held in Seoul, Republic of Korea from 17 September through 5 October 1988. One hundred fifty-nine nations attended the Olympics with 8,465 athletes competing (6,279 men and 2,186 women).

On 30 September 1981, Seoul was nominated by the IOC as the host city over Nagoya, Japan by a vote of 52-27 at the 84th IOC Session in Baden-Baden, Germany. The choice was highly controversial as many prominent nations in the Olympic Movement, notably the Soviet-bloc nations, did not have diplomatic relations with the Seoul government. There was widespread concern that another boycott would ensue because of this.

The problem became more complicated in July 1985 when North Korea demanded that it be allowed to co-host the Games with the Republic of Korea. Over the next three years the IOC negotiated with North Korea and offered to allow it to stage several events. However, no IOC concession was ever enough for the North, which wanted equal co-host status and an equal number of events. It demanded this despite the fact that the Games were close at hand and it had no possible hope of building the necessary facilities in time. When the IOC would not concede further to the North's demands, North Korea announced that it would definitely boycott the Seoul Olympics.

By then, however, most of the Soviet-bloc countries had agreed to compete in Seoul, making 1988 the first Summer Olympic competition in 12 years between the United States, the Soviet Union and the German Democratic Republic. After the North Korean's official boycott announcement, Cuba and Ethiopia also made it official that they would not attend the Olympics, out of solidarity with North Korea. Nicaragua, Albania, and the Seychelles also did not attend the Olympics, although their reasons were less clear and may not have been directly related to any boycott.

Thus, although there was a boycott of the 1988 Olympics, it encompassed only six nations and had minimal effect on the Games themselves. The Seoul Games went on and saw the largest participation in Olympic history. There were more nations represented than ever before. The Games themselves were excellent and very well run. Controversies and political intrusions, unlike the Games of the last 20 years, were relatively few and comparatively minor.

The sporting events were dominated by three swimmers and one female track & field athlete. In the pool, the GDR's Kristin Otto broke all sorts of records by winning six gold medals, an unmatched performance by a woman at the Olympics. Her only rival for swimming supremacy was America's Janet Evans who won three gold medals. On the men's side of the pool, Matt Biondi was attempting to equal Mark Spitz's record of seven gold medals. He failed in his first two events, taking a silver and a bronze, but won gold medals in his last five events.

On the track, the world was stunned by the performances of sprinter Florence Griffith Joyner. At the Olympics she won the 100 and 200, setting a world record in the 200 finals, and helped the American women win a gold medal in the 4x100 relay. She also ran anchor on the 4x400 relay team, adding a silver medal to her three golds.

The biggest media event of the 1988 Olympic Games was the disqualification of sprinter Ben Johnson, after he had won the 100 meters in a world record time of 9.79, defeating Carl Lewis. Johnson tested positive for an anabolic steroid and was disqualified, with Lewis receiving the gold medal. After the uproar of the scandal, the Canadians organized an investigation into drug use in international athletics, the Dubin inquiry. At the inquiry, Johnson admitted that he had used steroids for several years.

The 16th Olympic Winter Games (1992)   The 16th Olympic Winter Games were held in Albertville, France from 8 to 23 February 1992. Sixty-four nations attended with 1,801 athletes competing (1,313 men and 488 women). At the 91st IOC Session in Lausanne on 17 October 1986, Albertville was chosen by the IOC on the fifth round of voting over a large field of candidate cities: Sofia, Bulgaria (fifth round); Falun, Sweden (fifth round); Lillehammer, Norway (fourth round); Cortina d'Ampezzo, Italy (third round); Anchorage, Alaska, USA (second round); and Berchtesgaden, Germany (first round).

This was the third Olympic Winter Games to be held in France, and the second to be held in the French Savoie, after the 1924

Games in Chamonix in the Haute-Savoie. The 1968 Games in Grenoble (Isère), were in the Dauphiné area of the French Alps. The Games were awarded to Albertville but they were actually spread over several small towns and villages of the French Savoie in the French Alps. Problems with transportation between the villages did not materialize and the Games were extremely well run.

Another innovation was the introduction of a number of new Olympic sports and events to the Winter Games. Women competed in biathlon for the first time. Men and women competed in short-track speed skating skated in a pack style. Freestyle skiing, which had been a demonstration sport in 1988, returned with the moguls being a full medal sport. Speed skiing and the other two freestyle disciplines, ballet and aerials, were demonstration events.

The biggest news at the Olympics was the introduction of several new teams because of the political upheavals which had occurred in the past two years. Germany competed as a single team and independent nation for the first time since 1936. Because of the break-up of the Soviet Union, the Baltic states of Estonia and Latvia competed for the first time since 1936, and Lithuania for the first time since 1928. Two newly independent nations which had been former states of Yugoslavia, Croatia and Slovenia, competed at the Olympics for the first time as independent nations. The Soviet Union, which no longer existed, was represented instead by the Unified Team, representing a portion of the Commonwealth of Independent States. Russia, Belarus (formerly Byelorussia), the Ukraine, Kazakhstan, and Uzbekistan made up the states of the Unified Team at Albertville.

Athletically the biggest winners were two male cross-country runners from Norway and two female cross-country runners from the Unified Team. Yelena Välbe and Lyubov Yegorova won five medals in the women's events while Vegard Ulvang and Bjørn Dæhlie won four medals in the men's events.

The Games of the XXVth Olympiad (1992)   The Games of the XXVth Olympiad were held in Barcelona, Spain from 25 July through 9 August 1992. At the 91st IOC Session in Lausanne on 17 October 1986, Barcelona (47 votes) was awarded the Games on the third ballot over Paris, France (23 votes); Brisbane, Australia (10 votes); and Belgrade, Yugoslavia (5 votes). Other candidate cities which were eliminated earlier in the voting were Birmingham, England, Great Britain (second round); and Amsterdam, The Netherlands (first round). One hundred sixty-nine nations attended the Games with 9,367 athletes competing (6,659 men and 2,708 women).

The Barcelona Olympics were the Games of the New World Order. They were the most highly attended Olympics in history, both in terms of countries and athletes attending. After four consecutive Olympics with some form of protest or boycott, the Barcelona Olympics were boycott-free.

Since Seoul in 1988, the world had taken on a new face. The Soviet Union no longer existed but the Commonwealth of Independent States did. Estonia, Latvia, and Lithuania were once again free countries. East and West Germany were no more, replaced again by a unified Germany. Yugoslavia was now split into several republics. North and South Yemen had merged into one. All of these new national groupings appeared at Barcelona. South Africa had eliminated, at least constitutionally, apartheid, and competed at the Olympics for the first time since 1960. The Commonwealth of Independent States competed as a "Unified Team" for the last time, representing all the former republics of the Soviet Union, save for the Baltic States.

The Games were opened beautifully and dramatically as archer Antônio Rebollo lit the Olympic flame via bow and arrow. The drama and beauty of Catalonia continued on stage throughout the 16 days of the Olympics. There was concern about terrorist activity because the area was home to some terrorist groups, but heightened security and vigilance helped avoid any problems.

The competition was excellent. For the first time since 1972, all the major nations of the world attended. The most publicized athletes were the American basketball players. The U.S. was allowed to use professional players from the NBA (National Basketball Association), since all the other nations were by now using professionals. The NBA All-Star team, nicknamed "The Dream Team," did not disappoint, putting on a clinic for all nations and winning the gold medal unchallenged. It was led by professional greats Magic Johnson, Michael Jordan, and Larry Bird.

Many East European countries and the former Soviets continued to dominate certain sports, such as gymnastics and weightlifting. There were many great athletic performances but, other than the Dream Team, no one athlete seemed to capture these Games like so many had in the past. It was probably fitting, for then no athlete seemed larger than the Games themselves; fitting, for Barcelona was possibly the finest manifestation yet seen of the Olympic Movement.

The 17th Olympic Winter Games (1994)   The 17th Olympic Winter Games were held in Lillehammer, Norway from 12 to 27 February 1994. Sixty-seven nations attended with 1,737 athletes competing (1,217 men and 520 women). At the 94th IOC Session in Seoul on 15 September 1988, Lillehammer was chosen on the third round (45 votes) over Östersund, Sweden (39 votes, third round); Anchorage, Alaska, USA (second round); and Sofia, Bulgaria (first round).

For the first time, the Olympic Winter Games were not scheduled for the same year as the Games of the Olympiad. The IOC had decided to hold the Olympic Winter Games in the second year after the Olympic Games, thus shortening the cycle so that an Olympic Games or Olympic Winter Games would be held in a rotation every two years. The decision was ostensibly because this would result in greater advertising and sponsorship money.

Before the Lillehammer Olympics began, they were haunted by tragedy and controversy. There was the Nancy Kerrigan–Tonya Harding story, in which Harding's bodyguard and ex–husband admitted to attacking Kerrigan prior to the U.S. Olympic Trials, a story which was ubiquitous in the U.S. press and television. Two weeks before the Olympics, skiing medal favorite Ulrike Maier of Austria was killed when she fell and broke her neck in a downhill race. U.S. ice dancer Elizabeth Punsalan's father was savagely stabbed to death one week before the Olympics, allegedly by her brother and his son. For the Norwegians, they were stunned in October 1993 when their greatest sporting hero, Vegard Ulvang, tragically lost his brother who was killed in the Arctic wilderness while running. They also had to deal with the death of one of the Alpine ski coaches for the Norwegian team, Slovenian Ales Gartner, who suddenly died in December 1993. Finally, only days before the Games, Ole Gunnar Fidjestøl, the Norwegian ski jumper who was to ski jump the torch into the stadium at the opening ceremonies, crashed during a practice jump, sustaining a concussion. He had to be replaced by his understudy, Stein Gruben.

Most tragically, Lillehammer was haunted by the recent news from its sister Olympic Winter city of a decade ago, Sarajevo. Sarajevo, which had hosted a beautiful Olympic Winter Games, now lay in ruins, its stadia and people destroyed by a senseless war in which the Serbs attempted an "ethnic cleansing" of Bosnia–Herzegovina, killing many of their former Muslim brethren.

Stein Gruben performed beautifully at the Opening Ceremonies, as did all of Norway. The Ceremonies began a fairy-tale-like two weeks, which ended all thoughts of the tragedy and controversy that had preceded them, and reminded us again of what the Olympics and sport can bring to the world. The Olympic Winter Games had gone from the ridiculous to the sublime.

There were many great athletic feats at the Lillehammer Games. Manuela Di Centa won five medals in cross–country skiing. Norway's Johann Olav Koss won three speed skating gold medals in world record time. Dan Jansen won the hearts of sports fans everywhere when he finally won a gold medal in the 1,000 meter speed skating. But through it all, the champions seemed to be the small town of Lillehammer and the people of Norway itself.

There were also many poignant memories of Sarajevo. Katarina Witt skated her long program to "Where Have All the Flowers Gone?" in memory of the citizens who had lost their lives in that senseless war. On the next-to-last night, at the figure skating exhibition, Jayne Torvill and Christopher Dean skated "Bolero" as they had done so hauntingly in 1984. Koss donated a major portion of his Olympic bonus (about $33,000 [US]) to Olympic Aid for the citizens of Sarajevo. And during the Lillehammer Olympics, IOC President Samaranch visited Sarajevo, seeing in person the stark contrast between the Olympic City and the Sarajevo of 1994. At the Closing Ceremonies, Samaranch also spoke movingly about Sarajevo.

In summing up the Lillehammer Olympics, Leigh Montville said it best: "The XVII Winter Olympics did not exist. Norway did not exist. These were the fairy-tale Games, drawn from the imagination, staged in the pages of a children's book. They could not exist. Reality cannot be this good." (*Sports Illustrated*, 7 March 1994, p. 90)

The Games of the XXVIth Olympiad (1996)   The Games of the XXVIth Olympiad are scheduled to be held in Atlanta, Georgia, USA from 19 July through 4 August 1996. Atlanta won the IOC nomination at the 96th IOC Session on 18 September 1990 in the 5th round (51 votes) over Athens, Greece (35 votes). Other candidate cities were Toronto, Ontario, Canada (fourth round); Melbourne, Australia (third round); Manchester, England, Great Britain (second round); and Belgrade, Yugoslavia (first round).

The 18th Olympic Winter Games (1998)   The 18th Olympic Winter Games are scheduled to be held in Nagano, Japan from 7 to 22 February 1998. At the 97th IOC Session in Birmingham, England on 15 June 1991, Nagano won the nomination in the fourth round (46 votes) over Salt Lake City, Utah, USA (42 votes, fourth round); Östersund, Sweden (third round); Aosta, Italy (second round); and Jaca, Spain (first round).

The Games of the XXVIIth Olympiad (2000)   The Games of the XXVIIth Olympiad are scheduled to be held in Sydney, New South Wales, Australia from 16 September to 1 October 2000. In a bitterly fought contest, Sydney was awarded the 2000 Olympics during the 101st IOC Session in Monte Carlo on 23 September 1993 over Beijing, China by only two votes (45-43) in the fourth round. Other candidate cities participating in the voting were Manchester, England (third round); Berlin, Germany (second round); and Istanbul, Turkey (first round). Brasilia, Brazil; Milan, Italy; and Tashkent, Uzbekistan also made bids to the IOC but withdrew before the final vote.

The 19th Olympic Winter Games (2002)   The 19th Olympic Winter Games are scheduled to be held in Salt Lake City, Utah,

United States in February 2002. At the 104th IOC Session in Budapest, Hungary on 16 June 1995, Salt Lake City was chosen as the host city in round one over three other finalist cities with 55 votes. The other finalist cities were Östersund, Sweden (14 votes); Sion, Switzerland (14 votes); and Québec City, Québec, Canada (7 votes). Ten cities made preliminary bids; the other six candidate cities were as follows: Almaty, Kazakhstan; Graz, Austria; Jaca, Spain; Poprad–Tatry, Slovakia; Sochi, Russia; and Tarvisio, Italy. On 24 January 1995, the IOC Evaluation Commission eliminated all but four bidding cities in a new effort to decrease time, effort, and costs by so many bid candidates.

INTRODUCTION TO THE OLYMPIC MOVEMENT

The Olympic Movement began with the Ancient Olympic Games which were held in Greece on the Peloponnesus peninsula at Olympia, Greece. The recorded history of the Ancient Olympic Games begins in 776 B.C., although it is suspected that the Games had been held for several centuries by that time. The Games were conducted as religious celebrations in honor of the god Zeus. The Ancient Olympic Games were contested through 393 A.D., when they were stopped by imperial decree of the Roman Emperor Theodosius I.

For almost 15 centuries, the world did not have Olympic Games, although they were not forgotten and were often mentioned in literature. In the 19th century, a series of attempted revivals of the Olympic Games were held in various parts of the world. The most prominent of these were the Much Wenlock Olympian Games, held in Shropshire, England and beginning in 1850, and the Zappas Olympic Games, held in Athens, Greece, which were first conducted in 1859. The Zappas Olympic Games were held four times and were strictly Greek national sporting festivals. The Much Wenlock Olympian Games were the brainchild of Dr. William Penny Brookes. Modern scholars of the Olympic Movement give much credit to Brookes as a man who possibly originated the idea of reviving the Ancient Olympic Games.

However, full credit for the renovation of the Olympic Games is usually given to the Frenchman Baron Pierre de Coubertin. To Coubertin, in particular, should be given credit for instituting the Modern Olympic Movement, a Movement which encompasses far more than simply the Olympic Games themselves. For his efforts, Coubertin has been termed *le rénovateur*.

Coubertin first publicly suggested the idea of modern Olympic Games at a meeting of sports dignitaries at the Sorbonne in 1892, but nothing came of this. In 1894, he was in charge of the Paris International Athletic Congress, which was held ostensibly to discuss amateurism. However, Coubertin had different ideas and suggested the resurrection of the Olympic Games. His idea met with favor among the candidates and the Modern Olympic Games began two years later in Athens, Greece.

Since that time, the Olympic Games have been held every four years, with the exception of 1916, 1940, and 1944, when they were not held because of World Wars. In addition, in 1906, the Greeks held an Olympic Games, usually termed the Intercalated Olympic Games. The 1906 Olympics are not always given official recognition, but they are important because of their contribution to strengthening the revival of the Olympic Games.

In 1924, the first Olympic Winter Games were held in Chamonix, France. These Winter Olympics have since been contested every four years, save 1940 and 1944 (see above), until 1992. In that year, the cycle for Olympic Winter Games changed and the next ones were contested in 1994, with a new four-year cycle to ensue such that the next Winter Olympics will be held in 1998. This will ensure that the Olympic Games and the Olympic Winter Games are not held in the same calendar year.

In 1894, Coubertin was responsible not simply for suggesting the revival of the Olympic Games, but also for the formation of the International Olympic Committee (IOC). The IOC has existed since 1894 as a multi-national group whose responsibilities include the planning and staging of the Olympic Games and spreading the philosophy of the Olympic Movement, usually termed Olympism.

The IOC, and its responsibilities and philosophy, have evolved greatly over its first century of existence. Originally the IOC basically consisted of a group run by Coubertin. Although there were other members, he was in charge and the ideas and plans he espoused were usually accepted without argument by the other members of the IOC. Coubertin initially ran the IOC out of his home in Paris at 20 rue Oudinot. In April 1915, he moved to Lausanne, Switzerland and established the IOC headquarters in that city, where it has remained since that time.

Through World War II, and even until the early 1960's, the IOC, the Olympic Games, and the Olympic Movement did not change a great deal, although they all became a bit larger and better known. However, the IOC was still run basically by its President and a small headquarters staff, and with relatively small financial backing.

In the 1960's, television began to realize the importance of televising the Olympic Games and, since that time, things have changed greatly. With network telecasts of the Olympic Games came huge fees paid by the networks for that right. The money generated has given the IOC and the Olympic Movement significant financial freedom. This has enabled the IOC to expand its horizons in an effort to spread its philosophy of Olympism, and also to lend financial support to various structures within the Olympic Movement via Olympic Solidarity.

In the 1980's, the IOC began to seek other sources of financing its operations, via a commission of the IOC termed the Commission for New Sources of Financing. This has only served to strengthen the financial picture of the IOC and allow it to pursue its purpose even more aggressively.

With the increasing economic independence, however, has come great problems. The Olympic Games became so publicized that they also became subject to great political manipulation, ending in several boycotts. In 1968, political activists in Mexico City protested the Mexican government's staging of the Olympic Games. The

Mexican army and police intervened and killed several hundred protesters. In 1972, Arab terrorists kidnapped most of the Israeli Olympic team in the Olympic Village and, eventually, after hours of negotiations, savagely murdered 11 of the Israelis. Between 1968 and 1988, all the Olympic Games saw some form of protest or boycott.

Coubertin hated politics, stating, "We have not worked, my friends and I, to restore the Olympic Games to have them made a museum piece or a movie, nor for commercial or political interests to take over."[1] And so, the IOC has attempted to remain non-political. However, this is changing.

The IOC, and current IOC President Juan Antonio Samaranch, have more recently been quoted as saying that the mere act of declaring the group non-political is, in itself, a political statement. The IOC realizes it cannot operate in a vacuum, attempting to divorce itself from all the political problems of a world which, superficially at least, appears to have no desire to pursue freedom for all people and more internationalism. Samaranch's philosophy of not allowing the IOC to be politically isolated is best exemplified by his negotiations with respect to the 1988 Seoul Olympics, in which he attempted to negotiate with DPR Korea (North) in an effort to allow it to host several Olympic events.

The purpose of the IOC may seem to the rest of the world to be to stage Olympic Games. But the IOC would state that its primary reason for existence is to spread the philosophy of Olympism via the Olympic Movement. It is not easy to define either Olympism or the Olympic Movement. Both are defined in the Olympic Charter, basically the constitution of the IOC, and full definitions are given within this dictionary.

The Olympic Charter states simply that "The Olympic Movement, led by the IOC, stems from modern Olympism." The IOC has, however, defined the phrase more fully in some of its press releases. It has stated that the Olympic Movement encompasses the International Olympic Committee (IOC), the International Federations (IFs), and the National Olympic Committees (NOCs) and that the IOC is the supreme authority of the Olympic Movement. The Olympic Movement should also include the Organizing Committees of the Olympic Games (OCOGs or COJOs) which are groups formed in the host cities, whose only purpose is the staging of the Olympic Games.

The International Federations are the international governing bodies of the individual sports on the Olympic Program, and also of the IOC affiliated sports. The IOC gives the IFs almost complete autonomy in designing, organizing, and regulating the Olympic competitions under their aegis. The IFs define amateurism for each sport and thus Olympic eligibility. The IFs provide the international officials who conduct the Olympic events. The IFs also set qualifying regulations for the Olympic sports, as it would not be possible for all athletes who wish to compete at the Olympic Games to do so.

National Olympic Committees are the governing bodies of Olympic sports in their respective countries or areas. (This is an important distinction as not all NOCs represent autonomous nations.) The NOCs are responsible for fielding Olympic teams to represent their nation or NOC. The NOCs also work closely with groups termed National Governing Bodies (NGBs). NGBs are the national governing organizations for individual sports. They come under the umbrella both of their own NOC and their own IF. Thus, for example, U.S.A. Track & Field (USATF), which governs track & field in the United States, is a subset of both its NOC, the U.S. Olympic Committee, and its IF, the International Amateur Athletic Federation.

The philosophy of Olympism is even more difficult to define with precision, but certainly stems from the writings and philosophy of Coubertin. The IOC defines Olympism in the Olympic Charter as follows: "Olympism is a philosophy of life, exalting and combining in a balanced whole the qualities of body, will and mind. Blending sport with culture and education, Olympism seeks to create a way of life based on the joy found in effort, the educational value of good example, and respect for universal fundamental ethical principles. The goal of Olympism is to place everywhere sport at the service of the harmonious development of man, with a view to encouraging the establishment of a peaceful society concerned with the preservation of human dignity."[2]

However, most scholars of the Olympic Movement would tell you that Olympism is even more encompassing than the above rather broad definition. Coubertin considered sport a method of education, and stated that "sport is not a luxury activity, or an activity for the idle, or even a physical compensation for cerebral work. It is, on the contrary, a possible source of inner improvement for everyone. Sport is part of every man and woman's heritage and its absence can never be compensated for."[3]

This basically outlines Coubertin's philosophy of "sport for all," a concept which is a cornerstone of the modern Olympic Movement. In 1919, Coubertin defined this philosophy thusly: "All sports for all people. This motto will no doubt be criticized as utopian lunacy, but that doesn't worry me. I have given it considerable thought and I believe its realization is just and possible."[4] He also noted, "Class distinctions should have no place in sport."[5]

On Olympism, Coubertin defined it as ". . . not a system but a state of mind. It may be applied to the most diverse situations and is not the exclusive monopoly of any one race or time. The Olympic spirit is a state of mind created by the cultivation of both effort and eurhythmy . . . which in a paradoxical sense are the basis of all absolute virility."[6]

Coubertin was not a great classics scholar, but he understood a great deal about the religious and philosophical aspects of the

Ancient Olympic Games. His philosophy of Olympism was based on the ancient Greek ideal of *kalokagathia*, or the harmonic combination of beauty and goodness. Certainly, his philosophy of sport for all is also based somewhat on the Greek motto of *Mens sana in corpore sano*, or "a sound mind in a sound body."

To the bulk of the world, however, the Olympic Movement *is* the Olympic Games, and nothing else. Certainly they are the best publicized aspect of the Olympic Movement. The Olympic Games themselves now see politicians, philosophers, and the IOC itself wrestling with several controversial issues.

One is the commercialization of the Olympic Games. While the IOC has become financially independent, this is not always considered a good thing. Many sports historians and philosophers of sport yearn for the days when Avery Brundage was IOC President and the IOC was run on a financial shoestring. Though it was less glamorous, Brundage simply did not allow commercialism and fought its encroachment into the Olympic Games to his dying day.

Coupled with commercialism is the concept of amateurism, a concept which has engendered multiple philosophical imbroglios since its inception in Victorian England. Coubertin actually tired of debating the concepts of amateurism, finally declaring, "All I ask of the athlete . . . is loyalty to sport."[7] The Ancient Olympic Games are considered by many journalists and the lay public to have been contested by "amateur" athletes, but that is almost certainly false. In fact, the Ancient Greeks did not even have a word for the modern term "amateur," and all of the greatest Greek athletes were paid, and paid well, for their efforts.

Amateurism with respect to the Olympic Games is also dying out. Each International Federation is now responsible for providing its own definition of amateurism. The IOC leaves Olympic eligibility requirements to the International Federations and this situation has allowed professionals to compete in the Olympic Games in many sports: track & field athletics, basketball, cycling, football (soccer), figure skating, and volleyball, among them.

Some sporting purists would demur, stating that the Olympics should remain an amateur festival, but they usually have only a neophyte's understanding of the original meaning of the Olympic Games and the Olympic Movement. In today's world, many of the top international athletes are highly paid for their performances, and to exclude them would prevent the world's greatest athletes from competing in the world's greatest sporting event – the Olympic Games. It is very unlikely, however, that prize money will be given at the Olympic Games. It is offered at many of the International Federation's World Championships, but Samaranch has noted, "I think the Olympic Games are different."[8]

"Gigantism" is a term which deals with the increasing size of the Olympic Games and the commensurate increase in costs. This concept is interwoven with the commercialism of the Olympic Games, because as the Games increase in size and thus become more expensive, increased financial resources must be generated to conduct the Olympic Games and run the Olympic Movement.

Gigantism of the Olympic Games is a very difficult problem to solve. To make the Olympic Games smaller, only two real solutions exist: 1) decrease the number of sports and events, or 2) decrease the number of competitors in each sport. But all the world's sports want to be allowed on the Olympic showcase. Currently, the IOC recognizes 31 International (Sports) Federations and has 19 affiliated federations. However, the General Association of International Sports Federations (GAISF) has over 80 member federations, all of which would like to have their sports in the Olympics. Were the IOC to acquiesce, the Olympics would not only not be smaller, they would be three times larger than they are now.

Decreasing the number of competitors also raises difficult philosophical questions. The simple solution would be to limit each event only to the top-rated athletes in the world in that event. But this would virtually eliminate many of the world's sporting nations. Of the 197 National Olympic Committees (NOCs) currently recognized by the IOC, only a few can be considered sporting powers. Sports facilities and training techniques are simply not available to many of the world's athletes. To limit events to only the top competitors would prevent many of the world's NOCs from competing in the Olympic Games. This completely violates the IOC's ideals of sport for all and of promoting internationalism and international good will by bringing together the youth of all nations in a great sporting festival.

Thus, we have come full circle, from a small, simple religious festival in Ancient Greece, to a huge festival seen on television by billions of people which American sportscaster Jim McKay has termed, "The largest peacetime gathering of humanity in the history of the world."[9] To the athletes, the Olympic Games are the supreme test of their abilities. But even to the athletes, the Olympic Games are more than that, witnessed by the statement of Al Oerter, an Olympic legend and four-time discus gold medalist: "There is no job, no amount of power, no money to approach the Olympic experience."[10]

Though "just" a big sporting event, even the politicians have realized that the Olympics are more than that. Former California Governor Jerry Brown once commented, "These are just games and people should see them for fun; there shouldn't be any ulterior motives to the Olympics. They're just games, frivolous things. They're not really necessary. But don't forget some of the least necessary things in life are the most important. Art, religion, friendship, leisure time, games – they make life worth living."[11]

And the Olympic Movement itself, as we have discussed above, encompasses much more than the Olympic Games. Via its philosophy of Olympism it attempts to bring together people of all nationalities in peaceful competition, creating an air of internationalism rarely seen in today's divisive world. This has perhaps been best summed up by the emotional speech of Lord Killanin, outgoing IOC President, at the closing ceremonies of the 1980 Lake Placid Winter Olympics. Referring specifically to the planned U.S.-driven boycott of the Moscow Olympics, Killanin stated, "Ladies and gentlemen, I feel these Games have proved that we do something to contribute to the mutual understanding of the world, what we have in common and not what our differences are. If we can all come together it will be for a better world and we shall avoid the holocaust which may well be upon us if we are not careful."[12]

****

[1]Speech to the sports youth of all nations at Olympia, Greece, 17 April 1927; quoted in *The International Pierre de Coubertin Committee*, p. 15. (Lausanne: International Pierre de Coubertin Committee, 1983)

[2]*Olympic Charter*, p. 10. Lausanne: International Olympic Committee, 1995.

[3]Durántez Corral, Conrado. *Pierre de Coubertin: The Olympic Humanist*, p. 27. Lausanne: International Olympic Committee and International Pierre de Coubertin Committee, 1994.

[4]*Ibid*, p. 29.

[5]*Ibid*, p. 29.

[6]*Ibid*, p. 36.

[7]*Ibid*, p. 33.

[8]*USA Today*, March 1995.

[9]Mallon, Bill. *The Olympics: A Bibliography*, p. ix. New York: Garland, 1984.

[10]*Ibid*, p. v.

[11]*Los Angeles Times*, 1982.

[12]Lord Killanin. *My Olympic Years*, p. 187. London: Secker & Warburg, 1983.

DICTIONARY OF THE OLYMPIC MOVEMENT

Aamodt, Kjetil André. [NOR-ASK]   B. 2 September 1971.   His record of five Olympic medals (one gold, two silver, two bronze) in Alpine skiing has only been matched by Vreni Schneider (SUI) Alberto Tomba (ITA) (*qq. v.*).   Aamodt's only gold medal came in the super giant slalom in 1992 when he also took bronze in the giant slalom.   In 1994, he took silver in the downhill and Alpine combined and bronze in the super giant slalom.

Acrobatics   Acrobatics has never been contested at the Olympic Games, even as a demonstration sport.   However, the International Federation of sports acrobatics is recognized by the IOC.

Aeronautics   Aeronautics is governed internationally by the Fédération Aéronautique Internationale, which was created in 1905 and is recognized by the IOC.   At the 1936 Olympic Games a gold medal for merit for aeronautics was presented to Hermann Schreiber.

Afghanistan [AFG]   Afghanistan first competed at the 1936 Olympics in Berlin, the same year in which its National Olympic Committee was recognized by the IOC.   The country has since competed at the Olympic Games of 1948, 1956–1972, 1980, and 1988.   Afghanistan has never competed at the Olympic Winter Games.   No Afghan athlete has won a medal, their best finish being fifth by Mohammed Ebrahimi in 1964 featherweight freestyle wrestling.

Albania [ALB]   Albania's Olympic Committee was founded in 1958, and recognized by the IOC in 1959, but Albania did not compete at the Olympics until 1972.   Albania then did not compete at the Olympics for 20 years, returning in 1992.   Albania has not won any medals.   The best finishes by Albanian athletes were ninth by Ymer Pampuri in 1972 featherweight weightlifting and ninth by Dede Dekaj in the 1992 110 kg. class weightlifting.

Alekseyev, Vasiliy Ivanovich. [URS-WLT]   B. 7 January 1942, Pokrovo–Shishkino, Ryazan Oblast.   Unbeaten from 1970 to 1978 he was the greatest super-heavyweight lifter in history. His feat of taking eight successive gold medals at the Olympic Games and World Championships (1970–1977) equaled the record of Americans John Davis (*q.v.*) and Tommy Kono. He also won eight European titles and set 79 world records. He was finally defeated at the 1978 World Championships when suffering from a damaged hip tendon.

Algeria [ALG]   Algeria formed a National Olympic Committee in 1963 which was recognized by the IOC in 1964. Algeria first competed officially at the 1964 Olympic Games. It has since competed at the Olympic Games of 1968, 1972, and all Olympics since 1980. It competed at the Winter Olympics for the only time to date in 1992. Through 1992, Algerians have won four medals, one in track & field athletics and three in boxing. Prior to Algeria's independence in July 1962, several Algerian athletes competed for France at the Olympics. The first was 1924 marathoner Mohammed Kader Ghermati. The 1928 marathon winner, Mohammed Bouguerra El Ouafi, and the 1956 marathon winner, Alain Mimoun O'Kacha, were both native Algerians.

Ali, Muhammad (né Cassius Marcellus Clay). [USA–BOX]   B. 17 January 1942, Louisville, Kentucky. Muhammad Ali first gained international prominence as Cassius Clay by winning the light-heavyweight gold medal at the 1960 Rome Olympics. In February 1964, he upset "Sonny" Liston to win his first heavyweight championship. Shortly after the fight he embraced the Muslim faith and took the name Muhammad Ali. No fighter defeated him for the rest of the 1960's. But Ali was defeated by the U.S. draft board when he refused induction to the service based on conscientious objection and he was stripped of the heavyweight title. Eventually, Ali won his battle in the Supreme Court but the best years of his career were lost. He returned in 1970 and the next year lost a much ballyhooed fight against Joe Frazier (*q.v.*). In 1974, Ali regained the heavyweight championship against George Foreman (*q.v.*) and, after losing to Leon Spinks in 1978, he would become the only man to hold the title three times by defeating Spinks in a rematch. Ali's career professional record was 56 wins, 37 by knockout, and 5 losses.

Alpine Skiing   Alpine ski racing is the newer form of ski racing, as Nordic, or cross-country, competitions were held in the Scandinavian countries for many years before Alpine racing was developed. The first known race was in 1911 at Montana, Switzerland, when the British organized a downhill race for a challenge cup given by Lord Roberts of Kandahar. The first slalom style race was held in 1922 at Mürren, Switzerland.

Alpine skiing was first placed on the Olympic program in 1936 at Garmisch-Partenkirchen. The only event that year was a combined competition of both downhill and slalom. In 1948, this was held along with separate downhill and slalom races. Alpine combined was then not contested at the Olympic Winter Games until 1988 when it returned to the Olympic program. In 1952, the giant slalom was added as an event, and in 1988, the super giant slalom became a fourth separate event.

Men and women contest Alpine Skiing separately. Events for both sexes were held in 1936, and have been at all Olympics since. Interestingly, the program for men and women has been identical at all Olympics. The sport is governed by the Fédération Internationale de Ski (FIS) which had 84 member nations through 1993.

The two greatest Alpine skiers among the men have been Toni Sailer of Austria and Jean-Claude Killy (*qq.v.*), both of whom won all three gold medals available, in 1956 and 1968, respectively. Kjetil André Aamodt of Norway, Alberto Tomba of Italy, and Vreni Schneider (*qq.v.*) of Switzerland have won the most Olympic medals with five each. Austria, Switzerland, and France have been the top nations in Olympic Alpine Skiing, with Italy and the United States not far behind.

Alpinism   Alpinism is governed internationally by the Union Internationale des Associations d'Alpinisme, which was created in 1932 and is recognized by the IOC. Gold medals for merit for alpinism were presented at the 1924, 1932, and 1936 Olympic Games.

American Football   See Football, American.

American Samoa [ASA]   American Samoa has competed at the 1988 and 1992 Olympics and the 1994 Olympic Winter Games. In 1992, Robert Peden won two matches in flyweight boxing to finish equal fifth of 30 in his class, the top finish to date from this small island country.

Ancient Olympic Games   The Ancient Olympic Games were one of the four great Panhellenic sporting festivals, along with the Isthmian, Nemean, and Pythian Games (*qq.v.*). The Olympic Games were considered to be the greatest of the ancient Greek athletic contests. The first recorded Olympics are known to have been held in 776 B.C. although it is probable that they began several centuries earlier. The Games lasted until 393 A.D. when they were banned by imperial decree by the Roman Emperor Theodosius I. The Ancient Olympic Games were held in Olympia, which is near the city-state of Elis on the Greek Peloponnesus. (They were *not* held on or near Mt. Olympus, as is often incorrectly written.) The Ancient Olympic Games were held quadrennially. Winners at the Ancient Olympic Games received crowns of wild olive.

The origins of the Ancient Olympic Games are uncertain, but several traditional explanations exist. One connects the Games to Pelops, after whom the Peloponnesus was named. Pelops was a Phrygian who made his way to the peninsula which would later take his name. There he defeated Oenomaus, King of Pisa, in a chariot race, which Oenomaus had ordered as a race in which Pelops could win the hand of his daughter, Hippodameia. Oenomaus was thrown from his chariot and killed and Pelops was worshipped as a hero. He took over the kingdom and the Games were supposedly held at his tomb and in his honor. Later beliefs, popularized by Pindar (*q.v.*), state that the Games originated to honor Hercules and he founded them after his victory over Augeas. Hercules declared the Games to be in honor of his father, Zeus.

Originally, the Ancient Olympic Games consisted of only a single footrace, one length of the Ancient Olympic stadium of about 192 meters, and now termed the *stadion* (*q.v.*) race. Champions are recorded in this event from 776 B.C. (Coroebus of Elis [*q.v.*]) until 269 A.D. A second race of two laps of the stadium, termed the *diaulos* (*q.v.*), was added in 724 B.C., followed in 720 B.C. by the *dolichos* (*q.v.*), which was a long distance race of about 20–25 laps of the stadium. Wrestling (*q.v.*) champions are recorded from 708 B.C., while boxing (*q.v.*) was added to the list of victors in 688 B.C. The pentathlon (*q.v.*), an all-around championship of five events, was also added at the Olympics of 708 B.C. The pankration (*q.v.*), which was a brutal combination of wrestling and boxing, was known to have been contested at the Ancient Olympics from 648 B.C.

In addition to the above, a number of horse races and chariot races were contested at the Olympic Games. There were events at Olympia for boys, which was defined as being older than 12 but less than 18 years old. Competitions for heralds and lyre-playing were also contested at the Ancient Olympics.

Athletes from the Peloponnesus dominated the earliest Olympics, winning the first 13 *stadion* events. Greeks from other city-states later produced many Olympic champions. Elis produced the most known Ancient Olympic champions with 110 recorded victories, followed by Sparta with 76 known victories. In the later years of the Ancient Olympics, athletes from the Roman Empire began to compete at Olympia, winning many titles. The Ancient Olympic Games reached their zenith in the Golden Age of Greece, dimming once the Roman Empire took over the celebrations.

Andersen, Hjalmar Johan "Hjallis." [NOR–SSK] B. 12 March 1923, Rødøy. Winner of three gold medals at the 1952 Winter Games (1,500 meters, 5,000 meters, 10,000 meters). His winning margin in the 5,000 meters was an astounding 11 seconds and he also won the 10,000 meters by a substantial margin. He retired after the 1952 Games but returned to competition in 1954 to win his fourth Norwegian title, having earlier won the World, European and Norwegian all–around titles in 1950–52. He set one world record at 5,000 meters and three at 10,000 meters.

Anderson, Paul Edward. [USA–WLT] B. 17 October 1932, Toccao, Georgia. D. 15 August 1994, Vidalia, Georgia. After winning the world heavyweight title by a record margin in 1955 he took the Olympic gold medal in Melbourne the following year. He was probably the strongest man who ever lived. Anderson set hundreds of records as a powerlifter, including a bench press of 625 lbs. (284 kg.), a squat with 1,200 lbs. (545 kg.), a dead–lift of 820 lbs. (373 kg.), and three repetitions in the squat with 900 lbs. (409 kg.) In addition he performed a back–lift off trestles, supporting 6,270 lbs. (2,850 kg.) – the greatest weight ever lifted by a human.

Andorra [AND] Andorra formed a National Olympic Committee in 1971, and received IOC recognition in 1975. Its first Olympic appearance came at the 1976 Olympic Winter Games in Innsbruck. It has competed at every Olympics, summer and winter, since. Its best finish has been ninth in 1988 by Emili Perez, in the cycling individual road race.

Andrianov, Nikolay Yefimovich. [URS–GYM] B. 14 October 1952, Vladimir. The most successful Olympic male gymnast of all time. Between 1972 and 1980 he won seven gold medals (six individual, one team), five silver and three bronze for a total of a record 15 medals. At the World Championships he won gold on the rings in 1974, the all–around and rings in 1978, and the team event in 1979. He also won seven silver medals at the World Championships. His international career started at the 1971 European Championships where he was a late substitute but won six medals, including a bronze in the all–around. In individual European Championships he eventually won eight gold, six silver, and two bronze medals.

Angola [ANG] Angola, whose National Olympic Committee was formed in 1979 and recognized in 1980, has competed at the 1980,

1988, and 1992 Olympics. It has not yet competed at the Olympic Winter Games. The top Angolan Olympic performance likely occurred in 1992 Barcelona when its basketball team qualified for the Olympics but drew the United States as a first-round opponent. It eventually finished 10th of 12 teams.

Antigua and Barbuda [ANT]   Although Antigua formed a National Olympic Committee in 1966, the Antigua and Barbuda Olympic Association, it was not until 1976 that it received IOC recognition. Antigua has competed four times at the Olympics – at the celebrations of 1976, 1984, 1988, and 1992. Antigua and Barbuda has not yet competed at the Olympic Winter Games. The best Antiguan performance probably came in 1984 when Lester Benjamin finished 15th of 31 athletes in long jump qualifying, even though he did not qualify for the finals.

Antilles (West Indies) [ANL]   See West Indies Federation.

Apene – Ancient Olympic Sport   The apene race was a chariot race in which two mules pulled the chariot. The first known winner was Thersias of Thessaly in 500 B.C. The event was discontinued after 444 B.C.

Arba-Puşcatu, Rodica (née Puşcatu). [ROM-ROW] B. 5 May 1962, Bucharest. Rodica Arba (née Puşcatu) has won four Olympic rowing medals, sharing that honor with fellow Romanian, Olga Bularda-Homeghi (*q.v.*), with whom she has won most of her titles. As Rodica Puşcatu she won an Olympic bronze in 1980 at Moscow in the eights. She and Bularda-Homeghi added a gold medal in 1984 at Los Angeles in the coxless pairs. Her 1984 gold started her on a winning pattern, as she and Bularda-Homeghi won the World Championships in coxless pairs in 1985–1987 and also at the 1988 Olympics. Arba added a silver in the eights at Seoul to give her her fourth Olympic medal.

Archery   Though only recently returned to the Olympic program, archery is one of the oldest known sports. Use of the bow and arrow for hunting can be traced back to the Aurignacians, a race of people existing 15,000 years ago. By the 14th century, archers were found to be valuable as soldiers and the English kings made archery practice mandatory for the British soldiers. Archery as a sport became popular in the 16th and 17th centuries. In 1676, the first organized group, the

Royal Company of Archers, was formed in England for the purpose of advancing the sport. This was followed in 1781 by the Royal Toxophilite Society. The first British championships were conducted in 1844. Archery is governed world-wide by the Fédération Internationale de Tir à l'Arc (FITA), which was founded in 1931. Through 1994, 103 nations were members of FITA. Archery was first held as a sport in the 1900 Paris Olympics and again in 1904, 1908, and 1920, but then left the Olympics program. In those years it was possible for an athlete to compete in multiple events and win several medals. The top Olympic medal winner is Hubert Van Innis of Belgium, who competed in the 1900 and 1920 Olympics, winning nine medals, six of them gold.

When the sport was returned to the Olympics in 1972, there was only one event for men and one for women. In 1988, team events for men and women were added to the program. Also, in 1988, the individual formats were changed. Previously (to 1972), men and women shot a Double FITA Round. Now, qualifying is contested over a Single FITA Round, and the archers then engage in single-elimination matches until a champion is crowned.

Argentina [ARG]   Argentina first competed officially at the 1924 Olympics in Paris. Prior to that, two Argentine athletes had competed at the Olympics, i.e., Henri Torromé in 1908 figure skating, and a boxer named Rodriguez in 1920. Since 1924, Argentina has competed at every Olympic Games with the exception of 1980. Argentina has competed at the Olympic Winter Games of 1928, 1948, 1952, and all Winter Games since 1960. Through 1994, Argentine athletes have won 47 medals, 13 of them gold. Argentina has won more Olympic medals than any other South American country.

Armenia [ARM]   The Olympic Committee of the Armenian Republic was recognized by the IOC after the break-up of the Soviet Union. Many Armenian athletes competed from 1952 through 1988 for the Soviet Union, and Armenian athletes were present at Barcelona in 1992 as members of the Unified Team (*q.v.*). Armenia competed as an independent nation for the first time at the 1994 Olympic Winter Games in Lillehammer, represented by Joseph Almasian and Kenneth Topalian, who finished 36th in two-man bobsledding.

Art Contests   Art competitions were held at the Olympics of 1912, 1920, 1924, 1928, 1932, 1936, and 1948. The winners of the competitions were awarded gold, silver, and bronze medals, similar to the winners of the athletic competitions. The events were inspired by Pierre de Coubertin (*q.v.*), who wished to meld the competitions in sports with competitions in the arts. The art competitions were dropped from the Olympic program because of the difficulty of determining the amateur status of the artists. Competitions were held in Architectural Designs, Designs for Town Planning, Sculpture – Medals, Sculpture – Reliefs, Sculpture – Any Kind, Applied Graphics, Drawings and Water-Colors, Other Graphic Arts, Paintings, Dramatic Works, Epic Works, Literature – All Kinds, Lyrics, Musical Compositions for One Instrument, Musical Compositions for Orchestra of All Kinds, Musical Compositions of Songs for Soloist or Choir, With or Without Instrumental Accompaniment, Music – All Kinds, Merit for Aeronautics, and Merit for Alpinism. Two artists won three medals – Alex Walter Diggelmann of Switzerland (all in applied graphics) and Joseph Petersen of Denmark (one in epic works and two in literature – all kinds). Jean Jacoby of Luxembourg was the only artist to win two gold medals in the art competitions; one in drawings and water-colors and one in paintings. In 1912, the founder of the Modern Olympic Games and the art competitions, Pierre de Coubertin, won a gold medal in the literature category. Coubertin's gold medal was for his work entitled "Ode to Sport" which he entered under the dual pseudonym of Georg Hohrod and Martin Eschbach.

Aruba [ARU]   Aruba's Olympic Committee was formed in 1985 and recognized by the IOC in 1986. Aruba competed in the Olympic Games for the first time in 1988 at Seoul and also competed in 1992 at Barcelona. The best Aruban performance has been 53rd in the 1992 men's marathon by Kimball Reynierse.

Association des Comités Nationaux Olympiques [ACNO]   The Association des Comités Nationaux Olympiques (ACNO) was formed in 1968 by Giulio Onesti, then the President of the Italian Olympic Committee, as a method of uniting the various National Olympic Committees. Originally entitled the PGA, or Permanent General Assembly of National Olympic Committees, this would allow them a more unified voice to present their concerns to the International Olympic Committee. This union of NOCs greatly displeased then IOC President Avery Brundage (*q.v.*). The group was later renamed the Association of National Olympic Committees (ANOC). ACNO is currently based in Paris and its President, as of 1994, is Mexico's Mario Vazquez Raña. Formation of the ACNO has been responsible for the foundation of various continental and regional associations of National Olympic Committees. (See also: Association des Comités Nationaux Olympiques d'Afrique [ACNOA]; Association des Comités

Nationaux Olympiques d'Europe [ACNOE]; Oceania National Olympic Committees [ONOC]; Olympic Council of Asia [OCA]; Organización Deportiva Centroamericana y del Caribe [ODECABE]; and Pan American Sports Organization [PASO]).

Association des Comités Nationaux Olympiques d'Afrique [ACNOA] This group consists of the National Olympic Committees from the African nations. The association has its headquarters in Yaoundé, Cameroon. The President of the ACNOA (in 1994) is Jean–Claude Ganga of the Congo.

Association des Comités Nationaux Olympiques d'Europe [ACNOE] See European Olympic Committees (EOC).

Association Générale des Fédérations Internationales de Sports [AGFIS] See General Association of International Sports Federations (GAISF).

Association of Summer Olympic International Federations [ASOIF] On 20 May 1983, 21 International Federations governing sports on the program of the Olympic Games met in Lausanne and established the Association of Summer Olympic International Federations (ASOIF). The ASOIF constitution defines its purpose as "To coordinate and defend the common interests of its members to ensure close cooperation between them, the members of the Olympic Movement and those of other organizations, with the aim of preserving the unity of the Olympic Movement while maintaining the authority, independence and autonomy of the member International Federations." The ASOIF is currently based in Rome, Italy and its President, as of 1995, is Primo Nebiolo of Italy and the International Amateur Athletic Federation (IAAF).

Association of the International Winter Sports Federations [AIWF] In 1982, led by Marc Hodler of Switzerland and the International Ski Federation, the Winter Sports Federations formed their own group, the Association of the International Winter Sports Federations (AIWF). The group is based in Oberhofen, Switzerland. Hodler has been the President since the group's inception.

Association of the IOC Recognized International Sports Federations [ARISF] The IOC recognizes a number of international sports federations whose sports are not yet on the Olympic program. This recognition is important, for it is a first step towards getting a sport admitted to the Olympic program. At the end of 1994, the IOC has recognized the international federations for the following sports (in addition to those on the Olympic program): acrobatics, aeronautics, alpinism, bowling, bowls, golf, korfball, netball, orienteering, pelota basque, racquetball, roller skating, softball, squash, trampoline, triathlon, underwater aquatics, and water skiing. These IOC Recognized International Sports Federations have grouped together to form the Association of the IOC Recognized International Sports Federations (ARISF). They are headquartered in Leidschendan, The Netherlands, and as of 1995, the ARISF had 18 member federations. The statutes of the ARISF state that its aims are "to determine the consensus of the member federations on questions relating to the Olympic Movement, . . . and to coordinate and defend the common interest of its members in [that] context."

Athletics (Track & Field)   Athletics, or track & field, is the original Olympic sport. The first event contested in the Ancient Olympics was the stade race, a sprint race of about 190 meters. Recorded victors in this event are known as far back as 776 B.C. Other athletics events in the Ancient Olympics included longer races, races in armor, and a pentathlon consisting of the stade race, long jump, discus throw, javelin throw, and wrestling.

Throughout recorded sports history, athletics has always been practiced. Many of the attempted revivals of the Olympics in the 19th century consisted mostly of athletics contests. Since the revival of the Olympics in 1896, athletics has been the most publicized sport on the Olympic program. Today, athletics is rivaled only by football (soccer) as the sport practiced in the most countries in the world. The sport is governed internationally by the International Amateur Athletic Federation (IAAF), which was formed in 1912 and had 206 member nations at the end of 1994.

Athletics has been held at every Olympics. Women's athletics began in the 1928 Olympics and has been contested continually since. The program has varied but has been fairly standard since 1932. In addition, although women were first allowed to compete in only a few events, today they have a program with almost as many events as the men.

The United States' men have always been the top performers in the world in track & field athletics. Among the women, the Soviet Union and the GDR have been the top powers since their admission to the Olympics, and prior to their dissolution by the political events at the end of the 1980's.

Attempts at Revival   Prior to the 1896 Olympic Games in Athens, multiple efforts had been made at attempting to resurrect the Ancient Olympic Games (*q. v.*) and stage them with a program mainly containing contemporary events.   These include Robert Dover's Cotswold Olimpick Games, the Much Wenlock Olympian Games, and the Zappas Olympic Games in Athens (*qq. v.*).   Other attempts at Olympian–type festivals are known to have been held in Ramlösa, Sweden (near Helsingborg) in 1834 and 1836 under the initiative of Professor Gustav Johann Schartau of the University of Lund; in Montreal, Quebec, Canada, in the early 1830's and 1840's; in England held by the National Olympian Association from 1866 to 1883, which was an offspring of the Much Wenlock Olympian Games, as well as the Olympic Festivals of Liverpool (1862–1867); the Morpeth Olympic Games in Morpeth, England (1873–1958); and the Olympic Games at Lake Palić, held from 1880 to 1914 in Palić, a spa eight kilometers east of Subotica, then in Hungary and now in the Vojvodina province of Serbia.   In addition, various Highland and Caledonian Games were held in the 19th century, which brought together various peoples in athletic competition.   (See Appendix XVIII for listing of all known attempts at revival prior to 1896)   However, none of these events had the international flavor of Coubertin's revived Olympic Games.

Much of the impetus for revival in the 19th century was due to recent archaelogical finds at Ancient Olympia and other classical sites in Greece.   These digs were initiated by A. Blouet, a Frenchman, and continued by the Germans, notably Ernst Curtius. They were begun in 1875 by Curtius and his reports on his finds were issued between 1890 and 1897.   However, the German government published yearly reports between 1875 and 1881.

The idea of revival was also in the air for at least a century prior to Coubertin.   The term Olympic and Olympian was apparently used frequently to refer to any athletic contest.   Note Shakespeare's phrases from the late 1500's: " . . . such rewards as victors weare at the Olympian Games" (*Henry VI*, Act 2) and " . . . Olympic wrestling" (*Troilus and Cressida*, Act 4).   Milton discussed "As at th' Olympian Games or Pythian fields" in *Paradise Lost* in 1667.

Professor John Lucas of Penn State University discovered a letter from T. B. Hollis written in 1788 to Josiah Willard, President of Harvard University, in which Hollis states, "Our documents carry mention of an eventual rebirth of the Olympic Games in America. The friends of this latter [idea] want and pretend to be capable of it: after having acted according to Greek Principles, they must practice Greek exercises."

In 1793, Johannes C. F. Guts-Muths discussed the Ancient Olympics in his *Gymnastik für Jugend*, and by the second edition in 1804, he was considering a revival.   In 1813, the philologist and historian Bartold Georg Niebuhr wrote of " . . . a vast hall [in Rome] which, once properly decorated, could serve for the resumption of the Olympic Games."

Thus, Pierre de Coubertin (*q.v.*) did not come to his Olympic idea without help. However, a great deal of credit is due him as he was the visionary who, apart from William Penny Brookes (*q.v.*), really envisioned the possibility of a great international festival, bringing together the youth of all nations in peaceful competition. Without Coubertin's vision, it is almost certain that the Olympic Games would have been revived. But it is not as certain that they would be anything like the Olympic Games we know today.

Aussie Rules   See Football, Australian Rules.

Australia [AUS]   Australia, whose Olympic Committee was formed and recognized by the IOC in 1895, has competed at every summer Olympic Games. In 1908 and 1912 it competed as Australasia in a combined team with New Zealand. Australia has also competed at the Olympic Winter Games – those of 1936 and continuously since 1952. Australia has been successful in many sports, but particularly so in swimming and track & field. Through 1994, Australia has won 252 medals, 251 of them in the Olympic Games, and one at the Olympic Winter Games. Seventy-seven of these were gold medals. Australia has also hosted the Games of the XVIth Olympiad in 1956 in Melbourne, and is scheduled to host the Games of the XXVIIth Olympiad in 2000 in Sydney.

Australian Rules Football   See Football, Australian Rules.

Austria [AUT]   Austria competed at the first Olympics in 1896 and has missed only one Games since – those of 1920 when it was not invited as an aggressor nation in World War I. Austria has also competed at every Olympic Winter Games, where it has often been the dominant nation in Alpine skiing. It is one of only three countries (with Norway and Liechtenstein) to have won more medals at the Winter Olympics than at the Summer Olympics. Through 1994, Austrian athletes have won 128 medals (36 gold medals) at the Olympic Winter Games and 80 medals (18 gold medals) at the Summer Olympics. Austria has also twice hosted the Olympic Winter Games, those of 1964 and 1976.

Averof, Georgios. [GRE]   B. 15 August 1818, Metsovo, Greece. D. 15 July 1899, Alexandria, Egypt. A Greek merchant, resident in

Egypt, who acquired enormous wealth as a trader in Alexandria. Averof's donation of almost one million drachma for the excavation and rebuilding of the ancient Panathenaic stadium for the 1896 Games ensured that the first Modern Olympics were staged in an appropriate setting. A dedicated patriot, he had already given several schools and a military academy to the nation but as a man of a shy, retiring nature, he declined an invitation to be a guest at the Olympic Games that he had personally financed. His generosity was marked by the erection of a life–size statue which was unveiled shortly before the Games opened. His nephew was a member of the IOC from 1926 to 1930.

Azerbaijan [AZE]   As a former member of the Soviet Union, Azerbaijan has not yet competed independently at the Olympic Games, although Azerbaijani athletes were present at Barcelona in 1992 as members of the Unified Team (*q.v.*), and many Azerbaijani athletes competed from 1952 to 1988 for the Soviet Union.

********** B **********

Babashoff, Shirley Frances. [USA–SWI]   B. 31 January 1957, Whittier, California. Winner of a record eight Olympic medals, a total matched only among Olympic women swimmers by Kornelia Ender and Dawn Fraser (*qq.v.*). Her two gold medals both came in the 4x100 meter freestyle relay (1972, 1976) to which she added two silver medals in 1972 and four in 1976. She was the world champion at 200 meters and 400 meters in 1975 and set many world records in individual and relay events between 1974 and 1976.

Badminton   Badminton was invented in India. It was adopted by English soldiers there in the 19th century, who brought the game to Britain and eventually to many other countries. The game was originally called "Poona." The new sport took hold in England when it was exhibited there in 1873 at a party given by the Duke of Beaufort at his country estate, "Badminton" in Gloucestershire.
　　Badminton was contested as a demonstration sport at the 1972 Olympic Games in Munich. It made its debut as a full medal sport in 1992 at Barcelona. This is an unusual mode of entry into the Olympics. After 1972 it was not again a demonstration sport until its appearance at Barcelona on the medal program.
　　Badminton is governed by The International Badminton Federation (IBF), which was formed in 1934 and which had 122 members at the end of 1994.

Bahamas, The [BAH]   The Bahamas has competed at every Olympics from 1952 through 1976 and was again represented in 1984 through 1992. The Bahamas has never competed in the Olympic Winter Games. Bahamian athletes have won three medals. Its top sport has been yachting in which it has won two medals, one of them gold.

Bahrain [BRN]   The Bahrain Olympic Committee was organized in 1978 and recognizd by the IOC in 1979. Bahrain has competed at the Olympic Games of 1984, 1988, and 1992. The top finish by a Bahraini athlete was 14th in the 1992 men's hammer throw by Reyadh Rasheed Saad Al-Ameeri.

Baillet-Latour, Count Henri de. [BEL]   B. 1 March 1876, Antwerp. D. 6 January 1942, Brussels. Baillet-Latour was a Belgian aristocrat who proved himself to be an able administrator at an early age. Elected to the IOC in 1903 at the age of 27, he organized the Olympic Congress in Brussels two years later and, after playing a major role in securing the 1920 Games for Antwerp, he became President of the Belgian Olympic Committee in 1923, serving until 1942. He was named to the IOC Executive Board in 1921 and remained in that capacity until he took over as IOC President in 1925, following Coubertin's resignation. During his presidency, the IOC was concerned with the problems of the definition of an amateur and the program of the Olympic Games. Baillet-Latour remained President until his death in 1942.

Balczó, András. [HUN-MOP]   B. 16 August 1938, Kondoros. Balczó was the winner of a record six individual and seven team titles in the modern pentathlon at the World Championships. After placing fourth at the 1960 Olympics he won team gold and individual silver medals in 1968 and then, in 1972, he won the individual title and a silver medal in the team event for a total of six Olympic medals (three gold, three silver). Although the reigning world champion, he did not compete in the 1964 Games but his overall record is the greatest of any modern pentathlete.

Ballangrud, Ivar (né Ivar Eriksen). [NOR-SSK]   B. 7 March 1904, Lunner, Hadeland. D. 1 June 1969, Trondheim. His record of seven Olympic medals has only been matched by Clas Thunberg (FIN) (*q.v.*) among male speed skaters. In 1928, he won the 5,000 meters and, in 1936, he was the winner at 500 meters, 5,000 meters and 10,000 meters. He also won two silver medals (1932, 1936) and a bronze (1928). His record at the World Championships has never been approached; he won the 5,000 meters seven times, the 1,500 meters and 10,000 meters four times each and was a four-time winner of the overall title. He also set a total of five world records at 3,000 meters, 5,000 meters and 10,000 meters.

Bandy   Bandy was contested as a demonstration sport at the 1952 Olympic Winter Games. It is an outdoor form of ice hockey played on a large rink with 11 players to a side.

Bangladesh [BAN]   The Bangladesh Olympic Association was formed in 1979 and recognized by the IOC in 1980. Bangladesh did not compete in Moscow in 1980 but has been represented at the Olympics of 1984, 1988, and 1992. Bangladesh athletes have never competed at the Olympic Winter Games and the country has yet to win an Olympic medal.

Barbados [BAR]   The Barbados Olympic Association was formed in 1955, but, as an independent country, Barbados did not compete in the Olympics in 1968. Barbados has since competed at the Olympics of 1972, 1976, 1984, 1988, and 1992. It has not won a medal in those years. In 1960, Barbados competed with Jamaica and Trinidad representing the West Indies Federation. One of the Barbadan runners, James Wedderburn, ran with three Jamaicans as a member of the 4x400 meter relay team and helped win a bronze medal.

Baseball   Baseball is an American sport, the game having been invented in the early 19th century. Popular lore attributes its discovery to Abner Doubleday, but research indicates that it is unlikely he actually discovered the game. Its exact origins are unclear, although it is probably based somewhat on the British games of cricket and rounders.

American baseball has been contested at the Olympics as a demonstration sport in 1912, 1936, 1956, 1964, 1984, and 1988. In 1952, Finnish baseball was demonstrated at the Helsinki Olympics. American baseball became a full medal sport at Barcelona in 1992. The Americans no longer dominate this sport in international play, as the Cubans and several Central American countries produce excellent teams.

Internationally, baseball is governed by the International Baseball Association (IBA) which was founded in 1938 and has 89 members at the end of 1994.

Basketball   Basketball is one of the few sports for which the precise
origin is known.   The game was invented in 1891 by James W.
Naismith, an instructor at the International Y.M.C.A. Training
School in Springfield, Massachusetts, now Springfield College.   The
game was originally played with peach baskets and an attendant on a
ladder retrieved the ball after a made basket.   Naismith formulated 13
rules of the game, of which 12 still form the basics of the modern
game.
    In 1936, basketball made its first appearance as a medal sport
at the Olympics.   In 1976, women's basketball was added to the
program.   The United States has dominated international basketball
until recently.   The U.S. won all the Olympic titles until 1972 when it
was upset by the Soviet Union in a very controversial game.   It has
since won the 1976 and 1984 championships but was defeated again in
1988 at Seoul.   The Soviet women were originally the top team on the
female side, but the U.S. women now have surpassed them.
    Today, basketball has become one of the most popular sports
in the world.   U.S. college basketball is wildly popular in the United
States and the NBA has engendered international interest.   In
addition, multiple international leagues have added to the growth of
the sport.   In 1992, for the first time, the United States was allowed
to use professional players from the NBA.   This NBA All-Star Team,
dubbed the "Dream Team" (*q.v.*) by the world's media, is certainly
the greatest basketball team ever assembled and dominated the 1992
Olympic tournament.   The sport is governed world-wide by the
Fédération Internationale de Basketball Amateur (FIBA).   As a
measure of its popularity, FIBA had 198 member nations at the end of
1994.   (See Dream Team, The - 1992 USA Basketball; United States
Basketball Team - 1960; and United States Basketball Team - 1984)

Baszanowski, Waldemar.   [POL-WLT]   B. 15 August 1935,
Grudziądz.   Never weighing more than 70 kg., Baszanowski was one
of the greatest lifters ever pound-for-pound.   He won gold medals in
both 1964 and 1968 at the Olympics in the lightweight class and was
also World Champion in 1961 and 1964.   Baszanowski was a great
technician who did very well in the quick lifts of snatch and clean &
jerk, and was the first man to clean & jerk two-and-one-half times his
bodyweight.   He set 24 world records, capped by his greatest day, 26
June 1964, when he broke the world overall record three times in the
same competition.

Beach Volleyball   See Volleyball.

Beamon, Robert "Bob."   [USA-ATH]   B. 29 August 1936,
Jamaica, New York.   With a single performance, lasting no more than

a few seconds, Bob Beamon achieved sporting immortality at Mexico City in October 1968. His long jump of 8.90 meters (29' 2½") gave him the Olympic gold medal and a new world record by a massive margin. Rated by many as the greatest performance in track & field history his record was thought to be unbeatable but like all records it was inevitably surpassed and, in 1991, the record fell to Mike Powell (USA). Beamon never again approached the form he showed at the 1968 Olympics and he turned professional in 1972.

Bechuanaland.   See Botswana.

Belarus [BLR]   The National Olympic Committee of the Republic of Belarus was formed in 1991 after the break-up of the Soviet Union. Many Belarus (formerly Belorussia, or Byelorussia [White Russia]) athletes competed from 1952 to 1988 for the Soviet Union, and Belarus athletes were present at both Albertville and Barcelona in 1992 as members of the Unified Team (*q.v.*). Belarus competed as an independent for the first time at the 1994 Olympic Winter Games in Lillehammer, with 33 athletes who won two medals. Belarus has never hosted an Olympic Games, but in 1980, several preliminary football (soccer) matches were held in Minsk, the capital of Belarus.

Belgium [BEL]   Belgium has competed at every Olympic Games, with the exception of 1896 and 1904. Belgium began competing at the Olympic Winter Games in 1924, and also competed in figure skating and ice hockey in 1920, but the country missed the 1960 and 1968 Olympic Winter Games. Belgium has won 129 medals (35 gold medals) in the Olympic Games, four medals in the Olympic Winter Games, and eight medals in the now defunct Art Contests (*q.v.*) which were formerly held during the Games of the Olympiads. Belgium also hosted the Games of the VIIth Olympiad at Antwerp in 1920.

Belize [BIZ]   As British Honduras, this country formed a National Olympic Committee in 1967 and made three Olympic appearances in 1968, 1972, and 1976. As Belize it has been represented at the Olympics of 1984, 1988, and 1992. Belize has never competed at the Olympic Winter Games and has never won an Olympic medal. The best finish by this nation occurred in 1968 when Robert Hulse, a shooter representing British Honduras, finished 63rd of 86 competitors in the small-bore rifle, English match (prone).

Belousova, Lyudmila (later Protopopov). [URS-FSK]   B. 22 November 1935, Ulyanovsk. Partnering her husband, Oleg

Protopopov (*q.v.*), she won the Olympic pair skating title in 1964 and 1968. As the first Russian pair skaters to achieve international acclaim they provided the stimulus which ultimately led to many successes by future generations. They began skating as a pair shortly before 1957 and were married that year. In addition to their two Olympic gold medals they were World Champions four times (1965–1968). After losing their world title in 1969 they turned professional and later settled in Switzerland.

Belov, Sergey Aleksandrovich. [URS–BAS]   B. 23 January 1944, Nashchekova, Tomsk Oblast. Sergey Belov played guard for the Soviet national basketball team from 1967 until 1980. He won four Olympic medals, bronzes in 1968, 1972, and 1980, and a gold medal in 1972. In addition, Belov played on teams which won the World Championships in 1967 and 1974 and European Championships in 1967, 1969, 1971, and 1979.

Benin [BEN]   Benin was originally part of French West Africa, but became independent from France under the name Dahomey in 1960. Dahomey competed in the 1972 Olympics at Munich. The name was changed to Benin in 1975 and Benin has competed at the Olympics of 1980, 1984, 1988, and 1992. Benin has never competed in the Olympic Winter Games and has not yet won an Olympic medal. Benin's best Olympic performance came in 1980 when featherweight boxer Barthelemy Adoukonou received a first–round bye, won one match, and then lost in the third round to place equal ninth of 35 boxers.

Beresford, Jack, Jr. [GBR–ROW]   B. 1 January 1899, Chiswick, Middlesex. D. 3 December 1977, Shiplake-on-Thames, Oxfordshire. With five medals he was the most successful Olympic oarsman of all time. To his gold medals in the single sculls (1924), coxless fours (1932) and double sculls (1936), he added silver in the single sculls (1920) and the eights (1928). His remarkable career spanned five Olympic Games and it was almost certainly only the cancellation of the 1940 Games that prevented a sixth Olympic appearance. He was awarded the Olympic Diploma of Merit in 1949. At Henley, he won the Diamond Sculls four times (1920 and 1924–1926), the Nickalls Challenge Cup in 1928 and 1929 (coxless pairs with Gordon Killick), and the Double Sculls Challenge Cup in 1939 with Dick Southwood. He also won the Wingfield Sculls for seven consecutive years from 1920. His father, Julius Beresford (né Wisniewski), won an Olympic silver medal in the eights in 1912.

Bermuda [BER]   Bermuda has competed at the Olympics since 1936, failing to appear only in 1980. It has competed at the Olympic Winter Games of 1992 and 1994. Bermuda's athletes have won one medal, a bronze medal in boxing in 1976 by Clarence Hill.

Bhutan [BHU]   Recognized by the IOC in 1983, Bhutan has competed at the Olympics of 1984, 1988, and 1992. It has won no medals and has not yet competed at the Olympic Winter Games. Bhutan's athletes have thus far competed only in archery, its national sport. In 1984, Doriji Thieley finished 53rd of 62 archers in the men's individual event, the best finish by a Bhutanese athlete.

Biathlon   Attempts to introduce a winter multi–event, patterned after the modern pentathlon, began in 1948, when the winter pentathlon was contested at the St. Moritz Olympics as a demonstration sport. It consisted of cross–country and downhill skiing, and also shooting, fencing, and horse riding. Biathlon, which consists of cross–country skiing in which the runner stops at intervals to shoot a rifle at a target, was known in the 1920's but was not popular until the 1950's. The first World Championships were held in 1958 at Saalfelden, Austria. The sport quickly was placed on the Olympic program, showing up at Squaw Valley in 1960. Women's biathlon made its Olympic debut in 1992 as a full medal sport at Albertville.
    Biathlon is currently governed by the Union Internationale de Pentathlon Moderne et Biathlon (UIPMB), which oversees both biathlon and the modern pentathlon. There are currently 94 member nations in the UIPMB, which was formed in 1948.
    Biathlon events have consisted of a single men's race and a men's relay until 1980 when a second individual event was contested. The event is scored by time. In the longer individual race a one–minute penalty is assessed for a missed shooting bulls–eye, and a two–minute penalty is assessed for missing a target. In the shorter individual race and the relay, missing a target is penalized by requiring the skier to ski a 150 meter penalty loop. Women currently also compete in the Olympics in both a short (7.5 km.) and a long (15 km.) individual race, and a relay race.

Bicycle Polo   First played in Ireland in 1891, the game's growing popularity led to a demonstration match between Ireland and Germany being included in the program at the 1908 Olympic Games. Although the sport has been included in the Asian Games, the chances of it becoming an Olympic sport appear to be very remote.

Biondi, Matthew Nicholas. [USA-SWI]   B. 8 October 1965, Moraga, California. His total of 11 Olympic medals for swimming matched the record of Mark Spitz (*q.v.*). He was at his best at the 1988 Games winning seven medals (five gold, one silver, one bronze) and, although essentially a freestyle swimmer, he won his silver medal in the 100 meters butterfly. He set seven individual world records and won six gold medals at the World Championships (1986, 1991).

Blair, Bonnie Kathleen. [USA-SSK]   B. 18 March 1964, Cornwall, New York. With victories in the 500 meters in 1988, 1992 and 1994 she is the only woman to have won an Olympic speed skating event at three successive Games. She also won the 1,000 meters in 1992 and 1994 after taking the bronze in 1988, and her total of five gold medals has only been bettered by the Russian Lidiya Skoblikova (*q.v.*). She has won four World Championships, those being the World Short-Track Championships in 1986, and the World Sprints in 1989 (at which meet she set the current world record of 159.435 points for the sprint all-around), 1994, and 1995. She has set four world records in the 500 meters.

Blankers-Koen, Francina Elsje "Fanny" (née Koen). [NED-ATH]   B. 26 April 1918, Baarn. An outstanding all around athlete who made her Olympic debut as a high jumper in 1936. World War II deprived her of the opportunity of making further Olympic appearances until 1948 when, at the age of 30 and the mother of two, she was the star of the London Games. She won the 100 meters, 200 meters, 80 meters hurdles and ran the anchor leg on the winning relay team. She set world records at eight different events, won five European titles (1946-1950) and a statue was erected in her honor in her native Amsterdam. She married her coach, the Dutch Olympic triple jumper (1928), Jan Blankers.

Bleibtrey, Ethelda (later MacRobert, then Schlafke). [USA-SWI]. B. 27 February 1902, Waterford, New York. D. 6 May 1978, Atlantis, Florida. The first American female swimmer of international renown and the first female star of the Olympic pool. At the 1920 Games she won a gold medal in each of the three swimming events for women - 100 meters and 300 meters freestyle and relay - and would almost certainly have won a fourth had a backstroke event been included as she was, at the time, a world record holder in this style. She set seven world records before turning professional in 1922 after which she became a swimming instructor.

Blonay, Baron Godefroy de. [SUI]   B. 25 July 1869. D. 14 February 1937, Biskra, Algeria.   Blonay was appointed as the first Swiss IOC Member in 1899 and remained a member until his death in 1937.   He was a founder of the Swiss Olympic Committee in 1912 and was its first President (1912–1915).   During the latter part of World War I he served as provisional IOC President (1916–1919) when Coubertin (*q.v.*), who had enlisted in the French army, felt that it would not be appropriate for a military man to serve as head of the IOC.   After Coubertin was discharged from the military because of his age, Blonay relinquished his presidential duties and Coubertin again took over the presidency.   Blonay was a member of the IOC Executive Board from 1921 to 1937, and was President of the Executive Board from 1921 to 1925.   He then was Vice-President of the IOC from 1925 until his death in 1937.   Although Blonay was a close friend of Coubertin, when he attempted, as President of the Executive Board, to obtain certain administrative functions for this group, severe tensions developed between them.   A distinguished Egyptologist, Blonay lived in Paris for many years but eventually settled in Switzerland where he taught at the University of Neuchâtel.

Bobsledding   Bobsledding as a sport originated in Switzerland in 1888 when an Englishman, Wilson Smith, connected two sleighs with a board to travel from St. Moritz to Celerina.   Bobsledding was first practiced on the Cresta Run at St. Moritz but the run was not suitable for the faster bobsleds so a separate bob run was constructed there in 1904, the world's first.

Bobsledding was on the program of the first Olympic Winter Games in 1924 with a single four-man event.   In 1928, the event was one for sleds with either four or five men.   In 1932, the present program of two events, one for two-man sleds, and one for four-man sleds, began.   Bobsledding has been contested at all Olympic Winter Games except in 1960 at Squaw Valley.   Because of the distance to travel to California, only nine countries indicated that they would enter bobsled teams.   The Squaw Valley organizers thus decided not to build a bob run and the sport was not held that year.

Bobsledding has been dominated by the Swiss, the Italians, and, until 1992, the German Democratic Republic.   The sport is governed by the Fédération Internationale de Bobsleigh et de Tobogganing (FIBT), which was founded in 1923 and had 48 members at the end of 1994.

Bohemia [BOH]   Prior to becoming the largest province of Czechoslovakia in 1918, Bohemia appeared at the Olympics of 1900, 1906, 1908, and 1912.   In those Olympics, Bohemian athletes won six Olympic medals.

Bolivia [BOL] Bolivia formed a National Olympic Committee in 1932 and had a single swimmer at the 1936 Olympics in Berlin, but the nation did not compete at the Olympics again until 1964. It has since competed continuously with the exception of Moscow in 1980. Bolivian athletes have not yet won an Olympic medal. Bolivia has also competed five times at the Olympic Winter Games, sending Alpine skiers in 1956, 1980, 1984, 1988, and 1992. The best Bolivian performance occurred in 1972 when Roberto Nielsen-Reyes finished equal 22nd in the individual show jumping event.

Bosnia-Herzegovina [BIH, formerly BSH] Until 1992, Bosnia-Herzegovina was a republic in the state of Yugoslavia. In that year, Bosnia-Herzegovina, along with several other Yugoslav republics, declared its independence, but unfortunately, the Serbians declared war on the republic. Still, Bosnia-Herzegovina quickly formed a National Olympic Committee and, on the eve of the 1992 Olympics, was granted provisional recognition by the IOC and competed at Barcelona. Despite the civil war in the country, Bosnia-Herzegovina also valiantly sent competitors to the 1994 Olympic Winter Games in Lillehammer. The 14th Olympic Winter Games were held in Sarajevo in 1984 in what was then part of Yugoslavia, but Sarajevo is presently the capital city of Bosnia-Herzegovina.

Botswana [BOT] Botswana formed an Olympic Committee in 1978 and has competed at the 1980, 1984, 1988, and 1992 Olympic Games. Formerly called Bechuanaland, the country never made an Olympic appearance under that name. Botswanan athletes have yet to win an Olympic medal and the country has not yet competed at the Olympic Winter Games.

Bowling Ten-pin bowling (as opposed to lawn bowling or bowls [*q.v.*]) was a demonstration sport in Seoul at the 1988 Olympic Games. Its governing body, the Fédération Internationale de Quilleurs, is currently one of the IOC-recognized international federations.

Bowls Bowls has never been contested at the Olympic Games, even as a demonstration sport, but the Confédération Mondiale Sports Boules is currently one of the IOC-recognized international federations.

Boxing   Boxing was contested at the Ancient Olympic Games (*q.v.*) and many other sporting festivals in Ancient Greece. Boxing was a particularly brutal sport in Ancient Greece. The combatants wore leather thongs on their hands. Originally the thongs were simple straps of leather but later they were reinforced with sharp pieces of metal, and the glove was called a *cestus*. The first known Ancient Olympic boxing champion was Onomastos of Smyrna, who won in 688 B.C. The last known was Varasdates of Armenia, in 369 A.D., who is also the last known champion of the Ancient Olympic Games. Professional boxing has been around since the early 18th century, with a recognized list of professional champions dating from the late 1700's.

Boxing made its first Olympic appearance in 1904 at St. Louis. All the entrants were Americans and the event doubled as the AAU Championships for that year. Boxing was again contested at the 1908 Olympics in London. In 1912, boxing could not be on the Olympic program because boxing was illegal in Sweden at that time. Since 1920, boxing has been on the program of every Olympic Games.

The United States has traditionally been the premier nation in Olympic boxing. However, it has been surpassed in the last 20 years by first the Soviet Union and, more recently, Cuba. Two boxers have won three Olympic gold medals, László Papp of Hungary and Teófilo Stevenson of Cuba. A number of Olympic boxers have gone on to become professional World Champions, notably Cassius Clay (Muhammad Ali), George Foreman, Joe Frazier, and Sugar Ray Leonard (*qq.v.*).

Amateur boxing is governed by the Association Internationale de Boxe Amateur (AIBA), which has 182 member nations and was founded in 1946.

Boyarskikh, Klavdiya. [URS–NSK]   B. 11 November 1939, Verkhnyaya Pyshma, Sverdlovsk. To three gold medals (5 km., 10 km., and relay) at the 1964 Olympics she added two further golds at the 1966 World Championships to establish herself as the world's leading cross-country skier of the 1960's.

Boycotts and Politics   The Olympic Games have rarely been without the influence of politics since they became a major international event. The first significant intrusion of politics occurred in 1936 (see The Games of the XIth Olympiad) when several nations considered boycotting the Berlin Olympics to protest the policies of Germany's Adolf Hitler.

Minimal political intrusions occurred in 1948 and 1952. In 1956, however, a small boycott ensued because of the recent incursion of Soviet troops into Hungary, and because of an Egyptian–Israeli dispute over the Sinai peninsula. (See The Games of the XVIth Olympiad)

The Rome Olympics in 1960 were once again free of significant political conflicts. In 1964, a dispute arose concerning the eligibility of certain nations which had competed at the Games of the New Emerging Forces (GANEFO) in 1963. (See The Games of the XVIIIth Olympiad)

In 1968, the Mexican government faced numerous student protests over the presence of the Olympic Games in the Mexican capital despite the poverty and hunger of many of its citizens. As the protest movement gathered momentum leading up to the Games, the Mexican army took charge on the night of 2 October. As 10,000 people demonstrated in the Square of the Three Cultures in Mexico City, the army surrounded the crowd and opened fire. More than 250 people were killed and thousands were injured or imprisoned. (See The Games of the XIXth Olympiad)

The worst intrusion of politics into the Olympics occurred in 1972 when Arab terrorists representing the Black September movement entered the Olympic village and took as hostage 11 Israeli competitors and coaches. The hostages were all eventually murdered. (See The Games of the XXth Olympiad)

Shortly before the 1976 Olympics were due to start, they were marred by a boycott of 22 African countries, Guyana, and Chinese Taipei (then Taiwan). This was in protest of a recent tour of South Africa by the New Zealand national rugby team. As South Africa was ostracized from international sporting competition, the African nations demanded New Zealand not be allowed to compete at Montreal. However, as the IOC had no control of international rugby, New Zealand was properly allowed to start in the Olympics.

The Taiwan boycott occurred when the Canadian government did not allow its team to enter the country, as it did not recognize the island nation, in violation of its agreement as host country to admit all eligible nations in honoring the Olympic Charter. The Canadians eventually acquiesced and gave permission for the Taiwanese to compete, but refused to allow them to do so as the Republic of China, its official national name and the name by which it was then recognized by the IOC. Several other countries protested and threatened withdrawal, notably the United States. However, these protests were short-lived and the IOC finally gave in to the Canadian government. Taiwan withdrew and did not compete. (See The Games of the XXIst Olympiad)

The largest-scale Olympic boycott occurred in 1980. The Games were held in Moscow in July 1980. In December 1979, Soviet troops entered Afghanistan. The United States led a vocal protest and eventually boycotted the 1980 Olympic Games. It was joined by approximately 60 other nations who also boycotted. (See The Games of the XXIInd Olympiad)

In 1984, the Soviet Union exacted its revenge on the United States when it boycotted the Los Angeles Olympic Games. This was officially because of concerns over security and the safety of its athletes, but there was little doubt as to the reason. The Soviet Union boycott was joined, quite naturally, by other members of the Soviet bloc, including Eastern Europe and Cuba. Only Romania, among Soviet-bloc nations, defied the Soviet-led boycott. (See Games of the XXIIIrd Olympiad)

The IOC awarded the 1988 Olympics to Seoul. This was a highly controversial decision as many prominent nations in the Olympic Movement did not have diplomatic relations with the Seoul government. The problem became more complicated in 1985 when North Korea demanded that it be allowed to co-host the Games with the Republic of Korea. Over the next three years the IOC negotiated with North Korea and offered to allow it to stage several events. When the IOC would not concede further to the North's demands, North Korea announced that it would definitely boycott the Seoul Olympics.

By then, however, most of the Soviet-bloc countries had agreed to compete in Seoul, making 1988 the first Summer Olympic competition in 12 years between the United States, the Soviet Union and the German Democratic Republic. After North Korea's official boycott announcement, Cuba and Ethiopia also announced that they would boycott the Olympics. Nicaragua, Albania, and the Seychelles also did not attend the Olympics, although their reasons may not have been directly related to any boycott. (See The Games of the XXIVth Olympiad)

In 1992, the Olympics were held in Barcelona. These Games were remarkably free of political protest and intrusions. They were the first Olympic Games since 1968 which saw no form of boycott.

In addition to boycotts of the Olympic Games, political problems have haunted the IOC since the end of World War II. This has mostly been in terms of the official recognition of certain nations. In many cases, the nations have not been on good political terms with other IOC members, and these IOC members have protested their official recognition.

In particular, the IOC has dealt with the problems of the "two" Germanys (see Germany and the German Democratic Republic); the "two" Chinas (see China and Chinese Taipei); the "two" Koreas (see Korea, Democratic People's Republic of, and Korea, Republic of); and the question of recognition of South Africa (see South Africa) despite its apartheid policies. Similar problems existed in the later 1960's and early 1970's concerning Rhodesia (see Zimbabwe).

Brazil [BRA]   Brazil has competed at every Olympics since 1920, with the sole exception of 1928. It has competed at the Olympic

Winter Games in 1992 and 1994. Brazil's successes have come in a variety of sports. It has won medals in several different sports, and has always had one of the top basketball and football (soccer) teams. Brazilian athletes have won 39 Olympic medals, nine of them gold medals. Among South American countries, this places Brazil behind only Argentina in terms of Olympic medals won.

British Virgin Islands [IVB]   The British Virgin Islands has been represented at three Olympic Games, those of 1984, 1988, and 1992. In addition, Errolls Fraser competed in speed skating in 1984, representing the British Virgin Islands at Sarajevo. Its best Olympic performance came in 1988 when Matthew Arneborg finished 29th in boardsailing among 45 sailors.

Brookes, William Penny. [GBR]   B. 1809, Much Wenlock, England. D. 10 December 1895, Much Wenlock, England. William Penny Brookes was the founder of the Much Wenlock Olympian Games (*q.v.*), an early influence on the thinking of Coubertin (*q.v.*) towards the revival of the Olympics. Brookes was a doctor who was educated at various schools in Shropshire. He began his study of medicine at Guy's and St. Thomas's Hospitals in London in about 1827. He finished his studies in Paris and Padua, returning to Much Wenlock in 1831 to carry on the general practice of medicine which his father had started. He founded the National Olympian Association in 1865, the forerunner of the British Olympic Association. He was active in public affairs, serving as Justice of the Peace and Commissioner for Roads for the borough of Wenlock, and forming in 1841 the Wenlock Agricultural Reading Society. He eventually became a Licentiate of the Society of Apothecaries and, in 1881, a Fellow of the Royal College of Surgeons.

Brookes was an invited dignitary to Coubertin's Sorbonne Congress of 1894 which founded the Modern Olympic Games, but was unable to attend because of illness. He and Coubertin corresponded frequently and Brookes had Coubertin visit the Much Wenlock Olympian Games in October 1890. In 1881, Brookes was the first person who proposed that international Olympian Games be staged again, to be held in Athens. (See also Much Wenlock Olympian Games)

Brundage, Avery. [USA]   B. 28 September 1887, Detroit, Michigan. D. 7 May 1975, Garmisch-Partenkirchen, Germany. Brundage was an American who served as President of the IOC from 1952 to 1972, the longest reign ever aside from Coubertin (*q.v.*). As a participant in the track & field events in 1912 (decathlon and pentathlon), he is the only IOC President to have actually competed in the Olympics. Having made a fortune in the construction business, he enjoyed the financial freedom to devote his time to the administrative side of sport. He served seven terms as President of the Amateur Athletic Union (AAU), was President of the U.S. Olympic Committee for 25 years, and, after becoming a member of the IOC in 1936, he was elected to the Executive Board in 1937, and as IOC Vice–President in 1946 before becoming President six years later. His dedication to amateurism bordered on the fanatical and anachronistic, but he gradually lost his life–long battle to the rising tide of commercialism in sport. Although never terribly popular, and undoubtedly the most controversial IOC President ever, he traveled constantly in the cause of Olympism (*q.v.*) and did much to widen the international scope of the Olympic Movement (*q.v.*).

Brunei [BRU]   The Brunei National Olympic Council was formed in 1984 and recognized by the IOC in that year. Brunei has yet to compete at the Olympic Games, although it sent one official as an observer to both Seoul (1988) and Barcelona (1992).

Budo   *Budo* is a general term referring to the many different forms of Japanese martial arts. In 1964, the Japanese gave exhibitions of Japanese archery (*kyudo*), fencing (*kendo*), and wrestling (*sumo*) at the Tokyo Olympics.

Bularda–Homeghi, Olga (née Homeghi). [ROM–ROW]   B. 1 May 1958. Olga Bularda has won four medals in Olympic rowing, an equal number to that of fellow Romanian, Rodica Arba–Puşcatu (*q.v.*). As Olga Homeghi, her first medal was a bronze in the 1980 double sculls. She then began teaming with Arba–Puşcatu. In 1984, they won Olympic gold in the coxless pairs and they were World Champions in that event in 1985–1987. At Seoul in 1988, Bularda–Homeghi and Arba–Puşcatu won their fifth straight international championships in coxless pairs when they took their second Olympic gold medal. Olga Bularda–Homeghi also rowed with the Romanian eight which won a silver medal at Seoul.

Bulgaria [BUL]   Bulgaria first competed at the Olympic Games in 1924, and it has since missed only the Olympic Games of 1932, 1948, and 1984. Its first appearance in the Olympic Winter Games was in 1936 and it has competed at all celebrations since. Bulgaria has had its greatest successes in strength sports, mainly weightlifting and wrestling, and in the 1980's it was the premier nation in the world in weightlifting. Bulgarian athletes have won 168 Olympic medals, 40 of them gold.

Burghley, Lord; David George Brownlow Cecil, later the Sixth Marquess of Exeter. [GBR]   B. 9 February 1905, Stamford, Lincolnshire. D. 22 October 1981, Stamford, Lincolnshire. The Olympic 400 meters hurdles champion in 1928 and later a distinguished administrator. In 1933, at the age of 28, he was elected a member of the IOC and three years later he became Chairman of the British Olympic Association and President of the British Amateur Athletic Association. In 1946, he took over from Sigfrid Edström (*q.v.*) as President of the International Amateur Athletic Federation and was Chairman of the Organizing Committee for the 1948 Olympic Games. He failed in a bid for the IOC presidency in 1952, but from 1952 to 1966 he served as Vice-President.

Burkina Faso [BUR]   Burkina Faso sent a single competitor to the 1972 Olympics, representing Upper Volta. Taka Gangua and Taki N'Dio competed in the javelin throw in 1924 for France, but were nationals of Upper Volta. The country changed its name to Burkina Faso in 1984, and as Burkina Faso, its first Olympic participation occurred in 1988 at Seoul and it also competed in 1992. The best Olympic performance by a Burkina Fasan athlete was by Sounailla Sagnon in 1988 light-middleweight boxing, in which he finished equal ninth of 37 athletes.

Burma [BIR]   See Myanmar.

Burundi [BDI]   Burundi's National Olympic Committee was given official recognition by the IOC in September 1993, but the country has not yet competed at the Olympic Games.

Button, Richard Totten "Dick." [USA-FSK]   B. 18 July 1929, Englewood, New Jersey. Button was noted for bringing a new dimension of athleticism to figure skating. Between 1943 and 1952, he was only defeated twice and his many victories included the Olympics of 1948 and 1952 and he was the World Champion for five consecutive years (1948-1952). A Harvard-educated lawyer, he later became an award-winning television commentator and sports-event producer.

********** C **********

Cambodia [CAM]   Cambodia made its first Olympic appearance at the Equestrian Olympic Games of 1956 in Stockholm, although it did not compete at the Melbourne Olympics that year. It again participated in 1964 and 1972 but has not competed since. It has yet to win a medal. Briefly known as Kampuchea, the country has retaken the name Cambodia. Its current government does not have a recognized Olympic Committee. Cambodia has never competed at the Olympic Winter Games and the nation has won no Olympic medals.

Cameroon [CMR]   Cameroon made its Olympic debut in 1964 at Tokyo and has appeared at all Games since. It has not yet attended the Olympic Winter Games. Cameroon athletes have won two Olympic medals, both in boxing.

Canada [CAN]   Canada first appeared officially at the 1904 Olympic Games in St. Louis. However, in 1900, two Canadian citizens competed, both under U.S. colors. Since 1900, Canada has failed to be represented only at the 1980 Moscow Olympic Games. It has appeared at every Olympic Winter Games since their inception in 1924, and, in addition, its ice hockey team competed in the 1920 hockey tournament, winning decisively. This began a trend which continued until the Soviet Union entered the Olympic ice hockey tournaments, starting in 1956. Canada has won 258 Olympic medals (64 gold), 194 of them at the Olympic Games and 64 at the Olympic Winter Games. Canada has also hosted the Games of the XXIst Olympiad at Montreal in 1976, and the 15th Olympic Winter Games at Calgary in 1988.

Canadian Ice Hockey Teams [1920–1952]   Canada dominated ice hockey at the Olympics from 1920 through 1952, winning all the Olympic tournaments during that time with the exception of the 1936 Olympic Winter Games, when it was upset by a British team which contained a number of Canadians who held dual British citizenship. Canada was always represented by a club team during their ice hockey reign. The teams were as follows: 1920 – Winnipeg Falcons; 1924 – Toronto Granites (with the addition of two players from the Winnipeg Falcons and Montreal Victorias); 1928 – Toronto Varsity Graduate Team; 1932 – The Winnipegs (with the addition of two players from the Selkirk Fisherman); 1936 – Port Arthur Bearcats (with the addition of several players from the Montreal Victorias); 1948 – Royal Canadian Air Force Flyers; and 1952 – Edmonton Mercurys.

During this era of dominance, the Canadians posted a record of 35 wins, one loss, and three ties in Olympic competition. The loss was to Great Britain, 2–1, in 1936. The ties were in 1932 to the United States (2–2), in 1948 to Czechoslovakia (0–0), and in 1952 to the United States (3–3). In 1956, the Soviet Union entered the ice hockey tournament at the Olympic Winter Games and began its own period of dominance. (See Soviet Union Ice Hockey Teams [1956–1992])

Canoe & Kayaking   Many years ago, canoeing began as a means of transportation. Competition in canoes began in the mid–19th century. The Royal Canoe Club of London was formed in 1866 and was the first organization interested in developing the sport. In 1871, the New York Canoe Club was founded. Today competition is contested in either Canadian style canoes, similar to the dugout Indian style canoe, or kayaks, an enclosed shell surrounding the canoeist.

It is possible that canoeing first appeared in the Olympics at the Intercalated Games of 1906. The event usually listed as "single sculls" in rowing has recently been discovered to be listed in the official results as a canoe event. No other information exists concerning this and we have included the event's results with rowing, as is usually done.

In 1924, canoeing was on the Olympic program as a demonstration sport. Canoeing became a full medal sport in 1936 with both canoe and kayak events. The program has varied a great deal over the years with many events now discontinued and several new ones added. Women began Olympic canoeing, competing only in kayaks, in 1948. Whitewater canoeing, or slalom canoeing, has been held only at the 1972 Olympics in Munich and the 1992 Olympics in Barcelona, but is scheduled for the 1996 Olympics as well, and appears well established on the Olympic program.

Canoeing is governed world-wide by the Fédération Internationale de Canoë (FIC), which was founded in 1924 and had 86 member nations at the end of 1994. The top medal winners in Olympic canoeing history have been Sweden's Gert Fredriksson (*q.v.*) with eight (six gold), and Romania's Ivan Patzaichin with seven. Among women, Germany's Birgit Schmidt-Fischer (*q.v.*) has won six medals (four gold), and Sweden's Agneta Andersson has won five Olympic medals.

Cape Verde [CPV]   Cape Verde's Olympic Committee was formed in 1989 and given official recognition by the IOC in September 1993, but the country has not yet competed at the Olympic Games.

Čáslavská, Věra. [TCH–GYM]   B. 3 May 1942, Prague.
Attractive, vivacious and talented, Čáslavská was the outstanding
gymnast at the 1964 and 1968 Games. In Tokyo she won three gold
medals and a silver, and in Mexico she won four golds (one shared)
and two silvers. Having earlier won a silver medal in 1960 her total
of 11 Olympic medals has only ever been bettered by Larisa Latynina
(URS) (*q.v.*) among female gymnasts. After winning her final gold
medal in 1968 she married Czech Olympic silver medalist (1,500
meters in 1964) Josef Odložil (1938–1993), in Mexico. In 1989, she
was appointed President of the Czech Olympic Committee. In 1995
she was elected as a member of the International Olympic Committee
(*q.v.*).

Cayman Islands [CAY]   The Cayman Islands Olympic Committee
was formed in 1973 and was recognized by the IOC in 1976. The
Cayman Islands has been represented at the Olympic Games of 1976,
1984, 1988, and 1992. Its best Olympic performance was by
Michelle Bush in the 1988 women's marathon, when she finished
52nd of 69 runners. It has not yet competed at the Olympic Winter
Games.

Central African Republic [CAF]   The Central African Republic
first competed at the 1968 Olympic Games. It has since appeared at
the 1984, 1988, and 1992 Olympics as well. Its best finish occurred
in 1988 when Fidele Mohinga, a welterweight boxer, won one match
to place equal 17th of 44 competitors in the class. Central Africa has
not yet competed at the Olympic Winter Games.

Ceylon [CEY]   See Sri Lanka.

Chad [CHA]   Chad first competed at the Olympic Games of 1964.
It has since appeared at the Olympic Games of 1968, 1972, 1984,
1988, and 1992. Chad has not yet competed at the Olympic Winter
Games and has never won an Olympic medal. Chad's best finish at
the Olympics occurred in the high jump in 1964 track & field
athletics, when Mahamat Idriss finished ninth.

Chand, Dhyan. [IND–HOK]   See Dhyan Chand.

Chariot Races – Ancient Olympic Sport   Multiple chariot races
were contested at the Ancient Olympic Games (*q.v.*). These include

the apene (*q.v.*), the synoris (*q.v.*), a foals' synoris race, the tethrippon (*q.v.*), a foals' tethrippon, a chariot race for foals, a chariot race for 10 horses, and an event listed simply as chariot race. The last three were contested only in 65 A.D.

Charpentier, Robert. **[FRA–CYC]** B. 4 April 1916, Paris. D. 28 October 1966. Winner of the individual road race at the 1936 Games when he also won gold medals in the road race team event and the 4,000 meter team pursuit. Charpentier got started in cycling when he was an apprentice to a butcher and made his deliveries on his bicycle. He was runner–up at the 1935 amateur world championship road race. World War II prevented him from having any success after the 1936 Olympics as a professional.

Chile [CHI] In 1896, Luis Subercaseaux ran in a heat of the 100 meters, making Chile one of the 14 countries which was represented at the first Olympic Games. It did not appear again until 1912. Since that time, however, it has missed only the Games of 1932 and 1980. Chile first competed at the Olympic Winter Games of 1948 and since has competed 11 times in the winter celebrations, missing only 1972 and 1980. Chilean athletes have won eight Olympic medals, six silver and two bronze. Chile formed its National Olympic Committee in 1934 and was recognized by the IOC in the same year.

China, People's Republic of [CHN] Although the current NOC was recognized by the IOC in 1979, the first Chinese Olympic Committee was formed in 1910 and recognized in 1922. China competed at the Olympic Games of 1932, 1936, and 1948. In September 1949, Chinese Communists assumed control of the government, and many of the former rulers escaped to the island province of Taiwan, including many former members of the Chinese Olympic Committee (possibly as many as 19 of 26). Athletes from the Chinese mainland did compete at the 1952 Olympic Games in Helsinki. Thus began a 40–year political problem for the IOC: the question of the "two Chinas."

In May 1954, at the 50th IOC Session in Athens, the IOC voted by 23–21 to recognize both the Chinese Olympic Committee in Beijing (then Peking) (as the "Olympic Committee of the Chinese Republic," later [in 1957] as the "Olympic Committee of the People's Democratic Republic of China") and in Taipei (as the "Chinese Olympic Committee").

Both Chinas were invited to the 1956 Olympics in Melbourne. Beijing accepted the invitation on 20 November, which led Taipei to reject the invitation. However, Taipei changed its decision and elected to compete, which caused Beijing to withdraw in protest. At Melbourne, no athletes from mainland China competed, while 21 athletes from the island nation competed under the banner of the Republic of China. The Beijing committee withdrew from the IOC on 19 August 1958, in protest of the IOC's continued recognition of Taiwan.

A request to be recognized again was submitted in 1975. The IOC requested the All-China Sports Federation to send its rules for inspection, a standard procedure. The All-China Sports Federation took two years to comply, but its application was eventually approved on 25 November 1979.

In the interim, the IOC sent a three-member contingent, led by New Zealander Lance Cross, to inspect sporting facilities in China. Cross reported to the IOC at its 81st Session in Montevideo in April 1979. The IOC made the following recommendations at this Session: "In the Olympic spirit, and in accordance with the Olympic Charter, the IOC resolves: 1) to recognize the Chinese Olympic Committee located in Peking (now Beijing), and 2) to maintain recognition of the Chinese Olympic Committee located in Taipei. All matters pertaining to names, anthems, flags and constitutions will be the subject of studies and agreements which will have to be completed as soon as possible." The full Session approved this motion by 36-30. The IOC Executive Board modified this slightly, changing part two to read "to maintain recognition of the Olympic Committee located in Taipei."

China returned to the Olympic fold in 1980 at Lake Placid. It did not compete in 1980 at Moscow, but China has competed at all other Olympic Games since 1984. Chinese athletes have won 120 Olympic medals, 36 of them gold, all since 1984. Chinese women have won more medals (66 – 20 gold) than Chinese men (54 – 16 gold).

Chinese Taipei (aka Taiwan, Formosa, Republic of China) [TPE]
The Chinese Taipei Olympic Committee was first formed in 1949 by members of the mainland Chinese committee who had fled to the island. The IOC official policy at this time was that the mainland Chinese Olympic Committee had simply changed its address and was now located on the island of Taiwan. For many years thereafter, the country was embroiled in a dispute with mainland China over recognition by the IOC. (See also China, People's Republic of)

In October 1959, the IOC Executive Board recommended that the Olympic Committee in Taiwan be recognized as the "Olympic Committee of the Republic of China," but it also insisted that, at the 1960 Olympic Opening Ceremonies, this team should march behind a banner reading "Formosa." The banner eventually read "Taiwan/Formosa" but the placard bearer also posted a sign of his own, reading "Under Protest."

The greatest controversy concerning the participation of the athletes from Chinese Taipei occurred in 1976 at Montreal. In 1970, Canada had given political recognition to mainland China. Only a few weeks before the Montreal Olympics, Canada's government announced that it would not allow Chinese Taipei athletes to compete under the name of the "Republic of China." This was in complete violation of the Olympic Charter and the contract Montreal had signed as host of the Olympic Games, in which it agreed to allow all eligible athletes to enter the nation with the use of the Olympic Identity Card (*q.v.*). The United States Government protested vociferously, even threatening a boycott. Eventually, however, the U.S. athletes competed, although Chinese Taipei refused to compete under any name other than the Republic of China. On 11 July, only six days before the start of the Olympics, the IOC Executive Board gave in and proposed to the full IOC that the island nation should compete at Montreal as Taiwan. The IOC approved this recommendation by 58–2, with six abstentions. Chinese Taipei/Taiwan/Republic of China withdrew in protest and did not compete at the 1976 Olympics.

After competing for several years under the banner "China" or "Republic of China," the IOC eventually banned the country from competing under this name. The current NOC was recognized in its present form on 26 November 1979, and on 23 March 1981 it signed an agreement with the IOC in which the NOC agreed to change its name to the Chinese Taipei Olympic Committee and compete under a new flag and emblem.

Taiwan/Chinese Taipei first competed at the Olympic Games in 1956, and has competed at eight Olympic Games – those of 1956, 1960, 1964, 1968, 1972, 1984, 1988, and 1992. It has competed in the Olympic Games under various names – Taiwan (1960–1972), Chinese Taipei (1984–1992), and the Republic of China (1956). The nation has competed at six Olympic Winter Games: as Taiwan from 1972 to 1976, and as Chinese Taipei from 1984 to 1994. The nation has won four Olympic medals.

Chukarin, Viktor Ivanovich. **[URS/Ukraine–GYM]**   B. 9 November 1921, Mariupol (now Zhdanov). D. 26 August 1984, Lvov. A former World War II prisoner-of-war, he was 30 years old when the USSR first competed at the Olympic Games in 1952. Despite these handicaps, he dominated the gymnastics competition in Helsinki, winning the all-around title in addition to taking gold in the team event and two gold and two silver medals on the individual apparatus. In 1956, he successfully defended his all-around title and added two more gold, a silver and a bronze medal to bring his tally of Olympic medals to a then record total of 11. He was also World All-Around Champion in 1954 and, after retiring, he became head of gymnastics at the Lvov Institute of Physical Culture.

Citius, Altius, Fortius   See Olympic Motto.

Claudius, Leslie Walter. [IND-HOK]   B. 25 March 1927. He
shares with Udham Singh (*q.v.*) the distinction of being one of only
two players to win four Olympic medals for hockey. To his gold
medals in 1948, 1952 and 1956 he added a silver in 1960 when he
captained the team.

Clay, Cassius Marcellus. [USA-BOX]   See Muhammad Ali.

Coe, Sebastian Newbold. [GBR-ATH]   B. 29 September 1956,
Chiswick, London. The greatest 800 meter runner in history whose
world record (1:41.73) set in 1981 remains unbeaten after more than a
decade. He never won an Olympic title at this distance and had to
settle for a silver medal in 1980 and 1984, but he won a gold medal in
the 1,500 meters at both Games. A controversial omission from the
1988 British Olympic team denied him the opportunity of further
honors. A prolific record breaker, he set nine outdoor and three
indoor world records. After retirement, he continued to serve the
sport as an administrator and, in 1992, was elected a Member of the
British Parliament.

Colombia [COL]   Colombia first competed at the 1932 Olympic
Games, represented by a lone athlete, marathon runner Jorgé Perry
Villate. The country first formed a National Olympic Committee,
however, only in 1936 and this NOC was recognized by the IOC in
1939. Colombia has since competed at every Olympics with the
exception of 1952. It has yet to compete in the Olympic Winter
Games. Colombian athletes have won six Olympic medals through
1994.

Comăneci, Nadia. [ROM-GYM]   B. 12 November 1961, Onesti,
Moldavia. The first gymnast in Olympic history to be awarded the
perfect score of 10.0. She first achieved this landmark as a
14-year-old on the uneven parallel bars in 1976 and the judges
awarded her maximum marks a further seven times during the Games.
In the 1976 and 1980 Games she won a total of nine Olympic medals
(five gold, three silver, one bronze). Following the 1980 Games,
natural physical development began to inhibit her performance and
after a victory at the 1981 World Student Games she retired. In 1989,
she defected from Romania and settled in North America. She has
become engaged to American Olympic gymnastic medalist Bart
Conner.

Comité International Pierre de Coubertin   See International
Pierre de Coubertin Committee.

Commissions of the IOC   The International Olympic Committee
has created a number of Commissions which deal with specific issues
related to the Olympic Movement. The currently recognized
commissions are as follows: Commission for the International
Olympic Academy and Olympic Education; Eligibility Commission;
Athletes Commission; Centennial Olympic Congress and Congress of
Unity Study Commission; Cultural Commission; Finance
Commission; Juridical Commission; Medical Commission;
Commission for the Olympic Movement; Commission for New
Sources of Financing; Commission for the Olympic Program; Press
Commission; IOC Radio and Television Commission; Olympic
Solidarity Commission; Sport and Law Commission; Sports for All
Commission; Coordination Commission for the Olympic Games; IOC
Evaluation Commission for the Olympic Games and Olympic Winter
Games; the Pierre de Coubertin Commission; Sport and the
Environment Commission; and Olympic Collectors Commission.
Several of the IOC Commissions have Sub-commissions, notably:
Medical Commission - Sub-commission on Doping and Biochemistry
of Sport, Sub-commission on Biomechanics and Physiology of Sport,
Sub-commission on Sports Medicine and Coordination with the
NOCs, Sub-commission on Out of Competition Testing;
Coordination Commission for the Olympic Games - Summer 1996
Sub-commission, Winter 1998 Sub-commission, and Summer 2000
Sub-commission; Commission for the Olympic Program - Summer
Sub-commission, and Winter Sub-commission. In addition, the IOC
also recognizes several working groups which often have the status of
a commission, at least briefly. Currently, these include: Philatelic
Working Group, Council of the Olympic Order, and Bureau for the
Olympic Movement.

Commonwealth of Independent States [CIS]   In 1992, former
republics of the Soviet Union competed at the Olympic Games in
Barcelona and the Olympic Winter Games in Albertville. By then,
the former republics had formed the Commonwealth of Independent
States. Because of the short time after the break-up of the Soviet
Union, it was agreed that the former republics would compete as one
team, which was called the Unified Team, or Équipe Unifiée, and
which, loosely, represented the Commonwealth of Independent States.
(See also Unified Team and Union of Soviet Socialist Republics)

Comoros Islands [COM]   The Comoros Islands was given official recognition by the IOC in September 1993, but it has not yet competed at the Olympic Games.

Competition for Heralds – Ancient Olympic Sport   This event was held from at least 396 B.C. to 261 A.D. The last four known championships were won by Valerius Eclectus of Sinope.

Competition for Trumpeters – Ancient Olympic Sport   The competition for trumpeters was held from at least 396 B.C. to 217 A.D. The event was won consecutively from 328 B.C. through 292 B.C. by Herodoros of Megara.

Congo, Democratic Republic of the   See Zaire.

Congo, People's Republic of the [CGO]   The Congo has competed at six Olympic Games – 1964, 1972, 1980, 1984, 1988, and 1992. It has never competed at the Olympic Winter Games. Its best finish in the Olympics was sixth, albeit last, in women's handball in 1980.

Connolly, James Brendan. [USA–ATH]   B. 28 November 1865, South Boston, Massachusetts. D. 20 January 1957, Boston, Massachusetts. The first winner at the Modern Olympic Games and the first known Olympic champion since Varasdates in the fourth century A.D. Connolly achieved this distinction by winning the hop, step & jump (now known as the triple jump) on 6 April 1896. He also tied for second place in the high jump and placed third in the long jump in Athens but, in 1900, he narrowly failed to retain his hop, step & jump title. He did not take part in the 1904 Games and made his final Olympic appearance in 1906 when he failed to record a valid jump in either of the horizontal jumps. Unable to obtain a leave of absence from Harvard to travel to Greece for the first Modern Games he quit college but his place in Olympic history no doubt provided ample compensation. He later became well known as a writer of fishing stories.

Cook Islands [COK]   The Cook Islands Sports and Olympic Association was first organized and recognized by the IOC in 1986. The Cook Islands first competed at the 1988 Olympics in Seoul, and also competed in 1992 at Barcelona. The nation has not yet competed at the Olympic Winter Games and has not won an Olympic medal.

Coroebus of Elis. **[GRE-ATH]** *fl. ca.* 800 – 750 B.C. Coreobus was a cook in the city–state of Elis in Ancient Greece. His Olympic fame rests on the fact that he is the first recorded champion in Olympic history. In 776 B.C. he won the stadion race (*q.v.*). His feat was inscribed on his tomb.

Costa Rica **[CRC]** Costa Rica has competed at nine Olympic Games – 1936, and continuously since 1964. Its only medal to date was won by swimmer Silvia Poll who was second in the women's 200 meter freestyle in the 1988 Olympics. The nation has competed in four Olympic Winter Games – 1980, 1984, 1988, and 1992.

Cotswold Olimpick Games See Robert Dover's Games.

Coubertin, Baron Pierre de (né Pierre Frédy). **[FRA]** B. 1 January 1863, Paris. D. 2 September 1937, Geneva. Pierre de Coubertin is the founder of the Modern Olympic Movement. His inspirational idea to revive the ancient Greek festivals grew out of his general interest in physical education and, at the early age of 24, he began a campaign to restructure educational methods in France along the lines of the British Public School system, of which he was a great admirer. His idea of reviving the Olympic Games grew more from his interest in sociology, history and education than from any particular enthusiasm for competitive sports, but it was these sports that were to provide his lasting monument. In view of his aesthetic inclination, it must have been a source of satisfaction that he won the prize for literature in the Art Contests (*q.v.*) in 1912. His entry, "Ode to Sport," was submitted under a pseudonym. Taking over as President of the IOC from Demetrios Vikelas (*q.v.*) in 1896, Coubertin faced many problems in the turbulent early years of the Modern Olympic Movement and the current strength of the movement is a tribute to his dedication and diplomacy in the difficult pioneering days. From 1896 to 1924, he attended every celebration of the Games, except those of 1904 and 1906, but at the Paris Games of 1924 he resigned the presidency of the IOC at the age of 61 on the grounds that he was too old to continue in office. Surprisingly, his interest in Olympic matters seems to have declined rapidly but he recorded a message which was relayed at the 1936 Games in Berlin. The following year he collapsed and died from a heart attack while walking in Lagrange Park in Geneva and, although he is buried in Geneva, his heart is preserved in a marble stele at Ancient Olympia. Many other aspects of Coubertin's involvement with the Olympic Movement (*q.v.*) are covered in the separate entries on various subjects in this volume. (See also the Bibliography for a list of some of his published works on the Olympic Movement)

Cricket   Cricket was contested only at the 1900 Olympics, when a British squad beat a French team, which was actually made up of British residents of France.

Croatia [CRO]   Until the Yugoslavian civil war of 1991 Croatia had never competed at the Olympics as an independent nation. However, prior to 1991, many top Yugoslavian athletes were from Croatia, including several of the top Yugoslavian basketball players. Croatia made its Olympic debut at the 1992 Olympic Winter Games in Albertville and also competed at Barcelona where its best finish was the silver medal its basketball team won, losing only to the "Dream Team" (*q. v.*). Croatia won three medals at the Barcelona Olympics.

Croquet (Roque)   Croquet was contested at the 1900 Olympics in Paris, with three events. Two of the competitors were women, the first women to compete in the Modern Olympic Games. In 1904, roque, an American variant of croquet, was on the Olympic program as well. The sport has not been held at the Olympics since 1904. The name "roque" is derived by dropping the first and last letters from the name of its parent game of croquet.

Cuba [CUB]   In 1900, the fencer Ramón Fonst competed at the Olympic Games and actually won the first gold medal for the small Caribbean country. Fonst also competed in the 1904 Olympics along with a few other Cuban athletes. In 1924, Cuba was represented by nine competitors, while in 1928, the country had one competitor. In 1948, Cuba sent a full team to the London Olympic Games and its participation was continuous until it elected to boycott the 1984 Olympic Games in Los Angeles. In support of the North Korean government, Cuba also elected not to compete in 1988 in Seoul. Cuba returned to the Olympics in 1992. Cuban athletes have not yet competed in the Olympic Winter Games. Cuba has been successful in several sports, winning 83 Olympic medals, but by far its greatest success has come in boxing. Since the mid–1970's, Cuba has probably had the best amateur boxers in the world.

Curling   Curling was a demonstration sport at the 1924, 1932, 1988, and 1992 Olympic Winter Games. In addition, in 1936 and 1964, German curling (*Eisschießen*) was contested as a demonstration sport. Curling will be a full medal sport for the 1998 Olympic Winter Games in Nagano. The sport is governed by the World Curling Federation, founded in 1966, and with 31 member federations.

Cuthbert, Elizabeth "Betty." [AUS-ATH]   B. 20 April 1938, Merrylands, Sydney.   With two gold medals in the individual track sprints and a third gold in the relay at the 1956 Olympics, the 18-year-old Australian was instantly acclaimed as a national heroine by the Australian crowd.   Injury spoiled her chances at the 1960 Games but she came back to win the 400 meters in 1964 and claim her fourth Olympic gold medal.   Including relays, she set 18 world records and, sadly for such a fine athlete, she is now fighting multiple sclerosis.

Cycling   Bicycles were first developed in the late 18th century and have since been used as a form of transportation.   Originally the front wheel was much larger than the rear wheel and the rider was elevated a great deal, making them difficult to control and very dangerous.   In 1885, J. K. Starley of England devised the more modern bike with a chain and gearing to allow the wheels to be of equal size.   Although bike races had been held on the old "penny farthings," the new bikes stimulated the growth of bicycle racing as a sport.

From 1880 to 1900, cycling became immensely popular both in Europe and the United States.   The sport was primarily a professional one at that time.   The sport continues its grip on the European continent to this day, but bike racing ceased to be a popular sport in the United States at about the time of the depression.   Only the American Olympic victories at Los Angeles in 1984 and the recent exploits of Greg LeMond have again stimulated interest in bicycle racing in the United States.

Cycling is one of the few sports which has been on the program of every Olympic Games.   The program has varied but usually consists of a team and individual road race, and several different track races.   In 1984, women were admitted to Olympic cycling with a single road race.   In 1988, a sprint race on the track for women was also held and, in 1992, the women contested an individual pursuit track race.

The Europeans have dominated Olympic cycling, notably the French and Italians.   However, the East Europeans have also won many medals, especially on the track.   Mountain biking has recently become a very popular sport.   In 1993, the IOC approved mountain biking as an Olympic event which will appear on the program at the 1996 Atlanta Olympics.   Cycling is governed by the Union Cycliste Internationale (UCI) which was founded in 1900, and had 167 members as of 1995.

Cyprus [CYP]   The Cyprus National Olympic Committee was formed in 1974 and recognized by the IOC in 1978.   Cyprus has competed at the Olympic Games of 1980, 1984, 1988, and 1992.   Its first Olympic participation, however, occurred at the Olympic Winter Games of 1980 in Lake Placid, and it also sent competitors to the Winter Olympics in 1984, 1988, 1992, and 1994. In 1984, Petros Kyritsis posted the country's best Olympic performance when he finished 13th in skeet shooting.

Czech Republic [CZE]   Formerly a part of Czechoslovakia, the Czech Republic has been represented at the Olympics by many athletes. However, the Czech Republic did not compete officially at the Olympics as an independent nation until its appearance at Lillehammer for the 1994 Olympic Winter Games.

Czechoslovakia [TCH]   Athletes from what later became Czechoslovakia first competed at the 1900 Olympics, representing Bohemia (*q.v.*). In 1920, Czechoslovakia sent its first true Olympic team to Antwerp. Since that time, the only Olympic Games not attended, including the Olympic Winter Games, was the 1984 Los Angeles Olympics. Czechoslovakia has excelled in many different sports at the Olympics. The country's most noteworthy athletes have been distance runner Emil Zátopek and female gymnast Věra Čáslavská (*qq.v.*). Czechoslovakia split peacefully into the Czech Republic and Slovakia (*qq.v.*) on 1 January 1993. Athletes from Bohemia and Czechoslovakia won 174 Olympic medals, 38 of them gold.

********** D **********

Dæhlie, Bjørn. [NOR–NSK]   B. 19 June 1967, Råholt. With five gold medals Bjørn Dæhlie is the most successful male Nordic skier in Olympic history. In 1992, he won the combined pursuit, the 50 km. classical and was a member of the winning relay team, while in 1994, he was the winner of the 10 km. classical and the combined pursuit. To these gold medals he added silver in the 30 km. in 1992 and 1994, and a third silver in the relay in 1994. His total of eight Olympic medals has only been exceeded by Sixten Jernberg (SWE) (*q.v.*) among male Nordic skiers.

Dahomey   See Benin.

Daniels, Charles Meldrum. [USA-SWI]   B. 24 March 1885, Dayton, Ohio. D. 9 August 1973, Carmel Valley, California. His three Olympic gold medals for swimming in 1904 and one in 1906 were won against rather limited opposition but he proved his true worth in 1908 by winning the 100 meters freestyle against a truly international field. His total of four individual gold medals in swimming has not yet been beaten. He set seven world records over various distances between 1907 and 1911 but his most significant legacy to the sport was his development of the American crawl stroke. He was a fine all-round sportsman excelling at golf and squash and also at bridge.

Davis, John Henry, Jr. [USA-WLT]   B. 12 January 1921, Smithtown, New York. D. 13 July 1984, New York. John Davis was six times a world weightlifting champion and twice an Olympic gold medalist. His Olympic gold medals came in the unlimited class in 1948 and 1952 and he would undoubtedly have been a medal contender in 1940 and 1944. He set 18 world records between 1946 and 1951. Never defeated between 1938 and 1953, his only defeat prior to his retirement was a second-place at the 1954 World Championships to Doug Hepburn of Canada.

Dean, Christopher. [GBR-FSK]   See Jayne Torvill.

Decugis, Maxime Omer "Max." [FRA-TEN]   B. 24 September 1882, Paris. D. 6 September 1978, Biot. The winner of a record six Olympic medals (four gold, one silver, one bronze) for lawn tennis between 1900 and 1920. His victories included the mixed doubles in 1906 when he was partnered by his wife. Although the Olympic tournaments during that era attracted many of the world's top players his greatest achievement was to win the Wimbledon doubles with his countryman André Gobert in 1911 when they defeated the previously unbeaten holders, Tony Wilding (NZL) and Major Josiah Ritchie (GBR).

Demonstration Sports   Numerous sports have been contested at the Olympic Games and Olympic Winter Games as demonstration sports. These are usually sports which are being considered for the Olympic program, or a sport indigenous to the country hosting the Olympic Games. As of 1992, the IOC has decreed that demonstration sports will no longer be officially contested at the Olympic Games. (See also American Football, Aussie Rules Football, Badminton, Bandy, Basketball, Bicycle Polo, Bowling, Budo, Canoe & Kayaking,

Curling, Dogsled Racing, Freestyle Skiing, Gliding, Ice Dancing [in Figure Skating], Jeu de Paume, Judo [Women], Korfball, Lacrosse, Military Patrol, Pelota Basque, Roller Hockey, Short-Track Speed Skating, Skijöring, Speed Skating [Women], Speed Skiing, Taekwondo, Tennis, Water Skiing, and Winter Pentathlon)

Denmark [DEN]   Denmark has competed at every summer Olympic Games except 1904, including those of 1906. At the Olympic Winter Games, it has competed eight times – 1948, 1952, 1960, 1964, 1968, 1988, 1992, and 1994. Interestingly, its total number of athletes sent to the Olympic Winter Games, despite eight appearances, is only 21. Danish athletes have won 149 Olympic medals, 34 of them gold. Twenty-two of these have come in the Olympic Winter Games, of which five were gold medals.

Dhyan Chand. [IND-HOK]   B. 28 August 1905, Allahabad. D. 3 December 1979. Chand won three gold medals as a center-forward and is considered the greatest hockey player ever. He learned the game from British army officers and had his first international competition in 1926 on a tour of Australia and New Zealand. He led India to gold medals in 1928, 1932, and 1936. In 1947-48 he was still the star of the Indian team but declined selection to the 1948 team, which prevented him from being the only hockey player to have won four gold medals. His younger brother, Roop Singh, played on the 1932 and 1936 Olympic teams and his son, Ashok Kumar, won an Olympic bronze medal in 1972.

Diaulos Race – Ancient Olympic Sport   The diaulos race was one of the major running events of the Ancient Olympics. It consisted of a race of two laps of the stadium or about 385 meters. Champions are known from 724 B.C. (Hypenos of Pisa) through 153 A.D. (Demetrios of Chios). The greatest champions of the diaulos were Chionis of Sparta (664-656 B.C.), Hermogenes of Xanthos (81-89 A.D.), Astylos of Kroton and Syracuse (488-480 B.C.) and Leonidas of Rhodes (164-152 B.C.). An athlete from Argos also won the event four times, but his name is not known.

Dibiasi, Klaus. [ITA-DIV]   B. 6 October 1947, Solbad Hall, Austria. After winning a silver medal in the highboard diving at the 1964 Olympics he went on to win the gold at the next three Games (1968, 1972, 1976) and is the only Olympic diver to have won three successive gold medals. A silver in the springboard in 1964 gave him a record total of five Olympic medals. He also won the world platform title (1973, 1975), the European platform (1966, 1974) and the European springboard (1974). He was born in Austria of Italian parents who returned home when he was a child. He was coached by his father, a former Italian champion and a 1936 Olympian.

Di Centa, Manuela. [ITA-NSK]   B. 31 January 1963. In her first three Olympic appearances she failed to win a single medal but at Lillehammer in 1994 she uniquely won a medal in all five cross-country skiing events. To her gold medals in the 15 km. and 30 km. she added silver in the 5 km. and combined pursuit and a bronze in the relay.

Didrikson, Mildred Ella "Babe" (née Didriksen, later Mrs. Zaharias). [USA-ATH]   B. 26 June 1911, Port Arthur, Texas. D. 27 September 1956, Galveston, Texas. Considered by many authorities to be the greatest all-round sportswoman in history. At the 1932 Olympics, she won gold medals in the 80 meter hurdles and the javelin, and a silver in the high jump. She set new world records in each of these three disparate events. She was an All-American basketball player and held the world record for throwing the baseball but it was as a golfer that she excelled after giving up athletics. She won the U.S. Amateur title in 1946 and the U.S. Open in 1948, 1950 and 1954, her third victory being by a record margin of 12 strokes.

Diem, Carl. [GER]   B. 24 June 1882, Wurzburg. D. 17 December 1962, Köln. Carl Diem is one of the co-founders of the International Olympic Academy (*q.v.*) and is one of the most important writers and historians of the Olympic Movement (*q.v.*), authoring dozens of books and articles on Olympism (*q.v.*) and the Olympic Movement. He studied at the University of Berlin, after which, from 1917-1933, he was Secretary-General of the German Committee for Physical Education. He was Secretary-General of the Organizing Committee of the 1936 Olympic Games and conceived the idea of the Olympic Torch Relay (See Olympic Flame). From 1938-1944, at Coubertin's (*q.v.*) request, he served as director of the International Olympic Institute in Berlin. After World War II, Diem was a sports consultant to the German government. A sports university was founded in his honor, the Carl-Diem-Sporthochscule in Köln.

Dietrich, Wilfried. [FRG-WRE]   B. 14 October 1933. D. 3 June 1992. A competitor at five Olympic Games (1956-1972), he competed in seven Olympic tournaments (four freestyle and three

Greco–Roman) and won five medals (one gold, two silver, two bronze), a record for an Olympic wrestler. All his medals came in the unlimited class and unusually included a gold in the freestyle and a silver in the Greco–Roman style in 1960. He was the World Champion in 1961 and was unbeaten in the unlimited freestyle from 1955 to 1962. At the World Championships he also won two silver and two bronze medals between 1957 and 1969.

D'Inzeo, Piero *[B. 4 March 1923, Rome] and* **D'Inzeo, Raimondo** *[B. 2 February 1925, Poggio Mirteto, Rieti].* **[ITA–EQU]** Two Italian brothers who both competed in the equestrian events at eight Olympic Games (1948–1976), a record matched only by three other Olympians. They each won six Olympic medals (Raimondo – one gold, two silver, three bronze; Piero – two silver, four bronze), with their best collective performance coming in 1960 when they took the first two places in the individual show jumping. Raimondo was also the World Individual Champion in 1956 and 1960. Both brothers followed their father in making their career in the Italian cavalry.

Dityatin, Aleksandr. **[URS/Russia–GYM]** B. 7 August 1957, Leningrad. By winning a medal in all eight categories of gymnastics at Moscow in 1980 he established a record which remains unique in Olympic history. His three gold medals came in the team and individual all-around, and on the rings, to which he added four silver and a bronze medal. His finest performance was in the horse vault when he received the first perfect score (10) ever awarded to a male gymnast at the Olympics. He was equally dominant at the World Championships winning 12 medals (seven gold, two silver, three bronze).

Diving Diving is not considered to be a separate sport by the organizing body of world aquatics, Fédération Internationale de Natation Amateur (FINA). FINA contests four disciplines of aquatic competition – swimming, diving, synchronized swimming, and water polo. Usually the diving results are listed with the swimming. FINA was formed in 1908 and currently has 130 affiliated nations.

Diving contests are known to have been held in the 19th century though the sport is relatively modern. It was held at the 1904 Olympics in St. Louis, and its appearance on the Olympic program has been continuous since 1908.

The United States has absolutely dominated the sport of diving, perhaps more than any sport has been dominated in the Olympics. In the late 1980's the Chinese entered diving competition and posed the first serious threat to this dominance. While the United

States' Greg Louganis (*q.v.*), considered the greatest diver ever, was still competing, the Chinese men posted few victories but the Chinese women have been almost unbeatable of late.

Djibouti [DJI]   Djibouti competed at the 1984, 1988, and 1992 Olympics, its appearances highlighted by its excellent marathon runners, one of whom (Ahmed Salah) won a medal in 1988 at Seoul. Djibouti has not competed at the Olympic Winter Games.

Dogsled Racing   A dogsled race with seven dogs per team was held at the 1932 Olympic Winter Games as a demonstration sport (*q.v.*).

Dolichos Race – Ancient Olympic Sport   The dolichos race was the long–distance race of the Ancient Olympics, consisting of a running event of 20–25 laps (*circa* 4,000 – 5,000 meters). Champions are known from 720 B.C. (Akanthos of Sparta) through 221 A.D. The last known champion, Graos of Bithynia, is the only runner known to have won the race three times at Olympia.

Dominica [DMA]   Dominica was given official recognition by the IOC in September 1993, but the country has not yet competed at the Olympic Games.

Dominican Republic [DOM]   Albert Torres was the first Dominican Republic athlete to make an Olympic appearance, competing in the 1964 100 meter dash. The Dominican Republic has competed seven times since, never failing to appear since its debut. It has not yet competed in the Olympic Winter Games. Through 1994, the Dominican Republic has won one Olympic medal, a bronze by Pedro Nolasco in 1984 in bantamweight boxing.

Doping   Doping refers to the illegal use of drugs to enhance performance in sport and is considered illegal by the IOC and the IFs. The IOC rules against doping are contained in Rule 48 of the Olympic Charter (*q.v.*). Basically the IOC has a proscribed list of medications which are considered to be illegal for use by athletes taking part in its competitions. After each Olympic Games, all medalists, and certain other randomly selected athletes, are chosen to submit a urine sample which is then tested for these drugs. If any of the proscribed drugs are present in the athlete's urine in sufficient quantities, he or she may be disqualified from competition, pending further urine studies and, usually, legal hearings. In the 1980's and 1990's these penalties have been handed out and are virtually always contested by the athletes and their lawyers.

In addition, it is considered unlikely that previous IOC methods of testing for illegal drugs were sufficient to prevent athletes from using drugs. This is because athletes, coaches, and their doctors were able to learn enough about the drugs in order to know how long they had to be withdrawn from the athlete before a competition. This would enable the athlete to pass frequent drug tests despite being habitual users of the drugs. This is now being circumvented by IFs, NOCs, and National Governing Bodies performing random, out-of-competition tests of athletes at all times of the year.

Doping is not new. In the Ancient Olympics, trainers gave athletes various concoctions which they felt would improve their performance. The first physician to be considered a specialist in sports medicine was Galen, who prescribed as follows: "The rear hooves of an Abyssinian ass, ground up, boiled in oil, and flavored with rose hips and rose petals, was the prescription favored to improve performance." The name doping itself comes from the 19th century, when the term "dop" was used to describe a South African drink which was an extract of cola nuts to which was added xanthines (found in caffeine) and alcohol. The drink was intended to improve endurance and the term "doping" was derived from it.

Multiple doping scandals have existed in sports. The most famous occurred at the 1988 Seoul Olympics when 100 meter champion Ben Johnson was found to test positive for stanazolol, an anabolic steroid. At the 1960 Rome Olympics, Danish cyclist Knut Enemark Jensen collapsed and died during the cycling road race. He was later found to have been given amphetamines (Ronital) and nicotinyl tartrate (a nicotine-type of stimulant). In the 1967 Tour de France, the great British cyclist, Tommy Simpson, collapsed and died while ascending Mont Ventoux. He was found to have been heavily dosed with stimulants.

These two deaths alerted the sporting authorities to the dangers inherent in drug use in sports. At the 1968 Olympic Winter Games, the IOC tested for drugs for the first time. The first athlete to be disqualified in the Olympics for drug use was Sweden's Hans-Gunnar Liljenvall at the 1968 Olympic Games. Liljenvall was a modern pentathlete who had helped his team win a bronze medal. Prior to the shooting event he drank a few beers to help steady his nerves. This was commonplace among modern pentathletes in those days, but it cost him and his teammates a bronze medal.

In the 1970's and 1980's, the athletes of the GDR were suspected of doping violations which were never detected. No GDR athlete ever failed a doping test at the Olympics. After the fall of the Berlin Wall and the reunification of the two Germanys, former German athletes and coaches revealed that much of the success of the great GDR athletic machine was due to systematic use of illegal drugs. In the 1990's, the Chinese women swimmers and runners have been suspected of using similar practices to make great strides in their sports. Adding to this suspicion is that several of the former GDR coaches now coach in China. (See Appendix XVII for a complete list of all positive doping tests which have occurred at the Olympic Games.)

Dream Team, The - 1992 USA Basketball   The Dream Team was the basketball team which represented the United States at the 1992 Olympics. For the first time, all basketball professionals were declared eligible to compete at the Olympics, including members of the National Basketball Association (NBA), the United States' major professional league. This allowed the U.S. to field a team of multiple professional all-stars, which was certainly the greatest basketball team ever assembled. The team gained incredible attention from the media and fans, both in the United States and Spain, as well as throughout the world, and easily won the gold medal. The team members were Charles Barkley, Larry Bird, Clyde Drexler, Patrick Ewing, Earvin "Magic" Johnson, Michael Jordan (*q.v.*), Christian Laettner, Karl Malone, Chris Mullin, Scottie Pippen, David Robinson, and John Stockton.

Dresden Four, The - GDR Coxless Four Rowing Team [1968-72] Also known as the Einheit Dresden Four, this coxless four rowing team won Olympic gold medals in 1968 and 1972 and was never beaten in international competition. Representing the GDR, they were World Champions in 1966 and 1970, and European Champions in 1967 and 1971. The team members were Frank Forberger, Dieter Grahn, Frank Rühle, and Dieter Schubert.

********** E **********

Eagan, Edward Patrick Francis "Eddie." [USA-BOX/BOB]   B. 26 April 1898, Denver, Colorado. D. 14 June 1967, New York. Olympic light-heavyweight boxing champion in 1920 and a member of the winning four-man bobsled crew in 1932, he is the only man to have won an Olympic gold medal at both the Winter and Summer Games. While a Rhodes Scholar at Oxford University he made a second appearance at the Summer Games in 1924 when he was eliminated in the semi-finals of the heavyweight boxing.

Ecuador [ECU] Ecuador sent three track & field competitors to the 1924 Olympic Games – Alberto Jurado Gonzales, Luis Jarrin, and Belisario Villacis. A gap of 44 years then occurred before it returned to the Olympics at Mexico City and it has competed continuously since. It has never appeared at the Olympic Winter Games and has never won a medal. Its top performance has been a fourth-place finish in the 1972 200 meter butterfly swimming event by Jorgé Delgado Panchama.

Edström, Johannes Sigfrid. [SWE]. B. 21 November 1870, Morlanda, 65 km. north of Göteborg. D. 18 March 1964, Stockholm. As President of the IOC and the International Amateur Athletic Federation (IAAF), Sigfrid Edström was a man of immense sporting influence. Born in Sweden and educated partly there and in the United States and Switzerland (1891–1893), he was one of the organizers of the 1912 Olympic Games in Stockholm during which he took the initiative of founding the IAAF, for which he served as the first President, remaining in that office from 1913 until 1946. Edström founded the International Chamber of Commerce in 1918 (President, 1939–1945), the Federation of Swedish Industries in 1910 (Chairman, 1928–1929), and was Chairman of the Swedish Employers' Confederation from 1931–1942. His main business career was as Managing Director (1903–1933) and Chairman of the Board (1934–1949) for Allmåna Svenska Elektriska Aktiebolagel (ASEA), a world leader in the high-tension current industry. Edström was elected an IOC member in 1921 and became a member of the Executive Board when it was created in that same year. He chaired the Olympic Congresses (*q.v.*) in 1921 and 1925 and was appointed Vice-President of the IOC in 1937. Following the death of IOC President Henri de Baillet-Latour (*q.v.*) in 1942, Edström was, as a neutral, well placed to keep the Olympic Movement (*q.v.*) alive during the war years as a *de facto* President. In 1946, in the first post-war IOC Session in Lausanne, he was elected President by acclamation. On his retirement in 1952, at the age of 81, he was given the title of Honorary President of the IOC. In 1947, he was awarded the Olympic Cup (*q.v.*) for his contibutions to the Olympic Movement.

Edwards, Teresa. [USA-BAS] B. 19 July 1964, Cairo, Georgia. One of the greatest female guards to ever play basketball, she played collegiately at the University of Georgia, where she was a consensus All-American in 1984 and 1985. Her record is unmatched by women in international competition. She won gold medals at the 1984 and 1988 Olympics, and a bronze medal at the 1992 Olympics. She also was the playmaking leader of championship teams at the 1986 and

1990 World Championships, the 1986 and 1990 Goodwill Games, and the 1987 Pan-American Games. In 1991, she played on the U.S. team which won a bronze at the Pan-American Games. She was the USA Basketball player of the year in both 1987 and 1991.

Egerszegi, Krisztina. [HUN-SWI]   B. 16 August 1974, Budapest, Hungary. Krisztina Egerszegi has established herself as one of the greatest backstrokers in swimming history. When only 14 years old, she won a gold and silver in the two backstroke events at the 1988 Olympics. In 1992, she returned to win three individual gold medals, in the 100 meter backstroke, the 200 meter backstroke, and the 400 meter individual medley. At the European Championships she won three silver medals in 1989 and three gold medals in 1991 and 1993. At the 1991 World Championships, she won both backstroke events. She set two world records, one each in the 100 meter and 200 meter backstroke.

Egypt [EGY]   Egypt's first Olympic appearance was at the Intercalated Games of 1906. Its Olympic Committee was first formed and recognized by the IOC in 1910. Since then it has competed at all Olympics except those of 1908, 1932, 1956 (missing Melbourne, but not Stockholm), and 1980. Egypt has competed at the Olympic Winter Games only in 1984 at Sarajevo. From 1960 through 1968, Egypt competed as the United Arab Republic (UAR), joining in a union in 1960 with Syria, although all but three of the 74 UAR athletes were Egyptian. Egypt's greatest Olympic successes have come in the strength sports of weightlifting and wrestling.

El Salvador [ESA]   El Salvador's National Olympic Committee was formed in 1949, but it was not recognized by the IOC until 1962. Six years then passed before El Salvador competed at the Olympic Games in 1968. El Salvador has now competed at the Olympics of 1968, 1972, 1984, 1988, and 1992. It has won no Olympic medals to date and has not yet competed at the Olympic Winter Games. In 1988, light-flyweight boxer Henry Martinez posted the best Olympic finish ever by an El Salvadorean, when he won two matches to finish equal ninth.

Elvstrøm, Paul Bert. [DEN-YAC]   B. 25 February 1928, Gentofte (Hellerup), Copenhagen. One of the great Olympians who competed as a yachtsman in eight Games over a 40-year period. Although three other competitors have taken part in eight Games and another three have had a similarly lengthy Olympic career, none of them could match Elvstrøm's record of successes. He won the Firefly class in 1948 and the Finn class in 1952, 1956 and 1960 and was the first competitor in any sport to win individual gold medals at four successive Games. After being a reserve on the Danish team in 1964, he then competed in 1968 and 1972 without winning a medal. He also competed in 1984 and 1988 when his daughter, Trine, crewed for him.

Ender, Kornelia (later Matthes, then Grummt). [GDR–SWI] B. 25 October 1958, Plauen. One of only three women swimmers to have won a total of eight Olympic medals, a record she shares with Shirley Babashoff and Dawn Fraser (*qq.v.*). She won four gold medals in 1976 in the 100 meters and 200 meters freestyle, the 100 meters butterfly and the 400 meters medley relay. The most prolific record breaker of modern times, she set 23 world records (1973–1976) in currently recognized events and her total of 10 medals (eight gold, two silver) at the World Championships is also a record. She married first Roland Matthes (*q.v.*) and then Olympic decathlete Steffen Grummt.

Equatorial Guinea [GEQ]   Equatorial Guinea has competed at the Olympics only in track & field athletics in 1984, 1988, and 1992. The nation's best finish was a fourth place in a first round heat of the 1992 men's 100 meters by Gustavo Envela Mahua. The nation has never competed at the Olympic Winter Games.

Equestrian Events   Equestrian events have been on the Olympic program since 1900 when jumping events were held at the Olympics in Paris. However, equestrian events were not held again until 1912 in Stockholm. Since that year, the sport has always been on the Olympic program.

There are three equestrian disciplines contested, with an individual and team event in each, making six events on the Olympic program. These are jumping (or show jumping, or Grand Prix de Nations as a team event), dressage, and the three–day event. Jumping consists of jumping over a series of obstacles in an attempt to not disturb the fences. Dressage is a sort of ballet on horseback in which the rider has the horse perform certain intricate maneuvers of stepping. The scoring is done by judges who evaluate how well the horse executes the moves. The three–day event combines the above two disciplines, and adds a third competition of riding a cross–country course. Scoring is by a series of tables evaluating each day's performance. It actually occurs now over four days at the Olympics as two days are devoted to the dressage.

Equestrian sports are governed by the Fédération Equestre Internationale (FEI), which was formed in 1921 and had 106 member nations at the end of 1994. The top nations at the Olympics in equestrian events have been Germany, Sweden, the United States, and France.

Estonia [EST] As a separate nation, Estonia competed at the Olympic Games continuously from 1920 to 1936. Estonia also competed at the Olympic Winter Games of 1928 and 1936. From 1952 to 1988, Estonia was a republic of the USSR and thus did not compete as an independent nation, but many Estonian athletes competed for the Soviet Union. After the Soviet Revolution of 1991, Estonia declared and was granted its independence. The nation returned to the Olympic fold by competing in 1992 in both Albertville and Barcelona. Estonia has won 23 Olympic medals, 21 from 1920 to 1936, and 2 in Barcelona. Seven of these were gold medals, including an emotional victory for Erika Salumäe in women's match sprint cycling in 1992. Estonia has never hosted an Olympic Games, but in 1980, all of the yachting events of the Moscow Olympics were actually held in the Gulf of Finland off Tallinn, the capital of Estonia.

Ethiopia [ETH] Ethiopia made its first Olympic appearance in 1956. It has since missed only the 1976, 1984, and 1988 Olympics, all due to political boycotts. The country has made no appearances at the Olympic Winter Games. Ethiopia's top athletes have been distance runners. Heading this list is Abebe Bikila, Olympic marathon champion in 1960 and 1964, and generally considered the greatest marathoner of all time. Ethiopia has won 13 Olympic medals, 6 of them gold, all in track & field athletics.

European Olympic Committees [EOC] The affiliated National Olympic Committees from Europe have formed this group to further their interests with the International Olympic Committee. The EOC is headquartered in Rome, Italy. The President as of 1995 is Dr. Jacques Rogge of Belgium. The group's name was changed to European Olympic Committees (EOC) in November 1994 at its meeting in Atlanta. Prior to that time the group was known as the Association des Comités Nationaux Olympiques d'Europe (ACNOE).

Evans, Janet Elizabeth. [USA–SWI] B. 28 August 1971, Fullerton, California. Possibly the greatest female long distance swimmer of all time. She entered the 1988 Olympics as the world record holder in the 400 meters, 800 meters, and 1,500 meters and improved her own world record in winning the 400 meters in addition to taking gold medals in the 800 meters and the 400 meter individual medley. On her second Olympic appearance in 1992 she successfully defended her 800 meters title but suffered her first defeat in the 400 meters since 1986 when she place second to Dagmar Hase (GER). She won a host of medals at the World Championships, the Goodwill Games and other major championships and brought a new dimension to long distance swimming for women.

Ewry, Ray Clarence "R. C." [USA-ATH]   B. 14 October 1873, Lafayette, Indiana. D. 29 September 1937, Queens, New York. A victim of polio as a child, remedial leg-strengthening exercises resulted in his becoming the greatest exponent of the now defunct standing jumps. He was unbeaten in 10 Olympic competitions, winning the standing high jump and standing long jump (1900, 1904, 1906, 1908) and the standing triple jump (1900, 1904). His 10 individual gold medals remain an Olympic record for any sport. He retired after the 1908 Games having won 15 AAU (Amateur Athletic Union [USA]) titles and setting world records in each of his three speciality events.

Executive Board of the IOC   The Executive Board of the IOC manages the affairs of the IOC. It functions by making its recommendations to the IOC Sessions. These recommendations are rarely overturned, thus the Executive Board virtually runs the IOC. It consists of the President of the IOC, four Vice-Presidents, and six additional members. They are elected by the IOC Sessions. The Vice-Presidents and Board Members are elected for four-year periods.

********** F **********

Federal Republic of Germany [FRG]   See Germany.

Fencing   Fencing began as a form of combat and is known to have been practiced well before the birth of Christ. As a sport, fencing began in either the 14th or 15th century and both Italy and Germany lay claims to the origins of the sport. In 1570, Henri Saint-Didier of France gave names to fencing's major movements and most of that nomenclature remains.

Until the 17th century the fencing weapons were large and unwieldy like the combat weapons. However the combat sword evolved into the épée and, somewhat, into the sabre. The foil was originally a practice weapon for combat and became popular as a sporting event in the late 19th century. The foil is a light, quadrangular tapering blade in which only hits made with the blade point on the opponent's torso count. The épée, developed from the dueling weapons of European noblemen, is the same length as the foil, but is heavier and has a larger handguard. Hits also must be made with the tip of the blade but can be scored over the opponent's entire body. The sabre owes its origins to the Middle Eastern scimitar and the 18th century cavalry sabre. Hits may be scored with the tip of the blade, with its front edge, or with the last one-third of its back edge. The target area is from the bend of the hips up, including the head and arms.

Fencing was first contested at the 1896 Olympics and is one of the few sports to have been contested at every Olympic Games. Women's fencing first appeared in the Olympics in 1924. Today, men compete in the Olympics with three types of swords – the foil, the épée, and the sabre – in both team and individual events, thus six events in all. Women compete in the Olympics only in the foil, in both a team and individual event. Women's team and individual épée events have been added to the Olympic program for the 1996 Olympics in Atlanta. Electronic scoring has been used for the foil and épée for decades now, while electronic scoring for the sabre made its Olympic debut at Barcelona.

Fencing is governed world-wide by the Fédération Internationale d'Escrime (FIE), which was formed in 1913 and had 104 member nations affiliated as of 1994. Fencing has been dominated at the Olympics by France and Italy in the foil and épée, and Hungary in the sabre.

Figure Skating   Figure skating began in the mid- to late-19th century almost concurrently in Europe and North America, but two Americans are responsible for major developments in its history. In 1850, Edward Bushnell of Philadelphia revolutionized skating technology when he refined the use of steel-bladed skates. This allowed the creation of fancy twists and turns on the ice. Another American, Jackson Haines, a ballet master, visited Vienna in the 1860's and added the elements of music and dance to figure skating. Originally, free skating was subordinate to school figures, or the tracing of pretty patterns on the ice.

International figure skating competitions were held in Europe in the 1880's and the International Skating Union (ISU) was formed in 1892, the first true international governing body of any winter sport (now with 61 member nations). Originally men and women competed together, with the first world championship being held in what was then and is now St. Petersburg, Russia (formerly Leningrad) in 1896. The first women's championship was held in 1906.

Figure skating is the oldest sport on the Winter program. It was contested at the London Olympics of 1908 and again in 1920 at Antwerp. Events for men, women, and pairs were contested until 1972. In 1976, ice dancing, long a popular event, was added to the program as a fourth event, although it had been held as a demonstration sport (*q. v.*) in 1968.

Scoring has evolved during the century also, as the former predominance of compulsory figures in the scoring gave way in the early 1970's. A short program of free skating was added, primarily to equalize results among skaters who were excellent at compulsories but lesser free skaters, to those who were poor compulsory skaters but top-notch free skaters. This was exemplified in that era by Beatrix Schuba (AUT), who was an excellent skater in compulsories, but was a relatively poor free skater, and Janet Lynn (USA), who was a superb free skater but usually was beaten by Schuba because of her difficulty with the compulsories. This gave impetus to the movement to decrease the importance of compulsory figures. At the end of the 1980's the International Skating Union ruled that compulsory figures would no longer be held at international competitions. They last were contested at the 1990 World Championships and were not a part of the figure skating program in Albertville or Lillehammer.

Since World War II, figure skating has been dominated in the men's and women's singles by the United States which has won six men's gold medals and five women's gold medals. In pairs and ice dancing, by far the dominant nation has been the Soviet Union and its former republics. Since 1964, the Soviet Union (and its former republics) has won every pairs and dance gold medal available, with the exception of the 1984 ice dancing gold medal which went to Britain's Jayne Torvill (*q. v.*) and Christopher Dean.

Fiji [FIJ]   Fiji formed a National Olympic Committee in 1949 and first competed at the Olympics in 1956. Fiji has since competed at all the Olympics with the exception of 1964 and 1980. It has competed at the Olympic Winter Games in both 1988 and 1994. It has won no medals. Its best Olympic performance to date occurred in 1992, Anthony Philip finished tenth of 44 sailors in the Lechner boardsailing class.

Finland [FIN]   Finland first competed at the 1906 Intercalated Games in Athens and also appeared two years later at the 1908 London Olympics. Its first Olympic Winter appearance was in 1924 at Chamonix although it had two skaters entered in the figure skating events in 1920. Since those dates Finland's participation has been continuous, never missing an Olympic Games nor an Olympic Winter Games. Finland's greatest successes have come in the distance running events in the Summer Games. In those events, led by Hannes Kolehmainen, Paavo Nurmi, and Lasse Virén (*qq.v.*), Finland has been the preeminent nation. Prior to World War II, Finland was also the dominant nation in wrestling. In the Winter Games, Finland has excelled at Nordic Skiing and, in the early Games, at speed skating. Finland hosted the Games of the XVth Olympiad in Helsinki in 1952.

Flanagan, John Jesus. [USA/IRL–ATH]   B. 9 January 1873, Kilbreedy, County Limerick, Ireland. D. 4 June 1938, Kilmallack, County Limerick, Ireland. His three successive victories in the hammer throw (1900, 1904, 1908) remained an Olympic record for any track & field event until Al Oerter (*q.v.*) won his fourth consecutive gold medal in the discus in 1968. Flanagan would himself almost certainly have won four Olympic titles had the hammer been included in the program at the 1896 Games. Between 1896 and 1909 he improved the world best for the hammer no less than 18 times, his first record coming when he won the British title in 1896 shortly before he emigrated to the USA.

Football, American   American football was a demonstration sport (*q.v.*) at the 1932 Olympics.

Football, Association (Soccer)   Football (soccer) is the world's most popular sport, played in more countries than any other. The World Cup of football, the quadrennial competition played in the even year between Olympics (last in 1990), is considered the most watched single sporting event on the planet. The sport is governed internationally by the Fédération Internationale de Football Association (FIFA), which was formed in 1904 and had 168 members at the end of 1994.

The origins of football are vague. The Greeks played a game which loosely resembled its modern counterpart, as did the Romans. By the 14th century it was so popular in England that King Edward II issued a proclamation on 13 April 1314, forbidding the game "forasmuch as there is great noise in the city caused by hustling over large balls from which many evils might arise which God forbid; we commend and forbid, on behalf of the King, on pain of imprisonment, such game to be used in the city of the future." In 1349, Edward III objected to the game because it prevented the practice of archery, necessary for the military strength of the country. Banning the game had little effect, however, as similar edicts had to be issued in 1389

(Richard II), 1401 (Henry IV), 1436 (Henry VIII), 1457 (James II), and again in 1491.

Gradually, despite attempts to ban it, football spread throughout the world, becoming popular almost everywhere, with the United States being a notable exception. Football was contested as an exhibition at the 1896 Olympics. In 1900 and 1904, Olympic football tournaments were contested. The sport has been played at every Olympics with the exception of 1932 in Los Angeles.

The World Cup began in 1930 and brings together the world's top professional players. In recent years, Olympic eligibility has become a problem. Eastern European countries stated that they had no true professionals, although their players were state supported. Thus they often entered similar teams in both the World Cup and the Olympics, and the Eastern Europeans have been dominant in Olympic football since the 1950's. Recently, however, eligibility rules have changed as other countries may be allowed to use some of their professional players who have competed in the World Cup. The problem is not yet fully resolved. Currently, professional players may compete at the Olympics providing they are not more than 23 years old. There is some sentiment among IOC officials to change this and allow all professionals to compete.

Football (soccer) for women is now becoming more popular, with the first women's World Cup being contested in 1992. In September 1993, the IOC approved women's football as an Olympic sport which will appear on the Olympic program at Atlanta in 1996. (See Uruguay Football Teams [1924 and 1928])

Football, Australian Rules (Aussie Rules)   Australian Rules Football was a demonstration sport (*q.v.*) at the 1956 Olympics in Melbourne.

Foreman, George. [USA–BOX]   B. 22 January 1948, Marshall, Texas. George Foreman won the 1968 Olympic heavyweight championship. After the Olympics, Foreman quickly turned professional and began knocking out fighters left and right with his powerful punching ability. In 1973, he fought Joe Frazier (*q.v.*) for the heavyweight title, winning easily. Foreman defended the title twice but, on 30 October 1974, in Zaire ("The Rumble in the Jungle"), Muhammad Ali (*q.v.*) stopped him in eight rounds. Foreman was never a championship factor again in his "first" career. However, in 1987, George Foreman, by then weighing close to 300 pounds, began a comeback. Through 1990 he was not defeated in that comeback. In April 1991, he fought for the heavyweight title again and lost a 12–round decision to Evander Holyfield. In 1994, however, he defeated Michael Moorer to claim a portion of the world heavyweight championships at the age of 46 years.

Formosa   See Chinese Taipei.

France [FRA]   France can be said to be the home of the Modern Olympic Games, being the home of Pierre de Coubertin (*q.v.*), their founder. Not unexpectedly, it has competed at every celebration of the Olympic Games and at every Olympic Winter Games. In addition to appearing at all the Olympic Games, France has hosted five Olympic Games, second only to the United States. These were the Games of the IInd Olympiad in Paris in 1900, the Games of the VIIIth Olympiad in Paris in 1924, the 1st Olympic Winter Games in Chamonix in 1924, the 10th Olympic Winter Games in Grenoble in 1968, and the 16th Olympic Winter Games in Albertville in 1992. France's greatest athletic successes have come in the sports of cycling and fencing, sports at which it has often been the dominant nation. France has won 576 Olympic medals (176 gold) with 53 having been won at the Olympic Winter Games, of which 16 have been gold medals.

Fraser, Dawn Lorraine. [AUS-SWI]   B. 4 September 1937, Balmain, Sydney. The first of only three women swimmers to win a total of eight Olympic medals. She won four gold and four silver medals at the Games of 1956, 1960 and 1964, including three successive golds in 100 meters freestyle, a record for any Olympic swimming event. She was denied the opportunity of adding to her medal total when she received a lengthy suspension following misbehavior at the 1964 Games. She set 27 individual and 12 relay world records.

Frazier, Joseph "Joe." [USA-BOX]   B. 12 January 1944, Beaufort, South Carolina. Joe Frazier won a gold medal as a heavyweight at the 1964 Olympics. Frazier first won the heavyweight World Championship in 1970 by stopping Jimmy Ellis in five rounds. He defended the title four times before being knocked out by George Foreman (*q.v.*). Frazier later fought three tremendous battles with Muhammad Ali (*q.v.*). The first, in 1971, was the fight of the century, a battle of undefeated heavyweight champions, and Frazier won by a decision in 15. Frazier was on the losing end in the next two fights, but all three were great spectacles. After losing his heavyweight title, he continued to fight for a few years before retiring in the mid-1970's.

Fredriksson, Gert Fridolf. [SWE-CAN]   B. 21 November 1919, Nyköping. With eight medals (six gold, one silver, one bronze) between 1948 and 1960 he is the most successful canoeist in Olympic history. He was at his best in the K1-1,000 meters, winning a gold medal at three successive Games (1948–1956) and in the K1-10,000 meters, in which he won two gold medals (1948, 1956) and a silver (1952). He is one of only ten Olympians to have won gold medals at four or more consecutive Olympic Games. At the World Championships he won four individual titles and a further three in the relay. In 1956, Fredriksson was awarded the Mohammed Taher Trophy by the IOC. (See Appendix V)

Frédy, Pierre   See Coubertin, Baron Pierre de.

Freestyle Skiing   Freestyle skiing was held at the 1988 Winter Olympics as a demonstration sport (*q.v.*). In 1992, moguls was contested as a full-medal sport in Albertville. In Lillehammer in 1994, both moguls and aerials were full-medal events.

********** G **********

Gabon [GAB]   Gabon formed a National Olympic Committee in 1965 but did not compete at the Olympics until 1972. Gabon has competed at four Olympic Games, those of 1972, 1984, 1988, and 1992. It has never had an athlete compete at the Olympic Winter Games. Serge Bouemba can boast its best finish ever. A featherweight boxer in 1988, he received a first-round bye, and then won one match to finish equal ninth of 48.

Gambia, The [GAM]   The Gambia's National Olympic Committee was formed in 1972 and recognized by the IOC in 1976. The Gambia has competed at the Olympic Games of 1984, 1988, and 1992, but has never competed at the Olympic Winter Games. The Gambia has yet to win an Olympic medal. Its best performance came in 1988 men's athletics when Dawda Jallow qualified for the second round of the 400 meters.

Games of the Olympiad   See the chapter entitled "The Olympic Games and Olympic Winter Games."

Geesink, Antonius Johannes "Anton." [NED-JUD]   B. 6 April
1934, Utrecht.   With the introduction of judo to the Olympic program
in 1964, the Dutchman provided one of the surprises of the Games by
winning the open class.   He had, however, earlier destroyed the myth
of Japanese invincibility by becoming the first non-Japanese player to
win a world title in 1961.   Between 1953 and 1967, Geesink won 13
European titles in the open and unlimited classes.   He later became a
member of the IOC.

General Association of International Sports Federations [GAISF]
In the early 1960's, many sports federations were unhappy that they
had so little influence with the International Olympic Committee.
Led by the Frenchman Roger Coulon, President of the Fédération
Internationale des Luttes Amateurs (FILA – wrestling), in 1967 the
federations banded together to form the General Assembly of
International Federations (GAIF), later the General Association of
International Sports Federations (GAISF), or Association Générale
des Fédérations Internationales de Sports (AGFIS).   The headquarters
is currently in Monte Carlo and the President as of 1994 is Dr. Kim
Un-Yong (KOR).   As of 1994, there were 87 member federations.
The aims of the GAISF are "to act as a forum for the exchange of
ideas and for discussion on common problems in sport; to collect,
collate, and circulate information; to provide members with secretarial
and translating services, the organization of meetings, technical
documentation and consultancy; to collect news bulletins, technical
rules and regulations from members; to assemble and coordinate the
dates of main international competitions; and to publish a half-yearly
calendar."

Georgia [GEO]   Many Georgian athletes competed from 1952 to
1988 for the Soviet Union.   Its top sports were judo and wrestling
and, in fact, Georgian *judoka* won more medals for the Soviet Union
than any other republic, including Russia.   The most famous Georgian
Olympic athletes were wrestlers David Gobedzhishvili and Levan
Tediashvili, and track & field athletes Viktor Saneyev and Robert
Shavlakadze.   Georgian athletes were present at Barcelona in 1992 as
members of the Unified Team (*q.v.*).   Georgia's first Olympic
appearance as an independent nation occurred in 1994 at Lillehammer,
where it was represented by five athletes who competed in luge,
Alpine Skiing, and ski jumping.

Gerevich, Aladár. [HUN-FEN]   B. 16 May 1910, Jászbéreny.
D. 14 May 1991, Budapest.   One of the greatest of all Olympians.
His six successive gold medals in the sabre team event at every Games

from 1932 to 1960 stands as a record for any Olympic sport. In the sabre, he also won individual gold in 1948, silver in 1952, and bronze in 1936, and a further bronze in the foil team event in 1952. He confirmed his reputation as the world's greatest sabreur with three individual titles at the World Championships (1935, 1951, 1955). His wife, son and father–in–law were also Olympic medalists.

German Democratic Republic [GDR]   The German Democratic Republic (frequently termed East Germany) was formed on 7 October 1949 after the division of Germany into two countries after World War II. The problem of the "Two Germanys" perplexed the IOC for two decades. (See also Germany) From 1956 until 1964, the two nations purportedly competed at the Olympics as a single combined team. However, it should be noted that in 1952, a combined German team was planned and envisioned by the IOC but the GDR refused to start in an all–German team and no East German athletes competed on the 1952 "combined" team. In 1968 at Mexico City and Grenoble, the two Germanys competed as separate teams, but under the same banner, and using the same anthem and flag. The German Democratic Republic, however, was forced to use the name East Germany in 1968, a name which it detested. At the IOC Session in 1968, full recognition came to the German Democratic Republic when it was allowed to compete at the Olympics, beginning in 1972, using its correct name, with its own anthem, emblems, and uniforms.

Between 1956 and 1988, the GDR developed into a true Olympic powerhouse. Since the 1968 Olympics, with the United States and the Soviet Union, it was one of the three most powerful sporting nations in the world. The German Democratic Republic, competing as an independent nation, won 563 Olympic medals, 445 at the Olympic Games and 118 at the Olympic Winter Games. Of these, 202 were gold medals, 43 of which were won at the Olympic Winter Games. The sporting leviathan was fully state–supported, with the help of a highly advanced sports medicine program, and the athletes were treated royally in their country. After the re–unification of Germany, it was revealed that the GDR's sports medical program had helped develop many of its athletes by the use of drugs. (See Doping)

German Federal Republic [FRG]   See Germany.

Germany [GER/FRG]   Prior to World War II, Germany appeared at all Olympics (Winter and Summer) with the exception of 1920 and 1924, when, as an aggressor nation in World War I, it was not invited. Because of its actions in World War II, and because no true German state existed at the time, Germany was again not allowed to compete in 1948. After World War II, Germany split into two nations. The Federal Republic of Germany (FRG) (West) was proclaimed in Bonn on 23 May 1949 from the former United States, British, and French Zones of Occupation. The occupying powers restored civil status on 21 September 1949. The German Democratic Republic (GDR) (East) was formed on 7 October 1949 from the former Soviet Zone of Occupation. As well, the province of The Saar formed an independent country until 1956. The Saar competed independently in 1952, its only Olympic appearance. (See Saar)

From 1952 to 1968, the problem of the "two Germanys" was a major political problem for the IOC. The FRG Olympic Committee was formed on 24 September 1949 and requested IOC recognition immediately. On 29 August 1950, the IOC Executive Board gave provisional recognition to the FRG Olympic Committee. Full recognition came in May 1951 at the 46th IOC Session in Vienna. The GDR formed an Olympic Committee on 22 April 1951 and also asked for recognition. In 1952, a German team was entered at Oslo and Helsinki, made up entirely of athletes from the Federal Republic of Germany. (See also German Democratic Republic)

At the 51st IOC Session in Paris in 1955, the GDR was granted recognition by the IOC by a vote of 27–7. However, the proviso to this recognition was that both Germanys would compete at the Olympics with a combined team. Avery Brundage (*q.v.*) boasted, "We have obtained in the field of sports what politicians have failed to achieve so far."

In 1956, 1960, and 1964, a combined East and West German team competed under one flag. On 6 October 1965, at the 64th IOC Session in Madrid, the IOC gave the GDR the right to enter a separate team at the 1968 Olympic Games. However, the decision mandated that both Germanys compete with the same uniforms, using the same flag adorned with the Olympic Symbol (*q.v.*), and using the same anthem, the choral theme from Beethoven's Ninth Symphony. In addition, the GDR agreed to compete as East Germany, a name it did not recognize.

At the 68th IOC Session at Mexico City in 1968, the IOC voted 44–4 that, beginning in 1972, both the FRG and the GDR could compete separately at the Olympic Games, wearing their own uniforms, and using their own flag and anthem, and with the correct names of their nations.

On 3 October 1990, the GDR and the FRG dissolved their separate governments to once again form a single united German state. Competing in Albertville and Barcelona in 1992 was a single team representing a unified Germany.

Germany, wholly or separately, has always been one of the most powerful nations at the Olympics. Germany has also hosted three Olympic Games: the Games of the XIth Olympiad in Berlin in 1936, the 4th Olympic Winter Games in Garmisch-Partenkirchen, also in 1936, and the Games of the XXth Olympiad in Munich in 1972. In addition, the 1916 Olympic Games were originally planned for Berlin, and the 1940 Olympic Winter Games were rescheduled for Garmisch-Partenkirchen after Sapporo and then St. Moritz withdrew as hosts.

Germeshausen, Bernhard. [GDR-BOB]   B. 28 August 1951, Heiligenstadt. With his compatriot Meinhard Nehmer (*q.v.*) he won the two-man bob in 1976, and they were both members of the winning four-man crew in 1976 and 1980. The three Olympic gold medals they each won stand as the current Olympic record. Germeshausen also won silver in the two-man event at the 1980 Olympics (partnering Hans-Jürgen Gerhardt), and he was the winner at the World Championships in the two-man in 1981 (with Gerhardt) and in the four-man in 1977 and 1981.

Ghana [GHA]   Ghana first appeared at the Olympics in 1952, as the Gold Coast. It did not attend the 1956 Olympics, but competed from 1960 through 1972. After boycotting the 1976 and 1980 Olympics, Ghana has attended the 1984 through 1992 Olympics. Ghana has never competed at the Olympic Winter Games. Ghanian athletes have won four medals at the Olympic Games.

Gliding   A gliding exhibition was held at the 1936 Olympics in Berlin.

Gold Coast   See Ghana.

Golf   Golf has been held in the 1900 and 1904 Olympics. In 1900, men and women competed in separate individual events. In 1904, a men's individual match-play event and a team stroke-play event were contested. Golf was on the Olympic schedule in both 1908 and 1920 but was not contested in either year. There is a possibility that golf will be reinstated as a medal sport at the 2000 Olympics in Sydney, with individual competitions for both men and women. The World Amateur Golf Council is recognized by the IOC.

Goodwill Games   The Goodwill Games were held for the first time in 1985 in Moscow. They were the brainchild of Ted Turner of Atlanta, Georgia, the head of Turner Broadcasting and the Cable News Network. Turner was upset about the boycotts of the Olympics in both 1980 and 1984 and saw the need to hold a "peaceful" sporting festival outside of the Olympic Movement. They have been held in 1989 in Seattle, Washington, and in 1993 in St. Petersburg, Russia (the former Leningrad and Petrograd). With the break-up of the Soviet Union, the need for a Goodwill Games is now far from clear. In addition, the Games have lost significant amounts of money at each celebration and their future is in doubt.

Gould, Shane Elizabeth. [AUS-SWI]   B. 23 November 1956, Brisbane. A swimmer of phenomenal talent who became the first woman to hold the world freestyle record at every distance from 100 meters to 1,500 meters. She achieved this remarkable feat in December 1971, just three weeks after her fifteenth birthday. At the Olympic Games the following year she won the 200 meters and 400 meters freestyle and 200 meters individual medley, each in a new world record time, and, in addition to her three gold medals, she took the silver in the 800 meters and the bronze in the 100 meters freestyle. In 1973, still aged only 16, she retired but during her brief career she had become one of the legends of the sport.

Grafström, Gillis Emanuel. [SWE-FSK]   B. 7 June 1893, Stockholm. D. 14 April 1938, Potsdam, Germany. The supreme figure skater in the years following World War I, he won a record three Olympic gold medals (1920, 1924, 1928) and, in 1932, earned a silver medal in Lake Placid. He was also a three-time winner at the World Championships (1922, 1924, 1929). A noted amateur painter and sculptor, he skated more for aesthetic pleasure than for the competitive challenge. A professional architect, he worked mainly in Germany and spent little time in his native Sweden.

Great Britain [GBR]   Great Britain is the only nation which has never failed to be represented at the Olympic Games, including all the usual exceptions. It competed at the 1906 Intercalated Games in Athens, the 1908 figure skating events in London, the 1920 figure skating events in Antwerp, and at the 1956 Equestrian Olympics in Stockholm. Through 1920, Great Britain competed as a combined team with Ireland, which was still not an independent nation. Great Britain has won 640 Olympic medals, 181 of them gold, most of them at the Summer Olympics. Great Britain has twice hosted the Olympic Games, the Games of the IVth Olympiad in London in 1908, and the Games of the XIVth Olympiad in London in 1948.

Greece [GRE]   Greece is the home of the Olympics, the Ancient Games having been held there from at least 776 B.C. through 393 A.D. The Modern Olympic Games were revived and first held in Athens in 1896. Prior to 1896, several attempts at revival of the Olympics were contested in Greece, notably the Zappas Olympics (*q.v.*) of 1859, 1870, 1875, and 1889. Since 1896, Greek participation has been continuous at all Games of the Olympiad. Greece has also competed at the Olympic Winter Games, first appearing in 1936 and missing only the 1960 Squaw Valley Olympics. Greece hosted the Games of the Ist Olympiad in Athens in 1896, and also hosted the Intercalated Olympic Games of 1906. Greek athletes have won over 100 medals in the Olympics, with 83 of those occurring in 1896 and 1906.

Grenada [GRN]   Grenada has competed at the Olympics of 1984, 1988, and 1992. It has not competed at the Olympic Winter Games and it has not yet won an Olympic medal. The best Grenadan finish was equal ninth in 1984 welterweight boxing by Bernard Wilson.

Griffith Joyner, Delorez Florence (née Griffith). [USA–ATH] B. 21 December 1959, Los Angeles, California. A superb sprinter who completely dominated the women's track season in 1988. After setting a world record for 100 meters at the U.S. Olympic Trials, she won three gold and one silver medal at the Seoul Games. Victories in the 100 meters and 200 meters, in which she twice broke the world record, were followed by a third gold in the sprint relay and a silver in the 4x400 meters relay. She had previously won a silver medal in the 200 meters in 1984. The flamboyant outfits she wore on the track made her a darling of the media who gave her the name "Flo–Jo" after her marriage in 1987 to the 1984 Olympic triple jump gold medalist, Al Joyner.

Grishin, Yevgeny Romanovich. [URS–SSK]   B. 23 March 1931, Tula. The winner of gold medals for speed skating in the 500 meters and 1,500 meters at both the 1956 and 1960 Winter Games. He set world records at both distances but was at his best at 500 meters, winning six world titles and achieving the distinction of being the first skater to break the 40 seconds barrier. He became a coach with the national speed skating squad after he retired from competition.

Groß, Michael. [FRG–SWI]   B. 17 June 1964, Frankfurt. Michael Groß won six Olympic medals, three gold, mostly in the butterfly and sprint freestyle events. He was known as "The

Albatross" because of his enormous arm span of over seven feet (2.14 meters). At the World Championships he won a record 13 medals (five gold, five silver, three bronze), and he also won a record 18 medals at four European Championships (13 gold, four silver, one bronze). During his career he set ten world records in individual events. His top Olympics was 1984 when he won the 200 meter freestyle and the 100 meter butterfly, and took silver at the 200 meter butterfly and in anchoring the 4x200 meter freestyle relay.

Grøttumsbråten, Johan. [NOR-NSK] B. 24 February 1899, Sørkedalen, Oslo. D. 21 January 1983. Together with fellow–Norwegian, Thorleif Haug (*q.v.*), he dominated the Nordic skiing events at the early editions of the Winter Games. In 1924, he won silver at 18 km., bronze in the 50 km. and the Nordic combined event, and then in 1928 he won the 18 km. and the Nordic combined. He won his third gold and sixth medal overall in 1932 when he successfully defended his title in the Nordic combined event.

Guam [GUM]   Guam's initial Olympic appearance came at the 1988 Olympic Winter Games. It also competed at the 1988 Olympic Games in Seoul. In 1992, it competed in Barcelona but not Albertville, nor Lillehammer. Guam's best Olympic performance came in 1992 when female marathoner Jen Allred finished 36th of 47 runners.

Guatemala [GUA]   Guatemala first competed in the 1952 Olympics. It did not appear again until 1968 but has not missed an Olympic Games since. Guatemala appeared at its only Olympic Winter Games in 1988 at Calgary. Its top performances have been a tie for fifth (quarter-finals) by Carlos Mo Ha-Taracena in 1984 light-flyweight boxing, and a sixth-place finish by Edgardo Zachrisson in skeet shooting at Montreal in 1976.

Guiana, British   See Guyana.

Guinea [GUI]   Guinea has competed at the Olympic Games of 1968, 1980, 1984, 1988, and 1992. It has never competed at the Olympic Winter Games, nor has any Guinean athlete won a medal. Its best Olympic performance came in athletics in 1980 when Sékou Camara finished fifth in his heat of the first round of the 800 meters.

Guinea–Bissau [GNB]   The Olympic Committee of Guinea–Bissau was given official recognition by the IOC in June 1995 at the 104th IOC Session in Budapest.

Guyana [GUY]   Guyana has competed at 11 Olympic Games since 1948, missing only 1976. It competed from 1948 to 1964 as British Guiana, competing first as Guyana in 1968. Guyana has never competed at the Olympic Winter Games. Guyana claims one Olympic medal, a bronze in bantamweight boxing in 1980 by Michael Anthony.

Gyarmati, Desző. [HUN–WAP]   B. 23 October 1927, Miskolc. The greatest of all Olympic water polo players. His feat of winning medals at five successive Games (gold 1952, 1956, 1964; silver 1948; bronze 1960) has never been matched. A national hero, he coached the Hungarian team which won the Olympic title in 1976 and later became a member of Parliament. He married the 1952 Olympic 200 meters breaststroke champion Eva Székely. Their daughter, Andrea, was an Olympic silver medalist in the 100 meters backstroke in 1972 and she later married Mihály Hesz, the 1968 Olympic canoeing champion.

Gymnastics   Gymnastics is an ancient sport, having been practiced in various forms in Ancient Greece and Rome. However, gymnastics competitions are relatively modern. The modern development of gymnastics began in the mid–19th century in Europe. Gymnastics societies were formed in Germany (Turnvereins) and Bohemia of the Austro–Hungarian Empire (Sokols). Similar societies were formed in France and Switzerland and then spread generally throughout Europe.

In 1881, the Fédération Internationale de Gymnastique (FIG) was formed to organize gymnastics competitions. Modern competitive gymnastics has developed from two systems – the German Turnverein system emphasizing apparatus work of a formal nature and stressing muscular development, and the Swedish system of free exercises concerned with developing rhythmic movements.

Gymnastics has been contested at every Olympic Games. The program has varied widely but since World War II it has been fairly constant. Men compete in teams on six apparatuses – still rings, floor exercises, horizontal bar, parallel bars, pommelled horse, and horse vault. The top competitors in the team event are eligible for the individual all–around event (maximum of three per nation). This is conducted again on all six apparatuses. The top performers in each apparatus are then advanced to the individual apparatus finals, again with a maximum of three performers from any nation per event.

Individuals must be all-around performers; it is not possible to specialize on a single apparatus and enter in that.

Women's competition is similar, except that they compete in only four events - uneven parallel bars, floor exercises, horse vault, and balance beam. In 1984, rhythmic gymnastics for women was added to the Olympic program.

At the Olympics, the Soviet Union and its republics have been dominant in the women's events. Romania has also had superb female gymnasts, notably the remarkable Nadia Comăneci (*q.v.*). Men's gymnastics has been divided almost evenly since World War II by the Japanese and Soviet Union. The Chinese men are also now of top calibre.

The sport is governed world-wide by the Fédération Internationale de Gymnastique (FIG), which was founded in 1881 and currently has 117 member federations.

********** H **********

Hackl, Georg. [FRG/GER-LUG]   B. 9 September 1966. Georg Hackl is the only luger to have won medals at three consecutive Olympics in singles luge. After a silver medal in 1988 at Calgary, Hackl also became the first man to defend the Olympic luge singles title, winning in both 1992 and 1994. In addition to his Olympic successes, Hackl was singles World Champion in 1989 and 1990, and also won the luge World Cup in those years. In 1993, he was second in the World Championships and the World Cup, after having placed third in the World Cup in the Olympic year of 1992.

Haiti [HAI]   Haiti has a curious Olympic history. A fencer named Léon Thiercelin represented it at the 1900 Olympics in Paris. Its next appearances were in 1924, 1928, and 1932, followed by a long gap before its return to the Olympic fold in 1960. Haiti did not attend the 1964 or 1968 Olympics. Despite having appeared in five Olympics through 1960, it had a total Olympic representation of twelve men to that date. Haiti has since appeared at the 1972, 1976, 1984, 1988, and 1992 Olympics. It has not yet competed in the Olympic Winter Games. Haiti has won two medals in the Olympic Games through 1994.

Hämäläinen-Kirvesniemi, Marja-Liisa (née Hämäläinen).
[FIN-NSK]   B. 10 September 1955, Simpele, Finnish South

Karelia. After competing without distinction in the 1976 and 1980 Winter Games she achieved unprecedented success at the 1984 Games. With victories in the 5 km., 10 km. and 20 km. she became the first woman to win three gold medals for Nordic skiing at one Games. She also won a bronze medal in the relay and won a second relay bronze in 1988 but illness prevented her from adding to her medal tally at her fifth Olympics in 1992. At the 1994 Olympic Winter Games, she finished her Olympic career with bronze medals in the 5 km. and 30 km. races, giving her a total of seven Olympic medals. After her triple victory in 1984 she married Harri Kirvesniemi, himself an Olympic bronze medalist. Hämäläinen-Kirvesniemi is the only woman, and one of three athletes, to compete in six Olympic Winter Games.

Handball (Team Handball)   Handball is a team sport which combines aspects of basketball, soccer, and water polo. It is played on a basketball sized court by teams of seven players who attempt to score goals by throwing a ball slightly smaller than a volleyball into a goal on the ground which is about the size of a lacrosse goal.

The game was invented in Germany in the early 20th century and became very popular in Europe. At the 1936 Olympics, the Germans added it to the program, but it was contested outdoors on a large field with 11 men to a side. It was not again on the Olympic program until 1972 when it was added to the Olympics at Munich. This time the sport was contested as described above with seven men to a side and indoors. In 1976, women's handball became an Olympic sport.

Handball is immensely popular in Europe, surpassed by only football (soccer), athletics (track & field), and, perhaps recently, basketball and volleyball. The same popularity has not extended to other areas of the world, notably the United States; thus the sport has been dominated by the Europeans. The sport is governed world-wide by the Fédération Internationale de Handball (IHF), which was founded in 1946 and had 136 members at the end of 1994.

Haug, Thorleif. [NOR-NSK]   B. 28 September 1894, Lier. D. 12 December 1934, Drammen. Winning all three Nordic skiing events (18 km., 50 km. and Nordic combination) at the 1st Winter Games in 1924, the 29-year-old Norwegian was the star of the Games. Although his feat has been equaled on many occasions, no Nordic skier has yet succeeded in winning more than three gold medals at one Games. In 1924, he was also awarded the bronze medal in the ski jump but 50 years later it was discovered that the scores had been incorrectly calculated and that Anders Haugen [USA] had finished third with Haug in fourth place. Haug's daughter later presented her father's bronze medal to the rightful owner.

Heiden, Eric Arthur. [USA-SSK]   B. 14 June 1958, Madison, Wisconsin.   Recognized as the greatest speed skater of all time, he completely dominated the 1980 Olympic Winter Games, taking the gold medal at all five distances.   He set new Olympic records in every event adding a world record in the 10,000 meters.   At the World Championships following the 1980 Olympics he suffered his first defeat since 1977 and this led to his immediate retirement.   He then turned to cycling and, after coming close to making the U.S. Olympic team in a second sport, he had a brief career as a professional.   His sister, Beth, was also an outstanding speed skater and cyclist.   He later finished medical school and now practices as an orthopaedic surgeon.

Henie, Sonja (later Topping, Gardiner, and Onstad). [NOR-FSK]   B. 8 April 1912, Oslo.   D. 12 October 1969, in flight, Paris–Oslo.   A triple Olympic gold medalist (1928, 1932, 1936), she did more to popularize figure skating than any other individual.   After winning ten world and three Olympic titles she turned professional in 1936 and soon amassed a fortune.   Her flair for showmanship ensured the success of the ten feature films she made in Hollywood and accelerated the public awareness of ice skating as a sport.   She toured the world with spectacular ice reviews achieving great popularity, particularly in the USA.   She was initially idolized in her native Norway, but had some image problems after World War II when she was perceived to be a Nazi sympathizer who failed to support war relief efforts in Norway.   She later suffered from leukemia and died during a flight from Paris to Oslo where she was to visit a specialist.

Hildgartner, Paul. [ITA-LUG]   B. 8 June 1952.   One of the few lugers to win three Olympic medals and two gold medals, Hildgartner uniquely won his gold medals 12 years apart.   In 1972, Hildgartner joined Walter Plaikner to win the Olympic doubles luge gold medal. He then turned to singles luge primarily, earning a silver medal in 1980 and winning the Olympic title in 1984 at Sarajevo.   Hildgartner was also World Champion in singles in 1978, and in doubles in 1971 (with Plaikner).   He was the singles World Cup leader in both 1981 and 1983.

Hockey (Field)   Hockey is the oldest known ball and stick game. Records exist of it having been played in Persia in 2000 B.C.   It became so popular by the Middle Ages that it was banned in England for a time because it interfered with the practice of archery, which was the basis for national defense.

The modern game of hockey, however, was developed in England in the late 19th century. It spread throughout the British Empire, as a result, and most of the dominant nations in the sport have been nations which are, or were, members of that Empire. This includes India, Pakistan, Australia, New Zealand, and the United Kingdom. India's dominance in this team sport is matched only by the United States' dominance of basketball, Hungary's dominance of water polo, and Canadian and Soviet dominance of ice hockey. Between 1928 and 1956, India won six gold medals and 30 consecutive games.

Hockey appeared on the Olympic program in 1908 and 1920. In 1928, it was held at Amsterdam and it has been an Olympic sport since. In 1980, hockey for women was first introduced as an Olympic sport. Hockey is governed internationally by the Fédération Internationale de Hockey (FIH), which was formed in 1924 and had 120 member nations at the end of 1994. (See also India Field Hockey Teams [1928–1964])

Honduras [HON]   Honduras has competed at the Olympics Games of 1968, 1976, 1984, and 1988. In 1992, Honduras competed at Albertville in its only appearance at the Olympic Winter Games to date. The best Honduran finish occurred in the 1976 20 kilometer walk when Santiago Fonseca finished 27th.

Hong Kong [HKG]   Hong Kong first competed at the 1952 Olympic Games and has since missed only the 1980 Moscow Olympics. Hong Kong has never competed at the Olympic Winter Games. Despite this long Olympic history, prior to 1992, no Hong Kong athlete had ever finished in the top ten. In 1992, Chai Po–Wa won four matches in women's table tennis singles to finish equal fifth, the best Olympic finish yet by a Hong Kong athlete. On 1 July 1997, China will regain sovereignty over Hong Kong, currently a dependency of the United Kingdom of Great Britain and Northern Ireland. Hong Kong's Olympic future as a dependency of China is uncertain.

Hoplite Race   See Race in Armor.

Hungary [HUN]   Hungary was one of the countries which attended the first Olympic Games in 1896 in Athens. A National Olympic Committee was formed in Hungary in 1895 by Dr. Franz Kémény, who was one of the founding members of the IOC. Hungary has missed only two Olympics, including the Winter Games.

Hungary was not invited to the 1920 Olympics in Antwerp, having been an aggressor nation in World War I, and Hungary chose not to attend the 1984 Los Angeles Olympics. Hungary has been very successful in a variety of sports, but by far its greatest honors have come in fencing. In one fencing discipline, the sabre, it has been the dominant nation, and in fact, between 1908 and 1960 Hungary won 9 of 11 team titles and 10 of 11 individual titles in this event.

********** I **********

Ice Dancing   See Demonstration Sports and Figure Skating.

Ice Hockey   Ice hockey is a Canadian sport which began in the early 19th century. Around 1860, a puck was substituted for a ball, and in 1879, two McGill University students, W. F. Robertson and R. F. Smith, devised the first rules, combining field hockey and rugby regulations. Originally the game was played nine to a side.

The sport became the Canadian national sport with leagues everywhere. In 1894, Lord Stanley of Preston, Governor-General of Canada, donated the Stanley Cup which was first won in 1894 by a team representing the Montreal Amateur Athletic Association.

Ice hockey was contested at the 1920 Summer Olympics at Antwerp, held in early April. These were also the first World Championships and were played by seven-man sides, the only time seven-man teams played in the Olympics. In 1924, the Olympics began using the current standard of six men on the ice at a time.

Ice hockey has been held at every Olympic Winter Games. Canada dominated early Olympic ice hockey tournaments as might be expected. In 1956, the Soviet Union first entered the Olympic Winter Games and won the ice hockey tournament quite handily. It has been the pre-eminent country since, its dominance interrupted only by major upset victories by the United States in 1960 and 1980.

Women's ice hockey has been proposed as an Olympic sport and it will appear on the Olympic program in 1998 at Nagano. The sport is governed by the International Ice Hockey Federation (IIHF), which was founded in 1908 and had 50 affiliated nations at the end of 1994. (See also Canadian Ice Hockey Teams [1920–1952] and Soviet Union Ice Hockey Teams [1956–1992])

Iceland [ISL]   Iceland sent one athlete to the 1908 Olympics, Johannes Josefsson, a wrestler. The country also sent two athletes to the 1912 Olympics, but did not again appear until 1936. Since that time it has never failed to be present at an Olympic Games. It has competed at all Olympic Winter Games since 1948, except for 1972. Iceland has won two medals in the Olympic Games, a silver in triple jump (track & field athletics) by Vilhjálmur Einarsson in 1956, and a bronze in half–heavyweight judo by Bjarni Fridriksson in 1984. It could be argued that Icelanders have won a gold medal. In 1920, Canada won a gold medal in ice hockey at Antwerp. Of the eight Canadians on that team, seven were of Icelandic origin and had dual citizenship.

Independent Olympic Participant [IOP]   In 1992, at Barcelona, several athletes from Yugoslavia were allowed to compete as Independent Olympic Participants. The United Nations Security Council Resolution #757 had placed a ban on Yugoslav teams competing internationally because of the war in Bosnia–Herzegovina. However, the IOC made arrangements allowing individual athletes to compete, providing they did not officially represent Yugoslavia.

India [IND]   India's first Olympic appearance can be traced to 1900 when Norman Pritchard, an Indian citizen, competed in the sprints at Paris, but represented the London Athletic Club and Great Britain. India's next Olympic appearance, and first real one, occurred in 1920, although India's NOC was not formed until 1927. In 1928, India entered its first field hockey team and won the gold medal. This was the first of six consecutive gold medals won by India in men's field hockey. Pritchard won two medals in the 1900 sprints, and one Indian wrestler has won a medal (Kha–Shaba Jadav – 1952 freestyle bantamweight bronze) but otherwise, all of India's 14 medals in the Olympics have been won by its field hockey team. India has competed at the 1964, 1968, 1988, and 1992 Olympic Winter Games.

India Field Hockey Teams [1928–1964]   India dominated Olympic hockey (field hockey) from its first appearance in 1928 through 1964. During that time, India won 30 consecutive Games (1928–1960), the streak being broken, 1–0, in the 1960 finals by Pakistan. India won the gold medal in seven of the eight Olympics between 1928 and 1964, inclusive, losing only in 1960 to Pakistan, but still taking a silver medal. India continues to be one of the top nations in Olympic hockey, winning a bronze medal in 1968 and 1972, and another gold medal in 1980. Since that time, India's best finish has been fifth in 1984. Overall, India has an Olympic hockey record of 69 wins, 15 losses, and 8 ties. It has outscored its opponents 371 goals to 91 goals. India's women have competed in

Olympic hockey since 1980 but with less success, not having won any medals to date.

Indonesia [INA]   Indonesia formed a National Olympic Committee in 1946 but did not compete at the Olympics until 1952. Indonesia missed the 1964 Olympic Games when it withdrew after several of its athletes were banned for their participation at the 1963 Games of the New Emerging Forces (GANEFO). (See Korea, Democratic People's Republic of, and The Games of the XVIIIth Olympiad) Indonesia also boycotted the 1980 Olympics. The country has never competed at the Olympic Winter Games. Indonesia's national sport is badminton (*q.v.*), at which it is one of the dominant countries in the world, and at which it has won five of Indonesia's six Olympic medals.

International Federations [IFs]   International Federations (IFs) are non-governmental organizations which administer sports on an international level. The IFs' role is to establish and enforce the rules governing the practice of their sport, promote development of their sport internationally, and assume responsibility for the technical control of their sport at the Olympic Games. The sports governed by the IFs may be admitted to the Olympic program if they satisfy the following requirements: Games of the Olympiad - the sports must be widely practiced by men in at least 75 countries and four continents and by women in at least 40 countries and three continents. Olympic Winter Games - the sports must be widely practiced in at least 25 countries and three continents. (See the individual sports of the Olympics, which give the names, dates of foundation, and number of member nations for the various International Federations)

International Olympic Academy [IOA]   The idea of an International Olympic Academy (IOA) was first conceived in the 1930's by Ioannis Ketseas (*q.v.*), an IOC Member in Greece, and Carl Diem (*q.v.*). The idea never died but it took many years of informal discussions before the foundation of an Academy, to be located at Olympia, was unanimously approved by the IOC during a session in Rome in 1949. Of the 80 invitations sent to NOCs for the first preliminary session, only four replies were received and all of these were in the negative. Ketseas, who was now working closely with Carl Diem, a German professor with a passionate interest in Olympic matters, persisted with his goal and with the assistance of Olympic and archaeological bodies from Germany and Greece, the Academy eventually came into being and has subsequently prospered. The first session was held from 16-23 June 1961. A plot of some 150 acres of land bordering the Ancient Olympic stadium was acquired by the IOA, buildings were erected, and the complex, which now provides accommodations, a library, and several sports facilities, is a popular center for students of the Olympic Movement (*q.v.*). The IOA holds an annual session each summer during which students of the Olympic Movement gather for several days to hear speeches and talks on Olympic subjects. In addition, many other international symposia are held at the IOA each year. The idea of Olympic Academies has now spread and, as of 1995, there are also 72 National Olympic Academies, helping to spread the message of Olympism (*q.v.*) and the Olympic Movement (*q.v.*).

International Olympic Committee [IOC] The International Olympic Committee (IOC) is the international governing organization of the Olympic Movement and the Olympic Games. It is a non-governmental, non-profit organization of unlimited duration, in the form of an association with the status of a legal person, recognized by decree of the Swiss Federal Council of 17 September 1981. The International Olympic Committee was founded by Pierre de Coubertin (*q.v.*) in 1894, at the Olympic Congress which re-established the Olympic Games. The IOC is currently based in Lausanne, Switzerland, and has been since Coubertin moved there during World War I. The mission of the IOC is to lead the Olympic Movement in accordance with the Olympic Charter (*qq.v.*).

The IOC consists of members who are chosen and co-opted to membership. IOC member nations may have one member on the IOC, although not all do. However, any nation which has hosted the Olympic Games or Olympic Winter Games is entitled to a second member on the IOC. IOC members are not considered to be members *from* their respective nations. Rather, they are considered to be IOC ambassadors *to* or *in* their respective nations. Members must now retire at the end of the calendar year in which they reach the age of 75.

The IOC is led by a President, four Vice-Presidents, and an Executive Board (*q.v.*). The President is elected initially for a term of eight years, but may be re-elected for subsequent terms of four years. Vice-Presidents and Executive Board members are elected for a term of four years. They may not be re-elected to the same position for consecutive terms, although they may return to that position on the Executive Board after a period of four more years.

IOC Sessions consist of meetings of the entire membership and are required to be held at least once a year. The IOC Session is considered to be the supreme organ of the IOC but may delegate its powers to the Executive Board. The Executive Board meets more frequently and works by making recommendations to the IOC Sessions, which is then responsible for enacting or denying its recommendations. Day-to-day decisions are delegated to the IOC President. The Olympic Charter is the document which specifies the principles, rules, and byelaws of the IOC. Only IOC Sessions have the power to modify and interpret the Olympic Charter. (See Olympic Charter, Executive Board of the IOC, Appendix I for list of IOC Presidents, Appendix IV for list of all IOC Members, and the separate biographies of IOC Presidents: Demetrios Vikelas, Baron Pierre de Coubertin, Count Henri de Baillet-Latour, J. Sigfrid Edström, Avery Brundage, Lord Killanin, and Juan Antonio Samaranch)

International Paralympic Committee [IPC]   The International Paralympic Committee governs the Paralympics. These are international sporting events which typically follow the Olympic Games, usually in the same city which hosts the Olympic Games, and are contested by athletes with specific disabilities.

International Pierre de Coubertin Committee   The International Pierre de Coubertin Committee was founded in 1976. It is committed to the dissemination and study of Coubertin's (*q.v.*) works and his humanitarianism. The first President of the International Pierre de Coubertin Committee was Dr. Paul Martin (SUI), followed in 1977 by Geoffroy de Navacelle, Coubertin's grand-nephew. The current president is Conrado Durántez Corral (ESP). Navacelle and IOC President Juan Antonio Samaranch (*q.v.*) are currently Honorary Presidents of the International Pierre de Coubertin Committee.

International Society of Olympic Historians [ISOH]   Founded in 1991 to promote and study the history of the Olympic Movement (*q.v.*) and the Olympic Games, the immediate world-wide response from Olympic historians provided a clear indication of the need for such an organization. A journal of the group is published three times per year. As of 1995 the officers are: Honorary President Erich Kamper (AUT); President Ian Buchanan (GBR); Vice-President Ture Widlund (SWE); and Secretary-General Bill Mallon (USA).

Iran [IRI, formerly IRN]   Iran first competed at the 1948 Olympic Games and its participation was continuous through 1976. It has competed in 1988 and 1992 but boycotted the Games of 1980 and 1984. It has competed at the Olympic Winter Games of 1956, 1964, 1968, 1972, and 1976. All of Iran's success has come in the strength sports of weightlifting and wrestling. Through 1994, it has won 33

Olympic medals (4 gold medals) with 24 medals won in wrestling and 9 won in weightlifting.

Iraq [IRQ]   Iraq formed its National Olympic Committee in 1948 and made its first Olympic appearance in that year. Iraq then did not compete until the Rome Olympics of 1960. Iraq missed the 1972 and 1976 Olympics but has competed continuously since, including the 1984 Olympic Games. Iraq has never competed at the Olympic Winter Games. One Iraqi athlete has won an Olympic medal, that being a bronze medal by Abdul Wahid Aziz in lightweight weightlifting in 1960.

Ireland [IRL]   Ireland formed a National Olympic Committee in 1922, shortly after it became independent of Great Britain in December 1921. Ireland first competed as a separate state in the 1924 Olympic Games at Paris. Prior to that time, however, many Irish athletes had competed – mostly for Great Britain. In addition many of the great American weight-throwers had been recent Irish immigrants. Ireland also entered separate teams in 1908 field hockey and the 1912 cycling road race. Since 1924, Ireland has competed at every Olympic Games except those of 1936. Ireland has competed at the Olympic Winter Games only in 1992. Through 1994, Ireland has won 15 Olympic medals: 5 gold, 5 silver, and 5 bronze.

Israel [ISR]   The formation of the state of Israel as an independent Jewish state occurred on 15 May 1948. Israel dates its National Olympic Committee to 1933, but that was a Palestine organization, and not truly a precursor of the current NOC. The original Palestine Olympic Committee was recognized by the IOC in 1934, and was to represent Jews, Muslims, and Christians from the Palestine region. However, the rules of the original Palestine NOC stated, "Palestine is the National Home of the Jews, and so the Palestine NOC represents the Jewish National Home." Given that manifesto, the Palestine NOC refused to compete at the 1936 Olympic Games, in protest of Hitler's policies. After World War II, the 1948 London Organizing Committee originally invited the Palestine NOC but later withdrew the invitation. The problem of the status of the Palestine Olympic Committee was solved in 1951 when the Israel Olympic Committee was formed.

Israel competed at its first Olympics in 1952 at Helsinki, the same year in which its National Olympic Committee was formally recognized by the IOC. Israel has missed only the 1980 Moscow Olympics since 1952. Israel made its first Olympic Winter Games appearance in 1994 at Lillehammer. The zenith of Israel participation came in 1992 when two Israeli *judoka* won the nation's first medals. The nadir occurred at Munich on 5 September 1972 when Arab terrorists savagely and cowardly murdered 11 Israeli athletes and officials.

Isthmian Games   The Isthmian Games were ancient sporting festivals which were held biennially. With the Olympic Games, Nemean Games, and Pythian Games (*qq.v.*), they were one of the four great sporting festivals of ancient Greece. The Isthmian Games were contested at the sanctuary of Poseidon at the Isthmus of Corinth. They are first known to have been held in 582 B.C. and lasted through the fourth century A.D. Their origin is attributed to Sisyphus, King of Corinth. Champions at the Isthmian Games originally received crowns of dry wild celery, which was later changed to a crown of pine wreath during Roman times. One report suggests that the Isthmian Games were highly commercialized.

Italy [ITA]   Italy has never missed an Olympic Winter Games and has missed only the Olympic Games of 1904. Although it is usually considered not to have competed in 1896, recent research has discovered that an Italian shooter named Rivabella did compete in 1896. Despite that, Italy did not form a National Olympic Committee until 1908, and it was not until 1915 that this committee was recognized by the IOC. Italy has had success in many different sports. It has often been the dominant country in cycling and fencing. Italy has won 477 Olympic medals, 178 of them gold. Of these, 67 medals and 25 gold have been won at the Olympic Winter Games. Italy also hosted the Games of the XVIIth Olympiad at Rome in 1960, and the 7th Olympic Winter Games at Cortina d'Ampezzo in 1956.

Ivory Coast [CIV]   Ivory Coast has competed in the Olympic Games since 1964, missing only the 1980 Games. The country has not yet appeared at the Olympic Winter Games. Ivory Coast can claim one Olympic medal, a silver won by Gabriel Tiacoh in the 400 meters (track & field athletics) in 1984.

********* J **********

Jamaica [JAM]   Jamaica has sent athletes to all the Olympic Games since 1948. In 1960, Jamaica, Barbados and Trinidad combined to form the West Indies Federation (*q. v.*) team. That team won two medals, one of which was won by George Kerr, a Jamaican, in the 800 meters, while the other was a bronze in the 4x400 meter relay. Three members of that team were Jamaican while one was from Barbados. In 1988, Jamaica competed at its first Olympic Winter Games, represented by the now famous Jamaican Bobsled Team, which also represented the nation at Albertville in 1992 and Lillehammer in 1994. A movie, *Cool Runnings*, was later made about the Jamaican bobsled team. Jamaica has won 24 Olympic medals through 1994, 23 of them in track & field athletics, led by its outstanding sprinters. The other medal was a bronze in cycling won by David Weller in the 1,000 meter time trial.

Japan [JPN]   Japan first competed at the 1912 Olympic Games, its delegation and Olympic Committee led by Dr. Jigoro Kano, the founder of judo. Japan has since failed to compete only at the Games of 1948, when, as an aggressor nation in World War II, it was not invited, and 1980, when it chose to boycott the Moscow Olympics. At the Olympic Winter Games, Japan first competed in 1928 and has since missed only 1948 when it was also not invited. Japan was the dominant country in men's gymnastics from 1956 until the mid-1980's. In addition, at times it has been the top country in swimming and one of the top in wrestling and weightlifting. Japan has won 283 Olympic medals (92 gold medals), of which 19 (3 gold) came at the Olympic Winter Games. Japan hosted the Games of the XVIIIth Olympiad in Tokyo in 1964 and the 11th Olympic Winter Games in Sapporo in 1972. In addition, the 18th Olympic Winter Games are scheduled to be held in Nagano, Japan in 1998. Prior to the outbreak of hostilities, Japan was also scheduled to host both editions of the 1940 Olympics; the Olympic Winter Games were scheduled for Sapporo, and the Games of the XIIth Olympiad were scheduled for Tokyo.

Jernberg, Sixten. [SWE-NSK]   B. 6 February 1929, Lima, Dalarna (Dalecarlia). The most successful male Olympic Nordic skier in history. Between 1956 and 1964, he won four gold, three silver and two bronze for a record total, for men, of nine Winter Olympic medals. He added three gold and two bronze medals at the 1954, 1958, and 1962 World Championships, including four medals in the 50 km. Between 1952 and 1964 he took part in 363 ski races, winning 134. In his prime years of 1955–1960, he won 86 of 161 races. Initially a blacksmith and then a lumberjack his daily work provided the essential stamina for the rigors of long distance cross-country skiing. In 1965, the IOC awarded him the Mohammed Taher Trophy. (See Appendix V)

Jeu de Paume (Court Tennis or Real Tennis)   *Jeu de paume,* or game of the hand, the original version of tennis, has been contested in the Olympics only in 1908, when the gold medal was won by American Jay Gould. In 1928, the sport was a demonstration (*q.v.*) event in Amsterdam.

Johansson, Ivar. **[SWE-WRE]**   B. 31 January 1903, Kuddby, Östergötland. D. 4 August 1979. One of only three men to have won Olympic gold medals in both styles of wrestling and also one of three wrestlers to have won a total of three Olympic gold medals. In 1932, he won the freestyle middleweight and the Greco-Roman welterweight titles and, in 1936, he won the Greco-Roman middleweight. He won nine European Championships between 1931 and 1939, six at Greco and three at freestyle. He was a 22-time Swedish champion, winning 13 at Greco and 9 at freestyle. His last Swedish title came in 1943 at the age of 40.

Jordan [JOR]   Jordan formed a National Olympic Committee in 1957 which was recognized by the IOC in 1963. However, it was not until 1980 that Jordan's athletes competed on Olympian fields. Jordan has competed at the 1980, 1984, 1988, and 1992 Olympic Games, but has not yet appeared in the Olympic Winter Games. In 1980, Mohamed Jbour finished 26th of 39 shooters in small-bore rifle, three positions, the best ever finish by a Jordanian Olympian.

Jordan, Michael Jeffrey. **[USA-BAS]**   B. 17 February 1963, Brooklyn, New York. Michael Jordan is considered by many experts to be the greatest basketball player of all time. He played collegiately at the University of North Carolina, where he helped it win an NCAA championship in 1983. In 1984, Jordan led the United States to an Olympic gold medal. (See United States Basketball Team – 1984) Turning to professional basketball after his junior year in college, he became the greatest scorer in the NBA (National Basketball Association [USA]), leading the league in scoring every year except one in which he sat out most of the season with injury. In 1991, Jordan finally achieved his greatest thrill, leading the Chicago Bulls to an NBA Championship, and completing his Triple Crown of titles. Jordan eventually led the Bulls to three NBA titles in 1991 to 1993 and then retired from basketball to pursue a career in professional baseball. However, he never got out of the minor leagues and after two years, he returned to the NBA in March 1995 amidst much ballyhoo. In 1992, Jordan also played on the Dream Team (*q.v.*) which won the basketball gold medal at Barcelona.

Judo   The founder of judo, Dr. Jigaro Kano, was a long-time member of the International Olympic Committee. Judo is a form of wrestling which was developed by Dr. Kano from the ancient Japanese schools of yawara and jujitsu. He founded his first *dojo* (judo school) in 1882, termed the *Kodokan*. The contestants are termed *judoka* and are classified into grades consisting of pupils (*Kyu*) and degrees (*Dan*). There are five classes of *Kyu*, advancing to first *Kyu*, and wearing a brown belt. Thereafter, the *judoka* achieve a *Dan*, beginning with first *Dan* (black belt) and advancing theoretically to 12th *Dan* (white belt). Fighting ability and technical knowledge advance a *judoka* to fifth *Dan*, after which advancement depends on service to the sport. Leading international *judoka* are usually fourth or fifth *Dan*. The 11th and 12th *Dan* have never been awarded.

Judo made its first Olympic appearance in 1964, but was not included on the program of the 1968 Olympic Games. Judo returned to the Olympic fold in 1972 and the 1992 Olympics included judo events for women for the first time. The sport, not surprisingly, has been dominated by the Japanese, followed by the Soviet Union, with the Koreans also winning many medals. The sport is governed internationally by the International Judo Federation (IJF), which was formed in 1951 and had 168 members through 1994.

********** K **********

Kalpe - Ancient Olympic Sport   The *kalpe*, or race for mares, was a truly curious event. It is not known how many laps of the hippodrome were contested but, on the last lap, the rider dismounted and ran alongside the mare to the finish. The race was first contested in 496 B.C. and was dropped in 444 B.C. although only one winner is known, that being Pataikos of Dymai in 496 B.C.

Kampuchea   See Cambodia.

Kania-Busch-Enke, Karin. [GDR-SSK]   B. 20 June 1961, Dresden. Initially a leading figure skater she later became a champion speed skater and is one of the very few athletes to have reached world class in both disciplines. As she felt that chances for improvement on her ninth place in the 1977 European Figure Skating Championships were limited, she turned to speed skating with considerable success. Her total of eight medals (three gold, four silver, one bronze) between 1980 and 1988 remains an Olympic record for speed skating and her record at the World Championships was even more impressive. She won the sprint title a record six times (1980, 1981, 1983, 1984, 1986, 1987) and her five victories in the overall event were also a record for the Championships even though she missed the 1985 Championships because of pregnancy.

Kato, Sawao. [JPN-GYM]   B. 11 October 1946, Sugadaira, Niigata Prefecture. Winner of a record (for men) eight gold medals for gymnastics. He was a member of the winning all-around team in 1968, 1972 and 1976, and also took the individual title on the first two occasions, but had to settle for a silver medal in 1976. His other gold medals came in the individual floor exercises (1968) and the individual parallel bars (1972, 1976).

Kazakhstan [KAZ, formerly KZK]   Kazakhstan's National Olympic Committee was recognized by the IOC in 1992 shortly after the break-up of the Soviet Union. Many Kazakhstani athletes competed from 1952 to 1988 for the Soviet Union, and Kazakhstani athletes were present at Barcelona and Albertville in 1992 as members of the Unified Team (*q. v.*). Kazakhstan first competed at the Olympics as an independent nation in 1994 at Lillehammer, where its great cross-country skier Vladimir Smirnov won three medals, one gold and two silver.

Keles - Ancient Olympic Sport   In the keles, or horse race, the horse with a rider covered six full laps of the hippodrome. The first known champion was in 648 B.C. (Krauxidas of Krannon), with champions known through 193 A.D. (Theopropos of Rhodes). Hieron, Tyrant of Syracuse, is the only known two-time champion - 476 and 472 B.C.

Kelly, John Brenden "Jack." [USA-ROW]   B. 4 October 1889, Philadelphia, Pennsylvania. D. 26 June 1960, Philadelphia, Pennsylvania. Jack Kelly is probably the greatest sculler the United States has ever produced. Kelly joined the Vesper Boat Club in 1909. Between 1909 and his competitive retirement after the 1924 Olympics, Kelly won every sculling title available to him, including the World Championship in both singles and doubles, the Olympics in singles and doubles, and many national titles in both boats. Kelly never won the Diamond Sculls at the Henley Regatta because he was denied entry as Vesper Boat Club was banned for, to the British, earlier professional activities. Kelly fathered two very famous children - John Kelly, Jr., another Olympic rower who was later U.S.

Olympic Committee President, and the late Grace Kelly, the American movie star who later became Princess Grace of Monaco.

Kendo (Japanese fencing)   See Budo.

Kenya [KEN]   Kenya first competed at the Olympics in 1956. After competing in 1960, 1964, 1968, and 1972, it joined the boycotts of 1976 and 1980, but returned to the Olympic fold in 1984 at Los Angeles. It has never competed in the Olympic Winter Games. Kenya has won 39 Olympic medals through 1994, nicely distributed with 13 of each color. Kenya has won seven medals in boxing but all of its other medals are due to its excellent distance runners, the most outstanding of these having been Kipchoge Keino.

Ketseas, Ioannis [GRE]   B. 16 September 1887, Athens. D. 6 April 1965. Ioannis Ketseas was the co-founder of the International Olympic Academy (*q.v.*) with Carl Diem (*q.v.*). His life-long interest in sports led to his becoming President of the Hellenic AAU (SEGAS) in 1929, and President of the Greek Federation of Lawn Tennis in 1939. From 1946 to his death in 1965, he was an IOC Member in Greece. His business was as general director of the National Bank of Greece from 1906–1928, and he also served the Greek government as Minister of Foreign Affairs from 1921–1922. He and Diem founded the IOC officially in 1961, although they had promulgated the idea for almost 30 years. Ketseas served as the first Chairman of the Ephoria of the IOA, its ruling council, from 1961–1965.

Killanin, Lord, of Dublin and Spittal; Sir Michael Morris. [IRL] B. 30 July 1914, London, England. Lord Killanin was elected as President of the Olympic Council of Ireland in 1950. He became an IOC member two years later. In 1967, he was elected to the Executive Board. In 1968, he ascended to third Vice-President of the IOC and in 1970 he was named first Vice-President. He was elected as President of the IOC in 1972 and held that office until his retirement in 1980, when he was awarded the Olympic Order (*q.v.*) in Gold. He was also elected Honorary President for Life of the IOC. A noted journalist, author, and film producer, Lord Killanin also served as a director of many leading Irish business companies.

Killy, Jean-Claude. [FRA-ASK]   B. 30 August 1943, Saint-Cloud, Seine-et-Oise. At his Olympic debut in 1964 he only placed fifth in the giant slalom but four years later he matched Toni Sailer's (*q.v.*) 1956 record by winning Olympic gold in all three Alpine skiing events. Unlike Sailer, who won his events by substantial margins, all Killy's victories were narrow ones and he only won the slalom after the controversial disqualification of the Austrian, Karl Schranz. Killy was also World Champion in the Alpine combination (1966, 1968) and downhill (1966) and was a convincing winner of the first two World Cup competitions (1967, 1968). Following his retirement at the end of the 1968 season he amassed a fortune from endorsements and he also became involved in motor racing, films and professional ski racing. He was Co–President of the Organizing Committee for the 1992 Winter Games in Albertville. He then became President of the Amaury Group, which controls the Tour de France, the Paris–Dakar auto rally, and *L'Équipe*, the French sporting daily newspaper. Killy is the only person to have won an Olympic gold medal and been awarded the Olympic Order (*q.v.*) in Gold. In addition, in 1995 Killy was elected as a member of the International Olympic Committee (*q.v.*).

Kim Soo-Nyung. [KOR-ARC] B. 5 April 1971, Choong Chung Book Province. In only a few short years, she established herself as the greatest woman archer of the modern era. In 1988, Kim won an individual and team gold medal in archery at the Olympics. Nicknamed "Viper," she was women's individual and team world champion in both 1989 and 1991. Through 1990, she held every women's world record at all distances, and overall as well. At the Barcelona Olympics she again helped Korea to the team gold but finished second in the individual event.

Kiraly, Charles F., "Karch." [USA-VOL] B. 3 November 1960, Jackson, Michigan. Kiraly is regarded by many as the greatest volleyballer ever. In 1986, the FIVB declared him the top player in the world, the first time that distinction had been given. He won gold medals at the 1984 and 1988 Olympics, 1985 World Cup, 1986 World Championships, and 1987 Pan–American Games. He played at UCLA in college, where he led them to three NCAA championships and was twice named most valuable player of the NCAA Tournament. Playing professionally in Italy, he helped Il Messaggero win the 1991 World Club Championship. Now a star at beach volleyball, he has been the leading professional money winner at that sport from 1991 to 1994.

Klimke, Reiner. [FRG/GER-EQU] B. 14 January 1936, Münster. His six gold and two bronze medals in dressage events stand as the Olympic record for any of the equestrian disciplines. He won team gold in 1964, 1968, 1976, 1984 and 1988 and the individual gold in 1984. His two bronze medals came in the individual event in 1968 and 1976. He also had a fine record at the World Championships, winning six gold medals (two individual [1974, 1982] and four team [1966, 1974, 1982, 1986]).

Kolehmainen, Johan Pietari "Hannes." [FIN-ATH]   B. 9 December 1889, Kuopio. D. 11 January 1966, Helsinki. The first of the great Finnish distance runners. At the 1912 Olympics, he won the 5,000 meters with a new world record, the 10,000 meters and the individual cross-country race in which he also won a silver medal in the team event. He also set a world record for 3,000 meters in a heat of the team event. The cancellation of the 1916 Games undoubtedly prevented him from winning further Olympic honors but he returned in 1920 to take the gold medal in the marathon.

Kono, Tommy Tamio. [USA-WLT]   B. 27 June 1930, Sacramento, California. Between 1953 and 1959 he was undefeated as a weightlifter in world and Olympic competition, adding six straight world titles to his two Olympic gold medals in 1952 lightweight class and 1956 light-heavyweight class. He also won three straight gold medals in the Pan-American Games, in 1955, 1959, and 1963. He is the only man to ever set world records in four different classes, and he won 11 AAU championships - in three different weight classes.

Korbut, Olga Valentinovna. [URS/Belarus-GYM]   B. 16 May 1955, Grodno, Belarus, USSR. Olga Korbut burst onto the world's gymnastics scene at the 1972 Olympics in Munich, amazing experts with her flexibility and daring moves. A fall on the uneven parallel bars dropped her to seventh overall in the all-around individual. However, she won three gold medals; two individual on the balance beam and floor exercises, and one with the Soviet all-around team. Korbut never defeated her teammate, Lyudmila Turishcheva (*q.v.*), but she was the darling of the fans and the media for her courage to try new moves, and her willing smile. She later won the 1973 World University Games all-around title, and was second at the 1973 Europeans and 1974 World Championships in all-around. She competed at the 1976 Olympics, winning a gold medal in the team event and a silver on the balance beam. Korbut retired from competition in 1977 and has now settled in Atlanta, Georgia.

Korea, Democratic People's Republic of (North) [PRK]   The Democratic People's Republic of Korea (often termed North Korea) proclaimed its establishment on 9 September 1948. DPR Korea applied to the IOC for recognition in June 1956 and received provisional IOC recognition in 1957, on the understanding that it would only be allowed to compete at Rome in 1960 as a combined team with the Republic of Korea.

DPR Korea received full IOC recognition for its Olympic Committee in March 1962. Originally, the IOC policy was for both Koreas to form a combined team, similar to Germany in 1956–1964. DPR Korea agreed to this, but Korea (South) said it was impossible. DPR Korea then competed at the Innsbruck Olympic Winter Games in 1964, but with a flag that did not conform to the IOC decision made at the 1963 session in Baden-Baden.

DPR Korea was to make its début at the Olympic Games in 1964 in Tokyo but withdrew. This was because, in November 1963, DPR Korea had competed at the Games of the New Emerging Forces (GANEFO). These were highly controversial games (See The Games of the XVIIIth Olympiad), which were not recognized by the IOC because GANEFO organizers refused admission to Israel and Taiwan. All athletes competing in shooting, swimming, and athletics at GANEFO were banned by their international federations from competing at Tokyo in 1964. This included several athletes from DPR Korea, including its greatest athlete, 800 meter world-record holding runner Dan Sin-Kim. When these athletes were not allowed to compete, DPR Korea withdrew in protest.

GANEFO II was held from 25 November to 6 December 1966 and DPR Korea again competed at these games. Because of this, the track & field athletes from DPR Korea who had competed at GANEFO II were subsequently barred from the 1968 Mexico City Olympics, and the nation withdrew again, choosing not to send any athletes.

The 1968 withdrawal was also partly motivated by anger over a recent IOC decision. At the 68th Session in Mexico City shortly before the Olympics, the IOC decided that, after 1 November 1968, the nation would be referred to as the Democratic People's Republic of Korea, but that at Mexico City, the nation would compete under its geographic name of North Korea. Precisely similar decisions were made with respect to East Germany and Taiwan, who were forced by the IOC to compete at Mexico City under those names, rather than their proper names of the German Democratic Republic and Republic of China.

DPR Korea made its first Olympic appearance at the Olympic Winter Games in Innsbruck in 1964. The nation has also competed at the Winter Games of 1972, 1984, 1988, and 1992. DPR Korea has competed at the Olympic Games of 1972, 1976, 1980, and 1992, also skipping the 1984 Los Angeles Olympics and the 1988 Seoul

Olympics. DPR Korea withdrew from the 1984 Olympics in obvious sympathy with the Soviet boycott of the Los Angeles Olympics. DPR Korea has won 23 Olympic medals through 1994, including 6 gold medals. DPR Korea withdrew from the 1988 Olympics in protest of the hosting of the Games by the rival government in South Korea. Long political discussions were held from 1985 to 1988 between representatives of the NOCs of the two countries. These dealt with demands by the North Koreans to co-host the 1988 Olympics or at least host several of the events. The Korean Olympic Organizing Committee and the IOC were never able to satisfy the demands of the North Koreans and talks eventually broke off, resulting in the North Korean boycott. (See The Games of the XXIVth Olympiad)

Korea, Republic of (South) [KOR]   The Republic of Korea, as we know it today, was created on 15 August 1948, after the end of World War II. Korea first officially competed at the 1948 Olympic Games in London. However, in both 1932 and 1936, during the occupation of the country by the Japanese (1910–1945), several Korean athletes competed at the Olympic Games wearing the colors of Japan. Korea has competed at all Olympics since 1948 with the exception of 1980, when it boycotted the Moscow Olympics. Korea also made its first Olympic Winter Games appearance in 1948 and has since missed only the Winter celebration of 1952.

Since 1948, the Koreans have done well in combative sports, winning virtually all of their medals in boxing, wrestling, judo and weightlifting. The women have also medaled in volleyball, basketball, field hockey, table tennis, and archery. Korea has won 111 medals through 1994, 38 of them gold. Ten of these were won at the Olympic Winter Games. Korea ably hosted the Games of the XXIVth Olympiad in Seoul in 1988. (See also Korea, Democratic People's Republic of [North])

Korfball   Korfball was contested as a demonstration sport (*q. v.*) at the Olympics of 1920 and 1928. The International Korfball Federation is a recognized federation by the IOC.

Koss, Johann Olav. [NOR-SSK]   B. 29 October 1968, Drammen. Winner of the 1,500 meters, 5,000 meters, and 10,000 meters speed skating events at the 1994 Winter Games, setting a new world record in each event. He had earlier won Olympic gold in the 1,500 meters and silver in the 10,000 meters in 1992. In 1994, he donated his first gold medal cash bonus to Olympic Aid for Sarejevo and retired shortly after the Lillehammer Games to pursue a career in medicine. Koss was world all-around champion in 1990, 1991, and 1994, and was also World Cup champion at the distance events in 1991.

Kraenzlein, Alvin Christian. [USA-ATH]   B. 12 December 1876, Milwaukee, Wisconsin. D. 6 January 1928, Wilkes Barre, Pennsylvania. At the 1900 Games he won the 60 meters, the 110 and 200 meter hurdles, and the long jump, and his four individual gold medals remain the record for a track & field athlete at one Games. His pioneering technique of straight-leg hurdling brought him two world hurdle records in addition to his five world records in the long jump. Although a qualified dentist he never practiced, preferring to become a track coach notably of the German and Cuban national teams and at the University of Michigan.

Kurland, Robert Albert. [USA-BAS]   B. 23 December 1924, St. Louis, Missouri. Bob "Foothills" Kurland was the first dominating seven-footer to play college basketball; so dominant, in fact, that he caused the rules-makers to outlaw goaltending, because he could block almost every shot from going into the basket. In 1945 and 1946, he led his Oklahoma A&M team to the NCAA championship and then went on to play for six years with the Phillips 66ers, being named AAU All-America every year he played. While playing with Phillips, Kurland became the first man to play on two Olympic championship teams.

Kuwait [KUW]   Kuwait's National Olympic Committee was formed in 1957 and recognized by the IOC in 1966. Kuwait has competed continuously at the Olympic Games since 1968. It has yet to win a medal and it has never competed at the Olympic Winter Games. Its best finish was equal fifth in 1980 football (soccer).

Kyrgyzstan [KGZ]   Kyrgyzstan's National Olympic Committee was recognized by the IOC in 1992 shortly after the break-up of the Soviet Union. Several Kyrgyzstani athletes competed from 1952-1988 for the Soviet Union, and Kyrgyzstani athletes were present at Barcelona in 1992 as members of the Unified Team (*q.v.*). Kyrgyzstan's first Olympic appearance as an independent nation occurred in 1994 at Lillehammer, represented by Yevgeniya Roppel, a biathlete who finished 66th and 67th in her two events.

Kyudo (Japanese archery)   See Budo.

********** L **********

Lacrosse   Lacrosse has been contested in the Olympics as a full-medal sport in 1904 and 1908. In addition lacrosse was contested as a demonstration sport (*q.v.*) at the 1928, 1932, and 1948 Olympics.

Laos [LAO]   Laos formed a National Olympic Committee in 1975 and saw it recognized by the IOC in 1979. Laos's first Olympic appearance was in 1980 at Moscow. The country competed again in 1988 and 1992. It has not competed at the Olympic Winter Games and has never won a medal.

Latvia [LAT]   Prior to its annexation by the Soviet Union in 1940, Latvia competed at the Olympics of 1924, 1928, 1932, and 1936, winning three medals. Latvia also competed at the Olympic Winter Games of 1924, 1928, and 1936. From 1952 to 1988, many Letts (preferred to Latvians) competed for the USSR. After the Soviet revolution of 1991, Latvia declared and was granted its independence. Its National Olympic Committee was recognized by the IOC in 1991. Latvia returned to the Olympic fold in 1992 by competing in both Albertville and Barcelona and also competed in 1994 at Lillehammer. Latvia won three more Olympic medals at Barcelona in 1992.

Latynina, Larisa Semyonova (née Diriy). [URS-GYM]   B. 27 December 1934, Kherson. A Russian gymnast whose total of 18 Olympic medals is a record for any sport. Between 1956 and 1964 she won nine gold, five silver and four bronze medals with individual gold coming in the floor exercises (1956, 1960, 1964) and all-around (1956, 1960). She dominated other major championships to a similar extent and at the Olympic, World and European Championships won 24 gold, 15 silver and five bronze for a total of 44 medals. This phenomenal record was achieved despite the fact that her career was interrupted when she gave birth to two children.

Lebanon [LIB]   Lebanon has sent athletes to every Olympics since 1948 with the exception of the 1956 Olympics when it boycotted in protest of Israeli occupation of the Sinai. It has participated at every Olympic Winter Games since 1948, with the exception of 1994. All of its four Olympic medals have come in the strength sports of wrestling and weightlifting.

Lednev, Pavel Serafimovich. [URS/UKR-MOP]   B. 25 March 1943, Gorkiy. Although he never won the Olympic individual modern pentathlon title, he won a record seven medals. In the team event, he took gold in 1972 and 1980 and silver in 1976 and in the individual event he won silver in 1976 and bronze in 1968, 1972 and 1980. In contrast to his Olympic record, he was the individual winner at the World Championships four times (1973, 1974, 1975, 1978) and was twice a member of the winning team (1973, 1974).

Lee, Willis Augustus, Jr. [USA-SHO]   B. 11 May 1888, Natlee, Kentucky. D. 25 August 1945, Portland, Maine. The only man to win five gold medals for shooting at one Games. He achieved this feat in 1920 when he also won a silver and a bronze and all seven medals were won in team events. A U.S. Naval Academy graduate, he enjoyed a highly successful naval career and commanded the U.S. Pacific fleet during World War II, eventually rising to the rank of Vice-Admiral. Lee was a member of champion Navy rifle teams in 1908, 1909, 1913, 1919, and 1930. He was a distant relative of Robert E. Lee.

Lemming, Eric Otto Valdemar. [SWE-ATH]   B. 22 February 1880, Göteborg. D. 5 June 1930, Göteborg. Lemming was the first of the great modern javelin throwers. He was Olympic javelin champion in 1906, 1908 and 1912, winning both the orthodox and freestyle event in 1908. He would almost certainly have been the champion in 1900 had the javelin been on the program but, in the absence of his speciality event, he competed in six other field events, placing fourth in the pole vault and the hammer. In 1906, he also won bronze medals in the shot, pentathlon and tug-of-war. As a 19-year-old, he set a world best of 49.32 meters (161'10") in 1899 and made 13 further improvements to the record, culminating with a mark of 62.32 meters (204'5") in 1912 which was later accepted as the first official IAAF record.

Leonard, Ray Charles, "Sugar Ray." [USA-BOX]   B. 17 May 1956, Wilmington, North Carolina. He won a gold medal at the 1976 Olympics in Montreal rather easily. After the Olympics, Leonard immediately became one of the top welterweights. In 1979, Ray Leonard won his first world title by defeating Wilfred Benitez for the WBC version of the welterweight championship. He eventually won world titles in five different weight classes, from welterweight to light-heavyweight. One of the fastest boxers ever, his skills were virtually unmatched and he deserves comparison as a fighter to his namesake, Sugar Ray Robinson. His popularity also enabled him to command ring fees that made him one of the wealthiest athletes ever.

Leonidas of Rhodes [GRE–ATH] *fl. ca.* 180–130 B.C. Leonidas of Rhodes was the greatest runner and sprinter of the Ancient Olympic Games (*q.v.*). He won 12 Olympic titles, the most by any athlete, ancient or modern. In 164, 160, 156 and 152 B.C. he was proclaimed *triastes* or Olympic champion in three events, the stadion, diaulos, and race in armor (*qq.v.*).

Lesotho [LES]   Lesotho has competed at five Olympic Games – those of 1972, 1980, 1984, 1988, and 1992. Lesotho has never competed at the Olympic Winter Games and has never won an Olympic medal. Motsapi Moorosi has the best finish ever by a Lesothan. He advanced through one round of the 200 meters in 1972, finishing fifth of seven sprinters in a quarter–final heat.

Lewis, Frederick Carlton "Carl." [USA–ATH]   B. 1 July 1961, Birmingham, Alabama. Considered by many to be the greatest track & field athlete of all time and, with eight Olympic gold medals and seven at the World Championships, it is a justifiable claim. His Olympic gold medals came in 1984 (100 meters, 200 meters, 4x100 meters relay, long jump), 1988 (100 meters, long jump) and 1992 (4x100 meters relay, long jump). His four victories in 1984 matched the record set by Jesse Owens (*q.v.*) at the 1936 Games. He twice set individual world records at 100 meters (1988, 1991) and in the relays he was a member of the teams which posted new world records at the 4x100 meters six times and the 4x200 meters three times. He was also a frequent winner at the NCAA championships and the Pan–American Games and was the winner of the Sullivan Award in 1981.

Liberia [LBR]   Liberia first competed at the Olympics in Melbourne in 1956. It has since missed the Olympic Games of 1968, 1976, 1980, and 1992. Liberia has not competed at the Olympic Winter Games and has not won an Olympic medal through 1994. Samuel Stewart, a light–flyweight boxer, won one match in 1988 to finish equal ninth of 35 boxers in his class. This is Liberia's best Olympic performance to date.

Libya [LBA]   Libya competed at the 1968, 1980, 1988, and 1992 Olympics. Libya has not competed at the Olympic Winter Games and has not won an Olympic medal through 1994. In 1988, Fathi Aboud finished 35th of 43 triple jumpers in the qualifying round, the best Olympic finish yet by a Libyan athlete.

Liechtenstein [LIE]   Liechtenstein made its first Olympic appearances at the Games of 1936, both Winter and Summer. Since that time it has failed to appear only at the 1952 Oslo Winter Olympics, the 1956 Melbourne Olympics, and the 1980 Moscow Olympics. Liechtenstein has the rare distinction of having won medals at the Olympic Winter Games (nine, two gold) but not at the Games of the Olympiad. This is because of the country's outstanding Alpine skiers, and especially two families, the Frommelts and the Wenzels.

Lipa-Oleniuc, Elisabeta (née Oleniuc). [ROM-ROW]   B. 26 October 1964. Elisabeta Lipa-Oleniuc is the only woman to win five Olympic medals for rowing. In 1984, as Miss Oleniuc, she won the double sculls (with Marioara Popescu) and after her marriage she took the silver medal in this event in 1988 (with Veronica Cogeanu) and 1992 (with Veronica Cochelea-Cogeanu). She also won a second gold in the single sculls in 1992 and a bronze in the quadruple sculls in 1988. Lipa was also World Champion in 1989 in single sculls.

Lithuania [LTU, formerly LIT]   Prior to its annexation by the Soviet Union in 1940, Lithuania competed at the Olympic Games of 1924 and 1928, but failed to win any medals. Lithuania also competed at the 1928 Olympic Winter Games. From 1952 to 1988, many Lithuanians competed for the USSR. After the Soviet revolution of 1991, Lithuania declared and was granted its independence, and its National Olympic Committee was recognized by the IOC in 1991. Lithuania returned to the Olympic fold in 1992 by competing in both Albertville and Barcelona. At Barcelona, Lithuania won two medals, a bronze by its men's basketball team and a silver by Romas Ubartas in the discus throw in men's track & field athletics.

Louganis, Gregory Efthimios. [USA-DIV]   B. 29 January 1960, San Diego, California. Louganis is considered the greatest diver of all time. After winning Olympic silver in the platform in 1976 he missed the 1980 Games because of the boycott but returned to take the springboard-platform double in both 1984 and 1988. He also took both titles at the World Championships of 1982 and 1986, having earlier won the platform in 1978. Of Samoan and European descent, he studied classical dance for many years and this training provided the basis for the elegance and artistry of his performances. His superiority over his contemporaries was considerable and he held many records for the highest marks ever achieved in competition.

Louis, Spyridon. **[GRE–ATH]** B. 12 January 1873, Maroressi. D. 26 March 1940. As the winner of the first Olympic marathon at Athens in 1896 his place in sporting history is assured. Having only placed fifth in one of the Greek trial races, he was not favored to win the Olympic title but his unexpected triumph gave Greece its only victory in a track & field athletics event at the Games and Louis was accorded the status of a national hero. Despite the acclaim, he returned to his village of Amarousi, where he worked as a shepherd, and never raced again. He remained an Olympic legend and was a guest of the Organizing Committee at the 1936 Games in Berlin.

Luding–Rothenburger, Christa (née Rothenburger). **[GDR–SSK/CYC]** B. 4 December 1959, Weißwasser. The only woman to win medals at both the Winter and Summer Games. A speed skating gold medalist at 500 meters (1984) and 1,000 meters (1988), she also won a silver in the cycling sprint in 1988. She also earned a speed skating silver medal in 1988 and bronze medal in 1992 in the 500 meters. She was a World Champion at both sports, winning the speed skating sprint title in 1985 and 1988 and the cycling sprint gold medal in 1986. Although many athletes have demonstrated the affinity between cycling and speed skating, few have competed at the top level in both sports at the same time and only Sheila Young (USA) approaches Luding–Rothenburger's success at both sports.

Luge Tobogganing is one of the oldest winter sports. Descriptions of it in the 16th century are found in literature. As a racing sport, it can be traced to the mid–19th century when British tourists started sledding on the snowbound roads of the Alps. The original form of the sport was the skeleton sleds which were used on the Cresta Run at St. Moritz. Twice this sport was contested in the Olympics, in 1928 and 1948, both times when the Winter Games were held at St. Moritz.

Luge spread to Switzerland in the 1890's as a variant of the skeleton race. The first recorded competitions took place in 1890 at the Innsbruck–based Academic Alpine Club. An International Tobogganing Association was formed in 1913 and the first European Championships were held in 1914 at Reichenfeld, Austria.

At the IOC meeting in Athens in 1954, luge tobogganing was recognized as an official Olympic sport but luge events were not contested in the Olympics until 1964. The first world luge championships were contested in Oslo in 1955. It was planned to introduce the sport at the 1960 Olympic Winter Games but the Squaw Valley organizers had decided not to build a bob run and not to hold bobsled events, and they likewise opposed building a luge run for the participation of only a few countries. Thus luge's Olympic debut was delayed until 1964. Since that time luge has been contested at all Olympic Winter Games, with a singles and doubles event for men, and a singles event for women. The sport has been dominated by the Germans, Austrians, and Italians. Luge is now governed by the Fédération Internationale de Luge de Course (FIL), which was formed in 1957 and currently has 45 members.

Luxembourg [LUX]   Luxembourg is usually considered to have first competed at the 1912 Olympic Games, the same year in which it formed its National Olympic Committee. However, it was recently discovered by French athletics historian, Alain Bouillé, that Michel Theato, the winner of the 1900 marathon, was from Luxembourg, not France, as previously believed. Thus, Luxembourg has competed at a total of 18 celebrations of the Olympiad, missing only the 1932 Los Angeles Games since 1912. It has also competed at the Olympic Winter Games of 1928, 1936, 1988, 1992, and 1994. Luxembourg claims five Olympic medals (two gold) in sports (two at the Olympic Winter Games), and won three Olympic medals in the now-defunct Art Contests (*q.v.*).

********** M **********

Macedonia, Former Yugoslav Republic of (FYROM) [MKD, formerly MCD]   This former Yugoslav republic declared its independence from Yugoslavia on 8 September 1991. The Olympic Committee of the Former Yugoslav Republic of Macedonia was formed in 1992 and recognized by the IOC in 1993. The republic has not yet competed at the Olympics as an independent nation. The name of the newly independent nation, since its independence from Yugoslavia, is very controversial. Greece, Bulgaria and Albania all lay claim to pieces of Macedonia and the name. The European Community has decided not to recognize Macedonia's independence until it changes its name, a proposal it adamantly opposes. It is currently recognized by the European Community under the name "Former Yugoslav Republic of Macedonia (FYROM)." However, from 1924 to 1988 a few Yugoslav Olympians were from Macedonia. The best represented sport at the Olympics among Macedonians has been wrestling. Both Šaban Trstena and Šaban Sejdi from Skopje won two wrestling medals at the Olympics between 1980 and 1988. In the Ancient Olympics, it is known that Macedonians, then part of Ancient Greece, won nine championships, including four in the stadion (sprint) race. Two of these were consecutive by Antigonos in 292–288 B.C. The greatest Olympic champion of ancient Macedonia was Philip II, the father of Alexander the Great, who won three Olympic titles.

Madagascar [MAD]   Madagascar has competed at six Olympic Games – those of 1964, 1968, 1972, 1980, 1984, and 1992. Madagascar's Olympic Committee was formed in 1963 and recognized by the IOC in 1964. Madagascar has never competed at the Olympic Winter Games and no Madagascan athlete has won an Olympic medal through 1994. Its top athlete has been the sprinter, Jean-Louis Ravelomanantsoa, who finished eighth in the 100 meters in 1968, the country's best finish ever.

Malawi [MAW]   Malawi has competed at the 1972, 1984, 1988, and 1992 Olympics. Malawi has never competed at the Olympic Winter Games and, through 1994, has never won an Olympic medal. In 1984, Peter Ayesu, a flyweight boxer, won two matches and lost one, to finish equal fifth of 32 competitors, the best finish ever by a Malawian Olympian.

Malaya   See Malaysia.

Malaysia [MAS, formerly MAL]   Malaysia has competed in the Olympics since 1956, missing only the 1980 Moscow Olympics. Its National Olympic Committee was formed in 1953 and recognized by the IOC in 1954. In 1956 and 1960, the country competed as Malaya. In 1963, Malaya joined with Singapore, North Borneo (now Sabah) and Sarawak to form the Federation of Malaysia. In 1964, Singapore competed as a part of the Malaysian team, but Singapore separated from Malaysia in 1965, and since then Singapore has competed on its own. The country has never competed in the Olympic Winter Games. Malaysia won its first Olympic medal, a bronze in men's badminton doubles, in 1992.

Maldives [MDV]   The Maldives has competed at the 1988 and 1992 Olympics. The nation has not yet competed at the Olympic Winter Games and has never won an Olympic medal. The Maldives Olympic Committee was formed in 1985 and recognized by the IOC in the same year.

Mali [MLI]   Mali has competed at the Olympic Games of 1964, 1968, 1972, 1980, 1984, 1988, and 1992.   It has never won a medal and it has not competed at the Olympic Winter Games.   Its best Olympic performance came in 1972 when discus thrower Namakoro Niaré finished 13th of 29 men.

Mallin, Harry William. [GBR-BOX]   B. 1 June 1892, Shoreditch, London. D. 8 November 1969, Lewisham, London. With victories in the middleweight division at the 1920 and 1924 Games he became the first man to successfully defend an Olympic boxing title.   Even in those days the competence and partiality of the judges posed problems and Mallin only won his second gold medal after the decision giving the quarter–final bout to home–town hero, Roger Brousse, had been overturned.   Mallin's record was incomparable; he was unbeaten in more than 300 fights and won five British amateur titles.

Malta [MLT]   Malta first competed at the Olympics in 1928.   It has participated rather sporadically since then, appearing again in 1936, 1948, 1960, 1968, 1972, 1980, 1984, 1988, and 1992.   It has never competed at the Winter Games.   Malta's top Olympic moment occurred in 1928 when its water polo team won one match, defeating Luxembourg 3–1, before losing to France in the second round.   This gave it a placing of equal fifth, of a starting field of 14 teams.

Mangiarotti, Edoardo. [ITA-FEN]   B. 7 April 1919, Renate Veduggio, Milan.   Winner of a record 13 Olympic medals (six gold, five silver, two bronze) for fencing from 1936 to 1960.   He was most successful in the épée team event winning four gold medals (1936, 1952, 1956, 1960) and a silver (1948).   His other gold medals came in the épée individual (1952) and the foil team (1960).   At the World Championships he won two individual épée titles and was a member of 13 winning teams in the épée and foil.   He later became secretary–general of the Fédération Internationale d'Escrime (FIE). His brother, Dario, was also a member of the Italian medal winning Olympic épée teams in 1948 and 1952.

Mathias, Robert Bruce, "Bob." [USA-ATH]   B. 19 November 1930, Tulare, California.   The first of only two men to win successive Olympic decathlon titles.   His first gold medal came in 1948 when, as a 17–year–old, he became the youngest–ever winner of an Olympic track & field event.   He set his third world record in defending his title in 1952 but the following year he forfeited his amateur status by starring in a film of his life. Although now a professional, he was, as a Marine officer, eligible to compete in the 1956 Inter-Services championships when he won his eleventh and final decathlon competition to maintain his unbeaten record in the event. First elected as a Republican Congressman for California in 1966 he served four terms before losing out in the Democratic landslide of 1974. In 1973, he introduced legislation to amend the U.S. Olympic Charter which effectively created a Bill of Rights for amateur athletes.

Matthes, Roland. [GDR–SWI]   B. 17 November 1950, Pössneck. With victories in the 100 meters and 200 meters backstroke at both the 1968 and 1972 Games he is the most successful of all Olympic backstroke swimmers. He also won two silver and one bronze medals in the relays and added his eighth Olympic medal (a bronze) in the 1976 100 meter backstroke. He set 16 world backstroke records (eight at each distance) but was also a world class performer in other events, winning silver medals at the European Championships in the freestyle and butterfly and setting three European butterfly records.

Mauritania [MTN]   Mauritania has competed at the Olympic Games of 1984, 1988, and 1992. Oddly, its National Olympic Committee was actually formed in 1962 although it was not recognized by the IOC until 1979. It has never competed at the Olympic Winter Games and has never won an Olympic medal. Its best Olympic performance occurred in 1988 when Babacar Sar won two freestyle wrestling matches in the heavyweight class.

Mauritius [MRI]   Mauritius formed a National Olympic Committee in 1971 but did not compete at the Olympics until 1984 in Los Angeles. Mauritius has also competed at the Olympic Games of 1988 and 1992. Mauritius has never competed at the Olympic Winter Games and has never won an Olympic medal. Its best Olympic performance occurred in 1988 when Jose Moirt finished 17th of 22 weightlifters in the light-heavyweight class.

McCormick, Patricia Joan Keller (née Keller). [USA–DIV]   B. 12 May 1930, Seal Beach, California. With victories in both the springboard and platform at the 1952 and 1956 Olympics she became the only woman diver in history to win four Olympic gold medals. Her second double victory at Melbourne came only five months after the birth of her son. Her husband was the AAU champion at both springboard and platform and her daughter was on the U.S. diving team at the 1983 Pan-American Games. Her daughter, Kelly, competed for the United States at the 1984 and 1988 Olympics, winning a silver in 1984 and a bronze in 1988, both on the springboard.

McKay, James Kenneth (né James Kenneth McManus). [USA] B. 24 September 1921, Philadelphia, Pennsylvania. In the United States, Jim McKay achieved fame as the "Voice of the Olympics." He was host or co-host on the U.S. television network televising the Olympics an unprecedented seven times: six times for ABC Sports – 1960, 1976, and 1984 for the Olympic Games, and the Olympic Winter Games consecutively from 1976 through 1988. McKay was not the main studio host in 1972 at Munich, but it was there that he achieved his greatest fame as an Olympics host. He was called on to broadcast the news reports of the horrific Israeli hostage massacre, and was on the air in the United States for over 15 consecutive hours. He was awarded an Emmy for that broadcast, one of ten individual Emmys won by McKay, nine for sportscaster of the year, and one for lifetime achievement.

Meagher, Mary Terstegge. [USA-SWI]   B. 27 October 1964, Louisville, Kentucky. Mary T. Meagher is the greatest female butterfly swimmer ever. For her feats she earned the nickname of "Madame Butterfly." Meagher won three gold medals at the 1984 Olympics, in both butterfly events, and on the 4x100 meter medley relay. In 1988, by now past her prime, she earned a bronze in the 200 meter butterfly and a silver on the medley relay. Meagher would likely have won both butterfly events in 1980 had the United States not boycotted the Moscow Olympics. She was World Champion in 1982 over 100 meters and in 1986 over 200 meters. She set two world butterfly records over 100 meters, and five over 200 meters, beginning in 1979. Her performance at the 1981 U.S. Nationals remains her greatest effort when she set still-standing world records of 57.93 for 100 meters, and 2:05.96 for 200 meters. Through 1994, no swimmer other than Meagher has ever come within two seconds of the 200 meter mark.

Medved, Aleksandr Vasilyevich (né Oleksander Medvid [Ukraine]). [URS/UKR-WRE]   B. 16 September 1937, Belaya Tserkov, Kiev Oblast. With victories in the freestyle light-heavyweight (1964), heavyweight (1968) and super-heavyweight (1972) he is the only wrestler to win gold medals at three successive Olympic Games. He also won three world titles at light-heavyweight and four at super-heavyweight. His record was remarkable for the fact that his physique seldom matched that of his opponents and on his way to the Olympic super-heavyweight title in 1972 he overcame the giant American bronze medalist, Chris Taylor, who enjoyed an incredible weight advantage of almost 100 pounds (45 kg). His World Championships came at light-heavyweight (1962, 1963, and 1966), and at super-heavyweight (1967, 1969, 1970, and 1971). He was European champion in 1966, 1968, and 1972, competing less often at that meet.

Mexico [MEX]   Mexican athletes first competed at the 1900 Olympic Games when several polo players of mixed Mexican/Spanish ancestry played at Paris. Mexico did not compete again at the Olympics until 1924 and has competed since without fail. Mexico sent five bobsled competitors to the 1928 Winter Olympics and in 1932 they entered another bobsled team but it did not compete. Its next Winter Olympic appearances came in 1984, 1988, 1992, and 1994. Mexico has won 40 Olympic medals, nine of them gold, all at the Games of the Olympiad. Mexico also hosted the Games of the XIXth Olympiad at Mexico City in 1968.

Meyer, Deborah, "Debbie" (later Reyes). [USA–SWI]   B. 14 August 1952, Haddonfield, New Jersey. With victories in the 200 meters, 400 meters and 800 meters freestyle in 1968, she became the first woman swimmer to win three individual gold medals at one Olympic Games. She won each event by a large margin and achieved her unique Olympic treble despite the fact that she was handicapped by a severe stomach upset in Mexico City. Between 1967 and 1970 she set 15 world records and retired before her abilities had been fully extended.

Military Patrol   A military patrol event was held at the Winter Olympics in 1924, 1928, 1936, and 1948 as a demonstration sport (*q. v.*).

Milon of Kroton. [GRE–WRE]   *fl. ca.* 540–508 B.C. The son of the well-known athlete, Diotimos, Milon of Kroton was the greatest wrestler of ancient Greece and the Ancient Olympic Games (*q. v.*). He was champion six times at the Olympic Games (540 B.C in boys' wrestling, and 532–516 B.C. in wrestling), seven times at the Pythian Games, ten times at the Isthmian Games and nine times at the Nemean Games (*qq. v.*). In four Olympiads, he was *periodonikes*, meaning he won all of the four major festival titles. The base of his statue at Ancient Olympia reads, " . . . he had never been brought to his knees." Milon's strength was supposedly developed when he was a young boy and began carrying a wild heifer on his shoulders. As the heifer grew, Milon continued to carry her for exercise and his strength became legendary, but it eventually killed him. In a forest, he saw a tree which had been cut open with wedges in it. He decided to pull open the trunk with his massive hands, but when he did this the wedges flew out and the trunk trapped his hands. He was caught in the tree and wild beasts tore him to pieces that night.

Mittermaier, Rosi (later Neurather). [FRG–ASK]   B. 5 August 1930, Reit-im-Winkel. Mittermaier had a long career in international skiing, winning ten individual World Cup races between 1969 and 1976. In 1976, she was the World Champion in Alpine combined and led the overall World Cup, although she did not lead in any of the individual disciplines. Her greatest fame came at the 1976 Olympic Winter Games when she won the slalom and downhill. With the giant slalom still to come, she had a chance to equal the feats of Toni Sailer and Jean-Claude Killy (*qq.v.*) by winning all three available Alpine ski events. However, in the giant slalom, she finished second, losing out by 12/100 of a second to Canada's Kathy Kreiner. She later married Christian Neurather, another German Olympic skier.

Miyake, Yoshinobu. [JPN–WLT]   B. 24 November 1939. Yoshinobu Miyake was Japan's greatest lifter ever. He finished second in the 1960 Olympic bantamweight class but won gold medals at the 1964 and 1968 Olympics as a featherweight. He also won World Championships in 1962, 1963, 1965, and 1966. Miyake set 25 world records, including 10 consecutive records in the snatch and nine consecutive overall records in the 60 kg. class.

Modern Pentathlon   Modern pentathlon is a sport invented by the founder of the Olympic Games, the Baron Pierre de Coubertin (*q.v.*). It is better termed the "military pentathlon," as it supposedly mimics the skills needed by a soldier. He must first ride a horse and then fight off an enemy with a sword. He must then swim a river to escape, then fight off more enemies with a pistol, and finally, effect the final escape by running a cross-country course.

Coubertin was able to get the sport on the Olympic program in 1912. The order of the events has varied, but the current order is as in the soldier's trial – riding, fencing, swimming, shooting, and cross-country running. The riding is a cross-country steeplechase course. Fencing is a series of one-touch bouts done with épée swords. Shooting is with a rapid-fire pistol. The swim is 300 meters freestyle and the run is a 4,000 meter cross-country event. The final event is now arranged such that the runners leave the start in the order of their positions after four events. Further, the starts are arranged such that the time intervals correspond to the number of points separating the competitors. Thus, the finishing order in the run now corresponds exactly to the finishing order of the entire pentathlon, adding to the drama of the event.

Modern pentathlon was originally dominated by the Swedes. After World War II, the Hungarians and the Soviets have become the top countries. Scoring was originally on a points–for–place system with the lowest score winning, but the competition is now scored using tables for each of the five events.

Modern pentathlon is governed by the Union Internationale de Pentathlon Moderne et Biathlon (UIPMB), which was founded in 1948 and had 72 members at the end of 1994.

Moldova [MLD]   Moldova was formerly the Soviet Republic of Moldavia, which achieved independence after the Soviet break-up of 1991. Its National Olympic Committee was formed shortly thereafter and recognized by the IOC in 1993. Though the smallest of the former Soviet Republics, a few Moldavian athletes competed from 1952 to 1988 for the Soviet Union, and Moldavian athletes were present at Barcelona in 1992 as members of the Unified Team (*q.v.*). Moldova first competed at the Olympics as an independent nation in 1994 at Lillehammer, represented by one male and one female biathlete.

Monaco [MON]   Monaco competed at the 1920 Olympic Games and has since missed only the Games of 1932, 1956, and 1980. It has competed at the Olympic Winter Games of 1984, 1988, 1992, and 1994. At Calgary in 1988, Albertville in 1992, and Lillehammer in 1994, the country was represented in the bobsled events by Albert Grimaldi, Prince of Monaco, an IOC Member and the son of Prince Rainier and Princess Grace. No Monegasque athlete has won a medal in a sporting event but in 1924 Julien Médecin won a bronze medal in the architecture portion of the now–defunct Art Contests (*q.v.*).

Mongolia [MGL]   Mongolia has competed at the Olympic Games since 1964, its only absence being the 1984 Los Angeles Olympics, which it boycotted. Its first Olympic appearance was at the 1964 Innsbruck Olympics and it has since missed only the Olympic Winter Games of 1976. Mongolia claims the unusual distinction of having won the most Olympic medals (13 through 1994, all in the Olympic Games) of any country which has not yet won a gold medal.

Monti, Eugenio. **[ITA-BOB]** B. 23 January 1928, Dobbiaco, Bolzano. The greatest bobsled driver in history. After winning two Olympic silver medals in 1956 he was deprived of the opportunity of further honors in 1960 as the bobsled was not included in the program at Squaw Valley in 1960. At his second Olympics in 1964 he won two bronze medals and, in 1968, he took the gold medals in both events. The bobsled events at the 1968 Winter Games also carried the status of the World Championships and, including his Olympic victories, Monti won the world title in the two-man event eight times and was the world four-man champion three times. He retired after the 1968 Olympics and became the Italian team manager. In addition to his championships he is known for his sportsmanship at the 1964 Innsbruck Winter Olympics. Trailing the British team of Anthony Nash and Robin Dixon going into the final run, he lent them a bolt off his own sled when theirs failed. Nash and Dixon won the gold medal, but for this magnanimous action, Monti was awarded the International Fair Play Award.

Morocco [MAR] Morocco has competed at eight Olympics. First appearing in 1960, it has since missed only the 1980 Games. Morocco has sent athletes to the Olympic Winter Games in 1968, 1984, 1988, and 1992. Through 1994, Moroccan athletes have won nine Olympic medals, seven in track & field athletics, and two in boxing.

Morrow, Bobby Joe. **[USA-ATH]** B. 15 October 1935, Harlingen, Texas. Winner of gold medals in the 100 meters, 200 meters and the 4x100 meter relay at the 1956 Games. In winning the 200 meters he became the first man to set an official world record for this distance at the Olympic Games. He also equaled the world record for 100 meters three times during the Olympic year, equaled the world 100 yards record in 1957, and was a member of six world record-breaking teams in the sprint relays (4x100 and 4x200, or Imperial equivalent). Morrow won four AAU titles between 1955 and 1958 but he failed to make the 1960 U.S. Olympic team.

Motorboating Motorboating was contested at the Olympics only in 1908.

Mozambique [MOZ] Mozambique has competed in four Olympic Games, those of 1980, 1984, 1988, and 1992. Mozambique has not yet competed at the Olympic Winter Games and no Mozambican athlete has won an Olympic medal. Its top athlete has been the female distance running phenomenon, Maria Lurdes Mutola, who finished fifth in the 1992 800 meters and ninth in the 1,500 meters, while still only 19 years old.

Much Wenlock Olympian Games   The Much Wenlock Olympian Games were one of the various attempts at revival of the Ancient Olympic Games which preceded Coubertin's successful attempt. Much Wenlock is a small town in Shropshire, England, 12 miles south of Shrewsbury and 40 miles west of Birmingham. On 22 October 1850, these Games were held for the first time. They were the brainchild of British sports enthusiast, Dr. William Penny Brookes (1809–1895) (*q. v.*) .

The Games were only national in nature and the events were those of a British medieval country fair enriched by modern athletic sports disciplines. The original events in 1850 consisted of cricket, 14–a–side football, high and long jumping, quoits, a hopping race, and a running race. However, several athletic events were added in the next few editions. But, in 1855, a popular event was the blindfolded wheelbarrow race, and in 1858 a pig race was contested in which the pig "led its pursuers over hedge and ditch right into the town where it took ground in the cellar of Mr. Blakeway's house; and where it was captured by a man called William Hill." The most popular event became tilting–at–the–ring, which was first held in 1858. The competitors, compulsorily dressed in medieval costume, rode down a straight course and used their lances to spear a small ring, suspended from a bar over the course.

The Much Wenlock Olympian Games, altogether 45 in number up to 1895, achieved their high point in the 1860's and 1870's. In those years, representatives of the German Gymnastic Society (which was based in London) competed regularly. In 1859, Brookes contacted the Greeks and donated a £10 prize to the Zappas Olympic Games (*q. v.*). The winner of the long footrace at the 1859 Zappas Olympics, Petros Velissariou, was made an honorary member of the Much Wenlock Olympian Society.

In 1860, 1861, 1862, and 1864, Brookes also organized the Shropshire Olympian Games on a regional level in, respectively, Much Wenlock, Wellington, Much Wenlock, and Shrewsbury. These were followed by the Games organized by the National Olympic Association: 1866 (London), 1867 (Birmingham), 1868 (Wellington), 1874 (Much Wenlock), 1877 (Shrewsbury), and 1883 (Hadley).

The Much Wenlock Olympian Games were held more sporadically after Brookes' death in 1895, but they are actually still held today, sponsored by the Much Wenlock Olympian Society, which celebrated the 100th Much Wenlock Olympian Games in 1986. The Much Wenlock Olympian Games are important in the history of Olympic revivals because of their influence on Pierre de Coubertin (*q.v.*). Coubertin knew of Brookes' efforts and visited the Much Wenlock Olympian Games as a guest of honor in October 1890. In 1891, he donated a gold medal which was given to the winner of tilting-at-the-ring. However, as early as 1881, William Penny Brookes was the first person ever who proposed an International Olympic Festival to be staged in Athens.

Myanmar [MYA]   As Burma (name change in May 1989), Myanmar competed at all Olympics from 1948 through 1988, with the exception of the 1976 Olympics. Myanmar also competed at the 1992 Olympics in Barcelona. It has never attended the Olympic Winter Games nor has it won a medal. Its best finishes have been fifth in 1972 flyweight weightlifting by Gyi Aung and equal fifth in 1964 by featherweight boxer Tun Tim.

********** N **********

Naber, John Phillips. [USA-SWI]   B. 20 January 1956, Evanston, Illinois. At the 1976 Games he won four gold medals, each in a new world record time, and his records in the 100 meters and 200 meters backstroke remained unbeaten for seven years. He also won gold in the 4x100 meters freestyle relay and the medley relay and took the silver in the 200 meters freestyle. Perhaps the greatest of these fine performances came in the 200 meters backstroke where he became the first man to break two minutes for the distance. After winning three gold medals at the 1977 Pan-American Games he retired from international competition.

Nadi, Nedo. [ITA-FEN]   B. 9 June 1894, Livorno. D. 29 January 1940, Rome. The most versatile fencer in history, he uniquely won an Olympic title with each of the three weapons at the same Games. In 1912, he won the individual foil title and then, in 1920, he produced one of the greatest of all Olympic performances. He won the individual foil and sabre titles and led the Italians to victory in all three team events. His brother, Aldo, also won a gold medal in each of the three team events. After the 1920 Olympics, he taught as a professional in South America but on his return he was reinstated as an amateur and served as President of the Italian Fencing Federation.

Namibia [NAM]   Namibia's Olympic Committee was recognized by the IOC at its summer session in 1991. It competed in the 1992 Barcelona Olympics where sprinter Frank Fredericks won two medals for Namibia in track & field athletics. Namibia has not yet competed at the Olympic Winter Games.

National Olympic Academies [NOAs]   See International Olympic Academy.

National Olympic Committees [NOCs]   National Olympic Committees (NOCs) are the bodies responsible for the Olympic Movement in their respective countries. The Olympic Charter (*q.v.*) states that their mission "is to develop and protect the Olympic Movement in their respective countries, in accordance with the Olympic Charter." National Olympic Committees have not always been representative of autonomous national regions. Currently, Puerto Rico, which is a Commonwealth of the United States, has its own NOC. In the early part of this century, Bohemia was represented on the IOC, even though it was only a part of the Austro–Hungarian Empire. For the most part, however, NOCs represent independent nations. They are recognized by the IOC at the IOC Sessions. At the end of 1994, there were 195 National Olympic Committees.

   NOCs are supposed to be autonomous and resist political pressures and influences of any kind, but that principle has been recognized more in word than deed. Notably, prior to the fall of the Soviet bloc, all the Eastern European Communist nations had NOCs which basically were puppets of their governments. And, in 1980, the United States Olympic Committee (USOC) was coerced into boycotting the Moscow Olympics (against its wishes) by the U.S. President and government to protest the Soviet invasion of Afghanistan.

Nauru [NRU]   Nauru's Olympic Committee was recognized by the IOC at the 1994 Olympic Congress after having been given provisional recognition earlier in 1994. Nauru has not yet competed in the Olympic Games.

Nehmer, Meinhard. [GDR–BOB]   B. 13 January 1941, Boblin. A former nationally ranked javelin thrower, he only took up bobsledding after retiring from athletics. Although well past the age of 30, he formed a formidable partnership with Bernhard Germeshausen (*q.v.*) and they won the 1976 Olympic two-man and were both members of the winning four-man crew in 1976 and 1980 and they share the record for the most gold medals won by bobsledders. Nehmer also won an Olympic bronze medal in the two-man in 1980 with Bogdan Musiol. He was coach of the U.S. bobsled team for the 1992 Olympics.

Nemean Games   The Nemean Games were one of the four great Panhellenic sporting festivals, along with the Olympic Games, Isthmian Games, and Pythian Games (*qq.v.*). They were held biennially, with the first known Nemean Games being contested in 573 B.C. The Nemean Games were held in honor of Zeus. They were held in July in the Nemean sanctuary in Argolis. The Nemean sanctuary was near the site on the Peloponnesus where Hercules killed and skinned the Nemean Lion, the first of his famed twelve labors. Winners in the Nemean Games were crowned with a wreath of fresh wild celery.

Nepal [NEP]   Nepal has competed at the 1964, 1972, 1976, 1980, 1984, 1988, and 1992 Olympic Games. This Himalayan country has still not competed in the Olympic Winter Games. Its best Olympic performance was in 1964 when light-welterweight boxer Pun Omparsao won one match to finish equal ninth of 35 athletes in his class.

Netball   Netball has never been contested at the Olympic Games, even as a demonstration sport (*q.v.*). However, its governing body, the International Federation of Netball Associations, is recognized by the IOC.

Netherlands, The [NED, formerly HOL]   The Netherlands sent 27 athletes to the 1900 Paris Olympics. After missing the 1904 St. Louis Olympics, Holland has never missed an Olympic Games, although in 1956 it competed only at the Equestrian Games in Stockholm, boycotting the 1956 Olympic Games in protest of the Soviet invasion of Hungary. At the Winter Games, Holland appeared first in 1928, missed the 1932 Lake Placid Games, but has appeared continuously since. In the Summer Games, Holland has had a variety of successes in different sports but has never dominated any sport. In the Winter Olympics, however, Holland has always been one of the very top nations in speed skating. The Netherlands has won 219 Olympic medals, 59 of them gold. Of these, 50 medals and 14 gold medals were won at the Olympic Winter Games. The Netherlands hosted the Games of the IXth Olympiad in Amsterdam in 1928.

Netherlands Antilles [AHO]   The Netherlands Antilles first competed at the Olympics in 1952. It did not travel to Melbourne in 1956, and boycotted the 1980 Olympics, but has otherwise competed at every Olympic Games since 1952. The Netherlands Antilles made its Olympic Winter debut in 1988 at Calgary and also competed in 1992 at Albertville and in 1994 at Lillehammer. The Netherlands Antilles has won one Olympic medal, a silver by Jan Boersma in boardsailing in 1988.

New Zealand [NZL]   New Zealand was first represented at the 1908 Olympic Games. In that year it formed a combined team with Australia as Australasia. One New Zealander competitor, Harry Kerr, a walker, won a bronze in the 3,500 meter walk. In 1912, three New Zealanders competed with Australasia. Finally, in 1920 at Antwerp, New Zealand took part in the Olympic Games as a separate nation. New Zealand competed at its first Olympic Winter Games in 1952 at Oslo. It missed the Winter Games of 1956 and 1964, but has competed at the others since. New Zealand has had its greatest success in track & field with several of its middle–distance runners being Olympic champions. New Zealand has won 65 Olympic medals, 26 of them gold.

Nicaragua [NCA]   Nicaragua first competed at the Olympic Games in 1968. Its participation was continuous through 1984, but it did not compete in 1988 at Seoul, returning to the Olympics in 1992 at Barcelona. The country has never competed in the Olympic Winter Games. Its best Olympic performance occurred in 1992 when flyweight weightlifter Alvaro Marenco Ramos finished 11th of 17 lifters in his class.

Niger [NIG]   Niger has competed at the Olympics of 1964, 1968, 1972, 1984, 1988, and 1992. Niger has never competed at the Olympic Winter Games. Issaka Daborg won the only Olympic medal for this country in 1972 when he finished third in light–welterweight boxing.

Nigeria [NGR]   Nigeria first competed in the Olympics in 1952. It has since missed only the 1976 Games, owing to the African boycott. Nigeria has not yet competed at the Olympic Winter Games. Nigerians have won eight Olympic medals, but no golds. Five of these have come in boxing and three in track & field athletics.

Nordic Games   The Olympic Winter Games formally began in 1924 at Chamonix, although they were originally known as the *Semaine internationale des sports d'hiver* (International Week of Winter Sports). Prior to that time, winter sports events had been held during the Summer Games of 1908 (figure skating) and 1920 (figure skating and ice hockey). But there existed an earlier international winter sports festival, the Nordic Games, which began in 1901. Suggested by Sweden's Professor E. Johan Widmark, the initiative to hold Nordic Games was taken in 1899, the first ones being arranged in 1901. After this inaugural event in Stockholm, Sweden, Nordic Games were held in 1905, 1909, 1913, 1917, 1922, and 1926, always during February, mostly in Stockholm. They began, and were perpetuated, largely by the work of the influential Swedish sports administrator, Viktor Gustaf Balck. The Nordic Games were not without political problems, nor were they originally planned as precursors to the Olympic Winter Games, as often stated. In fact, despite Balck's influential status on the IOC, he and other Swedish and Norwegian sporting leaders opposed early suggestions to start Olympic Winter Games. The Olympic Winter Games themselves began only after several heated IOC debates concerning their merits. The Nordic Games ended after 1926, partly because of the growth of the Olympic Winter Games, partly because of Balck's death and the loss of his leadership, and partly because of the growth of the Fédération Internationale de Ski.

Nordic Skiing   Nordic skiing has been practiced in the Scandinavian countries since the 18th century. Competitions are known from the early 19th century. The sport has been on the Olympic program since the Chamonix games of 1924. The international governing body is the Fédération Internationale de Ski (FIS), which was founded in 1924 and has 86 members (1995).

Nordic skiing consists of three major disciplines: cross-country skiing, ski jumping, and Nordic combined, combining elements of both cross-country and ski jumping. All three disciplines have been contested at all Winter Olympics. Women compete only in cross-country skiing and first began to do so in 1952. Nordic skiing has been dominated, not surprisingly, by the Scandinavian countries and the Soviet Union and Russia.

Cross-country skiing consists of races varying from 15 to 50 kilometers for men, and from 5 to 20 kilometers for women, as well as relay races. The skiers race in time-trial fashion, starting at intervals. Ski jumping is contested on two hills, a 90 meter and a 120 meter hill. The size of the hill is not necessarily 90 or 120 meters, but those figures refer to the expected length of the jumps measured to the "norm" point of the hill. Nordic combined consists of a cross-country ski race and ski jumping with the results determined by a points table. In 1988, team events for men in both Nordic combined and ski jumping were added to the Olympic program.

In the 1980's, cross–country skiing underwent a revolution which was started by Bill Koch, the first American to be a top international skier. He changed from the classic cross–country of alternating legs and arms with the stride being pushed straight backwards, remaining in the ski track, to a style similar to skating on skis. The FIS was pushed to ban this style by the north Europeans, but it was decided instead to allow two styles. However, races are now designated as either "classic" or "freestyle," with skating being allowed in freestyle races. Men's 50 km. and women's 20 km. racers were permitted to use any style. In the relays, the classical style must be used for the first 100 meters, for safety reasons as the relays are a mass start, but after that the racers may use the skating technique.

North Borneo   See Malaysia.

Northern Rhodesia   See Zambia.

Norway [NOR]   Norway competed at the Olympics of 1900 and has missed only the 1980 Olympic Games since. Norway has competed at every Olympic Winter Games. Until 1984, Norway could claim to be the top nation at the Olympic Winter Games in terms of medals and gold medals won. In that year, however, the Soviet Union surpassed Norway in both categories. With the demise of the Soviet Union, Norway again tops the list of most medals won by a single country at the Olympic Winter Games with 214, 73 of them gold medals. Norway shares with Liechtenstein and Austria the unusual distinction of having won more medals in the Winter Games than in the Summer Olympics. Norway has twice hosted the Olympic Winter Games, in 1952 in Oslo and in 1994 in Lillehammer.

Nurmi, Paavo Johannes. [FIN-ATH]   B. 13 June 1897, Turku. D. 2 October 1973, Helsinki. An Olympic legend whose dedication to a rigorous training schedule and mastery of pace judgment brought a new dimension to distance running. Between 1920 and 1928 he won a record nine Olympic gold medals (seven individual; two team) and three individual silver medals. His medals came in a wide range of events: 1,500 meters, 3,000 meters (team), 5,000 meters, 10,000 meters, steeplechase and cross–country. In 1932, he was banned for alleged professionalism and missed the chance to add the 1932 marathon, for which he was one of the favorites, to his list of Olympic successes. Although subsequently reinstated as an amateur for domestic races, he continued to be excluded from international competition, a decision which left him embittered for the rest of his life. However, he returned to the Olympic arena in 1952 when he carried the torch at the Opening Ceremony. The incomparable "Flying Finn" set 22 official and 13 unofficial world records, and statues (done by Waino Aaltonen in 1925) honoring his feats stand in his hometown of Turku, outside the Olympic stadium in Helsinki, and in the park of the Olympic Museum (*q.v.*) in Lausanne.

Nykänen, Matti Ensio. [FIN-NSK] B. 17 July 1963, Jyvaskyla. Winner of a record four Olympic gold medals for ski jumping. At the 1984 Games he won on the large hill and placed second on the small hill before winning both events in 1988 when he won a further gold medal in the newly introduced team event. He was also the World Champion on the large hill in 1982 and won four World Cup titles. A controversial and often ill-tempered individual, he earned considerable respect for his sporting talents but little for his general behavior.

********** O **********

Oceania National Olympic Committees [ONOC] The Oceania National Olympic Committees, headquartered in Fiji, is a confederation of 12 National Olympic Committees from Oceania and is one of the recognized organizations of the International Olympic Committee. It was created on 25 September 1981 to promote the Olympic Movement and its ideals in Oceania, and to encourage and assist in the promotion and development of Olympic Sports in Oceania. The Presidents of ONOC have been Harold Austad (NZL; 1981-1983), Sir Lance Cross (NZL; 1983-1989), and currently, IOC Member Kevan Gosper of Australia (1989-1995).

Oerter, Alfred Adolph. [USA-ATH] B. 19 September 1936, Astoria, New York. The only track & field athlete to win four successive Olympic titles. He took the gold medal in the discus in 1956, 1960, 1964 and 1968, setting a new Olympic record on each occasion although he was never the favorite to win the event. His third victory in 1964 was remarkable for the fact that he overcame the handicap of neck and rib injuries but still managed to set a career best. He also won the Pan-American title in 1959 and set four world records, the first of which in 1962 gave him the distinction of being the first man to record a legal throw of over 200 feet (60.96 meters).

Olympiad   An Olympiad is a measure of time, designating a period of four consecutive years beginning with the opening of one edition of the Games of the Olympiad and ending with the opening of the following edition. The term is based on the Greeks who used the term Olympiad to measure the time between Olympic Games. Olympiad may be the term associated with the Olympics which is most often misused by the public, the media, and broadcasters. Specifically, the Olympic Games are not an "Olympiad." They are correctly termed the "Games of the Olympiad."

Olympic Anthem   See Olympic Hymn.

Olympic Ceremonies   A number of ceremonies accompany the Olympic Games, notably the Opening Ceremonies, the Closing Ceremonies, and the Victory, Medals, and Diplomas Ceremonies. These ceremonies are conducted according to strict protocols defined in Rule 69 of the Olympic Charter (*q.v.*) (Opening and Closing Ceremonies) and Rule 70 of the Olympic Charter (Victory, Medals, and Diplomas Ceremonies).

The Opening Ceremonies begin with the Head of State of the host country (normally) entering the stadium, accompanied by the President of the IOC and the President of the Organizing Committee of the Games. The parade of nations then follows, with the nations of all participating countries entering the stadium. The nations march in alphabetical order, using the alphabetical designation of the language of the host country. However, Greece always enters the stadium first, as the founding nation of the Ancient Olympic Games (*q.v.*), and the last nation to enter is always the host country. Each nation is led by a flag bearer carrying the flag of the nation or the National Olympic Committee.

The President of the Organizing Committee then speaks for no more than three minutes. The IOC President then speaks briefly and ends by inviting the Head of State of the host country to open the Olympic Games. He or she gives no speech but opens the Games by stating "I declare open the Games of ... (name of city) celebrating the ... Olympiad of the Modern Era (or the ... Olympic Winter Games)."

The Olympic Torch is then brought into the stadium and the Olympic Flame (*q.v.*) is lit by the final runner, followed by a symbolic release of pigeons, signifying peace. The flag bearers then form a semi-circle around the main rostrum and a competitor and an official of the host country take the Olympic Oath (*q.v.*) on behalf of all competitors and officials. The national anthem of the host country is then played, after which an artistic program entertaining the spectators is held. This program is usually designed to have some symbolic nature, representing both the Olympic Movement (*q.v.*) and the national features of the host country.

The Closing Ceremonies end the Olympic Games. The flag bearers of each nation first march into the stadium, followed by the athletes of all nations. The athletes march in no order and typically intermingle, signifying the friendships developed during the Olympic Games. (This change to the closing ceremony was suggested by John Ian Wing, a young British boy of Chinese origin, to the organizers of the 1956 Olympic Games in Melbourne.)

The President of the IOC and the Organizing Committee mount the rostrum in the center of the stadium. Three flags are then raised in the following order: the Greek flag on the right flagpole, the flag of the host country on the center flagpole, and the flag of the host country of the next Olympic Games (or Olympic Winter Games) on the left flagpole. All are raised to the playing of their respective national anthems.

The mayor of the host city then hands the official Olympic flag (*q.v.*) to the IOC President, who in turn hands it to the mayor of the host city of the next Olympic Games. The President of the Organizing Committee gives a brief speech. The IOC President then speaks briefly and ends the Olympic Games by stating, "I declare the Games of the ... Olympiad (or the ... Olympic Winter Games) closed and, in accordance with tradition, I call upon the youth of the world to assemble four years from now at ... (next host city) to celebrate with us there the Games of the ... Olympiad (or the ... Olympic Winter Games)." A fanfare then sounds, the Olympic flame is extinguished and while the Olympic Hymn (*q.v.*) is played, the Olympic flag is lowered from the flagpole.

The Victory, Medals and Diplomas Ceremonies consist of the awarding of these respective items. The medals are to be presented by the IOC President or an IOC Member designated by him. (In reality, the IOC President now awards only a very few medals.) The three place winners mount the victory platform, the winner on the highest step. Their names are announced and the medals are awarded to them. The national flags of the three medal winners are raised, the national flag of the winner on the central flagpole. While the flags are raised the national anthem of the champion is played.

Olympic Charter   The Olympic Charter is, effectively, the constitution of the International Olympic Committee and the Olympic Movement (*qq.v.*). It sets out, basically in an outline form, the principles, rules, and byelaws which govern the workings of both the IOC and the Olympic Movement, and stipulates the conditions for the celebration of the Olympic Games. The Olympic Charter was first adopted in 1908, based on a handwritten set of rules created by Pierre de Coubertin (*q.v.*) shortly after the formation of the IOC. The 1908 list of rules was not called the Olympic Charter but rather *Comité International Olympique: Annuaire* (in French only). Since that time, the IOC's governing rules have been published under multiple names, including *Olympic Rules, Protocol, Olympic Statutes, Olympic Statutes and Rules*, being first published officially as the *Olympic Charter* (*q.v.*) only in 1978.

Though the Olympic Charter is often held to be inviolate, it is, in fact, fairly easily modified and has been changed many times since its inception. Modifications, or amendments, can be made according to Rule 22.4 governing the sessions, which states, "The Session is the supreme organ of the IOC. It adopts, modifies, and interprets the Olympic Charter."

Olympic Code   See Olympic Creed.

Olympic Congresses   Olympic Congresses are gatherings of all the various bodies and individuals involved in the Olympic Movement (*q.v.*). The Olympic Charter now states that they are to be held, in principle, every eight years at a place and date determined by the IOC. It should be noted that this has not always been the case. Coubertin intended Olympic Congresses to be held from "time to time" to discuss the Olympic Movement. However, a gap of 43 years occurred from the ninth Olympic Congress until the 10th Olympic Congress in 1973. The Olympic Congress has no official power to make rules concerning the Olympic Games or to modify the Olympic Charter (*q.v.*) but only acts as a consultant to the Olympic Movement.

To date, 12 Olympic Congresses have been held. They have been as follows, with their themes following the name of the host city:

1st: 16 – 24 June 1894 – Paris – Re-establishment of the Olympic Games

2nd: 23 – 31 July 1897 – Le Havre – Sports hygiene and pedagogy

3rd: 9 – 14 June 1905 – Brussels – Sport and physical education

4th: 23 – 25 May 1906 – Paris – Art, literature, and sport

5th: 7 – 11 May 1913 – Lausanne – Sports psychology and physiology

6th: 15 – 23 June 1914 – Paris – Olympic regulations

7th: 2 – 7 June 1921 – Lausanne – Olympic regulations

8th: 29 May – 4 June 1925 – Prague – Sports pedagogy and Olympic regulations

9th: 25 – 30 May 1930 – Berlin – Olympic regulations

10th: 30 September – 4 October 1973 – Varna – Sport for a
world of peace – the Olympic Movement and its
future
11th: 23 – 28 September 1981 – Baden-Baden – 1. The
future of the Olympics Games; 2. International
co-operation; 3. The future Olympic Movement
12th: 29 August – 3 September 1994 – Paris – 1. The
Olympic Movement's contribution to modern
society; 2. The contemporary athlete; 3. Sport in
its social context; 4. Sport and the media

Olympic Council of Asia [OCA]   The Olympic Council of Asia is
a confederation of the National Olympic Committees from Asia,
which was formed in November 1982. The OCA is in overall charge
of sports in Asia, coordinates the activities of Asian countries in
sports at the regional and international level, and conducts the Asian
Games every four years. It is headquartered in Kuwait and, as of
1994, its President is Sheikh Ahmad Al-Fahad Al-Sabah of Kuwait.
There are currently 43 affiliated nations.

Olympic Credo   See Olympic Creed.

Olympic Creed   "The most important thing in the Olympic Games
is not to win but to take part, just as the most important thing in life
is not the triumph, but the struggle. The essential thing is not to have
conquered but to have fought well."
    This is the current form of the Olympic Creed (also termed
the Olympic Code, the Olympic Credo, an alternative Olympic Motto
or the Olympic Competition Motto – see Olympic Motto) as it
appears on the scoreboard at the Opening Ceremony of the Olympic
Games, although many permutations of this basic message have been
seen. The exact origin of this phrase is not clear, but it is felt that
Pierre de Coubertin (*q.v.*) adopted this creed after hearing Ethelbert
Talbot, the Bishop of Central Pennsylvania, speak at St. Paul's
Cathedral on 19 July 1908, during the London Olympics. The service
was given for the Olympic athletes who were all invited.
    Talbot was in London for the fifth Conference of Anglican
Bishops. During the conference, many of the visiting bishops spoke
in various churches. Talbot actually did not say anything close to the
above exact words during his speech, stating instead, "The only safety
after all lies in the lesson of the real Olympia – that the Games
themselves are better than the race and the prize. St. Paul tells us
how insignificant is the prize. Our prize is not corruptible, but

incorruptible, and though only one may wear the laurel wreath, all may share the equal joy of the contest."

However, Coubertin heard Talbot speak and, at a banquet at the Grafton Galleries on 24 July 1908, he interpreted Bishop Talbot's words as follows, "L'important dans ces Olympiades, c'est moins d'y gagner que d'y prendre part." ("The importance of these Olympiads is not so much to win as to take part.") He then went on to say that these very words were the foundation of a clear and sound philosophy: "L'important dans la vie ce n'est point le triomphe mais le combat. L'essentiel ce n'est pas d'avoir vaincu mais de s'être bien battu." ("The important thing in life is not the triumph but the struggle. The essential thing is not to have won but to have fought well.")

More recent research by Prof. David C. Young indicates that Coubertin probably had this thought in mind prior to hearing the speech of the Bishop of Central Pennsylvania. Young attributes the phrase to Ovid's *Metamorphoses*, which Coubertin had read in school. A sentence in that work reads, "Nec tam turpe fuit vinci quam contendisse decorum est," which can be translated as, "It was not so shameful to be beaten as it is honorable to have contended." Coubertin's knowledge of this statement is supplemented by a speech he gave in November 1894, given to the Parnassus Literary Society in Athens, in which he said, "Le déshonneur ne consisterait pas ici à être battu: il consisterait à ne pas se battre." This is literally translated as "The dishonor here would consist not of being beaten, it would consist of not contending."

In connection with the Olympic Games in Stockholm 1912 and Antwerp 1920, Coubertin again spoke of the words of the Bishop of Central Pennsylvania, but it did not attract any notice. At the Olympic Games in 1924 and 1928 no reference was made to Bishop Talbot's sermon in St. Paul's Cathedral in 1908. However, at the Olympic Games in Los Angeles (1932) the message appeared during the Opening Ceremonies on the great scoreboard of the Los Angeles Memorial Coliseum. It was finally established at the 1936 Olympic Games in Berlin when, at the Opening Ceremonies, Pierre de Coubertin's voice was heard over the loudspeaker, in a recording, delivering his message, "Important aux Jeux Olympiques, ce n'est pas tant d'y gagner que d'y avoir pris part; car l'essentiel dans la vie, ce n'est pas tant de conquérir que d'avoir bien lutté." ("Important in the Olympic Games is not winning but taking part; for the essential thing in life is not conquering but fighting well.")

Olympic Cup   The Olympic Cup was instituted by Baron de Coubertin (*q.v.*) in 1906. It is awarded to an institution or association with a general reputation for merit and integrity which has been active and efficient in the service of sport and has contributed substantially to the development of the Olympic Movement (*q.v.*). The Olympic Cup is one of the two awards currently given by the International Olympic Committee outside of the Olympic Games (*qq.v.*). (See Olympic Order and Appendix V for a list of recipients of the Olympic Cup)

Olympic Diplomas   Diplomas are given to the first eight finishers of all events at an Olympic Games. It is not well known that the first three finishers receive, in addition to their medals, these diplomas. In team events, the members of the first eight teams also all receive diplomas.

Olympic Films   Multiple Olympic Films and movies have been produced. The Organizing Committee of each Olympic Games now produces its own official Olympic Film celebrating in motion pictures "its" Olympics. This began with the 1936 Olympic Games in Berlin when German film producer Leni Riefenstahl, at the behest of Adolf Hitler, produced the most famous and haunting of all Olympic Films, *Olympia*. Prior to that, the filmed record of the Olympics came from cinema newsreels. Other famous official Olympic Films have been *Tokyo Olympiad*, celebrating the 1964 Olympic Games in Tokyo, and *Visions of Eight*, celebrating the 1972 Olympic Games in Munich.

In addition to official Olympic Films, many independent producers produce Olympic movies. The American television network which televises the Olympics now usually produces a cinematic summary of the Olympics and their coverage, often available to be bought and viewed on video-cassette recorders (VCRs).

The most prominent producer of Olympic Films has been the American Bud Greenspan, who was initially assisted by his late wife, Cappy Greenspan. Greenspan has produced a remarkable series of Olympic movies termed "The Olympiad Series." In addition, he has been the producer of the official Olympic Film five times: in 1984 (Los Angeles), 1988 (Calgary and Seoul), 1992 (Barcelona) and 1994 (Lillehammer).

Olympic Flag   The Olympic flag has a plain white background with no border. In the center is the Olympic Symbol, which consists of five interconnected rings. They form two rows of three rings above, and two below. The rings of the upper row are, from left to right, blue, black, and red. The rings of the lower row are yellow and green. The rings are thought to symbolize the five continents – Europe, Asia, Africa, Australia, and America. The colors of the rings are thought to have been chosen because at least one of these colors can be found in the flag of every nation. The origin of the flag's design is in some dispute. It is thought to be Coubertin (*q.v.*) who designed the symbol to honor and represent the 1914 Olympic Congress in Paris. Some sources state that Coubertin saw the rings at Delphi in 1913, but classics scholars believe this is highly unlikely and that they are of his own, modern invention. The idea of a flag was raised by the IOC in 1910 and a special committee worked to plan it. Several suggestions were made, notably by Theodore Cook (GBR) and Clarence von Rosem (SWE), but little progress was made until Coubertin came up with his design. He commented in the August 1913 edition of *Revue Olympique*, "These five rings represent the five parts of the world from this point on won over to Olympism and given to accepting fruitful rivalry. Furthermore, the six colors (including the white background) thus combined reproduce the colors of all the nations, with no exception." The flag was first flown at Chatsby Stadium in Alexandria, Egypt for the Pan-Egyptian Games on 5 April 1914. It was presented to the IOC by Baron Pierre de Coubertin at the Olympic Congress in 1914 at the Sorbonne in Paris, where it was officially approved on 15 June 1914. The flag was also flown in 1915 at the San Francisco Exhibition and at the 1919 IOC Session in Lausanne, before it made its Olympic debut in 1920 at Antwerp, Belgium. The "primary" Olympic flag was thus known as "the Antwerp flag," and has been the main Olympic flag flown at the stadium at all Olympic Games through 1984. In 1984, Seoul presented a new Olympic flag to the IOC, which was first flown at the 1988 Olympics. A second "primary" Olympic flag is used for the Olympic Winter Games, which was donated in 1952 by the host city of Oslo, Norway.

The Olympic flag is raised at the Opening Ceremonies and flies over the main stadium throughout the Olympic Games. It is lowered at the Closing Ceremonies of the Olympic Games. The mayor of the Olympic host city then presents the Olympic flag to the mayor of the next Olympic host city. The flag is to be kept in the town hall of the host city until the next Olympic Games.

Olympic Flame, Olympic Torch and Torch Relay   The Olympic flame is a symbol reminiscent of the Ancient Olympics, in which a sacred flame burned at the altar of Zeus throughout the Olympic Games. The flame was first used at the modern Olympics in Amsterdam in 1928, and again was lit thoughout the 1932 Los Angeles Olympics, but this marked the last time the flame was kindled at the site of the Games.

In 1936, Carl Diem, chairman of the organizing committee for the Berlin Olympics, proposed the idea of lighting the flame in ancient Greece, and transporting it to Berlin via a torch relay. This was done and has been repeated at every Olympics since.

The flame for the Olympic Games is lit in the altis of the Ancient Olympic stadium at Ancient Olympia, on the Greek Peloponnesus. The flame is lit during a ceremony by women dressed in robes similar to those worn by the ancient Greeks. The flame is lit naturally by the rays of the sun at Olympia, reflected off a curved mirror, and the high priestess then presents the torch to the first relay runner.

The flame for the Olympic Winter Games has not always been lit in Olympia. In 1952 and 1960 the flame for the Olympic Winter Games was lit at the hearth of Sondre Nordheim, the father of modern skiing, at his ancient home in Morgedal, Norway. In 1956 it was lit at the Temple of Jupiter in Rome for the Games in Cortina d'Ampezzo, Italy. Since 1964, the flame for the Olympic Winter Games has also been lit in Ancient Olympia. In 1994, a second, unofficial flame was lit in Morgedal for the Lillehammer Olympics, which greatly upset the Greeks who claim proprietary rights to the Olympic flame.

Olympic Games   The Olympic Games refer to the sporting festival which is held in the summer months, and is often referred to as the Summer Olympics. The proper name of the sporting celebration is the Games of the Olympiad. The Games of the Olympiad are always held during the first year of the Olympiad (See Olympiad) which they celebrate. The Olympic Games are entrusted to a single host city, which is now elected seven years in advance of the scheduled Olympic Games. (See discussions of the various Olympic Games in the chapter entitled The Olympic Games and Olympic Winter Games)

Olympic Hymn and Anthem   An Olympic Hymn, also called the Olympic Anthem, was composed for the 1896 Olympic Games by Greek composer Spyros Samaras (1863–1917), with words added by his colleague Kostis Palamas. The Olympic Hymn was first played at the 1896 Olympic Opening Ceremonies, performed by nine bands and a chorus. It was used again in 1906. Thereafter, a variety of musical offerings provided the background to the Opening Ceremonies until 1960. In 1954, the IOC launched a world-wide competition for a new version of an Olympic Hymn. From the 392 scores presented, the first prize went to Michael Spisak for his ultra-modern atonal work, with lyrics extracted from Pindar's (*q.v.*) odes. It was never terribly popular and Spisak's demands for excessive royalties led it not to be chosen as the official Olympic Hymn. It was elected to return to the Samaras/Palamas composition as the official Olympic Hymn.

The Samaras/Palamas hymn was played and sung at the 55th IOC Session in 1958 in Tokyo. It was such an impressive demonstration that IOC Member Prince Axel (DEN) suggested it be adopted as the official hymn. This was unanimously approved, although two years of legal work then took place dealing with the heirs of Samaras and Palamas. The Olympic Hymn was first used in that regard at the Opening Ceremonies in Rome three years later, since which time it has become an established part of the Olympic Ceremonies. The Olympic Charter (*q.v.*) currently terms this the Olympic Anthem.

Olympic Identity Card   The Olympic Identity Card is an important political document. It is given to all members of the Olympic Family, i.e., athletes, officials, IOC members and delegates, NOC members and delegates, and IF members and delegates. The importance of the Olympic Identity Card is that it establishes the identity of the holder and, with an appropriate national passport, is supposed to allow free passage into the country in which the host Olympic city is situated. Thus the card serves as, and supplants, a travel visa. Host cities must agree to recognize the right of all members of the Olympic Family to enter the country of the host city, based on a valid passport and the Olympic Identity Card, and not require a further visa.

Olympic Literature   The literature surrounding the Olympic Games is voluminous. The IOC now publishes multiple magazines, journals, press releases, and books. Each NOC and IF also may publish literature concerning the Olympic Games and often does so. The Organizing Committees publish a great deal of official information in addition to press releases and packets.

Private authors have also developed an enormous amount of Olympic literature. Books on the Olympics are now produced prior to and after each Olympic Games, in most of the major languages of the world. With the advent of advanced technology, some are now being produced on CD-ROMs to be read via computers.

No current up-to-date bibliography of Olympic literature exists. The two most complete and most recent are *The Olympics: A Bibliography*, compiled by Bill Mallon (New York: Garland Press, 1983) and *Bibliography: Geschichte der Leibesübungen, Band five, Olympische Spiele* (second edition), compiled by Karl Lennartz (Bonn: Verlag Karl Hofmann, 1983). (See also Olympic Magazine, Olympic Message, and Olympic Review)

Olympic Magazine   The *Olympic Magazine* is a relatively new publication of the International Olympic Committee. First published in February 1994, it is the official magazine of the Olympic Museum (*q.v.*). In its first year, it was published quarterly.

Olympic Medals   Olympic Medals are given as awards for finishing in the first three places in the events of the Olympic Games. The champion receives a gold medal, the runner-up a silver medal, and the third place finisher a bronze medal. At the 1896 Olympics, the winner received only a silver medal and the runner-up a bronze medal.

The medals must be at least 60 mm. in diameter and three mm. thick. They are designed by the Organizing Committee of the Olympic Games, upon approval by the IOC Executive Board. The "gold" medal is actually silver gilt which must be gilded with at least six grams of pure gold. The metal for the first and second place medals must be silver of at least 925/1000 grade.

Olympic Message   The *Olympic Message* has been a publication of the International Olympic Committee. It was first published in May 1982, and has been published three or four times per year since that time, but its publication has been discontinued as of the December 1994 issue (Volume 40). The *Olympic Message* was different from the *Olympic Review* (*q. v.*) in that each issue usually studied in detail a single theme of the Olympic Movement (*q. v.*).

Olympic Motto   The official Olympic Motto is "Citius, Altius, Fortius," a Latin phrase meaning swifter, higher, stronger. The Olympic Motto was adopted by Coubertin (*q. v.*) for the International Olympic Committee after hearing of its use by Reverend Father Henri Martin Didon of Paris, a Dominican friar and teacher. Didon, head master of Arcueil College, used the phrase while describing the athletic accomplishments of his students at that school. He had previously been at the school Albert Le Grand, where the Latin words were carved in stone above the main entrance. (See Olympic Creed)

Olympic Movement   The Olympic Movement is a phrase often used by the International Olympic Committee and practitioners and administrators of international sport. However, it is not well defined. The Olympic Charter (*q. v.*) states simply that "The Olympic Movement, led by the IOC, stems from modern Olympism." The IOC has, however, defined the phrase more fully in some of its press releases. They have stated that the Olympic Movement encompasses the International Olympic Committee (IOC), the International Sports Federations (IFs), and the National Olympic Committees (NOCs) and that the IOC is the supreme authority of the Olympic Movement. In addition, the IOC has stated its purpose and its fundamental principles as "to contribute to building a peaceful and better world by educating youth through sport practiced without discrimination of any kind and in the Olympic spirit, which requires mutual understanding with a spirit of friendship, solidarity, and fair play. The activity of the Olympic Movement is permanent and universal. It reaches its peak with the bringing together of the athletes of the world at the great sport festival, the Olympic Games."

Olympic Museum   An Olympic Museum had been a dream of the IOC for many years. In 1915, Coubertin (*q.v.*) announced his intention to set up an Olympic Museum in Lausanne to store the archives of the IOC and to become a public information center on the Olympic Movement (*q.v.*). IOC President Juan Antonio Samaranch (*q.v.*) made the dream a reality. He began his plans for an Olympic Museum in 1981, shortly after his election as IOC President, when the IOC bought a building at 18 avenue Ruchonnet in Lausanne and established a provisional museum. In 1984, the IOC acquired two plots of land in the Ouchy section of Lausanne, overlooking Lake Geneva. Construction on the permanent Olympic Museum began on this land in 1988. On 23 June 1993, the Olympic Museum was inaugurated on the 99th anniversary of the creation of the IOC. The Olympic Museum is intended to be the universal depository of the written, visual, and graphic memory of the Olympic Games. Samaranch has stated that "the Olympic Museum will be a global source of information on the impact of the Olympic tradition on art, culture, the economy and world peace. The focal point of the meaning of the Olympic Games and their role in modern society, the Olympic Museum will be both a witness and a center for reflection."

Olympic Oath   The Olympic Oath is a pledge to uphold the spirit of sportsmanship and is spoken at the Opening Ceremonies by representatives of the host country on behalf of all competitors and officials. In the July 1906 edition of the *Revue Olympique*, Coubertin (*qq.v.*) referred to the urgent need to introduce into the few but very important Olympic ceremonies an athletes' oath of fairness and impartiality. The protocol was first introduced at Antwerp in 1920 when the noted Belgian fencer, Victor Boin, performed the ceremony. A similar ceremony was conducted at the first Olympic Winter Games at Chamonix in 1924 when all competitors took the oath collectively, although they were led by France's Camille Mandrillon. The first woman to take the oath was the Italian skier Giuliana Chenal-Minuzzo at the 1956 Olympic Winter Games in Cortina d'Ampezzo. The first woman to take the oath at the Olympic Games was German track & field athlete Heidi Schüller at the 1972 Olympic Games in Munich.

Boin initially recited the following words: "We swear that we will take part in the Olympic Games in a spirit of chivalry, for the honor of our country and for the glory of sport." This oath was modified slightly in 1961, when the term "swear" was replaced by "promise," and "the honor of our country" by "the honor of our teams," in an obvious desire to eliminate nationalism from the Games.

The current edition of the Olympic Charter (*q.v.*) establishes the following text for the athletes' oath: "In the name of all the competitors I promise that we shall take part in these Olympic Games, respecting and abiding by the rules which govern them, in the true spirit of sportsmanship, for the glory of sport and the honor of our teams." Since 1972, the judges have also sworn an oath, the text of which, in conformity with the current Olympic Charter, is as follows: "In the name of all the judges and officials, I promise that we shall officiate in these Olympic Games with complete impartiality, respecting and abiding by the rules which govern them, in the true spirit of sportsmanship." (See Appendix 7 for the list of those who have spoken the Olympic Oath at the Opening Ceremonies of the Olympic Games.)

Olympic Order   The Olympic Order is the supreme individual honor accorded by the International Olympic Committee. It was created in 1974 and is to be awarded to "Any person who has illustrated the Olympic Ideal through his/her action, has achieved remarkable merit in the sporting world, or has rendered outstanding services to the Olympic cause, either through his/her own personal achievement(s) or his/her contribution to the development of sport." Originally, the Olympic Order was separated into three categories – gold, silver, and bronze. Currently, there is only a gold and silver category. (See Appendix V for a list of recipients of the Gold Olympic Order)

Olympic Programme, The   The Olympic Programme (TOP) is a fundraising program administered by the IOC which began in the 1980's. It is used to generate revenue for the IOC and has been very successful. TOP works by soliciting only a few sponsors, no more than 12 at a time to date, guaranteeing them exclusive marketing rights to the Olympic Symbol within their market niche, and providing that guarantee for a complete Olympiad. Each TOP edition thus lasts for four years. To date, there have been TOP I, TOP II, and TOP III. Because of the exclusivity of the program, the IOC has been able to command very large revenues from the sponsors, which has guaranteed the success of TOP.

Olympic Review   The *Olympic Review* is the official journal of the International Olympic Committee. It has been published under various titles relatively continuously since 1894. Originally published by Coubertin (*q.v.*), its first title was *Bulletin du Comité International des Jeux Olympiques*. From 1901 to 1914, it first took its current name in French, *Revue Olympique*. From 1938 to 1944, it was published in Berlin with the German title *Olympische Rundschau*, although French and English editions were also available. Other titles used during its publishing history include *Bulletin du Comité International Olympique*, *Bulletin Officiel du Comité International Olympique*, *Pages de critique et d'histoire*, and *Lettre d'information/Newsletter/Carta información*. It is now published monthly in French, English, German, and Spanish. Since 1970, the official title has remained *Olympic Review*, *Revue Olympique*, *Olympische Rundschau*, and *Revista Olímpica*.

Olympic Solidarity   Olympic Solidarity is a program in which the IOC helps the sporting development of underprivileged nations. Certain IOC fundraising is distributed via Olympic Solidarity to the NOCs which the IOC recognizes to be in the greatest need. This has taken the form of coaching assistance, technical assistance, and funds to help athletes travel to the Olympic Games and other international sporting events. The goals of Olympic Solidarity are quoted in the Olympic Charter (*q.v.*) to be "promoting the fundamental principles of the Olympic Movement (*q.v.*); developing the technical sports knowledge of athletes and coaches; improving the technical level of athletes and coaches; training sports administrators; and collaborating with the various IOC commissions."

Olympic Solidarity began in 1961 as the International Olympic Aid Committee at the suggestion of Count Jean de Beaumont (FRA). In 1968, this Committee became a Commission of the IOC (*q.v.*) while retaining the same name. In 1971, Adriaan van Karnebeek (NED) took the initiative for further developments by setting up an Olympic Solidarity Commission through the Permanent General Assembly of National Olympic Committees. (See Association des Comités Nationaux Olympiques [ACNO]) In 1972, the two groups merged to become what is now known as Olympic Solidarity. It was originally headquartered in Rome, but in 1979, at the 81st IOC Session, Olympic Solidarity was moved to its present headquarters in Lausanne. In 1982, Anselmo López became its first full-time director, a position he continued to hold through 1995.

Olympic Symbol   See Olympic Flag.

Olympic Torch and Torch Relay   See Olympic Flame.

Olympic Truce   It is often stated that in ancient Greece, a sacred Olympic Truce existed such that all wars ceased during the Olympic Games. In addition, all persons traveling to or from the Olympic Games were guaranteed free passage to Olympia, in the city–state of Elis, even if passing through lands or city–states which were at war. It is not certain if, in fact, the Olympic Truce existed fully in this form, and recent research by classical scholars indicates that this may be an oversimplification of the facts. It has been noted that the Olympic Truce "never stopped a war, nor indeed were the Eleans so foolishly utopian as to imagine they could achieve that." (Finley and Pleket, *The Olympic Games*, p. 98 [London: Chatto & Windus, 1976]) Apparently the Olympic law only forbade open warfare against the Eleans, and the truce was specifically meant only not to disrupt the Olympic Games.

Olympic Village   At each Olympics since 1924, the Organizing Committees have provided an Olympic Village which houses the athletes. In recent years with the spread of the Games over very large areas, many Organizing Committees have provided several Olympic Villages. Recently, the host cities to the Olympic Games have used the Olympic Villages to provide low–cost housing to their citizens at the end of the Olympics.

Olympic Winter Games   The Olympic Winter Games are held every four years. Originally they were held in the same year as the Olympic Games or Games of the Olympiad. Currently, they are contested every four years, but during the second calendar year following the beginning of the Olympiad. (See Olympiad) This ruling was made at the 91st IOC Session in 1986 in Lausanne, by a vote of 78-2, specifically to take advantage of the better use of advertising and television dollars to fund the Olympic Movement. (See discussions of the various Olympic Winter Games in the chapter entitled The Olympic Games and Olympic Winter Games)

Olympism   Olympism is a philosophy which is felt to be the cornerstone of the Olympic Movement. It is not easily defined and probably means different things to different people. The IOC defines Olympism in the Olympic Charter (*q.v.*) as follows: "Olympism is a philosophy of life, exalting and combining in a balanced whole the qualities of body, will and mind. Blending sport with culture and education, Olympism seeks to create a way of life based on the joy found in effort, the educational value of good example, and respect for universal fundamental ethical principles. The goal of Olympism is to place everywhere sport at the service of the harmonious development of man, with a view to encouraging the establishment of a peaceful society concerned with the preservation of human dignity."

Dr. John Powell, an eminent lecturer and author on Olympic ideals, has proposed another definition, which in 1986 was adopted by the Executive Committee of the Canadian Olympic Association, "Olympism is a harmony of ideas and ideals that affirm the value of Olympic sport in promoting and developing sound physical and moral qualities in individuals, and in contributing to a better and more peaceful world by enabling representatives of nations to meet in an atmosphere of mutual respect and international amity."

Oman [OMA]   Oman made its Olympic debut in 1984 at Los Angeles, represented by nine shooters and seven track & field athletes. Oman also competed in 1988 and 1992. Its best Olympic finish came in 1988 when Mohammad Al-Malky finished eighth in the 400 meters in track & field athletics. Oman has never competed at the Olympic Winter Games.

Ono, Takashi. [JPN-GYM]   B. 26 July 1931, Noshiro, Akita Prefecture. The first Japanese to win an individual Olympic gold medal for gymnastics, he barely lost the all-around title in both 1956 and 1960. He won the horizontal bar in 1956 and 1960, shared first place in the horse vault in 1960 and won team gold in 1956 and 1960. To his five gold medals he added four silver and four bronze medals. At the World Championships he won four silver medals and a bronze in 1958 and won the World Championships on the horizontal bar in 1962.

Organización Deportiva Centroamericana y del Caribe [ODECABE]   The Organización Deportiva Centroamericana y del Caribe (ODECABE) is a confederation of NOCs of the Central American and Caribbean region. The organization is headquartered in Mexico City and its President is José Joaquin Puello of the Dominican Republic.

Organización Deportiva Panamericana [ODEPA]   See Pan American Sports Organization (PASO).

Organizing Committees of the Olympic Games [OCOGs/COJOs]
The organization of each Olympic Games is entrusted by the IOC to an Organizing Committee which is then in charge of producing the Olympic Games. The committees are formed exclusively for the

purpose of putting on the Olympics and, as such, dissolve shortly after the Olympics are held.

Orienteering   Orienteering has never been contested at the Olympic Games, even as a demonstration sport (*q.v.*). However, the International Orienteering Federation is a recognized federation by the IOC.

Osburn, Carl Townsend. [USA-SHO]   B. 5 May 1884, Jacksontown, Ohio. D. 28 December 1966, Helena, California. The most successful Olympic marksman in history. At the Games of 1912, 1920 and 1924 he won five gold, four silver and two bronze medals for a record total of 11 medals. Three of his five gold medals came in 1920. He was a career Naval officer who graduated from Annapolis in 1906 and rose to the rank of Commander. Besides his Olympic shooting success, he competed internationally for the United States at the World Championships of 1921, 1922, 1923, and 1924, and at the Pan-American matches of 1913.

Otto, Kristin. [GDR-SWI]   B. 7 February 1966, Leipzig. Her six gold medals at one Games (1988) is a women's record for any sport and no other woman swimmer has won a total of more than four gold medals in an entire Olympic career. In Seoul she uniquely won gold medals in three different strokes, freestyle, backstroke and butterfly, and her overall performance at the 1988 Games ranks as one of history's greatest sporting achievements. At the World Championships (1982, 1986) she won seven gold medals. She set two individual world records and contributed to four relay world records in her career.

Owens, James Cleveland "Jesse." [USA-ATH]   B. 12 September 1913, Decatur, Alabama. D. 31 March 1980, Tucson, Alabama. An Olympic legend whose four gold medals at the 1936 Games (100 meters, 200 meters, 4x100 meters relay, and long jump) did much to undermine Hitler's myth of Aryan superiority. His place in sporting history had already been assured when he set six world records in one day (25 May 1935) and his long jump record of 26' 8¼" (8.13 meters) remained a world best for more than 25 years. At the end of the 1936 season he turned professional and in his later years he traveled extensively as a speaker promoting the cause of Olympism (*q.v.*) and related philosophies.

********** P **********

Pakistan [PAK]   Pakistan first competed at the Olympic Games in 1948. It did not attend the 1980 Moscow Olympics but has attended all Games since. It has never competed at the Olympic Winter Games. Pakistan owes almost its entire Olympic success to one sport – field hockey. It won a medal in this sport at every celebration from 1956 through 1984, finished fourth in 1948 and 1952, fifth in 1988, and again third in 1992. In 1960, it won the gold medal, defeating India in the final and ending its 32-year Olympic winning streak, a feat it repeated in both 1968 and 1984.

Palestine [PLE]   A Palestine Olympic Committee existed prior to World War II, formed in 1933. Palestine was ruled under a British mandate from 1921 through 1948. During those years, Palestine had an NOC which was recognized by the IOC, although it never competed at the Olympic Games. The Olympic Committee was titularly to represent Jews, Muslims, and Christians from the region of Palestine, but the rules of the original Palestine NOC stated that "(they) represent the Jewish National Home." Thus, that Olympic Committeee was more a precursor of the Israel Olympic Committee than of the current Palestine Olympic Committee. (See Israel)
        Palestine currently has no exact geographic boundaries, but was given provisional recognition by the IOC at its annual meeting in Monte Carlo in September 1993. This occurred shortly after the historic agreement signed between the Palestine Liberation Organization (PLO) and the state of Israel in that same month. As an independent nation, Palestine has not yet competed in the Olympic Games.

Pan American Sports Organization [PASO]   The Pan American Sports Organization (PASO) is a confederation of NOCs in the Americas. It was founded on 8 August 1948 and, in 1955, the current structure was put in place, and the current name of the group was adopted. The official languages of the group are English and Spanish and its name is listed as both the Pan American Sports Organization (PASO) and the Organización Deportiva Panamericana (ODEPA). The group's goals, as listed in its charter, are "To strengthen and tighten the bonds of friendship and solidarity among the peoples of America; to further the development and growth of the Olympic Ideal; to cooperate with the NOCs of the Americas; to ensure the periodic celebration of the Pan American Games; and to coordinate the Olympic and Pan American Solidarity Programs." The organization is headquartered in Mexico City and the current President (1994) is Mario Vazquez Raña of Mexico. At the end of 1994 there were 42 member nations.

Panama [PAN]   Panama was represented at the Olympics in 1928, 1948, and 1952 by a single athlete. It has sent larger contingents since 1960, although they did not attend the 1980 Moscow Olympics. It has never competed in the Olympic Winter Games. Its lone competitor in 1948 did quite well, as Lloyd LaBeach won Panama's only two Olympic medals to date, finishing third in both the 100 and 200 meter dashes.

Pankration – Ancient Olympic Sport   The pankration was a violent sport with virtually no holds barred, in which kicking played an important part. It was a very popular sport with the fans, and was actually less brutal than boxing as the pankratiasts wore no gloves which inflicted so much harm on the boxers. Plato described it as "a contest combining incomplete wrestling with incomplete boxing." The first recorded champion was Lygdamis of Syracuse in 648 B.C. Champions are recorded through Aurelius Phoibammon of Egypt in 221 A.D. Five separate athletes won at least three championships at Olympia in the pankration. A boys' pankration was held from 200 B.C. through 117 A.D. One of the most famous pankration champions, Arrikion of Figaleia, was killed while successfully defending his title in this sport. He was awarded the title post-humously when his opponent was disqualified.

Papp, László. [HUN-BOX]   B. 25 March 1926, Budapest. After winning the Olympic middleweight title in 1948 he won the light-middleweight crown in 1952 and 1956 to become the first boxer to win three Olympic gold medals. Possibly his finest victory in the Olympic ring came in the 1956 final when he beat José Torres [USA], a future world professional champion. A skillful, hard-punching southpaw, he was the first fighter from the Soviet bloc to turn professional and win the European middleweight title in 1962. However, in 1965, the Hungarian authorities withdrew its permission for him to fight professionally and the chance of a world title bout was denied him.

Papua–New Guinea [PNG, formerly NGU]   Papua–New Guinea has competed at the Olympic Games of 1976, 1984, 1988, and 1992. In 1992, Henry Kungsi posted its best Olympic performance yet. A lightweight boxer, he won one match to finish equal ninth of 29 competitors in his class. No athletes from Papua–New Guinea have competed in the Olympic Winter Games.

Paraguay [PAR]   Paraguay has competed at the Olympic Games of 1968, 1972, 1976, 1984, 1988, and 1992. It has not yet won a medal but its best Olympic finish came in 1992 when its football (soccer) team finished sixth of 16 teams. Paraguay has not yet competed at the Olympic Winter Games.

Parisi, Angelo. [GBR/FRA–JUD]   B. 3 January 1953, Italy. With four Olympic medals (one gold, two silver, one bronze) he is the most successful *judoka* in Olympic history. Italian born, he won a bronze in the open class in 1972 representing Great Britain and then represented France in 1980 and 1984, following his marriage to a French woman. In 1980, he won the unlimited class title and placed second in the open class and in 1984 he won his fourth medal with a silver in the unlimited class.

Pelota Basque   Pelota is a generic name for various hand–and–ball or racquet–and–ball games derived from the ancient French racquet sport of *jeu de paume* (*q.v.*). Pelota Basque, the Spanish variant played in the Basque regions and contiguous provinces of France and Spain, has thrice been an Olympic demonstration sport (*q.v.*) – in 1924, 1968, and 1992. The Federacíon Internacional de Pelota Vasca was founded in 1929 and is recognized by the IOC.

Pentathlon – Ancient Olympic Sport   The five events of the ancient pentathlon were jumping, a stadion race, the discus throw, the javelin throw, and wrestling. The origin of the event is attributed to Jason (of Argonaut fame). According to mythology, Jason was to award the prizes at an ancient games, and his friend Peleus was second in all the contests. So Jason combined the events out of a desire to honor his friend, and thus created the pentathlon.

   It is unclear how the winner of the pentathlon was decided. The precise order of the events is also unclear. It is only known with certainty that the last event was wrestling. If any athlete won any three events, he was immediately declared the winner, and the ancient term *triakter* is often seen, meaning the winner of three events. But scholars have not agreed on how the victor was determined.

People's Democratic Republic of Yemen [YMD]   See Yemen.

Peru [PER]   Peru first competed at the 1936 Olympic Games. It has since missed only the 1952 Games in Helsinki. The country has not competed at the Olympic Winter Games. Peru has won four Olympic medals, with one gold medal. Three of these were won in shooting and one in women's volleyball. Oddly the nation has won one medal each in 1948, 1984, 1988, and 1992.

Philippines, The [PHI]   The Philippines first competed at the Olympics in 1924, and has since missed only the 1980 Moscow Olympics. The Philippines has competed at the Olympic Winter Games of 1972, 1988, 1992, and 1994. The Philippines has won eight Olympic medals in boxing, swimming, and track & field athletics. Though the country has not yet won a gold medal in an official sport, in 1988 Arianne Cerdena won the women's bowling event in that exhibition sport.

Pietri, Dorando. **[ITA-ATH]**   B. 16 October 1885, Mandrio, Reggio Emilia. D. 7 February 1942. The most famous loser in Olympic history. Entering the stadium at the end of the 1908 Olympic marathon he held a comfortable lead over Johnny Hayes (USA) but he then collapsed five times and had to be helped across the finishing line. This assistance from well-meaning officials resulted in his disqualification but, in defeat, his fame far exceeded that of the winner. Queen Alexandra presented him with a large gold cup which was an exact replica of the one awarded to the Olympic champion, and Irving Berlin wrote the popular song "Dorando" in his honor. He soon turned professional and enjoyed a successful career in America and Europe.

Pindar. [GRE]   *fl. ca.* 520 – 440 B.C. Pindar was a Greek lyric poet, considered the greatest of the Greek choral lyricists. Few details remain of his life, but he was known to have been an aristocrat from Thebes who studied in Athens. He is best known for his *epinicia*, which were odes celebrating athletic victories. Forty-four of these have survived, most celebrating victories in the Olympic, Isthmian, Nemean, and Pythian Games (*qq.v.*). The odes were usually commissioned by the victor or his family.

Poland [POL]   Poland competed continuously at the Olympic Games from 1924 through 1980, and after boycotting Los Angeles, returned to the Olympic fold in 1988 at Seoul. Prior to 1924, several Poles probably competed for other countries. In 1908, Jerzy Gajdzyk, his name Americanized to George Gaidzik, won a diving bronze medal for the United States, and in 1912 the Polish–born Julius Beresford (né Wisniewski) won a silver medal with the British eight–oared crew. The 1912 Russian Olympic team included eight Poles. Poland has also competed at all the Olympic Winter Games since 1924. Through 1994, Poland has won 214 Olympic medals, 44 of them gold, with all but four of the medals coming at the Olympic Games.

Polo   Polo has been contested at the Olympics in 1900, 1908, 1920, 1924, and 1936.

Portugal [POR]   Portugal has competed at the Olympic Games continuously since 1912. Through 1984, Portugal had appeared at the Olympic Winter Games once with only one competitor. That was Duarte Espirito Santo Silva who competed in Alpine skiing events in 1952 at Oslo. However, Portugal also competed at the Olympic Winter Games in 1988 and 1994. Portugal has won 13 Olympic medals through 1994, two of them gold. It has yet to win a medal at the Olympic Winter Games.

Pound, Richard William Duncan, Q.C. [CAN]   B. 22 March 1942, St. Catharines, Ontario. A swimming finalist at the 1960 Olympic Games, he became President of the Canadian Olympic Association in 1977 and a member of the IOC the following year. In 1987, he was appointed a Vice-President of the IOC and in recent years he has exerted considerable influence in the financial sphere, particularly in negotiations with sponsors and the sale of TV rights. He has been chairman of the IOC Commission for New Sources of Financing since its inception. A Montreal based lawyer specializing in tax law, Pound earned his undergraduate and law degrees at McGill University in Montreal. His legal skills provided invaluable support to President Samaranch (*q.v.*) in the negotiations with North Korea over the 1988 Games.

Protopopov, Oleg Alekseyevich. [URS-FSK]   B. 16 July 1932, Moscow. The partnership with his wife Lyudmila (née Belousova) (*q.v.*) marked the emergence of the USSR as a figure skating nation. They won the Olympic pair event in 1964 and 1968, the world title for four consecutive years (1965-1968), and were the first Russian winners of either event. After losing their world title to fellow Russians Irina Rodnina (*q.v.*) and Aleksey Ulanov they turned professional and later settled in Switzerland.

Puerto Rico [PUR]   Puerto Rico first competed at the 1948 Olympics in London and has not failed to compete at the Olympic Games since then.   Puerto Rico has also competed at the Olympic Winter Games of 1984, 1988, 1992, and 1994; represented in 1984 and 1988 by George Tucker, a luger.   Puerto Rican athletes have won one silver and four bronze medals at the Olympic Games.

Pythian Games   The Pythian Games were one of the four great Panhellenic sporting festivals, along with the Olympic Games, Isthmian Games, and Nemean Games (*qq. v.*).   They were held in honor of Apollo at Delphi.   They were the only one of the four main Greek festivals which also featured musical contests.   The Pythian Games were first recorded in 582 B.C. and continued until the fourth century A.D.   The Pythian Games were held quadrennially, in the third year of each Olympiad (*q. v.*).   The victors at the Pythian Games were awarded a laurel crown.

********** Q **********

Qatar [QAT]   Qatar made its initial Olympic appearance in Los Angeles in 1984 with a team of eight track & field athletes, a football (soccer) team, and four shooters.   Qatar also competed in 1988 at Seoul and 1992 at Barcelona.   Qatar won its first Olympic medal (and only one to date) in 1992 when Mohamed Sulaiman finished third in the men's 1,500 meters in track & field athletics.

********** R **********

Race in Armor - Ancient Olympic Sport   The race in armor was contested at Olympia from 520 B.C. through at least 185 A.D.   It was also known as the *hoplite* event.   The event was held over two laps of the stadium, or about 385 meters.   Leonidas of Rhodes won four championships consecutively, from 164 to 152 B.C.

Rackets   Rackets has been contested as an Olympic sport in 1908 only, when a men's singles and doubles event was held in London.

Racquetball   Racquetball is decidedly different from rackets and is a very modern sport. It has not been contested at the Olympic Games but the International Racquetball Federation is recognized by the IOC.

Real Tennis   See Jeu de Paume.

Revival of the Olympic Games   See Attempts at Revival.

Revue Olympique   See Olympic Review.

Rhodesia [RHO]   See Zimbabwe.

Robert Dover's Games [Cotswold Olimpick Games]   Robert Dover's Games, or Cotswold Olimpick Games, were probably first contested in 1612, during Whitsun (Pentecostal) Week upon the Cotswold Hills. The Games were started by Robert Dover, a local lawyer who lived nearby in the Cotswold Hills. The Games were basically a medieval country fair type of festival but they achieved great fame. They were held from about 1612 to 1642 and were immortalized in a collection of 30 laudatory poems, entitled *Annalia Dubrensia*, and published about Robert Dover's Olimpick Games in 1636. Four of the poems were composed by great poets of the era: Ben Jonson, Michael Drayton, Thomas Heywood, and Sir William Davenant. It is slightly conjectural, but apparently even Shakespeare knew of these Games, possibly mentioning them in *Sir John Falstaff and the Merry Wives of Windsor*. "*Slender*: ' . . . How does your fallow greyhound, sir? I heard say he was outrun on Cotsall.'"
     The Cotswold Olimpicks did not end after 1642 but were simply suspended, during the Civil War in England. They were revived in the 1660s and were then held at unknown intervals for two centuries. In 1851, they were revived but were shortly thereafter suspended again. After another century, the Cotswold Olimpicks were revived in 1951, were briefly suspended and then resumed in 1963 to continue to this day.
     Though they were quite famous in their era, and though they have been contested for many centuries, the only justification to call them "Olympic" Games rests on the fact that they adopted that name and that they had been brought into contact with the Olympic, Pythian, Nemean, and Isthmian Games (*qq.v.*) via the *Annalia Dubrensia*. They had no significant influence on Coubertin (*q.v.*) or others who attempted to revive the Olympic Games.

Rodnina, Irina Konstantinova (later Zaitsev). [URS-FSK]   B. 12 September 1949, Moscow. The most successful pair skater in history. Olympic victories in 1972 with Aleksey Ulanov and in 1976 and 1980 with Aleksandr Zaitsev gave her a record total of three gold medals. Her record at the World Championships was even more impressive. She won the title for ten successive years (1969–1978), the first four with Ulanov and the next six with Zaitsev. She married Zaitsev in 1973 and their successes in the latter part of their partnership were as husband and wife.

Roller Hockey   In 1992, roller hockey was contested as a demonstration sport (*q.v.*) at the Barcelona Olympics. Roller hockey and roller skating have never been contested at the Olympics at any other time. Their governing body, however, the Fédération Internationale de Roller–Skating, is recognized by the IOC.

Roller Skating   See Roller Hockey.

Romania [ROM]   Romania first competed at the 1924 Olympic Games, and has missed only the 1932 and 1948 Olympics since. It defied pressure from its neighbors and valiantly was the only Warsaw Pact country to compete at the 1984 Olympics in Los Angeles. Romania has competed at the Olympic Winter Games since their inception in 1924, missing only 1960. It is best known for its outstanding women gymnasts, and has also produced excellent canoeists. Romania has won 220 Olympic medals, 124 by its men and 96 by its women, with 59 of them being gold medals.

Roque   See Croquet.

Rose, Iain Murray. [AUS-SWI]   B. 6 January 1939, Nairn, Scotland. Murray Rose was a triple gold medalist at the 1956 Games; he won the 400 meters and 1,500 meters freestyle and was a member of the world record breaking team in the 4x200 meters relay. After the Melbourne Games he enrolled at the University of Southern California and at the 1960 Olympics, he retained his 400 meters title, won silver in the 1,500 meters, and a bronze in the relay. His total of six Olympic medals would surely have been greater but for the fact that he was not selected for the 1964 Games as he refused to return from California for the Australian Championships. Earlier in the year he had set new world records for 880 yards and 1,500 meters and would certainly have been a medal contender in Tokyo. He continued to enjoy competitive swimming long after his Olympic career was over and, in 1981, he won the World Masters title in faster times than he recorded at the 1956 Games.

Rowing & Sculling   Rowing was first known as a means of transportation in the ancient cultures of Egypt, Greece, and Rome. Rowing as a sport probably began in Victorian England in the 17th and early 18th centuries. By the 19th century, rowing was popular in Europe and had been brought to America. Early races were usually contested by professionals, with heavy betting on races common. Competitive rowing precedes most of the other Olympic sports in its recorded modern history. The first Oxford–Cambridge race took place in 1828 and Yale and Harvard first rowed against each other in 1852.

Only in 1896 has rowing not been contested in the Olympics. It was actually on the program that year but rough seas forced cancellation of the events. There are multiple events for men in both sweep events (single oar used by alternate oarsmen) and sculling events (two oars used by a single sculler or by two or more scullers). These include races for single, double, and quadruple sculls, and in sweep events, races for two and four oarsmen, with and without coxswain, and the large boats with eight oarsmen and a coxswain. Women were admitted to the Olympic program in 1976. They compete in a streamlined program, with only one sweep event for two and four oarswomen, but they also compete in single, double, and quad sculls, and the eight-oar sweep event.

The United States was the dominant nation in Olympic rowing until about 1960. The Soviet Union quickly became a power in the sport, but the GDR in the 1970's and 1980's has been by far the dominant nation. The recent merger of the Germanys may change this, although it should be noted that the Federal Republic of Germany was also a rowing power, though not on the same level as its Eastern counterpart.

The rowing program for the 1996 Olympics has undergone a drastic change, with the introduction of lightweight events. The men's coxed pairs and coxed fours will be discontinued, replaced by the lightweight double sculls, and lightweight coxless fours. The women's coxless pairs will be discontinued, replaced by lightweight double sculls.

The world governing body of rowing is the Fédération Internationale des Sociétés d'Aviron (FISA), which was formed in 1892 and had 94 member nations through 1994. (See also Dresden Four, The – GDR Coxless Four Rowing Team [1968–1972])

Rudolph, Wilma Glodean. [USA–ATH]   B. 23 June 1940, St. Bethlehem, Tennessee. D. 12 November 1994, Brentwood,

Tennessee. Although born with polio and contracting scarlet fever and double pneumonia at the age of four, she overcame all these handicaps to become one the greatest women sprinters of all time. As a 16-year-old, she won a bronze medal in the relay at the 1956 Olympics and four years later she was the heroine of the 1960 Games. After setting a world 200 meter record (22.9) at the 1960 U.S. Championships she was a triple gold medalist at the Rome Olympics, winning the 100 meters, 200 meters and relay. A following wind deprived her of a world record in the 100 meters but she anchored the U.S. team to a new world record in the heats of the relay. The following year she equaled the world 100 meter record (11.3) and four days later posted a new record of 11.2 in addition to leading the U.S. to another world relay record. Her brilliant career ended with her retirement in 1962 after which she devoted herself to coaching and worked extensively with underprivileged children.

Rugby (Union) Football   Rugby Union has been contested at the Olympics in 1900, 1908, 1920, and 1924. Amazingly, the defending Olympic champions are the United States, which won the gold medals in 1920 and 1924.

Russia [RUS]   Prior to the Bolshevik Revolution, Russia competed at the Olympics of 1900, 1908, and 1912. Although at the first two celebrations its representation was only three and five athletes, respectively, in 1912, it sent a large team of 169 athletes. At those Olympics, Russia won one gold medal, four silver medals, and three bronze medals. After the Bolshevik Revolution, Russia became the largest republic of the Soviet Union (*q.v.*). The Soviet Union did not compete in the Olympics from 1920 to 1948, but returned to the Olympic Games at Helsinki in 1952, and competed in the Olympics through 1988. With the political events of 1991, Russia again became eligible to compete as an individual nation. At Albertville and Barcelona Russia joined with other former Soviet republics to compete as the "Unified Team," representing the Commonwealth of Independent States. Russia returned to the Olympic fold after an absence of 82 years in 1994 at Lillehammer, where its athletes won 23 medals and 11 gold medals. (See also Commonwealth of Independent States, Unified Team, and Union of Soviet Socialist Republics)

Rwanda [RWA]   Rwanda first competed in the Olympics in 1984 and also competed in 1988 at Seoul. To date Rwandan athletes have appeared only in track & field. Rwanda has not yet competed in the Olympic Winter Games and no Rwandan athlete has won an Olympic medal.

********** S **********

Saar, The   In 1952, the Saar was recognized as a separate Olympic Committee by the IOC and competed at the Helsinki Olympics, represented by 31 athletes but winning no medals. The Saar was reunited with the Federal Republic of Germany in 1956. Its athletes were absorbed by the combined German teams and the Saar Olympic Committee was dissolved on 20 September 1956. Its best finish in 1952 was equal eighth by Erich Schmidt in lightweight Greco–Roman wrestling.

Sailer, Anton "Toni." [AUT-ASK]   B. 17 November 1935, Kitzbühel. The greatest Alpine skier in Olympic history. Although his feat of winning all three Alpine events at the 1956 Winter Games was matched by Jean–Claude Killy (*q.v.*) 12 years later, Sailer's overall performance was far more impressive. He won the downhill by 3.5 seconds, the slalom by 4.0 seconds and the giant slalom by a remarkable 6.2 seconds, whereas Killy's margins of victory were far narrower. Sailer was also World Champion at Alpine combination (1956, 1958) and the downhill and slalom (1958). His career at the international level lasted only four seasons before he retired to become a hotelier and an occasional film actor and singer. A national hero, he was appointed technical director of the national Alpine team in 1972.

Saint Kitts and Nevis [SKN]   See St. Kitts and Nevis.

Saint Lucia [LCA]   Saint Lucia was given official recognition by the IOC in September 1993, but the country has not yet competed at the Olympic Games.

Saint Vincent and the Grenadines [VIN]   See St. Vincent and the Grenadines.

Salnikov, Vladimir Valeryevich. [URS-SWI]   B. 21 May 1960, Leningrad. At the 1980 Games he won gold medals in the 400 meters, the 1,500 meters (with the first ever sub–15 minute time), and the 4x200 meters relay. He remained the world's greatest long distance swimmer but the Soviet boycott of the 1984 Games denied him the opportunity of further Olympic honors. He set six world records at 400 meters (1979–1983), four at 800 meters (1979–1986), and three at 1,500 meters (1980–1983), and at the World Championships he won the 400 meters and 1,500 meters in both 1978 and 1982.

Salumäe, Erika. [URS/EST-CYC]   B. 11 June 1962. Erika Salumäe came to sports late; she took up cycling in 1981 and made the Soviet national team in 1984. She won the 1987 and 1989 world sprint championship and in 1988 and 1992 was Olympic match sprint champion. Her victory in 1992 at the Olympics was poignant as it was the first victory for Estonia at the Olympic Games after its independence from the Soviet Union. She also set several world records for the 200 meters (flying start) and 1,000 meters time trial from a standing start.

Samaranch (Torrelos), Juan Antonio, Marquis de Samaranch. [ESP]   B. 17 July 1920, Barcelona. The current and seventh President of the IOC. First appointed to the IOC in 1966, he became a Vice-President in 1974 before succeeding Lord Killanin (*q.v.*) as President in 1980. During this period he was also appointed as Spanish Ambassador to the Soviet Union in 1977. His period of office as President of the IOC has been marked by the transformation of the Olympic Movement (*q.v.*) into a vast business-like organization although not all the changes have met with the approval of the traditionalists. Ably supported by a dedicated group of Vice-Presidents he has taken the Olympic Movement into the modern era. Although not unique among IOC Presidents in having to face situations which threatened the fabric of the Olympic Movement, his diplomatic skills were invaluable in such matters as containing the boycotts of the 1984 and 1988 Games. In 1991, he was ennobled by the King of Spain for his services to Olympism (*q.v.*) and, in 1994, he announced his intention to retire at the end of his current term of office.

Samoa, American   See American Samoa.

Samoa, Western   See Western Samoa.

San Marino [SMR]   San Marino has competed at eight Summer Olympics – those of 1960, and all those from 1968 to 1992. It has competed at the Olympic Winter Games of 1976, 1984, 1988, 1992, and 1994. The best finish by an athlete from San Marino was fifth in small-bore rifle (prone) shooting in 1984 by Francesco Nanni.

São Tomé and Príncipe [STP]   São Tomé and Príncipe was given official recognition by the IOC in September 1993, but the country has not yet competed at the Olympic Games.

Saudi Arabia [KSA, formerly SAU]   Recognized by the IOC in 1965, Saudi Arabia has competed at the Olympics of 1972, 1976, 1984, 1988, and 1992. It has never competed in the Olympic Winter Games. Its best Olympic finish ever was 42nd of 58 fencers by Majed Habeebullah in 1984 men's individual foil.

Schemansky, Norbert. [USA-WLT]   B. 30 May 1924, Detroit, Michigan. Schemansky is the only man in history to win four medals in Olympic weightlifting. After placing second to John Davis in the heavyweight division at the 1947 World Championships he again finished as runner-up to Davis at the 1948 Olympics. He then took the gold medal at the 1952 Games and the bronze in 1960 and 1964. When he won his fourth medal (1964) he had passed his fortieth birthday and is the oldest man ever to win a medal in Olympic weightlifting.

Schenk, Adrianus "Ard." [NED-SSK]   B. 16 September 1944. On his Olympic debut in 1968 he tied for second place in the 1,500 meters speed skating but four years later he won three gold medals (1,500 meters, 5,000 meters, 10,000 meters). Each victory was by a wide margin and he posted new Olympic records in the 500 meters and 10,000 meters. He emphasized his superiority over his rivals two weeks later when he became one of only four men to win all four events at the World Championships. He set 18 world records at distances from 1,000 meters to 10,000 meters between 1966 and 1972 after which he turned professional.

Schmidt-Fischer, Birgit (née Fischer). [GDR/GER-CAN]   B. 25 February 1962, Brandenburg. The greatest woman canoeist of all time. Her total of 20 gold medals (1977-1994) at the World Championships has never been approached and her six (four gold) Olympic medals is also a record. Representing East Germany (GDR) she won the Olympic K1 title in 1980 (as Miss Fischer) and the K2 and K4 in 1988. After a three-year break from competition, during which she gave birth to her second child, she won the K1 in 1992 as a member of the unified German team. In addition to her four Olympic gold medals, she also won silver medals in the K1 (1988) and the K4 (1992). Her husband, Jörg, was a World Champion and Olympic silver medalist.

Schneider, Vreni. [SUI-ASK]   B. 26 November 1964, Elm. With five medals, Vreni Schneider has won the most Alpine skiing Olympic medals of any female, a number matched among men only by Kjetil André Aamodt (NOR) and Alberto Tomba (ITA) (*qq. v.*). Schneider won both the slalom and giant slalom at the 1992 Olympic Winter Games. In 1994 at Lillehammer, she won three more medals, repeating as champion in the slalom, while earning a silver in the Alpine combined, and a bronze in the giant slalom. At the World Championships she won the giant slalom in 1987 and 1989, and the slalom in 1991. She was overall World Cup champion in 1989, winning the following event championships: 1986, 1987, 1989, and 1991 giant slalom; and the 1989, 1990, 1992, and 1993 slalom. Among women, her 55 victories trails only Austria's Annemarie Moser-Proll in overall World Cup race wins.

Schollander, Donald Arthur. [USA-SWI]   B. 30 April 1946, Charlotte, North Carolina. In 1964, he became the first swimmer to win four gold medals at one Olympic Games. His victories came in the 100 meters and 400 meters individual freestyle and in both relays, and in all but the 100 meters he set a new world record. He was unfortunate that the 200 meters was not on the program at the Tokyo Games as he would set nine world records at this, his best distance (1963-1968). He also posted three world records at 400 meters and shared in eight world records in the freestyle relays. At the 1968 Games he was unable to defend his 100 meters and 400 meters Olympic titles as he failed to make the U.S. team at these distances, but he won his fifth gold in the 4x200 meters relay and took the silver in the 200 meters freestyle.

Scotland [SCO]   Scotland competed as a separate country in 1908 field hockey, finishing third, and with a separate team in the 1912 cycling road race. In all other Olympics, and in all the other sports at the 1908 and 1912 Olympics, Scotland has competed as a member of the United Kingdom of Great Britain and Northern Ireland. Scotland has also hosted one Olympic event as, in 1908, the 12 meters yachting was held on the River Clyde in Scotland, near Glasgow.

Senegal [SEN]   Senegal first competed at the 1964 Olympic Games and has competed at every Olympics since. It has competed at the Olympic Winter Games in 1984, 1992, and 1994. Amadou Dia Bâ won the nation's only medal to date, a silver in the 1988 400 meter hurdles in track & field athletics. Prior to Dia Bâ's medal in 1988, it can be argued that Senegal had won a medal in 1960. In that year, Abdoulaye Seye won a bronze in the 200 meters while representing

France. Seye was a Senegalese national, but the country was still a French territory, so he had to compete under the French flag. The first Senegalese national to compete in the Olympics was probably Cire Samba who competed for France in the javelin throw in 1924.

Serbia   Serbia competed at the 1912 Olympics, the only time Serbia has been represented at the Olympics as an independent nation. In that year, Serbia, later the largest province in Yugoslavia (*q.v.*), sent two athletes to the Olympic Games. Dragutin Tomasević did not finish the marathon race, and Dušan Milosević finished third in his heat of the 100 meters. However, it is likely that Momcilo Tapavica, who competed in 1896 in wrestling and tennis and is usually listed as representing Hungary, was actually a Serbian student from Belgrade studying in Budapest. On 4 December 1918, Serbia became part of the country that was then termed the Kingdom of Serbs, Croats, and Slovenes and would later become Yugoslavia. Serbian athletes competed under that banner through 1988. With the breakup of Yugoslavia in 1991, Yugoslavia now consists solely of the former provinces of Serbia and Montenegro. Thus Serbian athletes still compete at the Olympics under the Yugoslav flag. (See also Yugoslavia)

Sex Testing   Men and women compete in most Olympic events separately. (They compete against each other in certain shooting events, equestrian events, and yachting and also compete concurrently in figure skating [pair and dance]. They have previously competed concurrently in mixed doubles in tennis and will do so in mixed doubles in badminton beginning in 1996.)

The two sexes compete separately in most events because of the physical advantage claimed by men. Men posing as women would have a significant competitive advantage over natural women. At the 1936 Olympics, Dora Ratjen of Germany finished fourth in the women's high jump, but was later found (1938) to be a hermaphrodite. There were several other similar examples in the 1930s, notably Czechoslovakia's Zdenka Koubková, who competed in track & field events internationally, but never competed at the Olympics. The 1932 women's 100 meter Olympic champion was Stanisława Walasiewiczówna of Poland. At her death in 1980, her autopsy revealed she had mixed sexual characteristics. Her original birth certificate was later examined and "she" was found to have been christened Stefania Walasiewiczówna.

In the 1960s, concern about this problem of men posing as women to gain a competitive advantage led to the introduction of sex testing. At that time, several of the women track & field athletes were suspected of being genetically male. Sex testing began at the

Baron Pierre de Coubertin *Baron Pierre de Coubertin of France, the man who is considered responsible for the restoration of the Modern Olympic Games.*

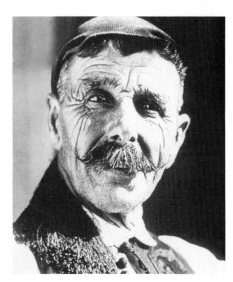

Spyridon Louis
Spyridon Louis, the Greek shepherd who won the first Olympic marathon at Athens in 1896. He is shown here as he appeared when he was a guest at the opening ceremonies of the 1936 Olympic Games.

Abebe Bikila *Ethiopian Abebe Bikila winning his second consecutive marathon gold medal at Tokyo in 1964. Bikila, usually considered the greatest marathoner ever, later was paralyzed below the neck in a car accident.*

Edwin Moses *Edwin Moses, the greatest 400 meter hurdler ever, who was unbeaten at his specialty from 1976 through 1986, and won gold medals in both 1976 and 1984.*

Paavo Nurmi At Paris in 1924, Finland's Paavo Nurmi, considered the greatest distance runner ever, leads his countryman Ville Ritola.

Al Oerter
America's Al Oerter, who won the discus throw at four consecutive Olympics—1956, 1960, 1964, and 1968.

Wilma Rudolph
Wilma Rudolph, who won three gold medals as a sprinter at the 1960 Olympics, receives her 100 meter gold medal. On her right is Britain's Dorothy Hyman, the silver medalist, and on her left is bronze medalist Giuseppina Leone of Italy.

Jim Thorpe
Jim Thorpe, the American Indian, who won both the decathlon and the pentathlon at the 1912 Olympics and is usually considered the greatest all-around athlete ever.

Michael Jordan
His Airness, Michael Jordan, as he appeared in his college days playing for North Carolina, at about the time of his 1984 Olympic gold medal.

Joe Frazier
Later a great heavyweight champion, in 1964 at Tokyo, American Joe Frazier won the gold medal in the heavyweight division.

Gert Fredriksson
On the left is Gert Fredriksson of Sweden, winner of a record eight medals in Olympic canoeing. He is being congratulated by Romanian canoeist Leon Rotman.

Larisa Latynina   Soviet gymnast Larisa Latynina, winner of the all-time record of 18 Olympic medals.

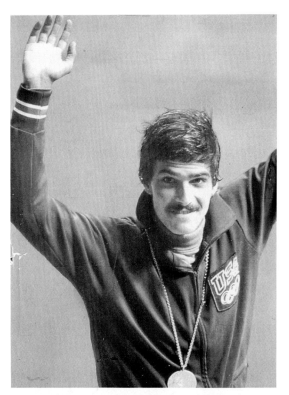

Mark Spitz
American swimmer Mark Spitz, who in 1972 at Munich won seven gold medals in seven events—all in world record times. Spitz finished his Olympic career with eleven medals, nine gold.

Dawn Fraser
Dawn Fraser of Australia, winner of eight medals and four gold medals in swimming. Fraser won the 100 meter freestyle in 1956, 1960, and 1964, the only swimmer to win the same event at three consecutive Olympics.

Johnny Weissmuller *On the right is American swimmer Johnny Weissmuller, who would later become famous as "Tarzan." He is flanked by the great Swedish swimmer Arne Borg.*

Paul Elvstrøm
Danish yachtsman
Paul Elvstrøm uniquely
won the same sailing
event at four consecutive
Olympics—1948, 1952,
1956, and 1960.

Jean-Claude Killy
France's Jean-Claude
Killy, triple gold medalist
in Alpine skiing at the
1968 Winter Olympics.
He would later be co-pres-
ident of the organizing
committee for the 1992
Olympic Winter Games, a
recipient of the Olympic
Order in gold, and a
member of the IOC.

Toni Sailer *Austrian skier Toni Sailer, who in 1956 at Cortina won all three Alpine skiing gold medals by huge margins.*

Eugenio Monti *Italian Eugenio Monti, second from the right, is embraced on the victory platform by British sledders Robin Dixon and Tony Nash, who won the gold medal in the two-man bob at the 1964 Olympics thanks to Monti, who lent them a bolt from his sled after Dixon and Nash's sled broke.*

Sixten Jernberg
No man has
ever won more
Nordic skiing
medals than
Sweden's
Sixten Jernberg.
Jernberg won
nine medals,
four gold, at the
1956, 1960, and
1964 Winter
Olympics.

Belousova/Protopopov
The superb Soviet
figure skating pair of
Lyudmila Belousova
and Oleg Protopopov,
who won gold medals
in pairs figure skating at
the 1964 and 1968
Olympic Winter Games.

Sonja Henie *Norway's Sonja Henie won three gold medals (1928, 1932, 1936) in ladies figure skating. She also won ten World Championships and later became a world-famous movie star, which made her a very wealthy woman.*

Ard Schenk
*Dutch speedskater Ard
Schenk won three gold
medals at the 1972 Olympic
Winter Games. Schenk won
the 1,500 meters, 5,000
meters, and 10,000 meters,
but lost his chance for a
gold medal sweep when he
fell during the 500 meters.*

Clas Thunberg
*Finnish speedskating legend
Clas Thunberg won seven
Olympic medals and five gold
medals in the speedskating
events at the 1924 and 1928
Winter Olympics.*

1966 European Athletics Championships, and began at the Olympics in 1968. At the 1966 European Athletics Championships, Ewa Kłobukowska of Poland was disqualified from further international competition. Kłobukowska had won a gold and bronze medal at the 1964 Olympic Games. Because of the obvious emotional and psychological trauma entailed in such an announcement, all subsequent sex testing results have not been released publicly.

Since 1968, all women wishing to compete in the Olympics have been required to undergo sex testing. (With one exception, that being Princess Anne of Great Britain, who competed in the 1976 Olympics in the equestrian events.) Testing until recently has been done by obtaining a buccal smear, or a scraping of the cells of the inner wall of the mouth. The cells were examined for the presence of a Barr body, which occurs almost exclusively in females. Females are genetically labeled as XX, while men are labeled as XY, those being the classifications of the respective sex chromosomes. The second X chromosome possessed by women contains a structure termed the Barr body.

Though some men did attempt to breach the rules and compete as women, the entire subject of mixed sexual characteristics is a highly complex and emotional one. A number of people with mixed sexual identity may have elected to compete as women for psychological reasons. In addition, doctors typically label babies with indeterminate genitalia as women. And in certain cases of mixed sex classification, some people who would be considered women lack a Barr body, and would thus have been disqualified. Because of these problems, the test has now been changed and the buccal smear is no longer used. Women are now cleared for international competition by doctors after simply undergoing a physical examination.

Seychelles [SEY]   The Seychelles has competed at three Olympic Games, those of 1980, 1984, and 1992. For reasons not precisely clear, The Seychelles did not compete in 1988 at Seoul. Its best Olympic performance came in 1992 when light–heavyweight boxer Roland Raforme won two matches to finish equal fifth of 27 in his class. The Seychelles has never competed at the Olympic Winter Games. A Seychelles national, Henri Dauban de Silhouette, represented Great Britain in the javelin throw at the 1924 Olympic Games.

Shakhlin, Boris. [URS/Ukraine–GYM]   B. 27 January 1932, Ishim, Tyumen Region. His six gold medals in individual gymnastic events remains an Olympic best for men, bettered only by Věra Čáslavská (*q. v.*). Between 1956 and 1964, he won a total of 13 medals (seven gold, four silver, two bronze) with his strongest individual event being the pommelled horse in which he won gold in 1960 and 1964. He also won a total of 14 medals at the World Championships. Unusually tall for a gymnast, his height and reach were a distinct advantage on the horizontal bar but he was weak at the floor exercise.

Sheridan, Martin Joseph. [USA-ATH] B. 28 March 1881, Bohola, County Mayo, Ireland. D. 27 March 1918, New York. The world's finest all-round athlete until the arrival of Jim Thorpe (*q.v.*). In addition to winning the discus at the 1904, 1906 and 1908 Olympic Games, he won the shot in 1906 and the Greek-style discus in 1908. To these five gold medals he added three silver medals in 1906 in the stone throw and the standing jumps and a bronze medal in the standing long jump in 1908. Between 1904 and 1911, he won 11 AAU titles at a variety of events including three in the All-Around Championship. He was at his best before world records were officially recognized but from 1902 to 1911 he set no less than 15 new "World Bests" in the discus, although irregularities in the specification of the throwing circle would have precluded some of these performances from being officially recognized under more stringent modern conditions. Irish-born, he emigrated to the USA at the age of 16 and died from pneumonia on the eve of his 37th birthday while serving with the New York Police Department.

Shooting   Shooting originated as a means of survival, as shooting was practiced to hunt game for food. In the 19th century, as the industrial revolution occurred and hunting for food became less necessary for more people, shooting as a sport evolved. The sport was first popular in English-speaking countries, notably England and the United States, but also in Ireland and South Africa. The National Rifle Association (USA) was formed in 1871 and provided the impetus for the development of organized shooting sport in the United States. The world governing body is the Union Internationale de Tir (UIT), which was formed in 1907 and had 148 member nations in early 1995.

Shooting has been contested at most of the Olympic Games. Baron Pierre de Coubertin (*q.v.*) was an avid pistol shot so he saw to it that the sport was included on the program in 1896. There were also events in 1900, but none were contested in 1904 at St. Louis. In 1928 at Amsterdam, shooting events were also not on the program.

The program has varied as much as any sport (with the possible exception of yachting). In 1908, 1912, 1920, and 1924, there were dozens of events, including multiple team events, and it was possible for shooters to win several medals at each Olympics. After the sport's hiatus in 1928, it returned to the Olympics in 1932 with only two events – one for pistols and one for rifles. Since World War II, the program has become relatively standardized. Women were first allowed to compete in Olympic shooting in 1968 and in that year, Mexico, Peru, and Poland each entered one female contestant. In 1976, Margaret Murdock (USA) won a silver medal in the small-bore rifle (three positions) event. In 1984, the UIT introduced separate events for women. Women now compete at the Olympics in four separate events. Men and women may compete together in skeet and trap shooting. The other events on the program are limited to men.

Short-track Speed Skating   See Speed Skating.

Sierra Leone [SLE]   Sierra Leone has competed at five Olympic Games, those of 1968, 1980, 1984, 1988, and 1992, but has never competed at the Olympic Winter Games. Its best Olympic performance came in 1984 when light-middleweight boxer Israel Cole won two matches to finish equal fifth of 34 in his class.

Singapore [SIN]   Singapore has competed independently at ten Olympic Games – those of 1948, 1952, 1956, 1960, 1968, 1972, 1976, 1984, 1988, and 1992. In 1964, Singaporean athletes also competed at the Olympic Games, but under the banner of Malaysia in a combined team with Malaya and North Borneo. Singapore left the Malaysian Federation in 1965. Singapore has not competed at the Olympic Winter Games. In 1960, Tan Howe-Liang won Singapore's only Olympic medal to date, a silver in lightweight weightlifting. (See also Malaysia)

Singh, Udham Kullar. [IND-HOK]   B. 4 August 1928. Of the seven Indian players to win three Olympic gold medals for hockey only Udham Singh and Leslie Claudius (*q.v.*) also won a silver medal. Singh won gold in 1952, 1956 and 1964 and a silver in 1960.

Skeleton   See Bobsledding.

Skijöring   Skijöring, originally called skid-körning, was held as a demonstration sport (*q.v.*) at the 1928 Winter Olympics in St. Moritz. Skijöring is a sport in which skiers are towed behind horses. It originally was a military competition in Norway and Sweden, and was part of the Nordic Games (*q.v.*) in 1901, 1905, and 1909. It is today only contested in Switzerland.

Skoblikova, Lidiya Pavlovna. [URS–SSK]   B. 8 March 1939, Zlatoust, Chelyabinsk. Winner of a record six Olympic gold medals for speed skating. She was a world class performer before speed skating for women was added to the Olympic program in 1960 at the Squaw Valley Games. In 1960, she won gold medals in the 1,500 meters, with a new world record, and the 3,000 meters. At the 1964 Winter Games, she became the first woman to win all four speed skating events at one Games, setting new Olympic records in the 500 meters, 1,000 meters, and 1,500 meters and was only deprived of a fourth record by adverse ice conditions in the 3,000 meters. After these successes her third Olympic appearance in 1968 was a disappointment when she finished 11th in the 1,500 meters. A teacher from Siberia, she set world records at 1,000 meters and 3,000 meters and was the world overall champion in 1963 and 1964, winning all four events in both years.

Sloane, William Milligan. [USA]   B. 12 November 1850, Richmond, Ohio. D. 11 September 1928, Princeton, New Jersey. The pioneer of the Olympic movement in America and a founding member of the IOC. A close friend and supporter of Coubertin (*q.v.*) he was the driving force behind the establishment, maintenance, and development of the strong links between the Olympic Movement and the United States. A professor of history at Princeton University and a distinguished academician, he later held the Roosevelt Chair at Berlin University but gave up most of his appointments after taking ill in 1921, although it was not until 1924 that he resigned from the IOC. His best known academic work was his four volume *Life of Napoleon Bonaparte*.

Slovakia [SVK]   Slovakia, which split from Czechoslovakia (*q.v.*) on 1 January 1993 along with the Czech Republic, competed in the Olympic Games as an independent nation for the first time at Lillehammer in 1994. Prior to the division, many Czechoslovakian athletes were actually from Slovakia. A Slovakian Olympic Committee was actually first formed in June 1939, and it attempted to revive its activities after World War II in 1945. However, in June 1947, it was coopted into the Czechoslovak Olympic Committee. The Slovakian Olympic Committee was recreated in October 1990, and was then formed officially on 19 December 1992, before its split from the Czech Republic on 1 January 1993. It received provisional recognition by the IOC on 16 March 1993 and official recognition at the 1993 IOC Session in Monaco in September 1993. At Lillehammer, Slovakia was represented by 34 men and eight women athletes. Its best finish was sixth by its ice hockey team.

Slovenia [SLO]   Prior to 1992, Slovenia had never competed at the Olympics as a sovereign nation.   However, many Yugoslav athletes were natives of Slovenia, notably Leon Štukelj (from Maribor) who won, between 1924 and 1936, more medals (six) and gold medals (three) than any other Yugoslav Olympian.   Slovenia was also responsible for all of Yugoslavia's (*q.v.*) medals in the Olympic Winter Games between 1984 and 1988.   Slovenia made its Olympic debut at both Albertville and Barcelona in 1992 after the Yugoslavian civil war.   At Barcelona, Slovenia won two bronze medals in men's rowing, and at Lillehammer in 1994, Slovenia won three more bronze medals, one in men's Alpine skiing and two in women's Alpine skiing.   Thus, Slovenia has so far won five Olympic medals as an independent nation, all bronze.

Smetanina, Raisa Petrovna. [URS-NSK]   B. 29 February 1952, Mokhcha, Komi.   With a total of ten Olympic medals for skiing she is the most successful competitor – man or woman – at any of the Winter Games disciplines.   Between 1976 and 1992 she won four gold, five silver and one bronze.   Her gold medals came in the 10 km. and relay in 1976, the 5 km. in 1980 and the relay in 1992.   Her fourth victory came only 13 days before her 40th birthday and gave her the distinction of being the oldest-ever skiing gold medalist.

Smith, John William. [USA-WRE]   B. 9 August 1965, Del City, Oklahoma.   John Smith is the most titled American wrestler ever.   A freestyler, he won two NCAA championships while at Oklahoma State.   His first major international victory was the Goodwill Games (*q.v.*) title in 1986.   In 1987, he won the Pan-American Championship and the World Championship.   In 1988 and 1992, he was Olympic champion, and from 1989–91 he won the World Championships.   In 1990 he also defended his Goodwill Games gold medal.   From 1986 through 1990, Smith's international record was 150–3.   He also received the Sullivan Award in 1990, the only American wrestler ever so honored.   He retired from competition and became coach at his alma mater where his team won the NCAA Championship in his first year of formal coaching.

Smyrna [SMY]   At the 1906 Intercalated Olympics, an international team represented Smyrna in the football (soccer) tournament and won a silver medal.   The athletes were actually all from Greece, France, and Great Britain.

Soccer (Association Football)   See Football (Association Football/Soccer).

Softball   Softball began in the 1890's as a variant of baseball, usually played by women. It was originally called mushball, kittenball, or indoor baseball, but acquired the name softball by the 1920's. In the United States the sport became organized with the formation of the Amateur Softball Association in 1933. Several variants of the sport exist in the United States, including both fast-pitch and slow-pitch. The international organization is the Fédération Internationale de Softball (ISF), which was formed in 1952 and had 90 member nations at the end of 1994. Softball has never been contested in the Olympics, but will make its debut as a full-medal sport for women at the 1996 Olympics in Atlanta.

Solomon Islands [SOL]   The Solomon Islands has competed at the Olympics of 1984, 1988, and 1992. Its best Olympic performance to date occurred in 1984 when Leslie Ata, a lightweight weightlifter, finished 16th of 19 in his class. The Solomon Islands has never competed at the Olympic Winter Games.

Somalia [SOM]   Somalia has competed at three Olympic Games – those of 1972, 1984, and 1988. Somalia entered the 1992 Olympics but did not compete, probably because of the famine in the country. It has competed only in track & field with 15 men competitors. The nation's best finish was eighth in the second semi-final of the 1988 800 meters by Ibrahim Okash Omar.

South Africa [RSA, formerly SAF]   With the exception of the Intercalated Games of 1906, South Africa's participation at the Olympic Games was continuous from 1904 through 1960. From 1964 to 1988, however, it was not allowed to compete at the Olympics. This was due to the country's policy of apartheid and, in particular, its use of the policy in choosing its athletic teams, which is forbidden by IOC policy. It is ironic that the first South African Olympians were two Zulu tribesmen who ran in the 1904 marathon; named Lentauw and Yamasini, they were both black men.
     The story of South Africa's banishment from the Olympics is one of the most complex issues which has ever faced the IOC. South Africa did not always practice apartheid as a sporting policy. In the 1930's, there was frequent inter-racial competition, but in June 1956, a South African law was passed requiring an end to inter-racial sport. In 1958, IOC Member Olav Ditlef-Simonsen of Norway informed IOC President Avery Brundage (*q.v.*) that his country would exclude an all-white South African team, if his nation were awarded the Olympics. In 1959, the Indians, Egyptians, and Soviets pressed the IOC for South Africa's ouster from the Olympics, but the IOC was

content with the promise that its 1960 Olympic team would be a multi-racial one. It was not.

In 1962, South Africa Interior Minister Jan de Klerk commented publicly that, "Government policy is that no mixed teams should take part in sports inside or outside the country." The IOC could scarcely ignore this message. At the 60th IOC Session in Moscow in 1962, the IOC voted to suspend the South African National Olympic Committee (SANOC) " . . . if the policy of racial discrimination practiced by the government . . . does not change before our Session in Nairobi which takes place in October 1963." SANOC was eventually suspended at the 62nd IOC Session in Innsbruck in January 1964.

Further problems arose in December 1966 in Bamako, Mali, when 32 African nations formed the Supreme Council for Sport in Africa (SCSA). The SCSA was to coordinate and promote sport, but its specific objective was to attack South Africa's apartheid policies in sport. At its founding conference, the SCSA resolved: " . . . to use every means to obtain the expulsion of South African sports organizations from the Olympic Movement and from International Federations should South Africa fail to comply fully with the IOC rules."

In mid-September 1967, an IOC commission visited South Africa to inspect the sporting facilities and see if the South Africa sporting groups were in violation of Olympic principles. The commission consisted of three IOC Members: future IOC President Lord Killanin (Ireland) (*q.v.*), Lord Reginald Alexander (Kenya – a white man), and Sir Adetokunbo Ademola (Nigeria – a black man). They presented their report to the IOC on 30 January 1968, and it was felt to be generally positive. By a mail ballot, the IOC voted to restore recognition to SANOC, allowing a multi-racial South African team to compete at the 1968 Olympics.

This prompted mass boycott hysteria among the African nations, which vehemently opposed this decision. The IOC Executive Board subsequently met in Lausanne on 20 April 1968, and decided to poll the IOC members. By a postal ballot of 47–17 (with eight abstentions), the IOC reversed its course and withdrew its recognition of SANOC, preventing a huge boycott of the 1968 Olympics. In May 1970, at the 70th IOC Session in Amsterdam, the South African Olympic Committee was expelled from the IOC by a vote of 35 to 28, with three abstentions.

In 1976, the South African question again became prominent when several African nations boycotted in protest of a New Zealand rugby team's having played several games on tour in South Africa. Ironically, rugby has not been an Olympic sport since 1924 and the New Zealand rugby team was named the All-Blacks.

In 1990, South Africa began to take steps to eliminate apartheid. In April 1991, the IOC, anticipating apartheid's elimination, gave provisional recognition to the South African Olympic Committee. On 9 July 1991, the International Olympic Committee granted full recognition to the South African Olympic Committee, and lifted its 21-year ban on its participation in the Olympics. In 1992 at Barcelona, South Africa competed on the Olympic stage for the first time in 32 years.

South Africa has also competed at the Olympic Winter Games in 1960 and 1994. South Africa has won 53 Olympic medals, 16 of them gold, none of them at the Olympic Winter Games. Of these, two silver medals came at South Africa's return to the Olympic stage in 1992.

Soviet Union [URS]   See Union of Soviet Socialist Republics (USSR).

Soviet Union Ice Hockey Teams [1956-1992]   The Soviet Union first entered the Olympic Winter Games in 1956 and immediately established itself as a dominant force in most winter sports. However, it was in ice hockey that the Soviet Union would be most dominant over the next 36 years. From 1956 through 1992, the Soviet Union won all but two of the Olympic gold medals in ice hockey (eight in all), losing only in 1960 and 1980 to the "hometown" United States' teams. Its last gold medal in 1992 was won as the Unified Team (*q.v.*), after the dissolution of the Soviet Union. During this time, Soviet and Unified ice hockey teams posted a record of 61 wins, 6 losses, and 2 ties.

Soviet Union Women's Gymnastics Teams [1952-1992]   The Soviet Union's women's gymnastics teams have produced a nonpareil record at the Olympic Games. They have never lost. From 1952 to 1988, and as the Unified Team (*q.v.*) in 1992, the Soviet Union has won every women's team all-around title in gymnastics, with the lone exception of 1984, when it did not compete because of the boycott.

Spain [ESP]   In 1900, Spain was represented by 14 athletes at the Paris Olympics. A Spanish NOC was formed in 1905, at the urging of the Greeks, and 20 Spanish athletes competed at Athens in 1906. Spain next appeared on the Olympic stage in 1920, and has since missed only the 1936 Berlin Olympics. In addition, Spain did not compete at Melbourne in 1956, although Spanish riders did compete in the Olympic Equestrian Games at Stockholm in 1956. Spain's first winter appearance was in 1936 at Garmisch-Partenkirchen and it has never failed to compete in the Olympic Winter Games since. Spain has won 49 Olympic medals, 18 of them gold, with 2 medals having been won at the Olympic Winter Games. In 1992, Barcelona hosted the Games of the XXVth Olympiad.

Speed Skating   Speed skating emerged on the canals of Holland as early as the 13th century. Competition is known to have been held in The Netherlands as early as 1676. The sport spread throughout Europe and national competitions were held in the 1870's. The first World Championships were contested in 1889, although the International Skating Union (ISU) held its first championships in 1893, one year after its formation.

Speed skating was contested at the 1924 Olympic Winter Games and has been on the Olympic Winter program since. Women first competed at the Olympics in 1932 when it was a demonstration sport (*q.v.*). Women's speed skating as a full medal sport began in 1960. The sport is governed by the International Skating Union (ISU), which also governs figure skating. The ISU was formed in 1892 and had 52 member nations at the end of 1994.

Olympic speed skating has almost always been contested in the European system of skating time trials in two–man pairs. In 1932 at Lake Placid, the Americans convinced the ISU to hold the events in the North American style of pack racing. Many Europeans boycotted the events as a result and the Americans won all four gold medals.

Short-track speed skating, racing in a pack indoors over a smaller rink, was contested as a demonstration sport (*q.v.*) in 1988 at Calgary. It became a full medal sport for both men and women in 1992 at Albertville.

The sport has been dominated by the Norwegians, the Dutch, and the former Soviet Union and its republics. In addition, the women of the former German Democratic Republic were outstanding speed skaters. The United States has produced excellent sprinters, winning many medals and gold medals by both men and women. In addition, in 1980, the United States' Eric Heiden (*q.v.*) won all five available gold medals, a dominance in speed skating matched only by the USSR's Lidiya Skoblikova (*q.v.*), who won all four women's events in 1964.

Speed Skiing   Speed skiing was a demonstration sport (*q.v.*) at the 1992 Olympic Winter Games in Albertville. The event was marred by the death of one of the course officials who was struck by a skier during a training run.

Spitz, Mark Andrew. [USA-SWI]   B. 10 February 1950, Modesto, California. An Olympic legend who won seven gold medals (four individual, three relay) for swimming, each in a new world record time, at the 1972 Olympics. At the 1968 Games he had won four medals (two gold, one silver, one bronze) and his overall total of 11 Olympic medals has only been matched by Matt Biondi (*q.v.*) among male swimmers. He set 26 individual world records and 6 in the relays and is arguably the greatest swimmer of all time. He returned to competition in 1991 with the aim of making the Olympic team the following year but, as he was over 40 years of age, it was a forlorn hope and an unfortunate end to a career of unrivaled achievements.

Squash Rackets   This sport is different from both rackets and racquetball (*qq.v.*) but it has never been contested at the Olympic Games, even as a demonstration sport. However, the World Squash Federation is recognized by the IOC.

Sri Lanka [SRI]   Sri Lanka, as Ceylon, competed at the Olympics from 1948 through 1968. After its name change to Sri Lanka (on 22 May 1972), it has competed at the Olympics of 1972, 1980, 1984, 1988, and 1992. Sri Lanka has yet to compete in the Olympic Winter Games. The first Ceylonese national to compete at the Olympics was Carl Van Geyzel, who competed for Great Britain in the 1928 high jump. In 1948, Duncan White won a silver medal in the 400 meter hurdles in track & field athletics for Ceylon. This is the only medal won in the Olympics by Ceylon or Sri Lanka.

St. Kitts and Nevis [SKN]   St. Kitts and Nevis was given official recognition by the IOC in September 1993, but the country has not yet competed at the Olympic Games.

St. Vincent and the Grenadines [VIN]   St. Vincent and the Grenadines first competed in the Olympics in 1988 at Seoul, when it was represented by six track & field athletes – five male and one female. The one woman, Jacqueline Ross, achieved the nation's best finish, 26th in the women's long jump. The nation also competed in 1992 at Barcelona, but has not yet competed at the Olympic Winter Games.

Stadion Race – Ancient Olympic Sport   The stadion race was the original Olympic event. It is a simple sprint of length of the Ancient Olympic stadium of approximately 192 meters. From this event, our modern word for stadium is derived. The first known champion was

Coroebus of Elis in 776 B.C. The last known champion of the stadion was Dionysios of Alexandria in 269 A.D. It is possible that, in the earliest Ancient Olympics, the stadion was the only event contested. Leonidas of Rhodes won four consecutive titles in this event from 164 to 152 B.C. Five other athletes are known to have won at least three titles.

Stevenson (Lorenzo), Téofilo. [CUB-BOX] B. 29 March 1952, Dcilias. One of only two men to win three Olympic gold medals for boxing (see also László Papp). On his way to winning the heavyweight title in 1972, 1976, and 1980, he had 12 scheduled bouts; one of his opponents withdrew, and he won nine of his 11 Olympic fights by a KO. His devastating punching power resulted in all four of his bouts at the 1976 Games ending in a knockout. At his peak he was undoubtedly the best heavyweight in the world but he resisted many lucrative offers to fight professionally. Had he done so there is little doubt that he would have been the world champion. And had Cuba not boycotted the 1984 Olympics, Stevenson would have been the favorite to win his fourth gold medal.

Strickland de la Hunty, Shirley Barbara (née Strickland). [AUS-ATH] B. 18 July 1925, Guildford, Western Australia. With seven Olympic medals she set a record for women's track & field which, although subsequently equaled by Irena Szewinska (*q.v.*), has never been beaten. The Australian sprinter-hurdler won three gold medals in the 80 meters hurdles (1952, 1956) and the 4x100 meters relay (1956). She also won one silver and three bronze medals in three Olympic appearances (1948-1956).

Sudan, The [SUD] The Sudan formed a National Olympic Committee in 1956, which was recognized by the IOC in 1959. The Sudan has competed at six Olympic Games, those of 1960, 1968, 1972, 1984, 1988, and 1992. It has never competed at the Olympic Winter Games. Its best Olympic performance came in 1984 when Omar Khalifa finished eighth in the men's 1,500 meters in track & field athletics.

Süleymanoğlu, Naim (né Naim Suleimanov, aka Naum Shalamanov). [BUL/TUR-WLT] B. 23 January 1967, Ptichar, Bulgaria. It is likely that Naim Süleymanoğlu is the strongest man who has ever lived, pound-for-pound. He set his first world record at age 15, and at the 1984 European Championships he became the second man to lift three times his bodyweight overhead.

Süleymanoğlu was also the first man to snatch two-and-a-half times his own bodyweight (27 April 1988). At the 1988 Olympics, Süleymanoğlu was absolutely dominant. He was born in Bulgaria but defected to Turkey at the 1986 World Cup finals. Born Naim Suleimanov and of Bulgarian Turkish descent, he was quite upset when the Bulgarians changed his name to Naum Shalamanov in 1985, to remove vestiges of its Turkish origins. Once in Turkey, he changed the name again to a more Turkish one. He was World Champion at 60 kg. in 1985, 1986, 1989, and 1991, and European Champion in 1984, 1985, 1986, and 1988. He did not compete in 1987 because of his defection. He also did not compete in 1990, retiring briefly before his successful comeback. In 1992 at Barcelona, he defended his Olympic championship despite his recent retirement.

Sumo Wrestling (Japanese Wrestling)　　　See Budo.

Suriname [SUR]　　　Suriname has competed at six Olympic Games since its debut in 1968, missing only the 1980 Moscow Olympics. In 1960, Suriname sent one athlete to the Olympics, Wym Essajas. Essajas was entered in the 800 meters but, after being told the heats were in the afternoon, slept through the heats which were held that morning. One Suriname athlete, Anthony Nesty, is responsible for both medals won at the Olympics by Suriname. A swimmer, Nesty won a gold medal in the 1988 100 meter butterfly and a bronze medal in the same event in 1992.

Swaziland [SWZ]　　　Swaziland has competed at four Olympic Games - those of 1972, 1984, 1988, and 1992, and one Olympic Winter Games - 1992. Its best Olympic performance was 17th by Richard Mabuza in the 1972 men's marathon.

Sweden [SWE]　　　With the exception of the 1904 St. Louis Olympics, Sweden has competed at every Olympic Games and every Olympic Winter Games. In addition to having been one of the top countries in the Winter Games, it has also been outstanding in equestrian sport, shooting, wrestling, and yachting at the Summer Olympics. Sweden has won 549 Olympic medals, 169 of them gold medals. Stockholm, Sweden hosted the Games of the Vth Olympiad in 1912. Stockholm also hosted the Equestrian Games of the XVIth Olympiad in 1956 when Australia was unable to hold the equestrian events in Melbourne because of the country's strict quarantine laws.

Swimming   Swimming is an ancient practice as prehistoric man had to learn to swim in order to cross rivers and lakes.   There are numerous references in Greek mythology to swimming, the most notable being that of Leander swimming the Hellespont (now the Dardenelle Straits) nightly to see his beloved Hero.   Swimming as a sport probably was not practiced widely until the early 19th century.   The National Swimming Society of Great Britain was formed in 1837 and began to conduct competitions.   Most early swimmers used the breaststroke or a form of it.   In the 1870's, a British swimming instructor named J. Arthur Trudgeon traveled to South America where he saw natives there using an alternate arm overhand stroke.   He brought it back to England as the famous trudgeon stroke – a crawl variant with a scissors kick.

In the late 1880's, an Englishman named Frederick Cavill traveled to the South Seas where he saw the natives there performing a crawl with a flutter kick.   Cavill settled in Australia where he taught the stroke which was to become the famous Australian crawl.

Swimming has been held at every Olympic Games.   The early events were usually only conducted in freestyle (crawl) or breaststroke.   Backstroke was added later.   In the 1940's, breaststrokers discovered they could go much faster by bringing both arms overhead together.   This was banned in the breaststroke shortly thereafter but became the butterfly stroke, which is now the fourth stroke used in competitive swimming.   Women's swimming was first held at the 1912 Olympics.   It has since been conducted at all the Olympics.

The United States has been by far the dominant nation in this sport at the Olympics.   At various times, Australia, Japan, and recently the GDR women, have made inroads into that dominance.   The governing body is the Fédération Internationale de Natation Amateur (FINA), which was formed in 1908 and had 155 member nations at the end of 1994.

Switzerland [SUI]   Switzerland first competed at the 1896 Olympic Games when it was represented by Louis Zutter, a gymnast from Neuchâtel.   Switzerland also competed at the first Olympic Winter Games in 1924, and was represented before that in 1920 at Antwerp in both the figure skating and ice hockey events.   It has been represented at every Olympic Games and every Olympic Winter Games, one of only three countries to make this claim (Great Britain and France are the others).   Switzerland has really never been the dominant country in any sport.   In the early Games it had top–notch gymnasts.   Until the GDR became dominant it was the top nation in bobsledding in the Winter Games.   St. Moritz, Switzerland hosted the 2nd Olympic Winter Games in 1928 and the 5th Olympic Winter Games in 1948.

Synoris - Ancient Olympic Sport   The synoris was a two-horse chariot race, lasting for eight circuits of the hippodrome (*circa* 9,000 meters). Champions are known from 408 B.C. (Euagoras of Elis) through 60 B.C. (Menedemos of Elis).

Syria [SYR]   Syria sent one athlete to the 1948 Olympic Games. In 1960, the United Arab Republic (Egypt and Syria) (UAR) competed at Rome with 74 athletes. Syria was a member of the UAR at that time but only three of the 74 athletes were Syrian. Syria and Egypt split their political alliance in 1961 and Syria did not compete in the 1964 Olympic Games. It returned to the Olympic fold in 1968, and has since missed only 1976. It has yet to compete in an Olympic Winter Games. In 1984, Joseph Atiyeh won Syria's only Olympic medal to date, a silver in heavyweight freestyle wrestling.

Szewińska-Kirszenstein, Irena (née Kirszenstein). [POL-ATH] B. 24 May 1946, Leningrad, USSR. With a total of seven Olympic medals in track & field she equaled the record of Australian Shirley Strickland (*q.v.*). She won gold medals in the 4x100 meters relay (1964), the 200 meters (1968) and the 400 meters (1976) and she also won two silver and two bronze medals. Her Olympic career ended in 1980 when, in her fifth Games, she pulled up with a muscle strain in the semi-finals of the 400 meters. Her tally of 13 world records included her Olympic victories of 1968 (200 meters) and 1976 (400 meters) and at the European Championships she won a record ten medals (five gold, one silver, four bronze). Born to Polish parents in the Soviet city of Leningrad she returned to Poland at an early age and during an outstanding career set 38 Polish records. In 1967 she married her coach, Janusz Szewiński.

********** T **********

Table Tennis   Table tennis was developed in the late 19th century, though its origins are not well documented. Several different sources for its invention are credited, but the modern game is said to have started with the introduction of the celluloid ball *circa* 1891. This development can be attributed to the Englishman, James Gibb, a world-record holding distance runner, who discovered the celluloid ball during a visit to America. This ensured the success of the game as a domestic pastime from which a competitive game emerged.

The sport is widely practiced throughout the world. However, it made an unusual entry into the Olympic program. Table tennis made its Olympic debut as a full medal sport in 1988 at Seoul. It was never contested at the Olympics as a demonstration sport (*q.v.*), which the IOC usually requires of new sports. Since the late 1950's, the Chinese have been by far the dominant factor in table tennis, although they are closely pushed by the Koreans. The governing body of the sport is the International Table Tennis Federation (ITTF), which was formed in 1926 and had 166 nations at the end of 1994.

Tadzhikistan [TJK]   As a former member of the Soviet Union, Tadzhikistan has not yet competed independently at the Olympic Games. Tadzhikistani athletes were present at Barcelona in 1992 as members of the Unified Team (*q.v.*). A few Tadzhikistani athletes competed from 1952 to 1988 for the Soviet Union.

Taekwondo   Taekwondo has been contested as a demonstration sport (*q.v.*) at the 1988 and 1992 Olympics. The World Taekwondo Federation was recognized by the IOC in 1973 and currently has 144 members. The sport has provisionally been admitted to the Olympic Program for the 2000 Olympic Games in Sydney.

Taiwan   See Chinese Taipei.

Tanganyika   See Tanzania.

Tanzania [TAN]   As Tanganyika, Tanzania had three athletes at the 1964 Olympic Games. As Tanzania it has competed at the 1968, 1972, 1980, 1984, 1988, and 1992 Olympics. It has never competed at the Olympic Winter Games. In 1980 at Moscow, Filbert Bayi won a silver medal in the steeplechase. In 1976, Bayi had been a co-favorite with New Zealand's John Walker in the 1,500 meters and the battle between them was anticipated to be one of the great races in track history. It never occurred as Tanzania joined the 1976 African boycott in protest of a New Zealand rugby team playing in South Africa. Tanzania's other Olympic medal also occurred in 1980 when Suleiman Nyambui finished second in the 5,000 meters in track & field athletics.

Team Handball   See Handball (Team Handball).

Television   Television is the method by which most of the world watches the Olympic Games. The rights fees paid by television are also critically important to the continued success of the Olympic Movement as they are the primary method of financing the Olympic Games and the activities of the International Olympic Committee (*q.v.*). The Olympic Games were televised for the first time in 1936 but with only a few viewers in Germany. The next few Olympiads also saw Olympic Games telecast within the host country but with no significant rights fees. Television first began world-wide broadcasts in 1960 at Rome, with most of Europe seeing the Games live, and the United States viewing them on tape delay. The rights fee paid by the U.S. host television network, CBS (Columbia Broadcasting System), was $395,000. By contrast, NBC (National Broadcasting Company), which televised the 1992 Barcelona Olympic Games in the United States, paid $401,000,000 for the rights to the Games. World-wide rights for the 1992 Olympics totaled $636,000,000. It was estimated that the gross cumulative television audience for 1992 was 24.6 billion people, and that 2.3 billion people (85% of all those with televisions) watched the 1992 Olympics at some time. While only one country was able to watch the Olympic Games of 1936, 1948, and 1956 on television, 21 nations watched the 1960 Olympics on television, and that number increased to 193 for the 1992 Olympics.

Tennis (Lawn Tennis)   Tennis, originally lawn tennis, was invented by Major Walter Wingfield, a British army officer, in 1873. The original name was "sphairistike." However, tennis variants are much older than that. Court tennis, or royal tennis, real tennis, or jeu de paume, was known to have been played in the Middle Ages.

Tennis was contested at every Olympic Games from 1896 through 1924 as a regular medal sport. It was then discontinued although it was on the schedule as a demonstration sport (*q.v.*) in 1968 and 1984. The reasons for dropping tennis as an Olympic sport probably are two: 1) the IOC was upset that many of the top tennis players, though considered amateurs, infringed upon its fine definition of amateurism; and 2) the tennis establishment, especially in Britain, was concerned that the Olympic events might become more important than Wimbledon, and did not wish that to occur.

Tennis returned to the Olympics as a full medal sport in 1988 and almost certainly will remain on the Olympic program. Full-scale professionals now compete in the Olympics, with no other qualifications. The governing body of the sport is the International Tennis Federation (ITF), which was founded in 1913 and had 190 members at the end of 1994.

Tethrippon - Ancient Olympic Sport   The tethrippon was a four-horse chariot race which was contested over 12 laps of the hippodrome (*circa* 14,000 meters). Champions are known from 680 B.C. (Pagondas of Thebes) through 241 A.D. (Titus Domitius Prometheus of Athens). Euagoras of Sparta was the only three-time champion in this event (548–540 B.C.).

Thailand [THA]   Competing in the Olympics since 1952, Thailand has missed only the 1980 Moscow Olympics. It has never competed in the Olympic Winter Games. Thai athletes have won four Olympic medals, one silver and three bronze, and all in boxing.

Theagenes of Thasos. [GRE–BOX/WRE]   *fl. ca.* 480–460 B.C. Theagenes is credited with over 1,400 victories in various sporting festivals in ancient Greece. Theagenes won at Olympia in 480 B.C. in boxing and in 476 B.C. in the pankration (*q.v.*). He and Kleitomachos of Thebes are the only two athletes to have won the boxing and pankration at Olympia.

The Thasians erected a statue to Theagenes in the town. A former athlete, who hated Theagenes, attacked the statue one night and it fell on him and killed him. The Thasians followed Draconian law and threw the statue into the sea. A great drought fell upon the island of Thasos, and crops suffered, with many animals dying as a result. The oracle at Delphi told them this could be corrected by bringing back to the country all their exiles. They did this but the drought and famine continued. They then consulted the wise Pythia at Delphi, who told them, "You have forgotten your great Theagenes, whom you threw in the sand, where he now lies, though before he won a thousand prizes." Several Thasian fishermen hauled the statue back in their nets, it was re-erected in its former position, and the drought ended. Later the Thasians sacrificed to Theagenes as a hero of healing.

Thessalonika [TSL]   At the 1906 Intercalated Olympics, a football (soccer) team represented Thessalonika and won a bronze medal. This is the only independent Olympic appearance by this province and city of Greece.

Thompson, Francis Morgan "Daley." [GBR–ATH]   B. 30 July 1958, Notting Hill, London. He shares with Bob Mathias (*q.v.*) the distinction of successfully defending an Olympic decathlon title. Thompson won his Olympic gold medals in 1980 and 1984, setting his fourth and final world record at the Los Angeles Games. He also competed in the 1976 and 1988 Olympics and is one of only two decathletes to have taken part in four Games. He was also the World

(1983), European (1982, 1986), and British Commonwealth (1978, 1982, 1986) champion.

Thorpe, James Francis (né Wa-tho-huck [Sac-and-Fox Indian name meaning "Bright Path"]). [USA-ATH]   B. 28 May 1888, Bellemont, Oklahoma. D. 28 March 1953, Lomita, California. Often described as the greatest all-round athlete in history, the accolade is well merited when judged by his superiority over his contemporaries. At the 1912 Olympics, he won the pentathlon and decathlon by huge margins, setting world records in both events. The following year, his name was struck from the roll of Olympic champions after it was revealed that he had earlier been paid for playing minor league baseball. The amount involved was miniscule ($15 [US] per week) but it was not until 1982 that the IOC reversed its decision and after an interval of 70 years the medals were returned, posthumously, to the family of their rightful owner. Part French and part Sac-and-Fox Indian, he attended Carlisle Indian School where he established an awesome reputation as a footballer being voted All-American in 1911 and 1912. He later played professionally for the Canton Bulldogs and played major league baseball for the New York Giants, Boston Braves and Cincinnati Reds.

Thunberg, Clas Arnold Robert. [FIN-SSK]   B. 5 April 1893, Helsinki. D. 28 April 1973, Helsinki. His record of five Olympic gold medals for speed skating was equaled by Eric Heiden (*q.v.*) in 1980 but has never been bettered. In 1924 he won the 1,500 meters, 5,000 meters and the combined event, placed second in the 10,000 meters and third in the 500 meters. Four years later, he won the 500 meters and successfully defended his 1,500 meters crown. Further Olympic honors seemed likely at the 1932 Games but, like many leading European skaters, he refused to compete at Lake Placid as a protest against the mass-start style of racing. An unusual character, he made his World Championship debut in 1922 at the age of 28 and his final appearance was in 1935, aged 42. During this period he missed three Championships (1926, 1930, 1935) but still won 14 individual titles and was the overall champion five times. He set five world records, the last in 1931 at the age of 38. He later became a Member of the Finnish Parliament.

Timmons, Stephen Dennis. [USA-VOL]   B. 29 November 1958, Newport Beach, California. With three Olympic medals, two of them gold, Steve Timmons has won more Olympic volleyball medals than any other man. Timmons led the U.S. to Olympic gold medals in both 1984 and 1988, being named most valuable player of the 1984

Olympic team. Between Olympics, he helped the U.S. win the 1986 World Championship and the 1985 World Cup. Timmons left the national team in 1989 to play professional volleyball for Il Messaggero in Rome. Timmons, with former U.S. star Karch Kiraly (*q.v.*), led Il Messaggero to the 1991 World Club Championship. He then returned to the national team to help the U.S. win a bronze medal at the 1992 Olympics. Timmons owns a beach sportswear company, and is married to the former Jeanne Buss, the daughter of the owner of the Los Angeles Lakers.

Togo [TOG]   Togo has competed at four Olympic Games – those of 1972, 1984, 1988, and 1992. The nation's best Olympic performance came in 1988 when welterweight boxer Abdoukerim Hamidou won one match to place equal ninth of 44 in his class. Togo has never competed at the Olympic Winter Games.

Tomba, Alberto. [ITA-ASK]   B. 19 December 1966, San Lazzaro di Savena, Bologna. An Olympic gold medalist in the slalom and giant slalom in 1988, he succesfully defended his giant slalom title in 1992 when he also took the silver medal in the slalom. At his third Winter Games in 1994 he placed second in the slalom giving him a total of five Olympic medals: a record for Alpine skiing which he shares with Kjetil André Aamodt and Vreni Schneider (*qq.v.*) who also won their fifth medals at the 1994 Games. Had Tomba chosen to compete regularly in the downhill and super giant slalom events he would surely have won even more medals. Surprisingly, in view of his Olympic successes, he had a poor record at the World Championships where he won a solitary bronze medal in 1987. In contrast, he enjoyed a superb record in the World Cup. A flamboyant, dashing character, both on and off the slopes, he was the idol of the Italian sporting public to whom he was always known as "La Bomba."

Tonga [TGA]   Tonga has competed at the 1984, 1988, and 1992 Olympics. Its best Olympic performance came in 1984 when heavyweight boxer Tevita Taufoou won one match to place fifth of 15 competitors in his class. Tonga has never competed at the Olympic Winter Games.

TOP [The Olympic Programme].   See Olympic Programme, The.

Torvill, Jayne (later Christensen) *[B. 7 October 1957, Nottingham]* **and Dean, Christopher Colin** *[B. 27 July 1958, Nottingham].*

[GBR-FSK]   The ice dance partnership of Jayne Torvill and Christopher Dean produced one of the legendary performances in Olympic history. Their interpretation of Ravel's "Bolero" at the 1984 Winter Games in Sarajevo drew the maximum score of 6.0 for artistic impression on all of the nine judges' scorecards. They were clear winners of the Olympic gold medal and set a new standard against which ice dancing was to be judged in the future. But only four weeks later they repeated their own superlative Olympic performance to win their fourth consecutive world title. A successful and lucrative professional career followed but, after Olympic eligibility had been restored, they took the bronze medal at the 1994 Winter Games, having earlier won the 1994 European title. Dean has twice been married to figure skating world champions: first to Isabelle Duchesnay, French pair world champion (1991), and currently to the 1990 world ladies' champion, Jill Trenary (USA).

Track & Field   See Athletics (Track & Field).

Trampoline   Trampolining has never been contested at the Olympic Games, even as a demonstration sport (*q.v.*). However, the International Trampoline Federation is recognized by the IOC.

Tretyak, Vladislav Aleksandrovich. [URS-ICH]   B. 25 April 1952, Moscow Oblast. Of the six ice hockey players to have won three Olympic gold medals he is the only one to have added a silver medal to his collection. Recognized as one of the greatest goalkeepers of all time, he won Olympic gold 1972, 1976, and 1984 and silver in 1980 when the Americans defeated the Soviets in a major upset. Tretyak was also on the winning team at nine World Championships and his talents attracted the attention of many NHL clubs. He was drafted by the Montreal Canadiens but the authorities in the USSR refused to let him play abroad, although he was later employed as a coach by the Chicago Black Hawks. He enjoys the distinction of being the only Soviet player in the Hockey Hall of Fame.

Triathlon   Triathlon is a relatively new sport which consists of running, swimming, and cycling. Its origins date to the 1970's when the first major triathlon, the Ironman Race, was first held in Hawaii. Triathlon is governed by the International Triathlon Union (ITU) which was recognized by the IOC in 1989, currently with 94 members. Triathlon has been provisionally admitted to the Olympic program for the 2000 Olympic Games.

Trinidad and Tobago [TRI]   Trinidad and Tobago has competed continuously at the Olympics since its debut in 1948, competing only as Trinidad through 1964. In 1960, it had one cyclist and one track & field athlete competing in a combined team with Jamaica and Barbados under the name of the West Indies Federation (*q.v.*), termed the Antilles by the Rome organizing committee. Though the Federation won two medals, no Trinidad athlete was a medal winner in 1960. Trinidad and Tobago competed in the Olympic Winter Games for the first time in 1994 at Lillehammer. Trinidad and Tobago has won seven Olympic medals, four in track & field athletics and three in weightlifting. Its only gold medal occurred in 1976 when Hasely Crawford won the men's 100 meters in track & field athletics.

Tug-of-War   In 1900, 1904, 1906, 1908, 1912, and 1920, tug-of-war was contested as a part of the track & field athletics program. The sport has not returned to the Olympics since. Three British athletes, Frederick Humphreys, Edwin Mills, and James Shephard, won three tug-of-war medals, two of them gold.

Tunisia [TUN]   Tunisia has competed at the Olympic Games since 1960, missing only the 1980 Olympic Games. It has never competed at the Olympic Winter Games. Tunisia has won five Olympic medals, four of them by Mohamed Gammoudi, a distance runner, and one by Habib Galhia, a boxer.

Turishcheva, Lyudmila Ivanovna (later Borzova). [URS-GYM] B. 7 October 1952, Grozny, Checheno-Ingushskaya, USSR. Lyudmila Turishcheva ranks with Larisa Latynina (*q.v.*) as one of the two greatest Soviet female gymnasts ever. But Turishcheva never won the fans' affections which were often reserved during her career for her teammates Olga Korbut (*q.v.*) and Nelli Kim. Turishcheva won nine Olympic medals, four of them gold. She was all-around champion at the 1972 Olympics, 1970 and 1974 World Championships, 1971 and 1973 European Championships and at the first World Cup in 1975, when she uniquely won all five individual events. She later married Soviet sprint great Valery Borzov and became coach of the Soviet gymnastics teams.

Turkey [TUR]   In 1907, Pierre de Coubertin (*q.v.*) visited Turkey and had as his guide Aleko Mulas, a young gymnast who was studying at the Galatasaray Lycée. Coubertin encouraged Mulas to attend the Olympic Games and, in 1908, Mulas became Turkey's first Olympic athlete when he competed in the gymnastic events. In 1912,

Turkey had two athletes at Stockholm, but it did not enter a real team until 1924 at Paris. Since then it has missed only the Games of 1932 and 1980. Turkey first competed at the Olympic Winter Games in 1936 and has since missed only the Winter Games of 1952, 1972, and 1980. Turkey has won 53 Olympic medals. Turkish wrestlers account for an outstanding 47 of these, with 24 gold medals in wrestling.

Turkmenistan [TKM]　　As a former member of the Soviet Union, Turkmenistan has not yet competed independently at the Olympic Games. A few Turkmen athletes competed from 1952 to 1988 for the Soviet Union, and Turkmen athletes were present at Barcelona in 1992 as members of the Unified Team (*q.v.*).

********** U **********

Ueberroth, Peter Victor. [USA]　　B. 2 September 1937, Evanston, Illinois. After the financial disaster of the 1976 Games and the boycott in 1980 there was no longer any great enthusiasm among cities to host the Olympic Games. Los Angeles was the only city to apply to stage the 1984 Games and under Ueberroth's able direction as President of the Organizing Committee they proved a great success. Although the Games had no public funding, a successful drive for corporate sponsorship and the sale of TV rights resulted in a surplus of over $200 million. This resulted in a world-wide revival of interest in hosting future editions of the Games. Although Ueberroth's methods were initially vilified by the European press, his marketing ideas have been adopted by the IOC and subsequent organizing committees and are now *de rigueur*. Ueberroth later served as commissioner of baseball in the United States but after he lost the support of the owners he did not seek re-election for a second term.

Uganda [UGA]　　Uganda competed at the Olympics for the first time in 1956. Its participation was continuous through 1972 – the highlight that year being John Akii-Bua winning the first Ugandan gold medal with his world record performance in the 400 meter hurdles. In 1976, after the overthrow of Idi Amin, and joining in the 1976 African protest, Uganda did not participate at Montreal. It did compete, however, in both 1980 and 1984. Uganda has never competed at the Olympic Winter Games. Ugandan athletes have won five Olympic medals, one by Akii-Bua and four by its boxers.

Ukraine, The [UKR]   As a separate nation The Ukraine had never competed at the Olympic Games until its debut in 1994 at Lillehammer. This is due mostly to the fact that, until the Soviet revolution of 1991, The Ukraine had only been truly independent in the 20th century for a brief period around the time of the Bolshevik Revolution (and was at civil war for most of that time). Many Ukrainians have competed for the Soviet Union at the Olympic Games, however. The Ukraine was second only to Russia among Soviet republics in terms of medals won. Ukrainian athletes were present at Albertville and Barcelona in 1992 as members of the Unified Team (*q.v.*). At Lillehammer, The Ukraine accounted for two Olympic medals, highlighted by the gold-medal-winning performance of Oksana Baiul in women's figure skating. The Ukraine has never hosted an Olympic Games, but in 1980 several preliminary football (soccer) matches were held in Kiev.

Ulvang, Vegard. [NOR-NSK]   B. 10 October 1963, Kirkenes. After achieving only modest success at the 1988 Winter Games he completely dominated the 1992 Games. At Calgary in 1988, he won a bronze medal in the 30 km. but four years later at Albertville he won three gold (10 km., 30 km. classical and relay) and a silver (combined pursuit). In 1994, he was no longer a major contender for individual honors but won his sixth Olympic medal with a silver in the relay. He competed injured in 1994, and also shortly after the trauma of his younger brother's being lost and dying while running in the woods in the autumn of 1993.

Underwater Swimming   Underwater swimming has never been contested at the Olympic Games, even as a demonstration sport (*q.v.*). However, the Confédération Mondiale des Activités Subaquatiques is recognized by the IOC.

Unified Team (aka CIS) [EUN]   Because of the Soviet revolution of 1991, the Unified Team represented the Commonwealth of Independent States (*q.v.*) at the 1992 Olympics in both Albertville and Barcelona. At Albertville, the Unified Team was a loose confederation of five former Soviet republics – Russia, Belarus (formerly Byelorussia), The Ukraine, Kazakhstan, and Uzbekistan. At Barcelona, the Unified Team had representatives from all the former Soviet republics, save for the Baltic states of Estonia, Latvia, and Lithuania, which competed independently. The Unified Team also included athletes from Georgia, which had not joined the Commonwealth of Independent States. In 1994 the republics competed independently and will do so in the future. (See also Commonwealth of Independent States [CIS])

Union of Soviet Socialist Republics (USSR) [URS]   The Soviet Union has had two distinct periods of Olympic participation. From 1900 through 1912 it competed at the Olympics as Russia. However, after the Bolshevik Revolution the Soviet Union withdrew from international sport until the late 1940's. After World War II it competed in the European Championships in track & field athletics but it did not return to the Olympics until 1952 at Helsinki. It made its inaugural Olympic Winter Games appearance in 1956 at Cortina. It has competed at every Olympics since with the exception of the 1984 Los Angeles Olympics. After returning to the Olympics the Soviet Union was a dominant force in almost all Olympic sports. The Soviet Union was disbanded in late 1991 after the August revolution. It no longer competes as a single nation at the Olympics but its 15 former republics now compete as independent nations. The Soviet Union hosted the Games of the XXIInd Olympiad in Moscow in 1980.

United Arab Emirates [UAE]   The United Arab Emirates has competed at the Olympics in 1984, 1988, and 1992. Its best Olympic finish ever was 101st in the 1988 individual road race cycling by Sultan Khalifa. Though this sounds unimpressive, he did defeat 35 of the 136 starters. It is no surprise that the United Arab Emirates has never competed at the Olympic Winter Games.

United Arab Republic [UAR]   See Egypt and Syria.

United States [USA]   The United States has competed at every Olympic Games with the exception of the 1980 Moscow Games, and has never failed to be repesented at the Olympic Winter Games. In addition, it had skaters present in both 1908 and 1920 when those events were held with the summer celebration. It has been the dominant country in terms of medals won since the inception of the Games. However, in the past three decades, the Soviet Union has won slightly more medals, and the German Democratic Republic threatened this dominance prior to its merger with West Germany in October 1990. The United States has also been host to the Olympic Games more than any other country. Three times the Games of the Olympiad have been held in the United States: 1904 in St. Louis, 1932 in Los Angeles, and 1984 in Los Angeles. The Olympic Winter Games have also been held in the United State three times: 1932 in Lake Placid, 1960 in Squaw Valley, and 1980 in Lake Placid. The Games of the XXVIth Olympiad are scheduled to be held in Atlanta in 1996.

United States Basketball Team - 1960   The United States 1960 Olympic basketball team was one of the greatest basketball teams ever assembled. It is almost certainly the greatest amateur team ever and its line-up would match up well with almost any professional team ever. The team easily won the gold medal at Rome in 1960. The team members were Burdette Haldorson, Jay Arnette, Walter Bellamy, Robert Boozer, Terry Dischinger, Darrall Imhoff, Allen Kelley, Lester Lane, Jerry Lucas, Oscar Robertson, Adrian Smith, and Jerry West. The starting line-up usually consisted of Robertson and West at guard, and as professionals, they would later be considered the two finest guards of their era.

United States Basketball Team - 1984   The United States 1984 Olympic basketball team rivaled the United States 1960 team as a great amateur unit. The team was coached by the redoubtable Bob Knight of Indiana University, and was never challenged in winning the gold medal. It was led by Michael Jordan (*q.v.*) of the University of North Carolina, who would later be considered the greatest professional player ever, and would also win a gold medal in 1992 with the Dream Team (*q.v.*). The team members were Steve Alford, Leon Wood, Patrick Ewing, Vern Fleming, Alvin Robertson, Michael Jordan, Joseph Kleine, Jon Koncak, Wayman Tisdale, Chris Mullin, Samuel Perkins, and Jeffrey Turner. Ewing and Mullin would also later play on the Dream Team.

United States' Virgin Islands [ISV]   The U.S. Virgin Islands has been represented at six Olympic Games, those of 1968, 1972, 1976, 1984, 1988, and 1992. It has competed in the Olympic Winter Games in 1988, 1992, and 1994. Peter Holmberg won a silver medal in 1988 Finn monotype yachting, the only medal yet won by an athlete from the U.S. Virgin Islands.

Upper Volta [VOL]   See Burkina Faso.

Uruguay [URU]   Uruguay first competed at the 1924 Olympics in Paris and has competed at every Games since, with the exception of the 1980 Games in Moscow. It had only one competitor in 1932 but he did quite well; Douglas Guillermo won a silver medal in the single sculls rowing. Uruguay has never competed at the Olympic Winter Games. Uruguay has won nine Olympic medals. Two of these were gold, the outstanding victories by the Uruguayan football (soccer) teams in 1924 and 1928 (*q.v.*).

Uruguay Football Teams [1924 and 1928]   In both 1924 and 1928 Uruguay won the gold medal in the Olympic football (soccer) tournament. This was considered a major upset in 1924, as Uruguay had never before even entered the Olympic football (soccer) tournament. In fact, after 1928, Uruguay has not entered the Olympic football tournament through 1992. In 1930, the Uruguay team revealed its greatness when several of its Olympic players helped Uruguay to win the inaugural World Cup in football. The players who played on both the World Cup team and at least one of Uruguay's gold medal teams were: Héctor Castro (1924, 1928 Olympic, 1930 World Cup); Pedro Cea (1928 Olympic, 1930 World Cup); José Nasazzi (1924, 1928 Olympic, 1930 World Cup); José Andrade (1924, 1928 Olympic, 1930 World Cup); Lorenzo Fernández (1928 Olympic, 1930 World Cup); Alvaro Gestido (1928 Olympic, 1930 World Cup); and Hector Scarone (1924, 1928 Olympic, 1930 World Cup).

Uzbekistan [UZB]   Many Uzbeki athletes competed from 1952 to 1988 for the Soviet Union, and Uzbeki athletes were present at Barcelona and Albertville in 1992 as members of the Unified Team (*q. v.*). Uzbekistan competed at the Olympics as an independent nation for the first time in 1994 at Lillehammer, represented by seven athletes. Lina Cheryazova won a gold medal in freestyle skiing aerials, the only medal won by Uzbekistan in 1994.

********** V **********

Val Barker Award   The Val Barker Award is given at each Olympic Games to the boxer who is judged to be the best overall technical boxer. It is named in honor of Val Barker of Great Britain, a former President of the AIBA. It was first awarded in 1936. Though typically it is given to one of the boxing gold medalists, three times it has been awarded to a non-champion, as follows: 1936 flyweight bronze medalist Louis Lauria (USA); 1968 featherweight bronze medalist Philip Waruinge (KEN); and 1988 light-middleweight silver medalist Roy Jones (USA).

Van Innis, Hubert. [BEL–ARC]   B. 24 February 1866, Elewyt. D. 25 November 1961, Zemst. The supreme Olympic archer who won a record six gold medals and a record total of nine medals at the Games of 1900 and 1920. Although the exceptional number of archery events at these Games clearly helped him towards his record medal total, this advantage was countered by his absence from the 1904 and 1908 Games and by the fact that archery events were not held at the 1912 Games. After his successes in 1920, archery was never again an Olympic sport during his lifetime but, in 1933, at the age of 67, he won a team gold medal at the World Championships and in all probability would have won further Olympic medals had he been given the opportunity. Van Innis was an architect by profession.

Vanuatu [VAN]   Vanuatu made its Olympic debut in 1988 at Seoul and also competed in 1992. Its best finish was probably Olivette Daruhi's performance in the 1988 women's 200 meter sprint. She finished fifth of seven competitors in a first-round heat. Vanuatu has not yet competed at the Olympic Winter Games.

Venezuela [VEN]   Venezuela formed a National Olympic Committee in 1935, and achieved IOC recognition in the same year. However, it was not until 1948 that Venezuelans competed at the Olympics. The Venezuelans have been represented at the Olympic Games without fail since 1948, one of only 25 countries to claim this. It has never competed in the Olympic Winter Games. Venezuela has won eight Olympics medals, five in boxing, and one each in men's track & field athletics, men's shooting, and men's swimming.

Vietnam [VIE]   The original NOC for Vietnam was founded on 25 November 1951 and was recognized by the IOC in 1952. After the Vietnam War the committee was restructured on 20 December 1976 and waited four years for IOC recognition. Vietnam appeared at every Summer Olympics from 1952 through 1972 and again competed in 1980 and 1988. It has never competed at the Olympic Winter Games. Its best Olympic finish occurred in 1988 when Quoc Cuong Nguyen finished equal 13th of 32 shooters in rapid-fire pistol.

Vikelas, Demetrios. [GRE]   B. 1835, Syra. D. 7 July 1908, Athens. Vikelas was the first IOC President (1894–1896). Although better known as a writer and for his interest in literature and the arts than for his sporting inclinations, because he lived in Paris and was well acquainted with Coubertin, he represented Greece and the Pan-Hellenic Gymnastic Club at the 1894 Olympic Congress in Paris. Early Olympic regulations stipulated that the IOC President should come from the country hosting the next Games and with Athens being awarded the 1896 Games, Vikelas was appointed President. Despite his lack of experience in sports administration he proved an able and enthusiastic President before handing the office over to Coubertin (*q.v.*) at the successful conclusion of the 1896 Games.

Virgin Islands, British [IVB]   See British Virgin Islands.

Virgin Islands, U.S. [ISV]   See United States' Virgin Islands.

Volleyball   Volleyball, like basketball, is a sport whose origin is known almost to the day. Oddly, both sports were invented at the same college and within a few years of one another. Volleyball was invented in 1895 by William G. Morgan, a student at Springfield College and a director of the Y.M.C.A. at Holyoke, Massachusetts. The game was originally called "minonette."
   Volleyball quickly spread around the world and became more popular in other countries than in the United States. The sport was introduced in the Olympics in 1964 by the Japanese, although it was never contested as a demonstration sport (*q.v.*) at the Olympics. No country has been truly dominant in volleyball, although the Soviet Union has won the most medals. Originally the Japanese had the world's best women's players while the United States has had the best men's team in the world for most of the 1980's.
   Volleyball has now reached great heights of popularity in the United States, spurred on by beach volleyball, a two-man outdoor sport played by the ocean or on any sand-covered court. In 1993, the IOC approved beach volleyball as an Olympic sport which will appear on the program at the 1996 Atlanta Olympics.
   The international governing body of volleyball is the Fédération Internationale de Volleyball (FIVB), which was formed in 1947 and had 210 member nations at the end of 1994. This makes volleyball the international federation with the most affiliated nations world-wide.

Volleyball, Beach   See Volleyball.

********** W **********

Wales   Wales competed as a separate country in 1908 field hockey, finishing third. In all other Olympics and, in all the other sports at the 1908 Olympics, Wales has competed as a member of the United Kingdom of Great Britain and Northern Ireland.

Walter-Martin, Steffi (née Martin). [GDR-LUG]   B. 17
September 1962, Schlema.   Walter-Martin is the only woman to win
two Olympic gold medals for luge.   She took the title in 1984 and
1988 and on each occasion led the East Germans to a clean sweep of
the medals.   She was also the World Champion in 1983 and 1985.

Watanabe, Osamu. [JPN-WRE]   B. 21 October 1940. It is
possible that Osamu Watanabe is the greatest wrestler ever,
pound-for-pound.   He had a very short career but he was never
beaten or scored upon during it.   It is known that he won at least 187
consecutive matches until his victory in the 1964 Olympics at Tokyo
when he won the featherweight freestyle gold medal.   In that
tournament, Watanabe won all of his matches without sacrificing a
single point.   This followed Watanabe's victories in the 1962 and
1963 World Championships.   He was not immensely strong, but was
very quick and his technical skills were unmatched in his era.

Water Polo   Water polo was developed in Europe and the United
States as two separate sports.   In the United States it was termed
softball water polo, as the ball was an unfilled bladder, and the sport
was very rough, often degenerating into numerous fights.   In 1897,
Harold Reeder of New York formulated the first rules for that sport,
which were intended to decrease the excessive roughness of the game.
   The European style of water polo predominated and today is
the form of the game practiced universally.   It is more scientific,
faster, and less dangerous than the American game.
   Water polo was played at the Olympics of both 1900 and
1904.   It was not on the 1906 Olympic program but has been
contested at all Games since.   Great Britain won four of the first five
Olympic tournaments, but by far the greatest exponents of water polo
have been the Hungarians.   Between 1928 and 1980, Hungary never
failed to medal in the sport at the Olympics.   Hungary did not
compete in 1984 and failed to medal in 1988 and 1992.
   Women's water polo is popular in several countries but has
yet to be admitted to the Olympics, although World Championships
are held in this sport.   Water polo, like swimming and diving, is
governed by the Fédération Internationale de Natation Amateur
(FINA), which was formed in 1908 and has 155 affiliated nations.

Water Skiing   Water skiing was a demonstration sport (*q.v.*) at the
1972 Olympics.   The sport is governed by the International Water Ski
Federation which was formed in 1946 and is currently recognized by
the IOC.

Weightlifting   Weightlifting in various forms has been popular for centuries. Strongmen of all types often performed at various fairs in the Middle Ages. In the 19th century, professional strongmen often toured with carnivals or vaudeville shows. Weightlifting as a sport became organized only in the late 19th century, however. The governing body is the International Weightlifting Federation (IWF), which had 156 member nations through 1994. The first governing body of weightlifting was founded in 1905 as the Amateur Athleten Weltunion. The current Federation was founded in 1920 as the Fédération Internationale Haltérophile in 1920, and adopted the name of the International Weightlifting Federation in 1972.

Weightlifting has been on the program of the Olympics except for the years of 1900, 1908, and 1912. The program has varied little except for the addition of more and more weight classes in recent years. Originally there were no weight classes, only an open competition, and in 1920 and 1924 there were also one-handed lifts. Beginning in 1928, the three Olympic lifts were standardized as the military press, the snatch, and the clean & jerk. Because of difficulties judging the press, and because there was some concern that the lift was biomechanically dangerous to lifters' backs, it was eliminated from international competition after the 1972 Olympics. Today lifters compete only in the snatch and the clean & jerk at the Olympics.

Weightlifting has been dominated by the Soviet Union since its entry to the Olympics in 1952. In the 1970's and 1980's, Bulgaria challenged that dominance, although a number of its lifters ran afoul of drug testing, notably in 1992. The United States was once a weightlifting power but has won only one Olympic medal since 1968 (and none since 1976), with the exception of the 1984 Olympics which were not attended by the East European nations.

Beginning in 1993, the weight classes in international weightlifting have been changed, with a completely new set of world records. This is to eliminate the possibility of earlier records having been set by drug users prior to strict drug controls.

Weissmuller, Johnny (né Petr Jánös Weiszmüller). [USA–SWI/WAP]   B. 2 June 1904, Freidorf, then Hungary. D. 20 January 1984, Acapulco, Mexico. Winner of the 100 meters freestyle in 1924 and 1928, the 400 meters freestyle in 1928 and a member of the winning relay team in both years. He set 28 world records and such was his margin of superiority over his contemporaries that many authorities still rate him ahead of Mark Spitz (*q.v.*) as the greatest swimmer of all time. Because of the limited number of events available to Weissmuller, his Olympic record cannot be fairly compared with that of Spitz but the longevity of his records is testament to his greatness. His 1927 world record for the 100 yard freestyle was unbeaten for 17 years, a remarkable length of time during a period of rapid development in the sport. Much of his success was due to his revolutionary high-riding stroke, flutter kick and head-turning breathing. Invited for a screen test for the role of Tarzan he was preferred to 150 other applicants and went on to become the most famous screen Tarzan of all, playing the role in 19 movies between 1934 and 1948.

Wenzel, Hanni. [LIE-ASK] B. 14 December 1956, Staubirnen, Germany. With a total of four medals, she trails only Vreni Schneider (*q.v.*) as the most successful of all women Olympic Alpine skiers. After winning a bronze medal in the slalom in 1976 she won gold in the slalom and giant slalom and a silver in the giant slalom in 1980. Born in Germany, Wenzel moved to Liechtenstein as an infant and was granted citizenship after winning the slalom at the 1974 World Championships. Both her brother and sister were Olympic Alpine skiers.

West Indies Federation In 1960, Jamaica, Barbados, and Trinidad competed as a combined team, representing the West Indies Federation. The Rome organizing committee called the "nation" the Antilles, a term which has, unfortunately, been often copied in many books. Since that time they have competed independently as separate nations. (See Barbados, Jamaica, and Trinidad & Tobago)

Westergren, Carl Oscar "Calle." [SWE-WRE] B. 13 October 1895, Malmö. D. 5 August 1958. Carl Westergren is the most successful Olympic wrestler in the Greco-Roman style. A four-time Olympian he won gold in 1920 (middleweight), 1924 (light-heavyweight) and 1932 (unlimited) but in 1928, when he was defending his light-heavyweight title, he was surprisingly defeated in the first round by Onni Pellinen of Finland and withdrew from the competition. His total of three Olympic gold medals is a record shared with Ivar Johansson and Aleksandr Medved (*qq.v.*) and he was the world middleweight champion in 1922. Westergren was a three-time European champion as well.

Western Samoa [SAM] Western Samoa has competed at the Olympic Games of 1984, 1988, and 1992. Marcus Stephan, a 1992 featherweight weightlifter, finished ninth of 31 in his class, this being the best finish by a Western Samoan in the Olympics. Western Samoa has not yet competed at the Olympic Winter Games.

Winkler, Hans Günter. [FRG-EQU]   B. 24 July 1926, Wuppertal-Barmen.   Hans Günter Winkler has the finest record ever of any German show jumper and his overall record internationally is rivaled only by France's Pierre Jonquères d'Oriola and Italy's Raimondo D'Inzeo (*q.v.*). Winkler won seven Olympic medals (five gold, one silver, one bronze), but only one in the individual event. That individual medal, a gold, came in 1956 when Winkler won the show jumping at the Melbourne Olympics. He led Germany to team golds in 1956, 1960, 1964, and 1972, a bronze in 1968, and a silver in 1976. Winkler's 1956 championship was his third consecutive internationally as he won the first two World Championships in show jumping which were held in 1954 and 1955.

Winter Pentathlon   In 1948 at St. Moritz, a winter pentathlon event was held as a demonstration sport (*q.v.*). The events of the winter pentathlon were cross-country skiing, shooting, downhill skiing, fencing, and horse riding.

Witt, Katarina. [GDR/GER-FSK]   B. 3 December 1965, Karl-Marx-Stadt (now Chemnitz). As a gold medalist in 1984 and 1988 Katarina Witt became the first woman figure skater to retain an Olympic title since Sonja Henie (*q.v.*). She was also a four-time World Champion (1984, 1985, 1987, 1988) and after taking the Olympic and world titles in 1988 she turned professional. With the return to Olympic eligibility of the professionals Witt took part in the Winter Games for a third time in 1994, but some of the magic of the earlier days had gone and she finished in seventh place.

Women at the Olympics   The first connection between women and the Olympic Games can be traced back to the 10th century B.C. when the Herean Games, which were exclusively for women, were held at Olympia, although not as part of the Ancient Olympic Games (*q.v.*).

Women were not allowed to compete at the Ancient Olympics, nor were they initially allowed to spectate. The Olympic boxing crown in 404 B.C. was won by Eukles, who was the son of Akousilaos and the grandson of Diagoras, who won the Olympic boxing championships in 464 and 448 B.C. To this time, legend has it that women were put to death if they were discovered watching the events, however, Eukles' mother attended his matches, disguised as a trainer. When he won, she leaped over the barrier behind the trainer's station and exposed herself as a woman. The judges withheld the death penalty "out of respect for her father and her brothers and son." (Finley and Pleket, *The Olympic Games: The First Thousand Years*, pp. 45-46) A rule was then enacted requiring all trainers to thereafter attend all Olympic contests fully naked, like the athletes.

In 396 B.C. the first female Olympic champion was crowned when Princess Kyniska of Sparta, the daughter of Sparta's King Archidamos, won the tethrippon, a four-horse chariot race. But it should be mentioned that in the Ancient Olympics, the winners of the chariot races were considered to be the owners of the chariots and horses, not the drivers.

No females officially competed in the first modern Olympics in 1896. There is fairly good evidence, however, that two women ran the marathon course near the time of the Olympic race after they were not allowed to compete in the actual race. These runners were Melpomene and Stamata Revithi, both Greeks.

The Games of 1900 saw the first official female Olympic participants when a total of 19 competitors from Bohemia, France, Great Britain, and the United States took part in croquet, golf, and tennis. The first known women to compete in the Olympics were two recently discovered French croquet players, Mme. Filleaul Brohy and Mlle. Marie Ohnier, who competed in the one-ball croquet singles beginning on 28 June 1900. By winning the tennis singles and mixed doubles on 11 July 1900, Charlotte Cooper of Britain became the first woman champion at the modern Olympic Games. In 1908, when Frances Rivett-Carnac (née Greenstock) (GBR) sailed aboard her husband's winning yacht in the seven-meter class, they became the first married couple to win Olympic gold medals.

Through the 1924 Olympics, women were not allowed to compete in track & field, the most well publicized sport at the Olympic Games. In response, women formed their own organization, the FSFI (Fédération Sportive Feminine Internationale) which sponsored the "Women's Olympics" in Paris in 1922 and the "Second International Ladies' Games" in Göteborg, Sweden in 1926. Only after these events proved that women could turn in credible athletic performances did the IAAF agree to allow them to compete in the 1928 Games, albeit only in five events.

All went well except in the 800 meters, when Lina Radke, the German winner, left a field of exhausted runners sprawled in various stages of collapse behind her. The IOC then banned women from any events beyond 200 meters, on the grounds that they were not physically equipped to run long distances. The ban remained in effect for 32 years, until the 1960 Olympics, when the 800 meters women's event was reinstated, with longer races to follow, beginning in 1972.

Coubertin (*q.v.*) resisted the notion of women competing at the Olympics and was a significant obstacle to their progress in sports. Despite this, the women's program has steadily enlarged and the evolution of the introduction of women's events to the Olympic program can be summarized as follows:

1900	Croquet*, Golf, Tennis
1904	Archery
1908	Figure Skating, Motorboating*, Yachting*
1912	Diving, Swimming
1924	Fencing
1928	Gymnastics, Track & Field Athletics
1936	Alpine Skiing
1948	Canoeing
1952	Equestrian Events*, Nordic Skiing
1960	Speed Skating
1964	Luge, Volleyball
1968	Shooting*
1976	Basketball, Handball (Team), Rowing
1980	Hockey (Field)
1984	Cycling, Shooting (separate women's events)
1988	Table Tennis
1992	Badminton, Biathlon, Judo
1996	Football (Soccer), Softball
1998	Curling, Ice Hockey (*qq. v.*)

* Indicates female participants in sports open to both sexes.

In 1956 at Cortina, Italian skier Giuliana Chenal Minuzzo was the first woman to take the Oath of the Athletes' on behalf of the competitors. At Mexico City in 1968, Enriqueta Basilio de Sotelo became the first woman to light the main Olympic Torch in the stadium, although Sweden's Karin Lindberg had lit one of the torches in 1956 at the Equestrian Olympic Games. Heidi Schüller (FRG) was the first woman to take the Athlete's Oath at the Summer Olympics in 1972 at Munich.

The IOC also resisted female membership, and it was not until 1981 that the first women became members of the IOC. Two were elected in that year – Flor Isava-Fonseca (VEN) and Pirjo Vilmi-Häggman (FIN). Through 1995, only eight women have served on the IOC.

Wrestling   Wrestling is the most ancient known competitive sport. Wrestling was introduced into the Ancient Olympics in 708 B.C., shortly after the Games' recorded history begins in 776 B.C. Ancient Olympic champions are recorded from Eurybatos of Sparta (708 B.C.) through Aurelius Aelix of Phoenicia (213 A.D.). The most titled champions at Olympia were Milon of Kroton who won five titles in wrestling (532–516 B.C.) and one in boys' wrestling (540 B.C.), and Hipposthenes of Sparta, who also won five wrestling titles (624–608 B.C.) and one boys' wrestling title (632 B.C.) at Ancient Olympia.

Only in 1900 has wrestling not been on the Olympic program.   There are four main forms of amateur competitive wrestling practiced in the world – Greco–Roman wrestling, freestyle wrestling, judo wrestling, and sombo wrestling. Judo is considered a separate sport at the Olympics. Sombo is a combination of freestyle and judo and is most popular in the Soviet Union but it has not yet been contested in the Olympics. Currently, both freestyle and Greco–Roman wrestling are contested at the Olympics and both have been held since 1920. Prior to that (except in 1908), only one form was used, usually Greco–Roman. Freestyle wrestling is similar to American collegiate style, or folkstyle wrestling. Holds are relatively unlimited, provided they are not dangerous, and can be applied to any part of the body. Greco–Roman wrestling limits holds to the upper body.

The dominant country in wrestling has been the Soviet Union and its former republics, especially in Greco–Roman style. The United States is close to the Soviets in freestyle, however. Other countries which produce good wrestlers include Iran, Turkey, and Mongolia. The wrestling international federation is the Fédération Internationale de Lutte Amateur (FILA), which was formed in 1912 and had 132 affiliated nations at the end of 1994.

********** Y **********

Yachting   Yachting began as a form of sailing, which has been practiced since antiquity as a means of transport. In the modern sense, yachting probably originated in the Netherlands, and the word seems to come from the Dutch "jaght" or "jaght schip," probably a light, fast naval craft.

The sport was brought to England by King Charles II about 1660 after his exile to Holland. International yacht racing began in 1851 when a syndicate of members of the New York Yacht Club built a 101-foot schooner named *America*. The yacht was sailed to England where it won a trophy called the Hundred Guineas Cup in a race around the Isle of Wight under the auspices of the Royal Yacht Squadron. The trophy was renamed The America's Cup, after the yacht, not after the United States, as is commonly thought. Yachting is now governed world-wide by the International Yacht Racing Union (IYRU), which was formed in 1907 and had 113 nations at the end of 1994.

Yachting was first contested at the 1900 Olympics. It made its next Olympic appearance in 1908 and has been on every Olympic program since that year. Yachting has had a very varied program which is usually changed every few Olympiads as the popularity of various boats waxes and wanes. Women have always been allowed to compete in Olympic yachting with men. In 1988, separate yachting events exclusively for women were introduced. In 1984, the popular sport of boardsailing (Lechner class) was also added to the Olympic program, and a separate boardsailing event for women was placed on the program for the first time in 1992.

Yegorova, Lyubov. **[EUN/Russia–NSK]** B. 5 May 1966. Winner of a record six gold medals for Nordic skiing. She won three gold in 1992 (15 km., combined pursuit, and relay), and a further three in 1994 (5 km. classic, combined pursuit, and relay). Additionally she won two silver medals in 1992 and one in 1994. She has been less successful in the World Championships, winning only one individual title, the 30 km. freestyle event in 1991.

Yemen [YEM] Yemen was formed on 22 May 1990 by combining the nations of the People's Democratic Republic of Yemen and the Yemen Arab Republic. It was shortly thereafter recognized by the IOC. Prior to the merger, the People's Democratic Republic of Yemen competed in 1988 at Seoul, while the Yemen Arab Republic competed at both the 1984 Los Angeles Olympics and the 1988 Seoul Olympics. The best performance by Yemen, the YAR, or the YMD, probably occurred in 1988 when Awad Saleh Nasser finished sixth in a heat of eight in the first round of the 800 meters.

Yemen Arab Republic (North) [YAR] See Yemen.

Yemen Democratic Republic (South) [YMD] See Yemen.

Yugoslavia [YUG] Yugoslavia first competed at the Olympics in 1920, although Serbia was represented by two athletes in 1912 at Stockholm. Since 1920, Yugoslavia has appeared at every Summer Olympic celebration, although in 1932 it was represented by a lone track & field athlete. It first appeared at the Olympic Winter Games at their inception in 1924 and has returned every four years with the exception of 1932 and 1960. Recent civil unrest in Yugoslavia caused the secession of many of the individual republics. Croatia and Slovenia competed at the 1992 Olympics in both Albertville and Barcelona. Bosnia–Herzegovina competed at Barcelona in 1992, and all three former Yugoslav republics competed at Lillehammer in 1994. It is possible that the Former Yugoslav Republic of Macedonia (FYROM) will attempt to compete independently at future Olympic Games. Yugoslavia now consists of only the former republics of

Serbia and Montenegro. Yugoslavia has won 90 Olympic medals, 26 of them gold. In 1984, Yugoslavia hosted the 14th Olympic Winter Games in Sarajevo, which is actually the capital of the former Yugoslav republic of Bosnia-Herzegovina, now an independent nation torn by civil war. (See Bosnia-Herzegovina; Croatia; Macedonia, Former Yugoslav Republic of; Serbia; and Slovenia)

########## Z ##########

Zaire [ZAI]   Zaire was formerly known as the Belgian Congo, but changed its name to the Democratic Republic of the Congo in June 1960. On 27 October 1971, the name was again changed to Zaire. As the Democratic Republic of the Congo, Zaire was represented by five cyclists at the Mexico City Olympics in 1968. Its second Olympic appearance came 16 years later in Los Angeles where it was represented by three track & field athletes – two men and a woman – and six boxers. Zaire also competed in 1988 at Seoul and 1992 in Barcelona. The country never competed in the Olympics as the Belgian Congo. Its best Olympic performance probably came in 1988 when Mobange Amisi finished 98th of 136 starters in the individual cycling road race.

Zambia [ZAM]   Formerly Northern Rhodesia, this nation took the name Zambia on 24 October 1964. Zambia has competed at the Olympic Games of 1968, 1972, 1980, 1984, 1988, and 1992. In addition, the country competed at Tokyo in 1964 as Northern Rhodesia. Zambia has never competed at the Olympic Winter Games. In 1984, Keith Mwila won a bronze medal in light-flyweight boxing, the only medal won by a Zambian athlete at the Olympics.

Zanzibar   See Tanzania.

Zappas, Evangelos. [GRE]   B. 1800, in what is now Albania. D. 1865. Evangelos Zappas was a wealthy landowner and businessman of Greek background, but he never set foot in Athens, where he would become famous for an early effort at Olympic revival which he sponsored. He lived most of his life in Romania, settling there after fighting for Greece in the Greek War of Independence. In early 1856, Zappas proposed to the Greek government a permanent revival of the Olympic Games, and offered to finance the project. The first of the

Zappas Olympic Games (*q.v.*) was held in 1859. Zappas had earmarked funds for restoration of the ancient Panathenaic Stadium but this was not done for the 1859 Games. After his death, his will provided ample money to support a permanent revival of the Ancient Olympic Games and for restoration of the stadium. Prior to the 1870 Zappas Olympics, the Panathenaic Stadium was restored, thanks to Zappas' largesse.

Zappas Olympic Games   Numerous attempts at revival of the Olympic Games occurred prior to the successful efforts of Baron Pierre de Coubertin (*q.v.*). (See Attempts at Revival) Perhaps the most significant of these were the Zappas Olympic Games. They are today usually called by this name, although in the 19th century, the Greeks termed them "Olympic Games for Greece."

The Zappas Olympic Games were conducted four times, in 1859, 1870, 1875, and 1889. They were held in Athens. The Games were the brainchild of Panagiotis Soutsos, but were sponsored by Evangelos Zappas (*q.v.*), a wealthy Greek who then lived in Romania. In 1856, he wrote to King Otto and offered to fund the entire Olympic revival himself. In early November 1859, a series of three festivals was conducted. The first was a series of agri-industrial contests. One week later, chariot races were conducted for professionals and laymen (the word "amateur" in reference to sports had not yet been invented).

On 15 November 1859, the athletic Games were conducted at Plateia Loudovikou, a city square on the edge of town. There were sprint races, a 1,500 meter race, two javelin throws (one for distance, the other for accuracy), and two discus throws (one for distance and one for accuracy). The winner of the 1,500 meters was Petros Velissariou, who came from Smyrna, and won a first prize of 280 drachmas, the largest prize of the first Zappas Olympics, because Brookes' (*q.v.*) Much Wenlock prize of £10 was included.

In 1870, the Zappas Olympics were moved to the ancient Panathenaic Stadium in the center of Athens. The stadium had been restored at Zappas' expense, although he had died in 1865. These Games, held on 15 November 1870, were the most successful of the Zappas Olympics, with the newspapers calling them a resounding success. Over 30,000 spectators attended these Games.

The 1875 Zappas Olympics are termed by classics scholar David Young a "disaster." In 1870, the winner of the 400 meters had been Evangelis Skordaras, a butcher, and the wrestling winner was Kardamylakes, a manual laborer. Several of Athens' elite then suggested that the Games be restricted only to athletes from the upper class and that the general public be banned. This early attempt at elitism and using the early British concepts of amateurism proved highly detrimental to the Zappas Olympics. Only 24 athletes took part in 1875, with a smaller crowd which left large sections of the stadium empty. The 1889 Zappas Olympics took place in May in a small gym, rather than in the stadium, and were not well organized. In fact, they were scheduled, begun, canceled, and then held again a few days later. Again, only a few privileged, upper-class athletes competed, and the crowd was much smaller. In 1891 and 1893, Panhellenic Gymnastic Society Games were contested, which were not organized by the Zappas Committee. Interestingly, several Greek athletes who competed in 1893 also competed at the 1896 Olympics. The Zappas Olympic Games rank with the Much Wenlock Olympian Games (*q.v.*) as the most significant attempts to revive the Ancient Olympic idea. They probably surpass the Much Wenlock Games because they were national sporting contests. Though he later denied any knowledge of them, Coubertin was keenly aware of the efforts of the Zappas Committee to hold Olympic Games, having been told of them by Demetrios Vikelas (*q.v.*), who would later be the first IOC President.

The Games themselves were fairly successful in 1859, and especially in 1870, but were "ruined" by elitism, anti-athleticism, bigotry, and attempts to apply an amateur-type code on the athletes. The Zappas Olympics never had the international flavor which Coubertin would instill in the modern Olympic Games. But they were the closest attempt yet to a true Olympic revival.

Zátopek, Emil. [TCH-ATH]   B. 19 September 1922, Koprivnice, Moravia. Emil Zátopek was a supreme distance runner whose rugged training regimen was rewarded with unprecedented success. At the 1948 Olympics he took the gold medal in the 10,000 meters and finished second in the 5,000 meters and then at Helsinki in 1952 he produced one of the greatest performances in distance running history. He won the 5,000 meters, successfully defended his 10,000 meters title and then took his third gold medal in his first-ever marathon race to complete a "triple" which remains unique in Olympic history. He closed his Olympic career four years later when he placed sixth in the marathon in Melbourne. Between 1949 and 1954, he set 18 world records at every distance from 5,000 meters to 30,000 meters, a remarkable display of versatility at the very highest level. His wife, Dana (née Ingrova), was the Olympic gold medalist in the javelin in 1952.

Zimbabwe [ZIM]   Zimbabwe was formerly Rhodesia, a British colony which was self-governing from 1923, and as Rhodesia, competed at three Olympic Games – those of 1928, 1960, and 1964. On 11 November 1965, Rhodesian Prime Minister Ian D. Smith announced his nation's unilateral declaration of independence from Great Britain. Britain termed the act illegal and demanded that Rhodesia broaden voting rights to provide for eventual rule by majority Africans. In May 1968, the United Nations Security Council condemned the white-dominated Rhodesian government, asking that Rhodesian passports not be accepted for international travel. Rhodesia did not compete at the 1968 Olympics, one reason being that the IOC did not recognize its independent status, another being that Mexico honored the U.N. Security Council ruling.

At the 71st IOC Session in Luxembourg in 1971, the IOC decreed that Rhodesian athletes could compete at the 1972 Olympics under the same conditions as in 1968 – using British uniforms, the Union Jack as a flag, and with "God Save the Queen" as an anthem. Initially, this placated the African nations. However, shortly before the 1972 Munich Olympics, the African nations threatened a mass boycott if Rhodesia was allowed to compete. The petition stated that the Rhodesians had entered Germany not on British passports, as still required by the U.N. Security Council, but using the Olympic Identity Card (*q.v.*). Two days before the 1972 Opening Ceremonies, the IOC narrowly voted (36–31, with three abstentions) to withdraw the invitation to Rhodesia for the 1972 Olympics.

In 1975, the IOC sent a three-member contingent to visit Rhodesia to inspect the sporting facilities and groups. Led by Major Sylvio Magalhães de Padilha of Brazil, this commission of inquiry was not kind to Rhodesian sports, and the IOC expelled the Rhodesian Olympic Committee, by a 41–26 vote.

After changing its constitution to allow black rule, and normalizing relations with Great Britain, Rhodesia became Zimbabwe on 18 April 1980. Zimbabwe first appeared at the Olympics in 1980 at Moscow and the highlight of its appearance was the gold medal performance of its women's hockey (field) team. This remains the only medal won by Zimbabwe at the Olympics. It has not competed at the Olympic Winter Games. Zimbabwe also competed at the 1984, 1988, and 1992 Olympic Games.

BIBLIOGRAPHY

Within each section, the books are listed first by Olympic Games, then alphabetically, and then chronologically, in cases where one author has several books listed. Also included are dissertations specifically concerned with the Olympic Games or certain aspects of them. In addition, a very few pertinent articles are listed, where no comprehensive book on a certain subject is available. All transliterated titles are from the native alphabet, using the *Encyclopaedia Britannica* as the source of the transliteration table.

Official Reports of the Games of the Olympiad

Current official reports (at least since 1960) are issued in both English and French, and usually in the language of the host nation. These are sometimes issued with parallel texts, and sometimes as separate editions for each language. In the following COJO is the acronym which stands for Comité d'Organisateur des Jeux Olympiques, the French name for Organizing Committee.

1896
The Baron de Coubertin; Philemon, Timoleon; Lambros, Spiridon P.; and Politis, Nikolaos G., editors. *The Olympic Games 776 B.C. - 1896 A.D.; With the approval and support of the Central Council of the International Olympic Games in Athens, under the Presidency of H.R.H. the Crown Prince Constantine.* Athens: Charles Beck, 1896. [This was issued in various versions, including several in parallel texts, as follows: Greek/English; Greek/French; Greek/French/English; and German/English. Also, multiple reprints of this first Official Report have been produced, most notably a 1966 edition with English/French/Greek parallel texts published by the Hellenic Olympic Committee, and also a 1971 German edition entitled *Die Olympischen Spiele 1896: Offizieller Bericht*, published by the Carl-Diem-Institut in Cologne, Germany.

1900
Merillon, Daniel, editor. *Concours Internationaux d'Exercices Physiques et de Sport: Rapports Publiés sous la Direction de M. D. Merillon, Délégué Général.* 2 vols. Paris: Imprimerie Nationale, 1901 (Vol. 1) and 1902 (Vol. 2).

1904
Sullivan, James E., compiler. *Spalding's Official Athletic*

Almanac for 1905: Special Olympic Number, Containing the Official Report of the Olympic Games of 1904. New York: American Sports Publishing, 1905.

1906
Savvidis, Panagiotis S., editor. *Leukoma ton en Athenais B'Diethnon Olympiakon Agonon 1906/Jeux Olympiques Internationaux 1906.* Athens: Estia, K. Maisner, N. Kargadouris, 1907.

1908
Cook, Theodore Andrea, editor. *The Fourth Olympiad: Being the Official Report of the Olympic Games of 1908 Celebrated in London Under the Patronage of His Most Gracious King Edward VII and by the Sanction of the International Olympic Committee.* London: British Olympic Council, 1909.

1912
Bergvall, Erik, editor. *The Official Report of the Olympic Games of Stockholm 1912 and V. Olympiaden. Officiel redogorelse for olympiska spelen i Stockholm 1912.* Stockholm: Wahlstrom & Widstrand, 1913.

1916
COJO Berlin 1916. *Denkschrift zur Vorbereitung der VI. Olympiade 1916, veranstaltet im Deutschen Stadion zu Berlin.* Berlin: author, n.d.

1920
Verdyck, Alfred, editor. *Rapport officiel des Jeux de la VIIème Olympiade, Anvers 1920.* Brussels: COJO Antwerp 1920, 1922.

1924
Avé, M.A., editor. *Les Jeux de la VIIIè Olympiade Paris 1924. Rapport officiel du Comité Olympique Français.* Paris: Librairie de France, 1925.

1928
Rossem, George van, editor. *IXe Olympiade. Officiel gedenkboek van de spelen der IXe Olympiade Amsterdam 1928; The Ninth Olympiad: Being the Official Report of the Olympic Games of 1928 Celebrated at Amsterdam Issued by the Netherlands Olympic Committee;* and *Olympiade Amsterdam 1928. Rapport officiel des Jeux de la IXè Olympiade Amsterdam 1928.* Amsterdam: J. H. de Bussy, 1930. Separate editions were published in Dutch, English, and French.

1932
Browne, Frederick Granger, editor. *The Games of the Xth Olympiad, Los Angeles, 1932: Official Report.* Los Angeles: COJO Los Angeles 1932, 1933.

1936
COJO Berlin 1936. *XI Olympiade, Berlin 1936: Amtlicher Bericht, Les XIè Jeux Olympiques, Berlin 1936: Rapport officiel,* and *The XIth Olympic Games, Berlin 1936: Official Report.* Berlin: W. Limpert, 1937. Separate editions were published in German, French, and English.

1940
COJO Tokyo 1940. *XIIth Olympic Games, Tokyo, 1940. Report of the Organizing Committee on Its Work for the XII. Olympic Games of 1940 in Tokyo Until the Relinquishment.* Tokyo: Isshiki, 1940.
COJO Helsinki 1940. *XII Olympiad Helsinki 1940,* and *Olympische Vorbereitungen für die Feier der 12. Olympiade Helsinki 1940.* Helsinki; author, 1940. Separate editions were issued in English and German.

1944
No report was ever issued.

1948
Lord Burghley, editor. *The Official Report of the Organizing Committee for the XIV Olympiad.* London: McCorquodale & Co., Ltd., 1951.

1952
Kolkka, Sulo, editor. *The Official Report of the Organizing Committee for the Games of the XV Olympiad Helsinki 1952, Le Rapport officiel du comité d'organisateur pour les Jeux Olympiques de la XVè Olympiade Helsinki 1952,* and *XV Olympiakisat Helsingissa 1952. Jarjestelytoimikunnan virallinen kertomus.* Porvoo, Finland: Werner Soderström Osakeyhtio, 1955. Three separate editions published in English, French, and Finnish.

1956
Doyle, E. A., editor. *The Official Report of the Organizing Committee for the Games of the XVI Olympiad, Melbourne 1956.* Melbourne: W. M. Houston, Government Printer, 1958.

1956 Equestrian Games
COJO Stockholm 1956. *Ryttaroolympiaden: The Equestrian Games of the XVIth Olympiad: Stockholm 1956.* Stockholm: Esselte Aktiebolag, 1959. Parallel texts in Swedish and English.

1960
Giacomini, Romolo, editor. *The Games of the XVII Olympiad, Rome 1960, Giochi della XVII Olimpiada Roma 1960,* and *Les jeux de la XVIIè Olympiade, Rome 1960.* 2 volumes. Rome: COJO Rome 1960, 1960. Three separate editions published in English, Italian, and French.

1964
COJO Tokyo 1964. *The Games of the XVIII Olympiad, Tokyo 1964. The Official Report of the Organizing Committee.* 2 vols. Tokyo: author, 1964.

1968
Trueblood, Beatrice, editor. *Mexico 1968. Mémoire officiel des Jeux de la XIX Olympiade/Commemorative Volumes of the Games of the XIX Olympiad.* 4 vols. Mexico City: COJO Mexico City 1968, 1968. Two separate editions were issued, one with parallel texts in French and English and one with parallel texts in Spanish and German. A fifth volume was also issued which contained entry tickets, programs, and other memorabilia. A supplement was also issued to the second volume.

1972
Diem, Liselott, and Knoesel, Ernst, editors. *Die Spiele: The Official Report of the Organizing Committee for the Games of the XXth Olympiad, Munich 1972.* 3 vols. Munich: ProSport, 1974. Separate editions of volumes 1 and 2 were issued in English, German, and French. Volume 3 was issued with parallel texts in English, French, and German.

1976
Rousseau, Roger, editor. *Games of the XXI Olympiad, Montreal 1976: Official Report,* and *Jeux de la XXIè Olympiade, Montréal 1976: Rapport officiel.* 3 vols. Montreal: COJO Montreal 1976, ca. 1978. Separate editions were issued in English and French.

1980
Novikov, I.T., editor. *Games of the XXIInd Olympiad Moscow 1980: Official Report of the Organizing Committee of the*

Games of the XXIInd Olympiad, and *Jeux de la XXIIè Olympiade Moscou 1980: Rapport officiel du Comité d'organisation des Jeux de la XXIIè Olympiade.* 3 vols. Moscow: Fitzkultura i Sport, 1981. Separate editions were issued in English and French.

1984
Perelman, Richard B., editor. *Official Report of the Games of the XXIIIrd Olympiad Los Angeles, 1984.* 2 vols. Los Angeles: COJO Los Angeles 1984, 1985. Separate editions were issued in French and English.

1988
Roh Sang-Kook, Lee Kyong-Hee, and Lee Bong-Jie, editors. *Official Report: Games of the XXIVth Olympiad Seoul 1988.* 2 vols. Seoul: Korean Textbook Co., Ltd., 1989. Separate editions were issued in French, English, and Korean.

1992
Cuyàs, Romà, editor. *Official Report: Games of the XXV Olympiad Barcelona 1992.* 4 vols. Barcelona: COJO Barcelona 1992, 1992. Separate editions were issued in English, French, Castilian Spanish, and Catalan Spanish.

Official Reports of the Olympic Winter Games

1924
No separate official report of the Chamonix Winter Olympics was ever issued. The report is found at the end of the report for the 1924 Olympic Games in Paris, *Les Jeux de la VIIIè Olympiade Paris 1924. Rapport officiel du Comité Olympique Français.* See above.

1928
Swiss Olympic Committee. *Rapport général du Comité Exécutif des IIèmes Jeux Olympiques d'Hiver et documents officiels divers.* Lausanne: author, 1928. Results were not included in this report but were issued in a separate volume as follows:
Swiss Olympic Committee. *Résultats des Concours des IIèmes Jeux Olympiques d'Hiver organisés à St. Moritz.* Lausanne: author, 1928.

1932
Lattimer, George M., editor. *Official Report: III Olympic Winter Games, Lake Placid 1932.* Lake Placid: COJO Lake Placid 1932, 1932.

1936

COJO Garmisch-Partenkirchen 1936. *IV. Olympische Winterspiele 1936. Garmisch-Partenkirchen 6. bis 16. Februar: Amtlicher Bericht.* Berlin: Reichssportverlag, 1936.

1940

Diem, Carl, editor. *Vorbereitungen zu den V. Olympischen Winterspiele 1940 Garmisch-Partenkirchen.* Munich: Knorr und Hirth, 1939. The Games did not take place. They were originally scheduled for Sapporo, Japan, and were later scheduled for St. Moritz, Switzerland, before being rescheduled to Garmisch-Partenkirchen. Sapporo and St. Moritz did not issue reports.

1944

No report was ever issued.

1948

Swiss Olympic Committee. *Rapport Général sur les Vès Jeux Olympiques d'Hiver St-Moritz 1948.* Lausanne: author, 1951.

1952

Petersen, Rolf, editor. *VI Olympiske Vinterleker/Olympic Winter Games: Oslo 1952.* English translation by Margaret Wold and Ragnar Wold. Oslo: Kirstes Boktrykkeri, 1956. Parallel texts in English and Norwegian.

1956

Comitato Olimpico Nazionale Italiano. *VII Giochi Olimpici Invernali/VII Olympic Winter Games: Rapporto ufficiale/Official Report.* Roma: author, ca. 1957. Parallel texts in Italian and English.

1960

Rubin, Robert, editor. *VIII Olympic Winter Games, Squaw Valley, California 1960: Final Report.* Sacramento: California Olympic Commission, 1960. Issued in English only.

1964

Wolfgang, Friedl, and Neumann, Bertl, editors. *Offizieler Bericht der IX. Olympischen Winterspiele Innsbruck 1964, Official Report of the IXth Olympic Winter Games, Innsbruck 1964,* and *Rapport du comité d'organisation des IXème Jeux Olympiques d'Hiver 1964.* Vienna: Österreichischer Bundesverlag, 1967. Separate editions were issued in German, French, and English.

1968
COJO Grenoble 1968. *Xème Jeux Olympiques d'Hiver: Grenoble 1968/Xth Olympic Winter Games Grenoble 1968: Official Report/X. Olympischen Winterspiele Grenoble 1968: Amtlicher Bericht.* Grenoble: author, 1968. Parallel texts in French, English, and German.

1972
COJO Sapporo 1972. *Les XI Jeux Olympiques d'Hiver: Sapporo 1972. Rapport officiel,* and *The 11th Olympic Winter Games: Sapporo 1972. Official Report.* Sapporo: author, 1972. Separate editions were published in French and English.

1976
Neumann, Bertl, editor. *Endbericht herausgegeben vom Organisationskomitee der XII. Olympischen Winterspiele Innsbruck 1976/Rapport final publié par le Comité d'Organisation des XIIèmes Jeux Olympiques d'Hiver 1976 à Innsbruck/Final Report Published by the Organizing Committee for the XIIth Winter Olympic Games 1976 at Innsbruck.* Innsbruck: COJO Innsbruck 1976, 1976. Parallel texts in German, French, English, and Russian.

1980
Madden Robert, and Lewi, Edward J., editors. *Final Report/Rapport Final. XIII Olympic Winter Games/XIII Jeux Olympiques d'Hiver. Lake Placid, NY.* New York: Ed Lewi Associates, 1981. Parallel texts in English and French. Oddly, no results were given in the Official Report, as is common now, but they were issued separately, with no publishing information given, as:
Official Results/Résultats Officiels/Offizielle Ergebnisse. No real text, but titles were given in English, French, and German.

1984
COJO Sarajevo 1984. *Final Report Published by the Organising Committee of the XIVth Winter Olympic Games 1984 at Sarajevo/Rapport Final publié par le Comité d'Organisation des XIVèmes Jeux Olympiques d'Hiver 1984 à Sarajevo/Završni Izvještaj Organizacionoh komiteta XIV zimskih olimipijskih igara Sarajevo, 1984.* Sarajevo: Oslobođenje, 1985. Parallel texts in English, French, and Serbo-Croatian (but written in Latin alphabet, thus Croatian as opposed to Serbian, which is written in the Cyrillic alphabet).

1988

COJO Calgary 1988. *Rapport officiel des XVes Jeux Olympiques d'hiver/XV Olympic Winter Games Official Report.* Calgary: author, 1988. Parallel texts in French and English.

1992
Blanc, Claudie, and Eysseric, Jean-Marc, editors. *Rapport officiel des XVIes Jeux Olympiques d'hiver d'Albertville et de la Savoie/Official Report of the XVI Olympic Winter Games of Albertville and Savoie.* Albertville: COJO Albertville 1992, 1992. Parallel texts in French and English.

Ancient Olympic Games

Diem, Carl. *Die Olympischen Spiele in Altertum und Gegenwart.* Eulau: n.p., 1933.
Finley, M. I., and Pleket, H. W. *The Olympic Games: The First Thousand Years.* London: Chatto & Windus, 1976.
Gardiner, E. Norman. *Athletics of the Ancient World.* Chicago: Ares, 1930.
Harris, H. A. *Sport in Greece and Rome.* Ithaca, New York: Cornell University Press, 1972.
Matz, David. *Greek and Roman Sport.* Jefferson, North Carolina: McFarland, 1991.
Raschke, Wendy J., editor. *The Archaeology of the Olympics.* Madison, Wisconsin: University of Wisconsin Press, 1988.
Renson, Roland, Lämmer, Manfred, Riordan, James, and Chassiotis, Dimitrios, editors. *The Olympic Games Through the Ages: Greek Antiquity and Its Impact on Modern Sport.* Athens: Hellenic Sports Research Institute, 1991.
Swaddling, Judith. *The Ancient Olympic Games.* London: British Museum Publications, 1980.
West, Gilbert. *Odes of Pindar, with Several Other Pieces in Prose and Verse, to Which Is Added a Dissertation on the Olympick Games.* London: R. Dodsley, 1753.
Young, David C. *The Myth of Greek Amateur Athletics.* Chicago: Ares, 1984.

Attempts at Revival

Burns, Francis. *Heigh for Cotswold! A History of Robert Dover's Olimpick Games.* Chipping Campden, England: Robert Dover's Games Society, 1981.
Kivroglou, A. "Die Bemühungenn von Ewangelos Sappas um die Wiedereinführung der Olympischen Spiele in Griechenland unter besonderer Berücksichtigung der Spiele von 1859."

Unpublished Diplomarbeit, Deutsche Sporthochschule Köln, 1981.

Lennartz, Karl. *Kenntnisse und Vorstellungen von Olympia und den Olympischen Spielen in der Zeit von 393-1896.* Schorndorf: Verlag Karl Hofmann, 1974.

Mullins, Sam. *British Olympians: William Penny Brookes and the Wenlock Games.* London and Birmingham: Birmingham Olympic Council and British Olympic Association, 1986.

Neumüller, B. "Die Geschichte der Much Wenlock Games." Unpublished Diplomarbeit, Deutsche Sporthochschule Köln, 1985.

Redmond, Gerald. *The Caledonian Games in Nineteenth-Century America.* Rutherford, New Jersey: Fairleigh Dickinson University Press, 1971.

Rühl, Joachim K. *Die "Olympischen Spiele" Robert Dovers.* Heidelberg: Carl Winter Universitätsverlag, 1975.

Svahn, Åke. "'Olympiska Spelen' i Helsingborg 1834 och 1836," In: *Idrott Historia och Samhälle,* (1983), pp. 77-105. Text in Swedish but with an English summary.

Young, David C. "Origins of the Modern Olympics," In: *International Journal of the History of Sport, 4* (1987), pp. 271-300.

Works on Specific Olympic Games

1896

Georgiadis, Konstantinos. "Die Geschichte der ersten Olympischen Spiele 1896 in Athen – ihre Entstehung, Durchführung und Bedeutung." Unpublished Diplomarbeit, Der Johannes Gutenberg Universitat Mainz, 1986/87.

Lennartz, Karl. *Geschichte der Deutschen Reichsaußchußes für Olympische Spiele: Heft 1 – Die Beteiligung Deutschlands an den Olympischen Spielen 1896 in Athen.* Bonn: Verlag Peter Wegener, 1981.

Lennartz, Karl, and Teutenberg, Walter. *Die deutsche Olympia-Mannschaft von 1896.* Frankfurt am Main: Kasseler Sportverlag, 1992.

Mandell, Richard D. *The First Modern Olympics.* Berkeley: University of California Press, 1976.

Tsolakidis, Elias. "Die Olympischen Spiele von 1896 in Athen: Versuch einer Rekonstruktion." Unpublished Diplomarbeit, Deutsche Sporthochschule Köln, 1987.

1900 and 1904

Lennartz, Karl. *Geschichte der Deutschen Reichsaußchußes für Olympische Spiele: Heft 2 – Die Beteiligung Deutschlands an*

den Olympischen Spielen 1900 in Paris und 1904 in St. Louis.
Bonn: Verlag Peter Wegener, 1983.

1904
Lucas, Charles J. P. *The Olympic Games 1904.* St. Louis:
Woodward & Tiernan, 1905.
Mallon, Bill. *A Statistical Summary of the 1904 Olympic Games.*
Durham, North Carolina: author, 1981.

1906
Lennartz, Karl, and Teutenberg, Walter. *Die Olympischen Spiele
1906 in Athen.* Kassel: Kasseler Sportverlag, 1992.

1916
Lennartz, Karl. *Die VI. Olympischen Spiele Berlin 1916.*
Cologne: Barz & Beienburg, 1978.

1920
Mallon, Bill. *The Unofficial Report of the 1920 Olympics.*
Durham, North Carolina: MOST Publications, 1992.

1936
Graham, Cooper. *Leni Riefenstahl and Olympia.* Metuchen, New
Jersey: Scarecrow Press, 1986.
Hart-Davis, Duff. *Hitler's Games: The 1936 Olympics.* London:
Century, 1986.
Holmes, Judith. *Olympiad 1936: Blaze of Glory for Hitler's
Reich.* New York: Ballantine, 1971.
Mandell, Richard D. *The Nazi Olympics.* New York: Macmillan,
1971.

1956
Lechenperg, Harald. *Olympische Spiele 1956: Cortina,
Stockholm, Melbourne.* Munich: Copress-Verlag, 1957.

1960
Lechenperg, Harald. *Olympische Spiele 1960: Squaw Valley,
Rome.* Munich: Copress-Verlag, 1960; and Zurich: Schweizer
Druckerei und Verlagshaus, 1960. Also published in English
as *Olympic Games 1960: Squaw Valley - Rome.* New York:
A.S. Barnes, 1960.

1964
Lechenperg, Harald. *Olympische Spiele 1964: Innsbruck, Tokyo.*
Munich: Copress-Verlag, 1964; Zurich: Schweizer Druckerei
und Verlagshaus, 1964; and Linz, Austria: Trauner, 1964.
Also published in English as *Olympic Games 1964: Innsbruck
- Tokyo.* New York: A.S. Barnes, 1964.

1972

Groussard, Serge. *The Blood of Israel: The Massacre of the Israeli Athletes: The Olympics, 1972.* New York: Morrow, 1975.

Leebron, Elizabeth Joanne. "An Analysis of Selected United States Media Coverage of the 1972 Munich Olympic Tragedy." Northwestern University, Unpublished Ph.D. Thesis, 1978.

Mandell, Richard D. *A Munich Diary: The Olympics of 1972.* Chapel Hill, North Carolina: University of North Carolina Press, 1991.

1976

Ludwig, Jack. *Five Ring Circus: The Montreal Olympics.* Toronto: Doubleday, 1976.

Auf der Maur, Nick. *The Billion Dollar Game: Jean Drapeau and the 1976 Olympics.* Toronto: J. Lorimer, 1977.

1980

Barton, Laurence. "The American Olympic Boycott of 1980: The Amalgam of Diplomacy and Propaganda in Influencing Public Opinion." Boston University, Unpublished Ph.D. Thesis, 1983.

Booker, Christopher. *The Games War: A Moscow Journal.* London: Faber & Faber, 1981.

Hulme, Derick L., Jr. "The Viability of International Sport as a Political Weapon: The 1980 U.S. Olympic Boycott (United States)." Fletcher School of Law and Diplomacy (Tufts University), Unpublished Ph.D. Thesis, 1988.

Hulme, Derick L., Jr. *The Political Olympics: Moscow, Afghanistan, and the 1980 U.S. Boycott.* New York: Praeger, 1990.

Wilson, Harold Edwin, Jr. "'Ours Will Not Go.' The U.S. Boycott of the 1980 Olympic Games." The Ohio State University, Unpublished Masters Thesis, 1982.

1984

Perelman, Richard B. *Olympic Retrospective: The Games of Los Angeles.* Los Angeles: COJO Los Angeles 1984, 1985.

Reich, Kenneth. *Making It Happen: Peter Ueberroth and the 1984 Olympics.* Santa Barbara, California: Capra Press, 1986.

Shaikin, Bill. *Sport and Politics: The Olympics and the Los Angeles Games.* New York: Praeger, 1988.

Ueberroth, Peter V. *Made in America: His Own Story.* With Richard Levin and Amy Quinn. New York: Morrow, 1985.

Wilson, Harold Edwin, Jr. "The Golden Opportunity: A Study of the Romanian Manipulation of the Olympic Movement During the Boycott of the 1984 Los Angeles Olympic Games." The Ohio State University, Unpublished Ph.D. Thesis, 1993.

1988
Kim Un-Yong. *The Greatest Olympics.* Seoul: Si-sa-yong-o-sa, Inc., 1990.
Park Seh-Jik. *The Seoul Olympics: The Inside Story.* London: Bellew, 1991.
Pound, Richard W. *Five Rings Over Korea.* Boston: Little Brown, 1994.

1992
Brunet, Ferrán. *Economy of the 1992 Barcelona Olympic Games.* Barcelona: Centre d'Estudis Olímpics Universitat Autónoma de Barcelona, 1993.

General Sporting Histories of the Olympic Games

Associated Press and Grolier. *The Olympic Story: Pursuit of Excellence.* New York: Franklin Watts, 1979.
Greenberg, Stan. *The Guinness Book of Olympics Facts & Feats.* Enfield, Middlesex, England: Guinness, 1983. Second edition issued as *Olympic Games: The Records,* same publisher, 1987. Third edition issued as *The Guinness Olympics Fact Book,* same publisher, 1991.
Henry, Bill. *An Approved History of the Olympic Games.* Four editions, those of 1948, 1976, 1981, and 1984. The last three editions were edited by Henry's daughter, Patricia Henry Yeomans. First edition: New York: G.P. Putnam, 1948. Second edition: New York: G.P. Putnam, 1976. Third/Fourth editions: Sherman Oaks, California: Alfred Publishing, 1981 and 1984.
Kamper, Erich. *Lexikon der Olympischen Winterspiele.* Stuttgart: Union Verlag, 1964. Parallel texts in German, French, English, and Swedish.
Kamper, Erich. *Enzyklopädie der Olympischen Spiele.* Dortmund: Harenberg, 1972. Parallel texts in German, French, and English. American edition issued as *Encyclopaedia of the Olympic Games* by McGraw-Hill (New York) in 1972.
Kamper, Erich. *Lexikon der 12,000 Olympioniken.* Graz, Austria: Leykam-Verlag, 1975. Second edition issued as *Lexikon der 14,000 Olympioniken,* same publisher, 1983.
Kamper, Erich, and Mallon, Bill. *The Golden Book of the Olympic Games.* Milan: Vallardi, 1993.

Kamper, Erich, and Soucek, Herbert. *Olympische Heroen: Portraits und Anekdoten von 1896 bis heute.* Erkrath, Germany: Spiridon Verlag, 1991.

Lord Killanin and Rodda, John, editors. *The Olympic Games.* London: Queen Anne Press, 1976. Second edition published as *The Olympic Games 1984: Los Angeles and Sarajevo,* Salem, New Hampshire: Michael Joseph, 1983.

Kluge, Volker. *Winter Olympia Kompakt.* Berlin: Sportverlag, 1992.

Mallon, Bill. *The Olympic Record Book.* New York: Garland, 1987.

Mező, Ferenc. *The Modern Olympic Games.* Budapest: Pannonia Press, 1956. Multiple editions were issued, in English, French, German, Spanish, and Hungarian.

Schaap, Richard. *An Illustrated History of the Olympics.* Three editions, those of 1963, 1967, and 1975. Last two editions list author's name as Dick Schaap. New York: Alfred A. Knopf, 1963, 1967, 1975.

Wallechinsky, David. *The Complete Book of the Olympics.* Three editions, followed by a separate edition for the Winter Olympics (see below). First edition: Middlesex, England: Penguin Books, 1983. Second edition: New York: Viking Penguin, 1988. Third edition: London: Aurum, 1991.

Wallechinsky, David. *The Complete Book of the Winter Olympics.* Boston: Little, Brown, 1993.

Wasner, Fritz. *Olympia-Lexikon.* Bielefeld, Germany: Verlag E. Gunglach Aktiengesellschaft, 1939.

Weyand, Alexander M. *Olympic Pageant.* New York: Macmillan, 1952.

General Political and Sociological Histories of the Olympic Games

Clark, Stanley James. "Amateurism, Olympism, and Pedagogy: Cornerstones of the Modern Olympic Movement." Stanford University, Unpublished Ed.D. Thesis, 1975.

Diem, Carl. *Ewiges Olympia.* Minden: np, 1948.

Espy, Richard. *The Politics of the Olympic Games.* Berkeley: University of California Press, 1979.

Fuoss, Donald E. "An Analysis of the Incidents in the Olympic Games from 1924 to 1948, with Reference to the Contribution of the Games to International Understanding." Columbia University, Unpublished Ph.D. Thesis, 1952.

Graham, Peter J., and Ueberhorst, Horst, eds. *The Modern Olympics.* Cornwall, New York: Leisure Press, *ca.* 1975.

Guttmann, Allen. *The Olympics: A History of the Modern Games.* Urbana, Illinois: University of Illinois Press, 1992.

Hill, Christopher R. *Olympic Politics.* Manchester: Manchester University Press, 1992.

Hoberman, John. *Olympic Crisis: Sport Politics and the Moral Order.* New Rochelle, New York: Caratzas, 1986.

Kanin, David B. *A Political History of the Olympic Games.* N.p.: Westview Books, 1981.

Landry, Fernand, Landry, Marc, and Yerles, Magdeleine, editors. *Sport: The Third Millennium/Le troisième millénaire.* Sainte-Foy, Quebec: Les presses de l'université Laval, 1991. A collection of papers with text in either French or English. Abstracts are provided in both languages.

Leiper, Jean Marion. "The International Olympic Committee: The Pursuit of Olympism, 1894–1970." University of Alberta (Canada), Unpublished Ph.D. Thesis, 1976.

Lucas, John. *The Modern Olympic Games.* New York: A.S. Barnes, 1980.

Lucas, John. *The Future of the Olympic Games.* Champaign, Illinois: Human Kinetics, 1992.

Messinesi, Xenophon Leon. *A Branch of Wild Olive.* New York: Exposition Press, 1973. Second edition issued as *A History of the Olympics*, published in 1976 by Drake Publishers of New York.

Miller, Geoffrey. *Behind the Olympic Rings.* Lynn, Massachusetts: H.O. Zimman, 1979.

Okafor, Udodiri Paul. "The Interaction of Sports and Politics as a Dilemma of the Modern Olympic Games." The Ohio State University, Unpublished Ph.D. Thesis, 1979.

Platt, Alan R. "The Olympic Games and Their Political Aspects: 1952 to 1972." Kent State University, Unpublished Ph.D. Thesis, 1976.

Segrave Jeffrey O., and Chu, Donald, editors. *The Olympic Games in Transition.* Champaign, Illinois: Human Kinetics, 1988.

Simson, Vyv, and Jennings, Andrew. *Lords of the Rings: Power, Money & Drugs in the Modern Olympics.* London: Simon & Schuster, 1991. Published in the United States as *Dishonored Games: Corruption, Money & Greed at the Olympics.* New York: S.P.I. Books, 1992.

Sun Byung-Kee, Lee Sei-Kee, Kim Sung-Kyu, Kogh Young-Lee, editors. *Olympics and Politics.* Seoul: Hyung-Seul, *ca.* 1984.

Tait, Robin. "The Politicization of the Modern Olympic Games." University of Oregon, Unpublished Ph.D. Thesis, 1984.

Tomlinson, Alan, and Whannel, Garry, editors. *Five Ring Circus: Money, Power, and Politics at the Olympic Games.* London: Pluto Press, 1984.

Histories of National Participation at the Olympic Games

Australia

Atkinson, Graeme. *Australian & New Zealand Olympians: The Stories of 100 Great Champions*. Canterbury, Victoria: Five Mile Press, 1984.

Blanch, John, and Jenes, Paul. *Australia at the Modern Olympic Games*. Coogee, New South Wales: John Blanch Publishing, 1984.

Howell, Reet, and Howell, Max. *Aussie Gold: The Story of Australia at the Olympics*. South Melbourne: Brooks Waterloo, 1988.

Lester, Gary. *Australians at the Olympics: A Definitive History*. Sydney: Lester-Townsend Publishing, 1984.

Phillips, Dennis H. *Australian Women at the Olympic Games*. Kenthurst, New South Wales: Kangaroo Press, 1992.

Bulgaria

Tsi. "g-r Petŭr Beron. *Olimpiyskite Igry 1896-1980 Shravochnyuk*. [Transliterated title] Sofia: Meditsina i fizkultura, *ca.* 1982.

Canada

Bryden, Wendy. *The Official Sports History and Record Book: Canada at the Olympic Winter Games*. Edmonton: Hurtig Publishers, 1987.

Cosentino, Frank, and Leyshon, Glynn. *Olympic Gold: Canadian Winners of the Summer Games*. Toronto: Holt, Rinehart and Winston, 1975.

Cosentino, Frank, and Leyshon, Glynn. *Winter Gold: Canada's Winners in the Winter Olympic Games*. Markham, Ontario: Fitzhenry & Whiteside Limited, 1987.

Roxborough, Henry. *Canada at the Olympics*. Three editions in 1963, 1969, and 1975. Toronto: Ryerson Press, 1963, 1969, 1975.

Czechoslovakia

Klír, M.; Kössl, Jiří; and Martíkovi, AaM. *Almanach Československých Olympioniků*. Prague: Stráž, 1987.

Estonia

Kivine, P. *Estonikie sportsmeny prisery Olimpiyskikh/Estonian Olympic Medal Winners/Die estnischen Olympiamedaillen-gewinner/Les Médaillés olympiques d'Estonie*. Tallinn: Perioodika, 1980. Parallel texts in Russian, English, German, and French.

France
Charpentier, Henri. *La Grande Histoire des Médaillés Olympiques Français de 1896 à 1988*. Paris: Editions Robert Laffont, *ca.* 1989.

German Democratic Republic
Gilbert, Doug. *The Miracle Machine*. New York: Coward, McCann & Geoghegan, Inc., 1980.

Great Britain
Buchanan, Ian. *British Olympians: A Hundred Years of Gold Medallists*. London: Guinness, 1991.

Greece
Tarasouleas, At[hanassios]. *Helliniki Simmetokhi Stis Sinkhrones Olympiades*. [Transliterated title] Athens: author, 1990.

Hungary
Mező, Ferenc. *Golden Book of Hungarian Olympic Champions/Livre d'Or des Champions Olympiques Hongrois*. Budapest: Sport Lap. És Könyvkiadö, 1955. Parallel texts in English and French.

India
Sanyal, Saraduni. *Olympic Games and India*. New Delhi: Metropolitan Book, Ltd., 1970.

New Zealand (see also Australia)
Atkinson, Graeme. *Australian & New Zealand Olympians: The Stories of 100 Great Champions*. Canterbury, Victoria, Australia: Five Mile Press, 1984.

Poland
Głuszek, Zygmunt. *Polscy Olimpijczycy 1924/1984*. Second edition. Warsaw: Sport i Turystyka, 1988. First edition published in 1980 as *Polscy Olimpijczycy 1924/1976*.

Slovenia
Levovnik, Tomo; Račič, Marko; and Rožman, Marko. *1920–1988: Naši olimpijci*. Ljublana: Grafos, 1992.

Soviet Union
Brokhin, Yury. *The Big Red Machine: The Rise and Fall of Soviet Olympic Champions*. New York: Random House, 1977 and 1978.
Khavin, B[oris]. *Vsyo ob Olimpiyskikh Igrakh*. [Transliterated title] Moscow: Fizkultura i sport, 1979.

Pavlov, S. P. *Olimpiyskaya Entsiklopediya.* [Transliterated title] Moscow: Fizkultura i sport, 1980.
Pavlov, S. P. *Olimpiyskaya Komanda SSSR.* [Transliterated title] Moscow: Fizkultura i sport, 1980.

Sweden
Glanell, Tomas, Huldtén, Gösta, et al., editors. *Sverige och OS.* Stockholm: Brunnhages Förlag AB, 1987.
Pettersson, Ulf, editor. *1896–1980 Guldboken om alla Våra Olympiamästare.* Stockholm: Brunnhages Förlag AB, 1980.

The Ukraine
Zinkewych, Osyp. *Ukrainian Olympic Champions.* Third edition. Baltimore: V. symonenko Smoloskyp Publishers, 1984.

United States
Mallon, Bill, and Buchanan, Ian. *Quest for Gold: The Encyclopaedia of American Olympians.* New York: Leisure, 1984.

Biographies of and by IOC Presidents

Demetrios Vikelas
Young, David C. "Demetrios Vikelas: First President of the IOC." In: *Stadion,* (1988), pp. 85–102.

Pierre de Coubertin
Boulongne, Yves-Pierre. *La vie et l'oeuvre de Pierre de Coubertin.* Ottawa, Quebec: Lemeac, 1975.
Durántez, Conrado. *Pierre de Coubertin: The Olympic Humanist.* Lausanne: IOC, 1994.
Durry, Jean. *Le Vrai Pierre de Coubertin.* Paris: Comité français Pierre de Coubertin, 1994.
Éyquem, Marie-Thérèse. *Pierre de Coubertin. L'Épopée Olympique.* Paris: Calman-Lévy, 1966.
Lucas, John Apostal. "Baron Pierre de Coubertin and the Formative Years of the Modern International Olympic Movement 1883–1896." University of Maryland, Unpublished Ed.D. Thesis, 1962.
MacAloon, John J. *This Great Symbol: Pierre de Coubertin and the Origins of the Modern Olympic Games.* Chicago: University of Chicago Press, 1981.
Müller, Norbert, editor. *Pierre de Coubertin: Textes Choisis.* 3 vols. Zurich: Weidmann, 1986.
Navacelle, Geoffroy de. *Pierre de Coubertin: Sa vie par l'Image.* Lausanne: IOC, 1986.

Henri de Baillet-Latour
Boin, Victor. "Graf Baillet-Latour," In: *Olympische Rundschau,* *17* (1942), pp. 6–11.
Diem, Carl. "Die Beisetzung (Graf Baillet-Latour)," In: *Olympische Rundschau, 17* (1942), p. 24.
Polignac, Melchior Marquis de. "Gedanken über Graf Baillet-Latour," In: *Olympische Rundschau, 17* (1942), pp. 17–22.

J(ohannes) Sigfrid Edström
Bring, Samuel E., editor. *J. Sigfrid Edström: Vänners hyllning på 75-årsdagen 21 november 1940.* Uppsala: Almqvist & Wicksell, 1940.
Edström, Ruth Randall. *J. Sigfrid Edström.* Västerås: Västmanlands Allehanda, 1946.
Bratt, K. A. *J. Sigfrid Edström – En Levnadsteckning.* 2 vols. Stockholm: P. A. Nordstedt & Söner, 1950 (Vol. 1) and 1953 (Vol. 2).

Avery Brundage
Schöbel, Heinz. *The Four Dimensions of Avery Brundage.* Translated by Joan Becker. Leipzig, GDR: Offizin Anderson Nexo, 1968.
Gibson, Richard Lee. "Avery Brundage: Professional Amateur." Kent State University, Unpublished Ph.D. Thesis, 1976.
Guttmann, Allen. *The Games Must Go On: Avery Brundage and the Olympic Movement.* New York: Columbia University Press, 1984.

Lord Killanin
Lord Killanin. *My Olympic Years.* London: Secker & Warburg, 1983.

Juan Antonio Samaranch
Miller, David. *Olympic Revolution: The Olympic Biography of Juan Antonio Samaranch.* London: Pavilion Books Limited, 1992.

Olympic Works by Coubertin
(Only Books On Sport and the Olympic Movement)

Coubertin, Pierre de. *L'éducation athlétique.* Paris: Imprimerie de Chaix, 1889.
Coubertin, Pierre de. *Notes sur l'Education publique.* Paris: Hachette, 1901.

Coubertin, Pierre de. *L'Education des Adolescents au XXe siècle. I: L'Education physique: La Gymnastique utilitaire. Saubetage - Défense - Locomotion.* Paris: Alcan, 1905.
Coubertin, Pierre de. *Une campagne de vingt-et-un ans (1887-1908).* Paris: Librairie de l'Education Physique, 1909.
Coubertin, Pierre de. *Une olympie moderne.* Lausanne: Olympic Review, 1909.
Coubertin, Pierre de. *Leçons de Gymnastique Utilitaire. Sauvetage - Défense - Locomotion. A l'usage des Instituteurs, Moniteurs, Instructeurs militaires, etc..* Paris: Payot, 1916.
Coubertin, Pierre de. *Leçons da Pédagogie sportive.* Lausanne: La Concorde, 1921.
Coubertin, Pierre de. *Mémoires olympiques.* Lausanne: Bureau international de pédagogie sportive, 1931.

Miscellaneous Olympic Works

Jackson, R., and McPhail, T., editors. *The Olympic Movement and the Mass Media: Past, Present, and Future Issues.* Calgary: Hurford Enterprises, 1989.
Leigh, Mary Henson. "The Evolution of Women's Participation in the Summer Olympic Games, 1900-1948." Ohio State University, Unpublished Ph.D. Thesis, 1974.
Lennartz, Karl. *Bibliographie: Geschichte der Leibesübungen, Band 5, Olympische Spiele.* Second edition. Bonn: Verlag Karl Hofmann, 1983.
Mallon, Bill. *The Olympics: A Bibliography.* New York: Garland, 1984.
Pappas, Nina K. "History and Development of the International Olympic Academy, 1927-1977." University of Illinois, Unpublished Ph.D. Thesis, 1978.
Welch, Paula Dee. "The Emergence of American Women in the Summer Olympic Games, 1900-1972." University of North Carolina at Greensboro, Unpublished Ed.D. Thesis, 1975.
Wenn, Stephen Robert. "A History of the International Olympic Committee and Television, 1936-1980." The Pennsylvania State University, Unpublished Ph.D. Thesis, 1993.

APPENDIX I

PRESIDENTS OF THE INTERNATIONAL OLYMPIC COMMITTEE

1894 – 1896	Demetrios Vikelas [Greece]
1896 – 1925*	Pierre Frédy, Baron de Coubertin [France]
1925 – 1942§	Count Henri de Baillet-Latour [Belgium]
1946 – 1952	J[ohannes] Sigfrid Edström [Sweden]
1952 – 1972	Avery Brundage [United States]
1972 – 1980	Sir Michael Morris, The Lord Killanin of Dublin and Spittal [Ireland]
1980 – date	Juan Antonio Samaranch Torellos, Marqués de Samaranch [Spain]

*During World War I, between December 1915 and February 1917, Baron Godefroy de Blonay of Switzerland served as an interim President of the IOC. This was at the request of Baron de Coubertin, who felt that the IOC President should represent a country which was neutral during the war.

§The IOC Presidency was technically vacant from 1942–1946, however, Sigfrid Edström served as interim President during that time.

APPENDIX II

THE GAMES OF THE OLYMPIADS: SITES, DATES, NATIONS, ATHLETES

	Site	*Dates*	*Nations*	*Athletes*	*Men*	*Women*
1896	Athens	6 – 15 Apr	14	245	245	--
1900	Paris	20 May – 28 Oct	26	1,225	1,206	19
1904	St. Louis	1 Jul – 23 Nov	13	687	681	6
1906	Athens	22 Apr – 2 May	20	826	820	6
1908	London	27 Apr – 31 Oct	22	2,035	1,999	36
1912	Stockholm	5 May – 27 Jul	28	2,414	2,360	54
1920	Antwerp	23 Apr – 12 Sep	29	2,668	2,591	77
1924	Paris	4 May – 27 Jul	44	3,072	2,941	131
1928	Amsterdam	17 May – 12 Aug	46	3,014	2,724	290
1932	Los Angeles	30 Jul – 14 Aug	37	1,408	1,281	127
1936	Berlin	1 – 16 Aug	49	4,066	3,738	328
1948	London	29 Jul – 14 Aug	59	4,099	3,714	385
1952	Helsinki	19 Jul – 3 Aug	69	4,925	4,407	518
1956	Total		72	3,342	2,958	384
	Stockholm	10 – 17 Jun	29	158	145	13
	Melbourne	22 Nov – 8 Dec	67	3,184	2,813	371
1960	Rome	25 Aug – 11 Sep	83	5,346	4,736	610
1964	Tokyo	10 – 24 Oct	93	5,140	4,457	683
1968	Mexico City	12 – 27 Oct	112	5,530	4,749	781
1972	Munich	26 Aug – 11 Sep	121	7,123	6,065	1,058
1976	Montreal	17 Jul – 1 Aug	92	6,026	4,779	1,247
1980	Moscow	19 Jul – 3 Aug	80	5,217	4,092	1,125
1984	Los Angeles	28 Jul – 12 Aug	140	6,797	5,230	1,567
1988	Seoul	17 Sep – 5 Oct	159	8,465	6,279	2,186
1992	Barcelona	25 Jul – 9 Aug	169	9,367	6,659	2,708

APPENDIX III

THE OLYMPIC WINTER GAMES:
SITES, DATES, NATIONS, ATHLETES

	Site	Dates	Nations	Athletes	Men	Women
1908	London	28 – 29 Oct	5	21	14	7
1920	Antwerp	23 – 29 Apr	10	86	74	12
1924	Chamonix	25 Jan – 4 Feb	16	258	245	13
1928	St. Moritz	11 – 19 Feb	25	464	438	26
1932	Lake Placid	4 – 15 Feb	17	252	231	21
1936	Garmisch	6 – 16 Feb	28	668	588	80
1948	St. Moritz	30 Jan – 8 Feb	28	669	592	77
1952	Oslo	14 – 25 Feb	30	694	585	109
1956	Cortina	26 Jan – 5 Feb	32	820	688	132
1960	Squaw Valley	18 – 28 Feb	30	665	522	143
1964	Innsbruck	29 Jan – 9 Feb	36	1,091	891	200
1968	Grenoble	6 – 18 Feb	37	1,158	947	211
1972	Sapporo	3 – 13 Feb	35	1,006	800	206
1976	Innsbruck	4 – 15 Feb	37	1,123	892	231
1980	Lake Placid	13 – 24 Feb	37	1,072	839	233
1984	Sarajevo	8 – 19 Feb	49	1,274	1,000	274
1988	Calgary	13 – 28 Feb	57	1,423	1,110	313
1992	Albertville	8 – 23 Feb	64	1,801	1,313	488
1994	Lillehammer	12 – 27 Feb	67	1,737	1,217	520

APPENDIX IV

MEMBERS OF THE
INTERNATIONAL OLYMPIC COMMITTEE

Dates of Service	Member [Nation]
1894–1925	Pierre Frédy, Baron Pierre de Coubertin [FRA] (*q.v.*)
1894–1897	Demetrios Vikelas [GRE] (*q.v.*)
1894–1895	Ferdinando Lucchesi Palli [ITA]
1894–1898	Arthur Oliver Russell, Lord Ampthill [GBR]
1894–1898	Duke Riccardo d'Andria Carafa [ITA]
1894–1900	General Aleksey Butowsky [RUS]
1894–1901	Count Maxime de Bousies [BEL]
1894–1905	Leonard A. Cuff [NZL]
1894–1906	Charles Herbert [GBR]
1894–1907	Dr. Franz Kémény [HUN]
1894–1907	José Benjamin Zubiaur [ARG]
1894–1913	Ernst Callot [FRA]
1894–1921	General Viktor Gustaf Balck [SWE]
1894–1924	Professor William Milligan Sloane [USA] (*q.v.*)
1894–1943	Dr. Jiří Guth–Jarkovský [Bohemia/TCH]
1896–1909	Karl August Willibald Gebhardt [GER]
1897–1919	Count Eugenio Brunetta d'Usseaux [ITA]
1897–1925	Count Alexandros Mercati [GRE]
1897–1927	Reverend Robert Stuart de Courcy Laffan [GBR]
1898–1924	Baron Frederik Willem Christiaan Hendrik van Tuyll van Serooskerken [NED]
1899–1902	Prince Gheorghe Bibesco [ROM]
1899–1903	Count Archambauld Talleyrand de Perigord [GER]
1899–1906	Niels V. S. Holbeck [DEN]
1899–1937	Baron Godefroy de Blonay [SUI] (*q.v.*)
1900–1903	Theodore Stanton [USA]
1900–1904	Caspar Whitney [USA]
1900–1908	Prince Sergey Beloselsky–Belotsersky [RUS]
1900–1911	Henri Hébrard de Villeneuve [FRA]
1900–1916	Count Nikolao Ribeaupierre [RUS]
1900–1948	Count Carl Clarence von Rosen [SWE]
1901–1903	François Reyntiens [BEL]
1901–1905	Prince Eduard Max Vollrath Friedrich of Salm-Horstmar [GER]
1901–1908	Sir Charles Edward Howard Vincent [GBR]

Dates of Service	Member [Nation]
1901–1931	Miguel de Beistegui [MEX]
1902–1921	Antonio de Mejorada del Campo, Marquis de Villamejor [ESP]
1903–1908	James Hazen Hyde [USA]
1903–1914	Count Caesar Erdmann von Wartensleben Carow [GER]
1903–1942	Count Henri de Baillet-Latour [BEL] (*q.v.*)
1904–1920	Count Albert Bertier de Sauvigny [FRA]
1905–1907	Henrik August Angell [NOR]
1905–1909	Alexander, Prince von Solms Braunfels [AUT]
1905–1909	Count Egbert Hoyer von der Asseburg [GER]
1905–1913	William Henry Grenfell, Lord Desborough of Taplow [GBR]
1905–1922	Don Carlos F. de Candamo [PER]
1905–1932	Richard Coombes [AUS]
1906–1912	Dimitri Tzokov [BUL]
1906–1912	Duke Antonio de Lancastre [POR]
1906–1912	Torben Grut [DEN]
1907–1908	Thomas Thomassen Heftye [NOR]
1907–1910	Manuel de la Quintana [ARG]
1907–1938	Count Géza Andrassy [HUN]
1908–1909	Prince Scipione Borghese [ITA]
1908–1910	Prince Simon Trubetskoy [RUS]
1908–1919	Baron Reinhold Felix von Willebrand [FIN]
1908–1920	Allison Vincent Armour [USA]
1908–1927	Johan Tidemann Sverre [NOR]
1908–1930	Selim Sirri Bey Tarcan [TUR]
1908–1939	Count Albert Gautier Vignal [MON]
1908–1949	Gheorghe A. Plagino [ROM]
1909–1914	Attilio Brunialti [ITA]
1909–1914	Baron Karl von Wenningen-Ullner von Diepburg [GER]
1909–1915	Sir Theodore Andrea Cook [GBR]
1909–1938	Jigoro Kano [JPN]
1909–1946	Gyula von Muzsa [HUN]
1910–1919	Count Adalbert von Francken-Sierstorpff [GER]
1910–1929	Jean-Maurice Pescatore [LUX]
1910–1933	Prince Léon Duroussof [RUS]
1910–1963	Angelo Christos Bolanaki [EGY/GRE]
1911–1914	Abel Ballif [FRA]
1911–1914	Oscar N. Garcia [CHI]
1911–1917	Evert Jansen Wendell [USA]
1911–1919	Otto, Prince zu Windisch-Grätz [AUT]
1911–1919	Rudolf, Count Colloredo-Mansfield [AUT]
1911–1921	John Hanbury-Williams [CAN]
1912–1921	Fritz Hansen [DEN]

Dates of Service	Member [Nation]
1912–1940	Count José Carlos Peñha Garcia [POR]
1912–1949	Svetomir V. Đukic [SER/YUG]
1913–1915	Georges Aleksandrovich Duperron [RUS]
1913–1919	Count Adolf von Arnim–Muskau [GER]
1913–1920	Algernon St. Maur Somerset, Duke of Somerset [GBR]
1913–1929	Dimitri Stancioff [BUL]
1913–1938	Baron Edouard–Émile de Laveleye [BEL]
1913–1938	Raul de Rio Branco [BRA]
1913–1944	Albert Glandaz [FRA]
1914–1919	Sydney Howard Farrar [RSA]
1914–1939	Carlo Montu [ITA]
1914–1950	Marquis Melchior de Polignac [FRA]
1918–1922	Bartow Sumter Weeks [USA]
1918–1929	Eduardo Dorn y de Alsua [ECU]
1918–1940	Pedro Jaime de Matheu [ESA/Central America]
1919–1922	Carlos Silva–Vildosola [CHI]
1919–1925	Arthur Marryatt [NZL]
1919–1929	Marquis Giorgio Guglielmi [ITA]
1919–1933	Count Justinien de Clary [FRA]
1920–1927	Sir Dorabji Jamsetji Tata [IND]
1920–1943	Henry Nourse [RSA]
1920–1946	Franjo Bucar [YUG]
1920–1948	Ernst Edvard Krogius [FIN]
1921–1923	Henrique Echevarrieta [ESP]
1921–1923	Nizzam Eddin Khoï [IRI/Persia]
1921–1932	Marcelo T. de Alvear [ARG]
1921–1933	Reginald John Kentish [GBR]
1921–1936	Francisco Ghigliani [URU]
1921–1946	James G. B. Merrick [CAN]
1921–1952	Johannes Sigfrid Edström [SWE] (*q.v.*)
1921–1954	Baron Guell de Santiago [ESP]
1921–1957	Wang Cheng–Ting [CHN]
1922–1924	Prince Stefan Lubomirski [POL]
1922–1931	Ivar Nyhölm [DEN]
1922–1936	Charles Hitchcock Sherrill [USA]
1922–1948	William May Garland [USA]
1922–1951	John Joseph Keane [IRL]
1923–1924	José Carlos Rincon Gallardo, Marquis de Guadalupe [MEX]
1923–1927	Joseph Pentland Firth [NZL]
1923–1927	Prince Samad Khan Momtazos Saltaneh [IRI/Persia]
1923–1929	Gerald Oakley, Earl of Cadogan [GBR]
1923–1936	Porfirio Franca y Alvarez de la Campa [CUB]
1923–1939	Jorgé Matte Gormaz [CHI]

Dates of Service	Member [Nation]
1923–1949	Ricardo Camillo Aldao [ARG]
1923–1957	Alfredo Benavides [PER]
1923–1961	Arnaldo Guinle [BRA]
1923–1962	José Ferreira Santos [BRA]
1924–1927	David Kinley [USA]
1924–1927	Fernando Alvarez, Duke d'Alba [ESP]
1924–1927	Jorgé Gomez de Parada [MEX]
1924–1928	Dr. Martin Haudek [AUT]
1924–1929	Oskar Ruperti [GER]
1924–1930	Prince Kasimierz Lubomirski [POL]
1924–1933	Seichi Kishi [JPN]
1924–1938	Theodor Lewald [GER]
1924–1944	James Taylor [AUS]
1924–1957	Pieter Wilhelmus Scharroo [NED]
1925–1943	Baron Alphert Schimmelpenninck van der Oye [NED]
1925–1953	Count Alberto Bonacossa [ITA]
1926–1930	Georgios Averof [GRE]
1926–1947	Janis Dikmanis [LAT]
1926–1956	Duke Adolf Friedrich von Mecklenburg–Schwerin [GER]
1927–1933	George Kemp, Lord Rochdale [GBR]
1927–1936	Ernest Lee Jahncke [USA]
1927–1950	Sir Thomas Fearnley [NOR]
1928–1930	Bernard Cyril Freyberg [NZL]
1928–1930	Marquis François Manuel de Pons [ESP]
1928–1932	Friederik Akel [EST]
1928–1932	Miguel Moises Saenz [MEX]
1928–1938	Theodor Schmidt [AUT]
1928–1939	Ignasz Matuszewski [POL]
1928–1939	Sir George McLaren Brown [CAN]
1929–1933	Don Alfredo Ewing [CHI]
1929–1944	Stepan G. Chaprachikov [BUL]
1929–1957	Clarence Napier Bruce, Lord Aberdare of Duffryn [GBR]
1929–1964	Karl Ferdinand Ritter von Halt [GER]
1930–1931	Augusto Turati [ITA]
1930–1932	Kremalettin Sami Pascha [TUR]
1930–1933	Nikolaos Politis [GRE]
1931–1933	Cecil J. Wray [NZL]
1931–1945	Stanislaw Rouppert [POL]
1931–1952	Count Federico Suarez de Vallelano [ESP]
1932–1952	Horacio Bustos Moron [ARG]
1932–1958	Axel Kristian George, Prince of Denmark [DEN]
1932–1964	Count Paolo Thaon di Revel [ITA]
1932–1966	Guru Dutt Sondhi [IND]

Dates of Service	Member [Nation]
1933–1936	Jotaro Sugimoura [JPN]
1933–1950	Sir Francis Noel Curtis Bennett [GBR]
1933–1951	Sir Harold Daniel Luxton [AUS]
1933–1952	Rechid Saffet Atabinen Bey [TUR]
1933–1981	David George Brownlow Cecil, Lord Burghley, The Sixth Marquess of Exeter [GBR] (*q. v.*)
1934–1948	Count Michimasa Soyeshima [JPN]
1934–1966	François Piétri [FRA]
1934–1967	Lord Arthur Espie Porritt [NZL]
1934–1968	Mohamed Taher Pascha [TUR]
1934–1973	Segura Marte Rodolfo Gomez [MEX]
1936–1939	Prince Iesato Tokugawa [JPN]
1936–1942	Joakhim Puhk [EST]
1936–1972	Avery Brundage [USA] (*q. v.*)
1936–1980	His Royal Highness Prince Franz–Josef II [LIE]
1936–1980	Jorge B. Vargas [PHI]
1937–1939	Henri Guisan [SUI]
1937–1948	Frédéric René Coudert [USA]
1937–1956	Joaquin Serratosa Cibils [URU]
1938–1942	Walther von Reichenau [GER]
1938–1955	Antonio Prado [BRA]
1938–1967	Johan Wilhelm Rangell [FIN]
1938–1969	Miguel Angel Moenck [CUB]
1939–1939	Arthur V. A. Lindbergh [RSA]
1939–1948	Miklós von Horthy [HUN]
1939–1949	Giorgio Vaccaro [ITA]
1939–1950	Matsuzo Nagai [JPN]
1939–1955	Kong Xiang–Xi [CHN]
1939–1957	Baron Gaston de Trannoy [BEL]
1939–1967	Shingoro Takaishi [JPN]
1946–1951	Johannes Dowsett [RSA]
1946–1954	John Coleridge Patteson [CAN]
1946–1955	Rodolphe William Seeldrayers [BEL]
1946–1956	José Joaquim Fernandes Pontes [POR]
1946–1964	Charles Ferdinand Pahud de Mortanges [NED]
1946–1965	Ioannis Ketseas [GRE]
1946–1965	Josef Gruss [TCH]
1946–1966	Benedikt G. Waage [ISL]
1946–1968	Albert Roman Mayer [SUI]
1946–1970	Armand Émile Massard [FRA]
1946–1975	Hugh Richard Weir [AUS]
1946–1982	Reginald Honey [RSA]
1946–	His Royal Highness Grand Duke Jean [LUX]
1947–1958	Shou Tung–Yi [CHN]
1947–1967	Sidney Dawes [CAN]
1947–1969	Manfred Mautner Ritter von Markhof [AUT]

Dates of Service	Member [Nation]
1947–1992	Raja Bhalindra Singh of Patiala [IND]
1948–1952	Enrique O. Barbosa Baeza [CHI]
1948–1952	Miguel Ydigoras Fuentes [GUA]
1948–1959	Stanko Bloudek [YUG]
1948–1961	Ferenc Mező [HUN]
1948–1961	Jerzy Loth [POL]
1948–1965	Bo Daniel Ekelund [SWE]
1948–1967	Olaf Christian Ditlev–Simonsen [NOR]
1948–1968	John Jewett Garland [USA]
1948–1976	Erik von Frenckell [FIN]
1949–1950	Rainier Grimaldi III, Prince of Monaco [MON]
1949–1956	Ahmed E. H. Jaffer [PAK]
1950–1951	James Brooks Bloodgood Parker [USA]
1950–1964	Pierre Grimaldi, Prince of Monaco [MON]
1950–1968	Ryotaro Azuma [JPN]
1951–1974	Sir Harold Lewis Luxton [AUS]
1951–1988	Ian St. John Lawson Johnston, The Lord Luke of Pavenham [GBR]
1951–1988	Konstantin Andrianov [URS]
1951–1990	Count Jean Robert Maurice Bonin de la Bonninie de Beaumont [FRA]
1951–1992	Giorgio de Stefani [ITA]
1952–1959	Enrique Alberdi [ARG]
1952–1967	Augustin A. Sosa [PAN]
1952–1968	Julio B. Bustamente [VEN]
1952–1970	Gustaf Peder Wilhelmsson Dyrssen [USA]
1952–1971	Aleksey Romanov [URS]
1952–1971	José de Jésus Clark de Flores [MEX]
1952–1980	Sir Michael Morris, The Lord Killanin of Dublin and Spittal [IRL] (q.v.)
1952–1984	Douglas Fergusson Roby [USA]
1952–1985	Pedro Ybarra y McMahon, The Second Marquis de Guell [ESP]
1952–1986	Julio Gerlein Comelin [COL]
1952–1987	Sheik Gabriel Gemayel [LIB]
1952–1987	Vladimir D. Stoychev [BUL]
1955–1960	Lee Ki–Poong [KOR]
1955–1980	Prince Gholam Reza Pahlavi [IRI]
1955–1984	Suat Erler [TUR]
1955–1985	Alejandro Rivera Bascur [CHI]
1955–	Alexandru Siperco [ROM]
1956–1991	Willi Daume [GER]
1957–1962	Saul Cristovão Ferreira Pires [POR]
1958–1964	His Royal Highness Prince Albert of Liège [BEL]
1958–1977	Ivar Emil Vind [DEN]

Dates of Service	Member [Nation]
1958-1982	Eduardo Dibos de Lima [PER]
1959-	Syed Wajid Ali [PAK]
1960-1974	Mario Luis José Negri [ARG]
1960-1987	Boris Bakrac [YUG]
1960-1990	Lord Reginald Stanley Alexander [KEN]
1960-1993	Ahmed El Demerdash Touny [EGY]
1961-	Mohamed Ben Hadj Addelouahed Benjelloun [MAR]
1961-	Wlodzimierz Reczek [POL]
1963-1974	His Majesty King Constantine [GRE]
1963-1975	Alfredo Inciarte [URU]
1963-1985	Sir Adetokunbo Ademola [NGR]
1963-1989	Raúl Cordiero Pereira de Castro [POR]
1963-	João Marie Godefrois Faustin Havelange [BRA]
1963-	Marc Hodler [SUI]
1964-1966	Lee Sang-Beck [KOR]
1964-1977	Jonkheer Herman Adriaan van Karnebeek [NED]
1964-1983	Arpád Csánadi [HUN]
1964-1983	Giulio Onesti [ITA]
1964-	Prince Alexandre de Merode [BEL]
1964-	Sylvio Magalhães de Padilha [BRA]
1965-1969	Amadou Barry [SEN]
1965-1981	František Kroutil [TCH]
1965-1981	Pyrros Lappas [GRE]
1965-	Gunnar Lennart Vilhelm Ericsson [SWE]
1965-	Mohamed Mzali [TUN]
1966-1971	Georg von Opel [FRG]
1966-1971	His Royal Highness Prince George Wilhelm von Hanover [IOA]
1966-1980	Heinz Schöbel [GDR]
1966-	Marquis Juan Antonio Samaranch Torrelos [ESP] (*q.v.*)
1967-1977	Chang Key-Young [KOR]
1967-1981	Paavo Honkajuuri [FIN]
1967-1981	Prince Tsuneyoshi Takeda [JPN]
1967-1989	James Worrall [CAN]
1967-	Jan Staubo [NOR]
1968-1971	Henri René Rakotoke [MAD]
1968-1976	Hamengku Buwono IX [INA]
1968-1981	José A. Bercasa [VEN]
1968-1982	Abdel Mohamed Halim [SUD]
1968-	Agustin Carlos Arroyo Yeroui [ECU]
1969-1976	Rudolf Nemetschke [AUT]
1969-1988	Sir Cecil Lancelot Stewart Cross [NZL]
1969-1989	Masaji Kiyokawa [JPN]
1969-1991	Raymond Gafner [SUI]

Dates of Service	Member [Nation]
1969–1994	Virgilio E. de Léon [PAN]
1969–	Louis Guirandou-N'Diaye [CIV]
1970–1976	Sven Alfred Thofelt [SWE]
1970–1988	Henry Heng Hsu [TPE]
1970–1994	Maurice Herzog [FRA]
1971–1974	Prabhas Charusathiara [THA]
1971–1987	Ydnekatcheu Tessema [ETH]
1971–	Vitaly Smirnov [URS/RUS]
1972–1988	Berthold Beitz [GER]
1972–1994	Pedro Ramírez Vázquez [MEX]
1973–1993	Manuel Gonzalez Guerra [CUB]
1973–	Ashwini Kumar [IND]
1973–	Kéba M'Baye [SEN]
1973–	Roy Anthony Bridge [JAM]
1974–1981	David Henry McKenzie [AUS]
1974–1986	Julian Kean Roosevelt [USA]
1974–1990	Dawee Chullasapya [THA]
1974–1991	Eduardo Hay [MEX]
1974–	Mohamed Zerguini [ALG]
1975–1977	Epaminondas Petralias [GRE]
1976–1993	Matts Wilhelm Carlgren [SWE]
1976–	José Dalmiro Vallarino Veracierto [URU]
1976–1994	Kevin Patrick O'Flanagan [IRL]
1976–	Peter Julius Tallberg [FIN]
1977–1983	Kim Taik-Soo [KOR]
1977–1986	Cornelis Lambert "Kees" Kerdel [NED]
1977–1988	Roberto Guillermo Peper [ARG]
1977–1989	Dadang Suprayogi [INA]
1977–1989	Lamine Keita [MLI]
1977–1990	German Rieckehoff [PUR]
1977–	Bashir Mohamed Attarabulsi [LBA]
1977–	Niels Holst-Sørensen [DEN]
1977–	Philipp von Schöller [AUT]
1977–	Richard Kevan Gosper [AUS]
1977–	Shagdarjav Magvan [MGL]
1978–1986	Nikolaos Nissiotis [GRE]
1978–1994	Kim Yu-Sun [PRK]
1978–	Honorable Tan Seri Hamzah Bin Haji Abu Samah [MAS]
1978–	René Essomba [CMR]
1978–	Richard William Duncan Pound [CAN] (*q. v.*)
1981–1990	Sheik Fahad Al-Ahmad Al-Sabah [KUW]
1981–1992	Günther Heinze [GDR/GER]
1981–1995	Flor Isava-Fonseca [VEN]
1981–	He Zhen-Liang [CHN]
1981–	Nikolaos Filaretos [GRE]

Dates of Service	Member [Nation]
1981–	Pirjo Vilmi–Häggman [FIN]
1981–	Vladimir Cernušak [SVK]
1982–1993	Mary Alison Glen–Haig [GBR]
1982–	Chiharu Igaya [JPN]
1982–	Franco Carraro [ITA]
1982–	Ivan Dibos [PER]
1982–	Philip Walter Coles [AUS]
1983–	Anani Matthia [TOG]
1983–	His Royal Highness Prince Faisal Fahd Abdul Aziz [KSA]
1983–	Pál Schmitt [HUN]
1983–	Roque Napoleon Muñoz Peña [DOM]
1983–	Zein El–Abdin Mohamed Ahmed Abdel Gadir [SUD]
1984–1985	Park Chong–Kyu [KOR]
1984–1988	Turgut Atakol [TUR]
1984–	David Sikhulumi Sibandze [SWZ]
1984–	Her Royal Highness Princess Nora [LIE]
1985–1991	Robert H. Helmick [USA]
1985–	Albert Grimaldi, Prince of Monaco [MON]
1985–	Carlos Ferrer Salat [ESP]
1985–	Francisco J. Elizalde [PHI]
1985–	Henry E. Olufemi Adefope [NGR]
1986–	Anita Luceete DeFrantz [USA]
1986–	His Excellency Jean–Claude Ganga [CGO]
1986–	Kim Un–Yong [KOR]
1986–	Lambis V. Nikolaou [GRE]
1987–	Antonius Johannes Geesink [NED] (q.v.)
1987–	Ivan Borissov Slavkov [BUL]
1987–	Seuili Paul Wallwork [SAM]
1987–	Slobodan Filipović [YUG]
1988–1992	Marat V. Gramov [URS/RUS]
1988–	Borislav Stanković [YUG]
1988–	Fidel Mendoza Carrasquilla [COL]
1988–	Francis Were Nyangweso [UGA]
1988–	Princess Anne, Her Royal Highness the Princess Royal [née Anne Elizabeth Alice Louise Windsor] [GBR]
1988–	Rampaul Ruhee [MRI]
1988–	Sinan Erdem [TUR]
1988–	Tennant Edward "Tay" Wilson [NZL]
1988–	Willi Kaltschmitt Lujan [GUA]
1988–	Wu Ching–Kuo [TPE]
1989–	Fernando F. Lima Bello [POR]
1989–	Walther Tröger [GER]
1990–	Antonio Radriguez [ARG]

Dates of Service	Member [Nation]
1990–	Carol Anne Letheren [CAN]
1990–	Charles Nderitu Mukora [KEN]
1990–	Nat Indrapana [THA]
1990–	Philippe Chatrier [FRA]
1990–	Richard L. Carrion [PUR]
1990–	Shun-Ichiro Okano [JPN]
1991–	Denis Oswald [SUI]
1991–	Jacques Rogge [BEL]
1991–	Mario Vazquez Raña [MEX]
1991–	Thomas Bach [GER]
1992–1994	Olaf Poulsen [NOR]
1992–	Sheik Ahmad Al-Fahad Al-Sabah [KUW]
1992–	Primo Nebiolo [ITA/IAAF]
1992–	Sergio Santander Fantini [CHI]
1994–	Alex Gilady [ISR]
1994–	Alpha Ibrahim Dialio [GUI]
1994–	Arne Ljungqvist [SWE]
1994–	Austin L. Sealy [BAR]
1994–	Craig Reedie [GBR]
1994–	Gerhard Heiberg [NOR]
1994–	James L. Easton [USA]
1994–	Mario Pescante [ITA]
1994–	Mohamed Hasan [INA]
1994–	Robin Mitchell [FIJ]
1994–	Shamil Tarpichev [RUS]
1994–	Valery Borzov [UKR]
1995–	Sam Ramsamy [RSA]
1995–	Antun Vrdoljak [CRO]
1995–	Reynaldo González López [CUB]
1995–	Jean-Claude Killy [FRA]
1995–	Patrick Hickey [IRL]
1995–	Toni Khouri [LIB]
1995–	Olegario Vázquez Raña [MEX]
1995–	Věra Čáslavská [CZE] (*q.v.*)
1995–	Mustapha Larfaoui [ALG/FINA]
1995–	Yuri Titov [URS/FIG]
1995–	René Fasel [SUI/IIHF]

APPENDIX V

AWARDS OF THE INTERNATIONAL OLYMPIC COMMITTEE

The International Olympic Committee has given out several awards, outside of the medals and diplomas given to Olympic athletes. Currently, the IOC presents only two awards, the Olympic Order and the Olympic Cup. Other awards by the IOC were discontinued at the 75th IOC Session in Vienna in 1974. These included the Olympic Diploma of Merit (first awarded in 1905), the Sir Thomas Fearnley Cup (donated in 1950), the Mohammed Taher Trophy (donated in 1950), the Count Alberto Bonacossa Trophy (presented in 1954), the Tokyo Trophy (presented in 1964), and the Prix de la Reconnaissance Olympique (presented in 1972).

Recipients of the Olympic Order

The Olympic Order is the supreme individual honor accorded by the International Olympic Committee. It was created in 1974 and is to be awarded to "Any person who has illustrated the Olympic Ideal through his/her action, has achieved remarkable merit in the sporting world, or has rendered outstanding services to the Olympic cause, either through his/her own personal achievement(s) or his/her contribution to the development of sport." Originally, the Olympic Order was separated into three categories – gold, silver, and bronze. The bronze Olympic Order has not been awarded since 1984 and currently, there is only a gold and a silver category. We have listed only the recipients of the Olympic Order in Gold. Through 1994, there have been 515 recipients of the Olympic Order in Silver, and 112 recipients of the Olympic Order in Bronze.

Gold [46]

1975	–	Avery Brundage [USA] (*q.v.*)
1980	–	Sir Michael Morris, the Lord Killanin [GBR] (*q.v.*)
1981	–	Lord Burghley, the Marquess of Exeter [GBR] (*q.v.*)
		His Majesty King Olaf of Norway [NOR]
		Amadou Mahtar M'Bow [SEN]
		Pope John Paul II (The Vatican)

1982	–	His Majesty King Pertuan Agung of Malaysia [MAS]
1983	–	Indira Gandhi [IND]
1984	–	François Mitterrand [FRA]
		Peter Victor Ueberroth [USA] (*q.v.*)
		Branko Mikulić [YUG]
1985	–	His Majesty King Juan Carlos de Borbon [ESP]
		Erich Honecker [GDR]
		Nicolae Ceauşescu [ROM]
1986	–	Li Wan [CHN]
1987	–	Todor Zhivkov [BUL]
		His Majesty King Bhumibol Adulyadej [THA]
		His Excellency Kenan Evren [TUR]
1988	–	Frank W. King [CAN]
		Mario Vazquez Raña [MEX]
		His Royal Highness Prince Rainier III [MON]
		His Royal Highness Prince Bertil Bernadotte of Sweden [SWE]
1989	–	Chevalier Raoul Mollet [BEL]
		His Imperial Majesty Emperor Akihito [JPN]
		His Excellency Raphael Hernandez Colon [PUR]
1990	–	Giulio Andreotti [ITA]
1991	–	Count Jean de Beaumont [FRA]
		Yoshiaki Tsutsumi [JPN]
		Willi Daume [FRG]
1992	–	Josep Miguel Abad [ESP]
		Michel Barnier [FRA]
		Javier Gomez–Navarro [ESP]
		Jean–Claude Killy [FRA] (*q.v.*)
		Pasqual Marragal [ESP]
		Jordi Pujol [ESP]
		Leopoldo Rodes [ESP]
		Carlos Salinas de Gortari [MEX]
		Narcis Serra [ESP]
		Javier Solana [ESP]
		Boris Yeltsin [RUS]
1994	–	Joaquin Leguina [ESP]
		Richard von Weizsäcker [GER]
		Dr. Mauno Koivisto [FIN]
		His Majesty King Harald of Norway [NOR]
		Gerhard Heiberg [NOR]
		Her Majesty Queen Sonja of Norway [NOR]

Recipients of the Olympic Cup

The Olympic Cup was instituted by Baron de Coubertin in 1906. It is awarded to an institution or association with a general reputation for merit and integrity which has been active and efficient in the service of sport and has contributed substantially to the development of the Olympic Movement.

1906	–	Touring Club de France
1907	–	Henley Royal Regatta
1908	–	Sveriges Centralförening för Idrottens Främjande
1909	–	Deutsche Turnerschaft
1910	–	Česka obec Sokolska
1911	–	Touring Club Italiano
1912	–	Union des Sociétés de Gymnastique de France
1913	–	Magyar Athletikai Club
1914	–	Amateur Athletic Union of America
1915	–	Rugby School, England
1916	–	Confrérie Saint-Michel de Gand
1917	–	Nederlandsche Voetbal Bond
1918	–	Equipes Sportives du Front Interallié
1919	–	Institut Olympique de Lausanne
1920	–	Y.M.C.A. International, Springfield, MA, USA
1921	–	Dansk Idræts Forbund
1922	–	Amateur Athletic Union of Canada
1923	–	Associación Sportiva de Cataluña
1924	–	Finnish Gymnastic and Athletic Federation
1925	–	National Physical Education Committee of Uruguay
1926	–	Norges Skiforbund
1927	–	Colonel Robert M. Thomson [USA]
1928	–	Junta Nacional Mexicana
1929	–	Y.M.C.A. World's Committee
1930	–	Association Suisse de Football et d'Athlétisme
1931	–	National Playing Fields Association, Great Britain
1932	–	Deutsche Hochschule für Leibesübungen
1933	–	Société Fédérale Suisse de Gymnastique
1934	–	Opera Dopolavoro Roma
1935	–	National Recreation Association of the USA
1936	–	Union of Hellenic Gymnastics and Athletics Associations, Athens
1937	–	Österreichischer Eislauf Verband
1938	–	Königl. Akademie für Körpererziehung in Ungarn
1939	–	"Kraft durch Freude"
1940	–	Svenska Gymnastik – och Idrottsföreningarnas Riksförbund
1941	–	Finnish Olympic Committee
1942	–	William May Garland [USA]
1943	–	Comité Olímpico Argentino
1944	–	City of Lausanne
1945	–	Norges Fri Idrettsforbund, Oslo

1946	–	Comité Olímpico Colombiano
1947	–	J. Sigfrid Edström [SWE] – IOC President
1948	–	The Central Council of Physical Recreation, Great Britain
1949	–	Fluminense Football Club, Rio de Janeiro
1950	–	Comité Olympique Belge
		New Zealand Olympic and British Empire Games Association
1951	–	Académie des Sports, Paris
1952	–	City of Oslo
1953	–	City of Helsinki
1954	–	Ecole Fédérale de Gymnastique et de Sports, Macolin [SUI]
1955	–	Organizing Committee of the Central American and Caribbean Games, Mexico
	–	Organizing Committee of the Pan-American Games, Mexico
1956	–	Not attributed
1957	–	Federazione Sport Silenziosi d'Italia, Milano
1958	–	Not attributed
1959	–	Panathlon Italiano, Geneva
1960	–	Centro Universitario Sportivo Italiano
1961	–	Helms Hall Foundation, Los Angeles
1962	–	IV Juegos Deportivos Bolivarianos, Barranquilla
1963	–	Australian British Empire and Commonwealth Games Association
1964	–	City of Tokyo
1965	–	Southern California Committee for the Olympic Games [USA]
1966	–	Comité International des Sports Silencieux, Liège [BEL]
1967	–	Juegos Deportivos Bolivarianos
1968	–	City of Mexico
1969	–	Polish Olympic Committee
1970	–	Organizing Committee of the Asian Games in Bangkok [THA]
1971	–	Organizing Committee of the Pan-American Games in Cali [COL]
1972	–	Turkish Olympic Committee
		City of Sapporo
1973	–	Population of Munich
1974	–	Bulgarian Olympic Committee
1975	–	Comitato Olímpico Nazionale Italiano (CONI)
1976	–	Czechoslovak Physical Culture and Sports Association
1977	–	Comité Olympique Ivoirien
1978	–	Comité Olympique Hellenic
1979	–	Organizing Committee of the 1978 World Rowing Championships in New Zealand

1980	–	Ginasio Clube Português
1981	–	Confédération Suisse
		International Olympic Academy
1982	–	Racing Club de France
1983	–	Puerto Rico Olympic Committee
1984	–	Organizing Committee of the 1st World Championships in Athletics at Helsinki
1985	–	Chinese Olympic Committee
1986	–	City of Stuttgart
1987	–	*L'Équipe* (French sporting daily newspaper)
1988	–	The People of Australia
1989	–	City of Calgary
		City of Seoul
		La Gazzetta dello Sport (Italian sporting daily newspaper)
1990	–	Panhellenic Athletic Club of Athens
1991	–	Japanese Olympic Committee
1992	–	Département de la Savoie (Région Rhône–Alpes)
		City of Barcelona
1993	–	Comité Olympique Monégasque

APPENDIX VI

FINAL OLYMPIC TORCH BEARERS

Games of the Olympiads

1936	Fritz Schilgen [GER]
1948	John Mark [GBR]
1952	Paavo Nurmi [FIN]
	Hannes Kolehmainen [FIN]
1956	Ron Clarke [AUS]
1960	Giancarlo Peris [ITA]
1964	Yoshinori Sakai [JPN]
1968	Enriqueta Basilio de Sotelo [MEX]
1972	Günter Zahn [FRG]
1976	Stéphane Prefontaine [CAN]
	Sandra Henderson [CAN]
1980	Sergey Belov [URS]
1984	Rafer Johnson [USA]
	Gina Hemphill [USA]
1988	Sohn Kee-Chung [KOR]
	Lim Chun-Ae [KOR]
	Chung Sun-Man [KOR]
	Kim Won-Tak [KOR]
	Sohn Mi-Chung [KOR]
1992	Herminio Menéndez Rodriguez [ESP]
	Juan Antônio San Epifanio Ruiz [ESP]
	Antônio Rebollo (archer) [ESP]

Olympic Equestrian Games

1956	Hans Wikne [SWE]
	Karin Lindberg [SWE]
	Henry Eriksson [SWE]

Olympic Winter Games

1952	Eigil Nansen [NOR]
1956	Guido Caroli [ITA]
1960	Kenneth Henry [USA]
1964	Joseph Rieder [AUT]
1968	Alain Calmat [FRA]
1972	Hideki Takada [JPN]
1976	Christl Haas [AUT]
	Josef Feistmantl [AUT]

1980	Charles Morgan Kerr [USA]
1984	Sandra Dubravčič [YUG]
1988	Robyn Perry [CAN]
1992	Michel Platini [FRA]
	François-Syrille Grange [FRA]
1994	Crown Prince Haakon Magnus [NOR]
	Stein Gruben (ski jumper) [NOR]
	Catherine Nottingnes [NOR]

APPENDIX VII

SPEAKERS OF THE OLYMPIC OATH

Games of the Olympiads – Athletes
1920	Victor Boin [Water Polo/Fencing]
1924	Georges André [Athletics]
1928	Harry Dénis [Football]
1932	George Calnan [Fencing]
1936	Rudolf Ismayr [Weightlifting]
1948	Donald Finlay [Athletics]
1952	Heikki Savolainen [Gymnastics]
1956	John Landy [Athletics]
1960	Adolfo Consolini [Athletics]
1964	Takashi Ono [Gymnastics]
1968	Pablo Garrido [Athletics]
1972	Heidi Schüller [Athletics]
1976	Pierre St. Jean [Weightlifting]
1980	Nikolay Andrianov [Gymnastics]
1984	Edwin Moses [Athletics]
1988	Huh Jae [Basketball]
	Son Mi-Na [Handball]
1992	Luis Doreste Blanco [Yachting]

Olympic Equestrian Games – Athlete
1956	Henri Saint Cyr [Equestrian]

Olympic Winter Games – Athletes
1924	Camille Mandrillon [Skiing]
1928	Hans Eidenbenz [Skiing]
1932	Jack Shea [Speed Skating]
1936	Wilhelm Bögner [Skiing]
1948	Riccardo "Bibi" Torriani [Ice Hockey]
1952	Torbjørn Falkanger [Ski Jumping]
1956	Guilliana Chenal-Minuzzo [Alpine Skiing]
1960	Carol Heiss [Figure Skating]
1964	Paul Aste [Bobsledding]
1968	Leo Lacroix [Alpine Skiing]
1972	Keichi Suzuki [Speed Skating]
1976	Werner Delle Karth [Bobsledding]
1980	Eric Heiden [Speed Skating]

1984	Bojan Križaj [Alpine Skiing]
1988	Pierre Harvey [Nordic Skiing]
1992	Surya Bonaly [Figure Skating]
1994	Vegard Ulvang [Nordic Skiing]

Games of the Olympiads – Officials

1972	Heinz Pollay [Equestrian official]
1976	Maurice Fauget [Athletics official]
1980	Aleksandr Medved [Wrestling official]
1984	Sharon Weber [Gymnastics official]
1988	Lee Hak-Rae [Judo official]
1992	Eugeni Asensio [Water Polo official]

Olympic Winter Games – Officials

1972	Fumio Asaki [Ski Jumping official]
1976	Willi Köstinger [Nordic Skiing official]
1980	"Terry" McDermott [Speed Skating official]
1984	Dragan Perović [Alpine Skiing official]
1988	Suzanne Morrow-Francis [Figure Skating official]
1992	Pierre Bornat [Alpine Skiing official]
1994	Kari Karing [Nordic Skiing official]

APPENDIX VIII

OFFICIAL OPENINGS OF THE OLYMPIC GAMES

Games of the Olympiads
1896 King Giorgios I [Greece]
1900 none
1904 President David Francis [Louisiana Purchase Exposition/United States]
1906 King Giorgios I [Greece]
1908 King Edward VII [England]
1912 King Gustaf V [Sweden]
1920 King Albert I [Belgium]
1924 President Gaston Doumergue [France]
1928 His Royal Highness Prince Hendrik [The Netherlands]
1932 Vice President Charles Curtis [United States]
1936 Reichsführer Adolf Hitler [Germany]
1948 King George VI [England]
1952 President Juho Kusti Paasikivi [Finland]
1956 His Royal Highness Philip, The Duke of Edinburgh [Scotland/United Kingdom]
1960 President Giovanni Gronchi [Italy]
1964 Emperor Hirohito [Japan]
1968 President Dr. Gustavo Díaz Ordaz [Mexico]
1972 President Dr. Gustav Heinemann [Federal Republic of Germany]
1976 Queen Elizabeth II [England]
1980 President Leonid Ilich Brezhnev [Soviet Union]
1984 President Ronald Wilson Reagan [United States]
1988 President Roh Tae-Woo [Korea]
1992 King Juan Carlos I [Spain]

Olympic Equestrian Games
1956 King Gustaf VI Adolf [Sweden]

Olympic Winter Games
1924 Under-Secretary for Physical Education Gaston Vidal [France]
1928 President Edmund Schulthess [Switzerland]
1932 Governor Franklin Delano Roosevelt [New York, United States]

1936	Reichsführer Adolf Hitler [Germany]
1948	President Enrico Celio [Switzerland]
1952	Her Royal Highness Princess Ragnhild [Norway]
1956	President Giovanni Gronchi [Italy]
1960	Vice-President Richard Milhous Nixon [United States]
1964	President Dr. Adolf Schärf [Austria]
1968	President General Charles de Gaulle [France]
1972	Emperor Hirohito [Japan]
1976	President Dr. Rudolf Kirchschläger [Austria]
1980	Vice-President Walter Frederick Mondale [United States]
1984	President Mika Spiljak [Yugoslavia]
1988	Governor-General Jeanne Sauvé [Canada]
1992	President François Mitterrand [France]
1994	King Harald V [Norway]

APPENDIX IX

MOST OLYMPIC MEDALS WON: SUMMER, MEN

Medals	Athlete [Nation–Sport]
15	Nikolay Andrianov [URS–GYM]
13	Edoardo Mangiarotti [ITA–FEN]
13	Takashi Ono [JPN–GYM]
13	Boris Shakhlin [URS–GYM]
12	Sawao Kato [JPN–GYM]
12	Paavo Nurmi [FIN–ATH]
11	Matthew Biondi [USA–SWI]
11	Viktor Chukarin [URS–GYM]
11	Carl Osburn [USA–SHO]
11	Mark Spitz [USA–SWI]
10	Aleksandr Dityatin [URS–GYM]
10	Raymond Ewry [USA–ATH]
10	Aladár Gerevich [HUN–FEN]
10	Akinori Nakayama [JPN–GYM]
9	Giulio Gaudini [ITA–FEN]
9	Zoltán von Halmay [HUN–SWI]
9	Sixten Jernberg [SWE–NSK]
9	Eizo Kenmotsu [JPN–GYM]
9	Carl Lewis [USA–ATH]
9	Heikki Savolainen [FIN–GYM]
9	Martin Sheridan [USA–ATH]
9	Konrad Stäheli [SUI–SHO]
9	Alfred Swahn [SWE–SHO]
9	Yury Titov [URS–GYM]
9	Mitsuo Tsukahara [JPN–GYM]
9	Hubert Van Innis [BEL–ARC]
9	Mikhail Voronin [URS–GYM]
8	Vilhelm Carlberg [SWE–SHO]
8	Philippe Cattiau [FRA–FEN]
8	Charles Daniels [USA–SWI]
8	Roger Ducret [FRA–FEN]
8	Gert Fredriksson [SWE–CAN]
8	Albert Helgerud [NOR–SHO]
8	Reiner Klimke [FRG–EQU]

Medals	Athlete [Nation-Sport]
8	Eugen Mack [SUI-GYM]
8	Roland Matthes [GDR-SWI]
8	Georges Miez [SUI-GYM]
8	Léon Moreaux [FRA-SHO]
8	Otto Olsen [NOR-SHO]
8	Louis Richardet [SUI-SHO]
8	Viljo "Ville" Ritola [FIN-ATH]
8	Henry Taylor [GBR-SWI]

APPENDIX X

MOST OLYMPIC MEDALS WON: SUMMER, WOMEN

Medals	Athlete [Nation–Sport]
18	Larisa Latynina [URS–GYM]
11	Věra Čáslavská [TCH–GYM]
10	Polina Astakhova [URS–GYM]
10	Ágnes Keleti [HUN–GYM]
9	Nadia Comăneci [ROM–GYM]
9	Lyudmila Turishcheva [URS–GYM]
8	Shirley Babashoff [USA–SWI]
8	Kornelia Ender [GDR–SWI]
8	Dawn Fraser [AUS–SWI]
8	Sofiya Muratova [URS–GYM]
8	Margit Plachyné–Korondi [HUN–GYM]
7	Mariya Gorokhovskaya [URS–GYM]
7	Karin Janz [GDR–GYM]
7	Ildikó Ságiné–Ujlakiné–Rejtő [HUN–FEN]
7	Shirley Strickland de la Hunty [AUS–ATH]
7	Irena Szewińska–Kirszenstein [POL–ATH]
6	Yelena Belova–Novikova [URS–FEN]
6	Daniela Hunger [GDR–SWI]
6	Nelli Kim [URS–GYM]
6	Olga Korbut [URS–GYM]
6	Olga Lemhényiné–Tass [HUN–GYM]
6	Tamara Manina [URS–GYM]
6	Kristin Otto [GDR–SWI]
6	Andrea Pollack [GDR–SWI]
6	Birgit Schmidt–Fischer [GDR–CAN]
6	Daniela Silivaş [ROM–GYM]
6	Renate Stecher–Meissner [GDR–ATH]

APPENDIX XI

MOST OLYMPIC GOLD MEDALS WON: SUMMER, MEN

Golds	Athlete [Nation–Sport]
10	Raymond Ewry [USA–ATH]
9	Paavo Nurmi [FIN–ATH]
9	Mark Spitz [USA–SWI]
8	Matthew Biondi [USA–SWI]
8	Sawao Kato [JPN–GYM]
8	Carl Lewis [USA–ATH]
7	Nikolay Andrianov [URS–GYM]
7	Viktor Chukarin [URS–GYM]
7	Aladár Gerevich [HUN–FEN]
7	Boris Shakhlin [URS–GYM]
6	Gert Fredriksson [SWE–CAN]
6	Rudolf Kárpáti [HUN–FEN]
6	Reiner Klimke [FRG–EQU]
6	Pál Kovács [HUN–FEN]
6	Edoardo Mangiarotti [ITA–FEN]
6	Nedo Nadi [ITA–FEN]
6	Akinori Nakayama [JPN–GYM]
6	Vitaly Shcherbo [EUN–GYM]
6	Hubert Van Innis [BEL–ARC]
5	Charles Daniels [USA–SWI]
5	Yukio Endo [JPN–GYM]
5	Morris Fisher [USA–SHO]
5	Anton Heida [USA–GYM]
5	Thomas Jager [USA–SWI]
5	Alfred Lane [USA–SHO]
5	Willis Lee, Jr. [USA–SHO]
5	Ole Lilloe–Olsen [NOR–SHO]
5	Takashi Ono [JPN–GYM]
5	Carl Osburn [USA–SHO]
5	Louis Richardet [SUI–SHO]
5	Viljo "Ville" Ritola [FIN–ATH]
5	Donald Schollander [USA–SWI]
5	Martin Sheridan [USA–ATH]
5	Konrad Stäheli [SUI–SHO]
5	Mitsuo Tsukahara [JPN–GYM]
5	John Weissmuller [USA–SWI]
5	Hans Günter Winkler [FRG–EQU]

APPENDIX XII

MOST OLYMPIC GOLD MEDALS WON: SUMMER, WOMEN

Golds	Athlete [Nation–Sport]
9	Larisa Latynina [URS–GYM]
7	Věra Čáslavská [TCH–GYM]
6	Kristin Otto [GDR–SWI]
5	Polina Astakhova [URS–GYM]
5	Nadia Comăneci [ROM–GYM]
5	Ágnes Keleti [HUN–GYM]
5	Nelli Kim [URS–GYM]
4	Evelyn Ashford [USA–ATH]
4	Yelena Belova-Novikova [URS–FEN]
4	Fanny Blankers-Koen [NED–ATH]
4	Betty Cuthbert [AUS–ATH]
4	Krisztina Egerszegi [HUN–SWI]
4	Kornelia Ender [GDR–SWI]
4	Janet Evans [USA–SWI]
4	Dawn Fraser [AUS–SWI]
4	Olga Korbut [URS–GYM]
4	Patricia McCormick [USA–DIV]
4	Birgit Schmidt-Fischer [GDR–CAN]
4	Ecaterina Szabó [ROM–GYM]
4	Lyudmila Turishcheva [URS–GYM]
4	Nicole Uphoff [FRG–EQU]
4	Bärbel Wöckel-Eckert [GDR–ATH]

APPENDIX XIII

MOST OLYMPIC MEDALS WON: WINTER, MEN

Medals	Athlete [Nation-Sport]
9	Sixten Jernberg [SWE-NSK]
8	Bjørn Dæhlie [NOR-NSK]
7	Ivar Ballangrud [NOR-SSK]
7	Veikko Hakulinen [FIN-NSK]
7	Eero Mäntyranta [FIN-NSK]
7	Bogdan Musiol [GDR-BOB]
7	Clas Thunberg [FIN-SSK]
6	Johan Grøttumsbråten [NOR-NSK]
6	Wolfgang Hoppe [GDR-BOB]
6	Roald Larsen [NOR-SSK]
6	Eugenio Monti [ITA-BOB]
6	Vladimir Smirnov [URS-NSK]
6	Gunde Anders Svan [SWE-NSK]
6	Vegard Ulvang [NOR-NSK]
5	Kjetil André Aamodt [NOR-ASK]
5	Peter Angerer [FRG-BIA]
5	Sergey Chepikov [EUN-BIA]
5	Fritz Feierabend [SUI-BOB]
5	Yevgeny Grishin [URS-SSK]
5	Harald Grønningen [NOR-NSK]
5	Eric Heiden [USA-SSK]
5	Knut "Kuppern" Johannesen [NOR-SSK]
5	Harri Kirvesniemi [FIN-NSK]
5	Johann Olav Koss [NOR-SSK]
5	Juha Mieto [FIN-NSK]
5	Matti Nykänen [FIN-NSK]
5	Aleksandr Tikhonov [URS-BIA]
5	Alberto Tomba [ITA-ASK]
5	Pal Tyldum [NOR-NSK]
5	Nikolay Zimyatov [URS-NSK]

APPENDIX XIV

MOST OLYMPIC MEDALS WON: WINTER, WOMEN

Medals	Athlete [Nation–Sport]
10	Raisa Smetanina [EUN/URS–NSK]
9	Lyubov Yegorova [EUN/RUS–NSK]
8	Karin Kania–Enke [GDR–SSK]
8	Galina Kulakova [URS–NSK]
7	Andrea Ehrig–Schone–Mitscherlich [GDR–SSK]
7	Marja–Liisa Kirvesniemi–Hämäläinen [FIN–NSK]
6	Bonnie Blair [USA–SSK]
6	Manuela Di Centa [ITA–NSK]
6	Lidiya Skoblikova [URS–SSK]
6	Yelena Välbe [EUN/URS–NSK]
5	Stefania Belmondo [ITA–NSK]
5	Alevtina Kolchina [URS–NSK]
5	Gunda Niemann–Kleemann [GER–SSK]
5	Anfisa Reztsova [EUN/URS–BIA/NSK]
5	Vreni Schneider [SUI–ASK]
5	Helena Takalo [FIN–NSK]
4	Tatyana Averina–Barabash [URS–SSK]
4	Christina "Stien" Baas–Kaiser [NED–SSK]
4	Lyubov Baranova–Kozyreva [URS–NSK]
4	Toini Gustafsson [SWE–NSK]
4	Antje Harvey–Misersky [GER–BIA]
4	Dianne Holum [USA–SSK]
4	Marjatta Kajosmaa [FIN–NSK]
4	Marjo Matikainen [FIN–NSK]
4	Kaija Mustonen [FIN–SSK]
4	Natalya Petruseva [URS–SSK]
4	Hilkka Riihivuori–Kuntola [FIN–NSK]
4	Cathy Turner [USA–SSK]
4	Hanni Wenzel [LIE–ASK]
4	Radya Yeroshina [URS–NSK]

APPENDIX XV

MOST OLYMPIC GOLD MEDALS WON: WINTER, MEN

Golds	Athlete [Nation–Sport]
5	Bjørn Dæhlie [NOR–NSK]
5	Eric Heiden [USA–SSK]
5	Clas Thunberg [FIN–SSK]
4	Ivar Ballangrud [NOR–SSK]
4	Yevgeny Grishin [URS–SSK]
4	Sixten Jernberg [SWE–NSK]
4	Johann Olav Koss [NOR–SSK]
4	Matti Nykänen [FIN–NSK]
4	Gunde Anders Svan [SWE–NSK]
4	Aleksandr Tikhonov [URS–BIA]
4	Thomas Wassberg [SWE–NSK]
4	Nikolay Zimyatov [URS–NSK]
3	Hjalmar "Hjallis" Andersen [NOR–SSK]
3	Vitaly Davydov [URS–ICH]
3	Anatoly Firsov [URS–ICH]
3	Bernhard Germeshausen [GDR–BOB]
3	Gillis Grafstrom [SWE–FSK]
3	Johan Grøttumsbråten [NOR–NSK]
3	Sven Tomas Gustafson [SWE–SSK]
3	Veikko Hakulinen [FIN–NSK]
3	Thorleif Haug [NOR–NSK]
3	Andrey Khomutov [EUN–ICH]
3	Jean-Claude Killy [FRA–ASK]
3	Kim Ki-Hoon [KOR–SSK]
3	Mark Kirchner [GER–BIA]
3	Viktor Kuzkin [URS–ICH]
3	Eero Mäntyranta [FIN–NSK]
3	Meinhard Nehmer [GDR–BOB]
3	Aleksandr Ragulin [URS–ICH]
3	Anton "Toni" Sailer [AUT–ASK]
3	Adrianus "Ard" Schenk [NED–SSK]
3	Alberto Tomba [ITA–ASK]
3	Vladislav Tretyak [URS–ICH]
3	Vegard Ulvang [NOR–NSK]
3	Ulrich Wehling [GDR–NSK]
3	Jens Weißflog [GER–NSK]

APPENDIX XVI

MOST OLYMPIC GOLD MEDALS WON: WINTER, WOMEN

Golds	Athlete [Nation–Sport]
6	Lidiya Skoblikova [URS–SSK]
6	Lyubov Yegorova [EUN/RUS–NSK]
5	Bonnie Blair [USA–SSK]
4	Galina Kulakova [URS–NSK]
4	Raisa Smetanina [EUN/URS–NSK]
3	Klavdiya Boyarskikh [URS–NSK]
3	Yvonne van Gennip [NED–SSK]
3	Sonja Henie [NOR–FSK]
3	Karin Kania-Enke [GDR–SSK]
3	Marja–Liisa Kirvesniemi-Hämäläinen [FIN–NSK]
3	Anfisa Reztsova [EUN–BIA]
3	Irina Rodnina [URS–FSK]
3	Vreni Schneider [SUI–ASK]
2	Tatyana Averina-Barabash [URS–SSK]
2	Myriam Bédard [CAN–BIA]
2	Lyudmila Belousova [URS–FSK]
2	Andrée Brunet-Joly [FRA–FSK]
2	Chun Lee-Kyung [KOR–SSK]
2	Deborah Compagnoni [ITA–ASK]
2	Manuela Di Centa [ITA–NSK]
2	Nina Gavrylyuk [RUS–NSK]
2	Marielle Goitschel [FRA–ASK]
2	Yekaterina Gordeyeva [URS/RUS–FSK]
2	Toini Gustafsson [SWE–NSK]
2	Trude Jochum-Beiser [AUT–ASK]
2	Petra Kronberger [AUT–ASK]
2	Larisa Lazutina [EUN–NSK]
2	Andrea Mead-Lawrence [USA–ASK]
2	Rosi Mittermaier [FRG–ASK]
2	Marie–Thérès Nadig [SUI–ASK]
2	Gunda Niemann-Kleemann [GER–SSK]
2	Barbara Petzold [GDR–NSK]
2	Tamara Tikhonova [URS–NSK]
2	Cathy Turner [USA–SSK]
2	Yelena Välbe [EUN–NSK]
2	Steffi Walter-Martin [GDR–LUG]
2	Hanni Wenzel [LIE–ASK]
2	Pernilla Wiberg [SWE–ASK]
2	Katarina Witt [GDR–FSK]

APPENDIX XVII

LIST OF ALL POSITIVE DRUG TESTS AT THE OLYMPIC GAMES

Listed after each athlete's name is his or her country, sport and event, finish before disqualification, and the name of illegal drug detected.

1968 Mexico City [1]
Hans-Gunnar Liljenvall [SWE] – Modern pentathlete; 3rd – Alcohol.

1972 Sapporo [1]
Alois Schroder [FRG] – Ice hockey; 7th – Ephedrine. [Note: The team doctor, Franz Schlickenrieder, was disqualified from serving in that capacity for life.]

1972 Munich [5]
Bakhaava Buida [MGL] – Judo, 63 kg. class; 2nd – drug unknown.
Miguel Coli [PUR] – Basketball; 6th – Ephedrine.
Richard DeMont [USA] – Swimming, 400 meter freestyle; 1st – Ephedrine.
Jamie Huelamo [ESP] – Cycling, individual road race; 3rd – Coramine.
Walter Legel [AUT] – Weightlifting, 67.5 kg. class; 15th – Amphetamines.

1976 Innsbruck [2]
Galina Kulakova [URS] – Nordic skiing, 5 km.; 3rd – Ephedrine. [Note: Kulakova also finished 3rd in the 10 km. and 1st on the 4x5 km. relay team at these Olympic Winter Games, but was allowed to keep those medals.]
František Pospíšil [TCH] – Ice hockey; 2nd – Codeine. [Note: The team doctor, Treffny, was disqualified from serving in that capacity for life.]

1976 Montreal [11]
Blagoi Blagoev [BUL] – Weightlifting, 82.5 kg. class; 2nd – Anabolic steroids.
Mark Cameron [USA] – Weightlifting, 110 kg. class; 5th – Anabolic steroids.

Paul Cerutti [MON] – Shooting, Trap shooting; 43rd – Amphetamines.

Valentin Khristov [BUL] – Weightlifting, 110 kg. class; 1st – Anabolic steroids.

Dragomir Ciorislan [ROM] – Weightlifting, 75 kg. class; 5th – Fencanfamine.

Phillip Grippaldi [USA] – Weightlifting, 90 kg. class; 4th – Anabolic steroids.

Zbigniew Kaczmarek [POL] – Weightlifting, 67.5 kg. class; 1st – Anabolic steroids.

Lorne Leibel [CAN] – Yachting, Tempest class; 7th – Phenylpropanolamine.

Arne Norback [SWE] – Weightlifting, 60 kg. class; eliminated – Anabolic steroids.

Petr Pavlašek [TCH] – Weightlifting, 110 kg. class; 6th – Anabolic steroids.

Danuta Rosani-Gwardecka [POL] – Track & field athletics, Discus throw; 14th in qualifying (DNQ) – Anabolic steroids.

1980 Lake Placid and Moscow [0]
No positive drug tests at either Games.

1984 Sarajevo [1]
Purevjalyn Batsukh [MGL] – Nordic skiing, 15 km.; 69th / 30 km.; 65th / 4x10 km. relay / 15th – Methandienone.

1984 Los Angeles [12]
Serafim Grammatikopoulos [GRE] – Weightlifting, Unlimited class; did not finish – Nandrolone.

Vesteinn Hafsteinsson [ISL] – Track & field athletics, Discus throw; 14th in qualifying round – Nandrolone.

Thomas Johansson [SWE] – Wrestling, Unlimited Greco-Roman class; 2nd – Methenolone.

Stefan Laggner [AUT] – Weightlifting, Unlimited class; 4th – Nandrolone.

Göran Petterson [SWE] – Weightlifting, 110 kg. class; 6th – Nandrolone.

Elji Shimomura [JPN] – Volleyball; 7th – Testosterone.

Mikiyasu Tanaka [JPN] – Volleyball; 7th – Ephedrine. [Note: The trainer of the Japanese volleyball team was banned from the Olympics for life.]

Ahmed Tarbi [ALG] – Weightlifting, 56 kg. class; 9th – Nandrolone.

Mahmoud Tarha [LBA] – Weightlifting, 52 kg. class; 4th – Nandrolone.

Gian-Paolo Urlando [ITA] – Track & field athletics, Hammer throw; 4th – Testosterone.

Martti Vainio [FIN] – Track & field athletics, 10,000 meters; 2nd – Methenolone.
Anna Verouli [GRE] – Track & field athletics, Javelin throw; 13th in qualifying round – Nandrolone.

1988 Calgary [1]
Jaroslav Morawiecki [POL] – Ice hockey; 10th – Testosterone.

1988 Seoul [11]
Alidad [AFG] – Wrestling, 62 kg. freestyle class; eliminated third round – Furosemide.
Kerrith Brown [GBR] – Judo, 71 kg.; 3rd – Furosemide.
Kálmán Csengeri [HUN] – Weightlifting, 75 kg. class; 4th – Stanozolol.
Angel Genchev [BUL] – Weightlifting, 67.5 kg. class; 1st – Furosemide.
Mitko Grablev [BUL] – Weightlifting, 56 kg. class; 1st – Furosemide.
Ben Johnson [CAN] – Track & field athletics, 100 meters; 1st – Stanozolol.
Fernando Mariaca [ESP] – Weightlifting, 67.5 kg. class; 13th – Pemoline.
Jorge Quezada [ESP] – Modern pentathlon; 24th – Propranolol.
Andor Szányi [HUN] – Weightlifting, 100 kg. class; 2nd – Stanozolol.
Alexander Watson [AUS] – Modern pentathlon; 61st – Caffeine.
Sergiusz Wołczaniecki [POL] – Weightlifting, 90 kg. class; 3rd – Stanozolol.

1992 Albertville [0]
No positive drug tests.

1992 Barcelona [5]
Madina Biktagirova [EUN] – Track & field athletics, Marathon; 4th – Norephedrine.
Bonnie Dasse [USA] – Track & field athletics, Shot put; 14th in qualifying round – Clembuterol.
Judson Logan [USA] – Track & field athletics, Hammer throw; 4th – Clembuterol.
Nijole Medvedeva [LTU] – Track & field athletics, Long jump; 4th – Meziocarde (a stimulant).
Wu Dan [CHN] – Volleyball; 7th – Stimulant with a strychnine base.

1994 Lillehammer [0]
No positive drug tests.

APPENDIX XVIII

ATTEMPTS AT OLYMPIC REVIVAL
PRIOR TO 1896

1834   Ramlösa, Sweden (near Helsingborg) – "Olympic Games" organized under the initiative of Professor Gustav Johann Schartau of the University of Lund.

1836   Ramlösa, Sweden – second, and last, Swedish attempt at revival.

1830–1840's Olympic–type festivals held in Montreal, Quebec, Canada.

1850   First Much Wenlock Olympian Games held in Much Wenlock, a small town near Shrewsbury, Shropshire, England. Altogether, 45 in number were held consecutively, failing only 1874, through 1895. They were later held sporadically and continue to the 1990's.

1859   First Zappas Olympic Games in Athens, Greece, sponsored by the Greek philanthropist Evangelis Zappas.

1860   First Shropshire Olympic Games organized in Much Wenlock, England by the Shropshire Olympic Society.

1861   Second Shropshire Olympic Games held in Wellington, Shropshire, England.

1862   Third Shropshire Olympic Games held in Much Wenlock, Shropshire, England.
First Grand Olympic Festival held in Liverpool, England, sponsored by the Liverpool Olympian Society.

1863   Second Grand Olympic Festival held in Liverpool, England, sponsored by the Liverpool Olympian Society.

1864	Fourth, and last, Shropshire Olympic Games held in Much Wenlock, England. Third Grand Olympic Festival held in Liverpool, England, sponsored by the Liverpool Olympian Society.
1866	First Olympic Games sponsored by England's National Olympian Association, held in London, England. Fourth Grand Olympic Festival held in Llandudno, Wales, sponsored by the Liverpool Olympian Society.
1867	Second Olympic Games sponsored by the National Olympian Association, held in Birmingham, England. Fifth, and last, Grand Olympic Festival held in Liverpool, England, sponsored by the Liverpool Olympian Society.
1868	Third Olympic Games sponsored by the National Olympian Association, held in Wellington, Shropshire, England.
1870	Second Zappas Olympic Games in Athens, Greece.
1873	First Morpeth Olympic Games held in Morpeth, England. The Games will be held almost annually until 1958.
1874	Fourth Olympic Games sponsored by the National Olympian Association, held in Much Wenlock, England.
1875	Third Zappas Olympic Games in Athens, Greece.
1877	Fifth Olympic Games sponsored by the National Olympian Association, held in Shrewsbury, England.
1880	Olympic Games at Lake Palić, held from 1880 to 1914 in Palić, a spa eight kilometers east of Subotica, then in Hungary and now in the Vojvodina province of Serbia. The Games will be held sporadically until 1914.

1883   Sixth, and last, Olympic Games sponsored by the National Olympian Association, held in Hadley, Shropshire, England.

1889   Fourth Zappas Olympic Games in Athens, Greece.

1891   First Panhellenic Gymnastic Society Games, modelled after the Zappas Olympics, held in Athens.

1893   Second Panhellenic Gymnastic Society Games, modelled after the Zappas Olympics, held in Athens.

April 1896   Games of the Ist Olympiad, celebrating the First Olympiad of the Modern Era, held in Athens, Greece, signalling the final re-birth of the Olympic Games after 15 centuries.

ABOUT THE AUTHORS

IAN BUCHANAN has now retired from a business career in the Far East where he spent many years as a director of a Reinsurance Company and compiled the first authoritative history of the Far Eastern and Asian Games. This is the fourth book he has co-authored with Bill Mallon and his many other published works include *British Olympians: A Hundred Years of Gold Medallists* (London: Guinness, 1991). He is a founding member and President of the International Society of Olympic Historians (ISOH), a member of the British Olympic Association, the British Society of Sports History, and the Association of Track & Field Statisticians.

BILL MALLON, a former professional golfer, is an orthopaedic surgeon, whose life-long interest in the Olympic Games became a second career while he was in medical school at Duke University. This is his eighth book on the Olympic Games. With Erich Kamper, he co-authored *The Golden Book of the Olympic Games* (Milan: Vallardi, 1993), and with Ian Buchanan he co-authored *Quest for Gold: The Encyclopaedia of American Olympians* (New York: Leisure Press, 1984). He is a co-founder and Secretary-General of the International Society of Olympic Historians and edits the ISOH journal, *Citius, Altius, Fortius*.